Welcome to Los Angeles

Los Angeles is a polarizing place, but there's truly a corner of the city for everyone. Drive for miles between towering palm trees, bodega-lined streets, and Downtown's skyscrapers, and you'll still never discover all of L.A.'s hidden gems. Scratch the surface to find people-watching on Rodeo Drive, historic bars on the Sunset Strip, and the glitz and grime of Hollywood Boulevard. From the humble and trendy East Side to the tony beach-adjacent cities of Venice and Santa Monica to the west, experience everything in the city's year-round idyllic weather.

D0124864

TOP REASONS

★ **Star Gazing:** Both through the telescope atop Griffith Park and among the residents of Beverly Hills.

★ **Eating:** From food trucks to fine dining, an unparalleled meal awaits your palate.

★ **Beaches and Boardwalks:** The dream of '80s Venice is alive in California.

★ **Shopping:** Peruse eclectic boutiques or window-shop on Rodeo Drive.

★ **Architecture:** Art deco wonders to Frank Gehry masterpieces abound.

★ **Scenic Drives:** You haven't seen the sunset until you've seen it from a winding L.A. road.

Contents

1 EXPERIENCE LOS ANGELES 7

20 Ultimate Experiences...............8
What's Where...............................16
Los Angeles Today.......................18
Famous Film Locations................20
Best Beaches. 22
Best Things to Eat and Drink.......24
Under-the-Radar L.A....................26
Best Celebrity Hangouts 28
Historic Restaurants....................30
Los Angeles with Kids 32
Los Angeles Sports Action 33
What to Read and
Watch Before Your Trip...............34

2 TRAVEL SMART LOS ANGELES 35

10 Things to Know
Before You Go...............................36
Getting Here.................................38
Before You Go...............................43
Essentials....................................44
Contacts 50
Best Tours in Los Angeles 51
Great Itineraries..........................57

3 SANTA MONICA AND THE BEACHES 61

Neighborhood Snapshot.............62
Santa Monica 63
Pacific Palisades..........................74
Venice...76
Malibu...83
El Segundo 88
Manhattan Beach 89
Hermosa Beach............................89

Redondo Beach............................90
Brentwood 91

4 BEVERLY HILLS, WEST HOLLYWOOD, AND THE WESTSIDE................................ 95

Neighborhood Snapshot.............96
Beverly Hills.................................97
West Hollywood 109

5 HOLLYWOOD AND THE STUDIOS........................... 123

Neighborhood Snapshot............124
Hollywood 125
Studio City...................................144
Universal City...............................145
Burbank.......................................148
North Hollywood 151

6 MID-WILSHIRE AND KOREATOWN................... 155

Neighborhood Snapshot............156
Mid-Wilshire and
Miracle Mile.................................157
Koreatown....................................161
Culver City...................................166

7 DOWNTOWN LOS ANGELES .. 167

Neighborhood Snapshot............168

8 PASADENA............................. 197

Neighborhood Snapshot............198

9 LOS FELIZ AND THE EASTSIDE............................ 209

A Day at Griffith Park.................210
South-of-the-Border Flavor.......212

Neighborhood Snapshot 214
Los Feliz 215
Silver Lake.....................................222
Echo Park 225
Atwater Village.............................228
Highland Park 231

10 ORANGE COUNTY AND
    CATALINA ISLAND 237
    Welcome to Orange County
    and Catalina Island 238
    Planning 240
    Disneyland Resort.......................242
    Knott's Berry Farm 252
    The Coast 254
    Catalina Island.............................266

    INDEX 273

    ABOUT OUR WRITERS 288

MAPS

Santa Monica, Pacific Palisades,
and Venice 64–65
The Beaches and Brentwood......84
Beverly Hills and
West Hollywood 98–99
Hollywood 126–127
Burbank, the Studios,
and North Hollywood.................150
Mid-Wilshire, Culver City,
and Koreatown 158–159
Downtown............................170–171
Pasadena and Environs......200–201
Los Feliz, Silver Lake,
Echo Park, Atwater Village,
and Highland Park..............216–217

Fodor's Features

Cruising the Sunset Strip 52
Along the Strand 80
LA's Historic Bars 191

Disneyland 244
The Orange County Coast..........257
Catalina Island.............................267

Chapter 1

EXPERIENCE
LOS ANGELES

20 ULTIMATE EXPERIENCES

Los Angeles offers terrific experiences that should be on every traveler's list. Here are Fodor's top picks for a memorable trip.

1 Walt Disney Concert Hall

Designed by Frank Gehry, the voluptuous curves of this stainless steel–clad masterpiece located downtown are a signature of the modern metropolis.The 2,265-seat Disney Hall is home to the Los Angeles Philharmonic. *(Ch. 7)*

2 Disneyland

"The Happiest Place on Earth" continues to delight children and all but the most cynical adults. *(Ch. 10)*

3 Santa Monica Pier

Spend a sunny day beside the Pacific Ocean riding the Ferris wheel and playing dozens of games for prizes at this popular family destination. *(Ch. 3)*

4 Universal Studios Hollywood

Universal is more a theme park with lots of roller coasters and thrill rides than a backstage pass, though its tour provides a good firsthand look at familiar TV and movie sets. *(Ch. 5)*

5 Los Angeles County Museum of Art

LACMA is the focal point of the museum district along Wilshire Boulevard. Chris Burden's *Urban Light* sculpture, with more than 220 cast-iron street lamps, marks the location. *(Ch. 6)*

6 Venice Beach Boardwalk

The bohemian vibe of this famous boardwalk is constantly threatened by gentrification. Still, the magicians, fortune-tellers, and Muscle Beach weight lifters survive. *(Ch. 3)*

7 El Pueblo de Los Angeles

This district showcases the city's oldest historical structures (11 of the 27 are open to the public), a plaza for festivals and celebrations, and a marketplace bustling with food and goods. *(Ch. 7)*

8 Pacific Coast Highway

Nothing epitomizes L.A. more than a drive down the scenic PCH. After taking in the sweeping views, stop at a seafood shack for ahi burgers or fish and chips. *(Ch. 3)*

9 The Broad Museum

Philanthropists Eli and Edythe Broad built this striking museum to house their art collection, which features work by Basquiat, Cindy Sherman, and Kara Walker. *(Ch. 7)*

10 TCL Chinese Theatre and the Walk of Fame

Stars have been imprintins their hands since 1927. Today, the Walk of Fame runs a mile along Hollywood Boulevard. *(Ch. 5)*

11 Chinatown

Marked by the dragon gate, Chinatown offers many authentic food and entertainment options. *(Ch. 7)*

12 Sunset Boulevard

This avenue began humbly in the 18th century as a route from El Pueblo de Los Angeles to the Pacific. Today, as it passes through West Hollywood, it becomes the sexy and seductive Sunset Strip. *(Ch. 4)*

13 Rodeo Drive

Dominated by exclusive fashion brands, Rodeo Drive is a shoppers' paradise. Along the cobblestoned Via Rodeo, you can drop $1,000 on python pumps or nosh on a $500 sushi dinner. *(Ch. 4)*

14 The Arts District

In the 1970s, artists began to create the Arts District when they built studios in abandoned warehouses. Today, it's filled with trendy bars and hip galleries. *(Ch. 7)*

15 Dodger Stadium

Unless it's a big game, tickets at Dodger Stadium are easy to come by—especially if you're willing to sit in the cheap bleacher seats. Don't forget to dress in blue and eat a Dodger Dog while you're there. *(Ch. 9)*

16 Hollywood Bowl

Nothing compares to spending a summer evening at the Hollywood Bowl. For a true local experience, pack a picnic and don't be afraid to share with your neighbors. *(Ch. 5)*

17 Paramount Pictures

This is the only surviving major studio from Hollywood's golden age. Paramount offers probably the most authentic studio tour, giving you a real sense of the film industry's history. *(Ch. 5)*

18 Little Ethiopia

This block-long stretch of Fairfax Avenue has a high concentration of Ethiopian businesses and restaurants that will transport you to the markets and eateries of East Africa. *(Ch. 6)*

19 Getty Center

On a hillside above Brentwood, the Getty Center houses airy galleries filled with Impressionist canvases, Greek antiquities, and French decorative arts. *(Ch. 3)*

20 Griffith Park

One of the most popular routes through this expansive park is up Mount Hollywood, with views of the L.A. basin, the Griffith Observatory, and the Hollywood Sign. *(Ch. 5)*

WHAT'S
WHERE

1 Santa Monica and the Beaches. In Santa Monica, a lively beach scene plays out daily. Venice is a more raffish mix of artists, beach punks, and yuppies, most of whom you can see on the Venice Boardwalk. Drive up the Pacific Coast Highway to Malibu, where the rich and famous reside.

2 Beverly Hills, West Hollywood, and the Westside. Go for the glamour, the restaurants, and the scene. Rodeo Drive is particularly good for a look at wretched or ravishing excess. West Hollywood is an area for urban indulgences—shopping, restaurants, nightlife—rather than sightseeing.

3 Hollywood and the Studios. Glitzy and tarnished, good and bad—Hollywood is just like the entertainment business itself. The Walk of Fame, TCL Chinese Theatre, Paramount Pictures studio, and the Hollywood Bowl keep the romantic past alive. Universal Studios Hollywood and Warner Bros. are in the Valley.

4 Mid-Wilshire and Koreatown. Mid-Wilshire is a glorious hodgepodge of

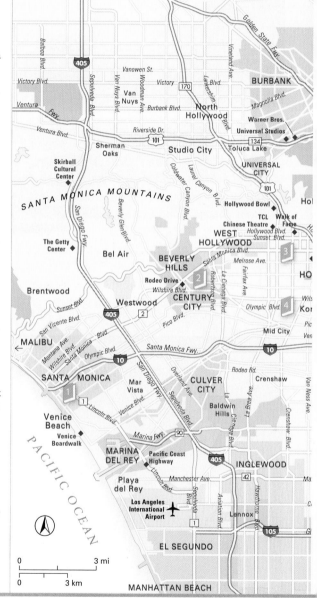

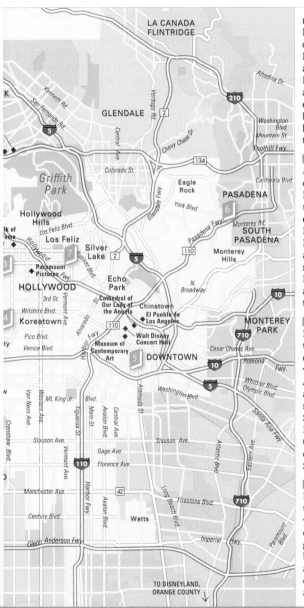

manicured lawns and Art Deco high-rises. Here you can also peruse art along Museum Row, or nosh along the stretch of Fairfax Boulevard known as Little Ethiopia. Just east is Koreatown, which boasts some of the best bars and restaurants in the city.

5 Downtown Los Angeles. One of the oldest parts of the city, DTLA shows off spectacular modern architecture, especially the Walt Disney Concert Hall. The MOCA and the Broad anchor a world-class art scene, while El Pueblo de Los Angeles, Chinatown, and Little Tokyo reflect the city's diversity.

6 Pasadena. Parts of Pasadena are even older than Downtown. It's a quiet, genteel area to visit, with outstanding Arts and Crafts homes and a pair of exceptional museums: the Norton Simon Museum and the Huntington Library, Art Collections, and Botanical Gardens in adjoining San Marino.

7 Los Feliz and the Eastside. If you've come to L.A. in search of bright young things, then head east. This is a land of good eats and better booze. Dine in Los Feliz and Silver Lake and go drinking in Echo Park and Highland Park.

Los Angeles Today

Starstruck. Excessive. Smoggy. Superficial…. There's a modicum of truth to each of the adjectives regularly applied to L.A., but the locals dismiss their prevalence as envy from those who aren't as blessed with year-round sunshine. Pop culture does permeate life here, its massive economy employing millions of Southern Californians, but the city where dreams are made accommodates those from all avenues of life.

DOWNTOWN'S CONTINUED UPSWING

Los Angeles has been archly described as "72 suburbs in search of a city." Hence the renaissance its once-desolate Downtown has experienced may come as something of a surprise. Long-neglected neighborhoods here have been spruced up, and streets even the police deemed irredeemable have been revitalized.

The Broad Foundation's 120,000-square-foot, three-story contemporary art museum, simply called "the Broad," has been a highly popular destination since opening its doors in 2015. Across the street from Walt Disney Concert Hall and the Los Angeles Museum of Contemporary Art, the honeycomb-shape structure holds more than 2,000 art objects and includes pieces by heavy hitters in the art world like Cindy Sherman and Andy Warhol.

The skyline is now a mixture of skyscrapers and cranes. It's a constantly evolving metropolis. The Wilshire Grand was completed in 2017, becoming the tallest building west of the Mississippi (though many place an asterisk next to this record, as it's the spiral that bested it over the U.S. Bank Tower, also in Downtown). The construction blitz shows no signs of stopping, with high-rises planned across the area.

ACCESS HOLLYWOOD

Hollywood may disappoint tourists looking to overdose on glitz; after all, most of its moviemakers departed for the San Fernando Valley decades ago, leaving the area to languish. Even after the much-hyped debut of the Hollywood & Highland Center, the area remains more gritty than glamorous, yet that's part of its charm.

Tourists continue to flock to the region, trodding over the stars on the Hollywood Walk of Fame or seeing how the size of their hand compares to celebrities both living and dead at the TCL Chinese Theatre.

SCOOTERS ARE IN, AIRBNB IS OUT (SORT OF)

It's no secret that L.A. is a hard town to maneuver without a car, but competing scooter companies—Bird, Lime, and Jump—have popped up throughout the city, especially in tourist-heavy areas on the Westside. The scooter invasion may have some residents griping that they're discarded on sidewalks like trash, but it's heavenly for the out-of-towner who doesn't want to hoof it along the long stretches between Metro stops.

Meanwhile, another tech solution for tourists is being heavily limited: the Los Angeles City Council has restricted Airbnb rentals. Beginning in 2019, property owners may only list their primary residence and only homes that are not under rent control.

GO NORTHEAST

First, it was Los Feliz. Then it was Silver Lake. Then it was Echo Park. Now it's Highland Park, Glassell Park, Cypress Park. The cool kids keep going farther and farther northeast. So, if you want to find the best bars in town, you'll have to keep venturing farther afield.

FOOD FOR THOUGHT

Star chefs continue to make their mark on Los Angeles. Recent big openings have included Majordomo, David Chang's exquiste west-coast debut, and Somni, José Andrés's stunning (and expensive) tasting menu–only eatery hidden inside perennial favorite, the Bazaar. For a solid brunch, don't miss Jessica Koslow's Sqirl on Virgil Avenue in Silver Lake, known for its seasonal rice bowls and house-made jams.

Eats in L.A. remain relatively egalitarian. Even posh places seldom require jackets, so the dress code is casual. Ditto for the menu. (In the city that invented fast food, it's no coincidence that Govind Armstrong flips gourmet burgers at LAX or that Wolfgang Puck built his reputation on pizza.) If you want to go budget, you can easily justify chowing down at McDonald's, Carl's Jr., and In-N-Out Burger; all qualify as "indigenous cuisine" having originated in the Five-County Area.

WHAT'S NEW

After a few delays, the Academy Museum of Motion Pictures will finally open in late 2019. The 300,000 square foot Renzo Piano–designed museum will unveil *Where Dreams Are Made,* a permanent exhibit that takes visitors inside *The Wizard of Oz, 2001: A Space Odyssey,* and the films of Charlie Chaplin. The first temporary exhibit will be a tribute to Japanese filmmaker Hayao Miyazaki and will include production materials from *Spirited Away* and *My Neighbor Totoro.*

You'll also be able to step inside another eagerly awaited cinematic wonder: Star Wars: Galaxy's Edge at Disneyland opened in 2019. Here you can pilot the Millennium Falcon, join the resistance, and go to the far, far away planet of Batuu.

A long time ago, L.A. lost both the Rams and the Raiders. The Rams came back, but the Raiders stayed away, replaced by the Chargers. The only problem was they had nowhere to play. In 2020, a brand-spankin'-new stadium will be open for business in Inglewood, hosting both teams.

Helping to ferry people to Inglewood in 2020 will be the newly opened Crenshaw/LAX line of the Metro, which connects the Expo Line in the north to the Green Line in the south. Commuters will be able to access Leimert Park and Hyde Park, and eventually, LAX. A few years later, in 2023, the Purple Line is scheduled to expand into Mid-City, connecting it with Downtown.

Famous Film Locations

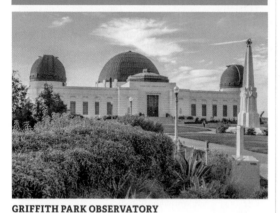

GRIFFITH PARK OBSERVATORY
Seen In: *Rebel Without a Cause.* Movie buffs will recognize this building in countless films like *Rebel Without a Cause* with James Dean (there's even a James Dean bust outside), *Charlie's Angels: Full Throttle,* and recent (almost) best picture Oscar winner, *La La Land.*

MILLENNIUM BILTMORE HOTEL
Seen In: *Ghostbusters, Splash, Beverly Hills Cop, Cruel Intentions.* A grande dame of L.A.'s Downtown hospitality scene, the hotel was opened in 1923 and was once the home of the Academy Awards Ceremony.

CIRCUS LIQUOR
Seen In: *Clueless.* If you happen to be hanging out in Burbank after a tour at the Warner Bros. lot, head over to Circus Liquor, which is known for its 32-foot clown sign. More famously, however, it's the parking lot where Cher Horowitz was mugged in *Clueless.* "It's an Alaïa!"

BEVERLY WILSHIRE HOTEL
Seen In: *Pretty Woman.* This iconic hotel was built in 1928 and has hosted the likes of Elvis, John Lennon, and Barack Obama. But it's mostly known as the setting for *Pretty Woman,* starring Julia Roberts. Fans of the movie can book the "Pretty Woman for a Day" experience at the hotel.

POINT DUME
Seen In: *Planet of the Apes.* Point Dume and Westward Beach are constantly in the movies. There's a good chance on any given weekday that you may spot a film crew here. It's been used in *The Big Lebowski* and *Iron Man.* But it's most famous claim to fame: the iconic ending of the original *Planet of the Apes.*

THE WESTIN BONAVENTURE HOTEL
Seen In: *In the Line of Fire, Interstellar, and Heat.* A behemoth hotel, the Bonaventure is actually the biggest in L.A. with more than 1,300 rooms. Its unique cylindrical towers have starred in a bevy of films. California's former governor, Arnold Schwarzenegger, rode a horse into the glass elevator in *True Lies.*

GAMBLE HOUSE

Seen In: *Back to the Future.* Head up to Pasadena and check out Doc Brown's house, a stunning example of American Craftsman style. Close your eyes, and you can picture Michael J. Fox wearing an orange windbreaker vest as he runs up to the front door.

USC CAMPUS

Seen In: *Legally Blonde, The Social Network, The Graduate, and Forrest Gump.* USC is known for its football team and stunning campus that also houses one of the best film schools in the country. So it shouldn't come as a surprise that a number of its graduates have taken time to film here.

BRADBURY BUILDING

Seen In: *Blade Runner.* Built in 1893, this DTLA architectural marvel is like an M.C. Escher painting come to life. With a series of interlocking wrought iron stairs and caged elevators, the Bradbury Building has been featured in *500 Days of Summer, Double Indemnity, D.O.A.,* and most famously, *Blade Runner.*

Best Beaches

EL MATADOR BEACH
Throngs of people flock to Malibu's worst-kept secret, from selfie-taking tourists to locals hoping for quiet spots to call their own. But don't worry about the crowds. El Matador's sweeping, sea-meets-land panoramas make up for it.

HERMOSA BEACH
Blazing orange sunsets draw sunning crowds and shutterbugs, but this is, without a doubt, a surfing beach. Even its famous landmark—the statue of Tim Kelly riding a swell—is a declaration of this fact.

SURFRIDER BEACH
There are two sets of people who frequent the sandy Malibu outpost—the surf nuts (hence, the name) and the anglers.

WILL ROGERS STATE BEACH
It's the sand-and-sun chasing things riddle this stretch in Pacific Palisades, taking on a game or two of volleyball while waiting for the epic sunsets this beach is known for. Out of L.A.'s top beaches, Will Rogers is probably the quietest.

ZUMA BEACH
On summer weekends, you'll be hard pressed to find a good place to lay your blanket, but this popular Malibu beach is two miles of gorgeous zigzagging shore.

VENICE BEACH
Even though Venice is now shockingly expensive, a colorful, artistic past still lingers. Along the boardwalk, vibrant street art adorn the modern retail and gastronomic spaces. Watch out for the tech bros that have taken over the neighborhood.

POINT DUME
Walk along the trail that meanders through this state beach and nature reserve, and you'll often see waves crashing against the wind-carved bluff, tide pools, the occasional migrating whale, and one of the most epic panoramas in Southern California.

MANHATTAN BEACH
A day at this beach might involve taking your cruiser for a spin along the bike trail, a bit of retail therapy, and a nosh at a restaurant serving freshly caught seafood.

LEO CARRILLO STATE PARK
This is a tale of two beaches. When the tide is in, it's a serene spot to gaze at the sea. When out, it's for those seeking exploration—that's when the tidepools and caves are unveiled. Camping is allowed, so pitch a tent and stay a while.

DOCKWEILER STATE BEACH
Beach bonfires are largely illegal in L.A., but at Dockweiler's 3.7-mile stretch, lighting up isn't just permitted, it's practically encouraged. It's for this reason that the beach is almost always a scene where 20- and 30-somethings roast marshmallows and guzzle beer.

Best Things to Eat and Drink

VEGAN FARE
And while you're on that health kick, why not sample some vegan dishes as well? L.A. is overflowing with restaurants catering to the meat-averse. Places like Café Gratitude and Kitchen Mouse are excellent plant-based dining stops.

L.A. HOTDOGS
While every major city in the country has their own take on street hot dogs, L.A.'s Mexican-inspired version is arguably the best. Wrapped in bacon and topped with grilled onions, bell peppers, ketchup, mustard, mayo, and jalapenos, it's practically a ritual for anyone stumbling home drunk to grab one. By the way, you should probably be drunk while eating them. Look for street carts in areas with a lot of bars—Spring Street and Staples Center in Downtown, Sunset Boulevard in Echo Park, and Normandie Avenue in Koreatown.

MEZCAL
If you're a fan of tequila, then it's time to elevate your taste buds with mezcal, the fermented agave spirit that hails from Oaxaca and is known as tequila's smokier, sexier cousin. Most bars in town keep it in stock, and many local mixologists use them to create their own spin on traditional cocktails. Pop into La Cuevita, the Corner Door, or Melrose Umbrella Co. to get your fix.

KOREAN BBQ
Los Angeles claims to have the biggest (and best) Koreatown in the world. So if there's one place you should feast on Korean BBQ—outside of South Korea, that is—it's here. There are so many Korean BBQ joints in the city, in fact, that it's hard to pick the best ones, though Park's BBQ and Magal certainly have our votes.

KOREAN BBQ TACOS
If you like Korean BBQ and you enjoyed those street tacos, then you might be ready for Korean BBQ tacos, which is one of the few culinary creations that originated in La La Land. They're exactly what it sounds like—tacos but with Korean BBQ meats, and the best place to get them is from one of Roy Choi's legendary Kogi food trucks. To find a location, go to kogibbq.com.

ORGANIC JUICE AND SMOOTHIES
Make fun of L.A.'s healthy juice obsession all you want, but they're actually surprisingly delicious, not to mention nutritious. Don't knock it until you try it. Naturewell and Pressed Juicery are good, popular spots to sample them.

STREET TACOS

This is a beautifully simple dish: grilled meat with chopped cilantro and onion, wrapped in corn or flour tortillas, drizzled with lime and salsa. They're not only delicious, but cheap. Every Angeleno has their own go-to spot, usually a stand or a truck, so ask your favorite local for recommendations.

ELOTE

This Mexican corn concoction is essentially just grilled corn smothered with butter, crema fresca (or mayo), cotija, chile powder, and lime then served on a cob or in a cup. But it's a delightful assault on your taste buds and a favorite Los Angelenos snack. Keep an eye out for street carts that tout it or take a chance at one of L.A.'s many farmers markets.

FILIPINO FOOD

The city is teeming with Filipino food joints that either champion traditional Filipino dishes like Pork Adobo, Kare-Kare and Pinakbet, or boast modern takes. For a traditional take, go to Max's in Glendale. For a modern twist, Ricebar in Downtown is a good spot. Regardless of your choice, leave room for dessert, as they're to die for.

IN-N-OUT

No L.A. food list is complete without the legendary In-N-Out. "Where's the closest In-N-Out" is asked by just about every tourist the moment they arrive.

Not that we blame them— In-N-Out burgers and fries are made fresh and made to order, which is why they're so good in the first place. But which location should you go to? Any of them! Whether it's the one near LAX as soon as you leave the airport or in Hollywood, which gets a lot of traffic.

Under-the-Radar L.A.

THE LAST BOOKSTORE

Built inside an abandoned bank, this Instagram-worthy book-paradise is a two-floor behemoth with more than 250,000 books, old and new, including rare first editions. As you wind through the maze of shelves, you'll be surprised to find tucked-away shops with curios, art, and even yarn.

WATTS TOWERS

It's probably not on most tourists' top lists, but that's a mistake considering the Watts Towers is on the U.S. National Register of Historic Places, a U.S. National Historic Landmark, a California Historical Landmark, and a Los Angeles Historic-Cultural Monument. The towers were built over 33 years by Italian immigrant Simon Rodia between 1921 and 1954 and consist of 17 interlaced iron spirals with mosaics and other architectural features.

BRONSON CAVES

Located in the southwest section of Griffith Park, the Bronson Caves are the remnants of an old quarry that was used in the early 1900s. Fans of the original '60s Batman TV show might recognize this spot as the Batcave.

THE MAGIC CASTLE

Up on a hill, just north of Hollywood Boulevard is a Victorian mansion that is home to the Academy of Magical Arts. Inside this secret spot is a magician's Shangri-La filled with multiple bars and stages. In order to get in, you need to be invited by a member, but there is a work-around. If you stay at the Magic Castle Hotel next door, they can get you inside without any hocus-pocus.

HOTEL CECIL/STAY ON MAIN

Fans of the macabre will find lots to love when they learn about the history of Downtown L.A.'s most notorious hotel. Originally built in 1924, the hotel was once home to multiple serial killers, including the Night Stalker, and the spot of many unsolved murders. The most recent occurred only a few years ago when they found the remains of a tourist inside the hotel's water tower.

MARILYN MONROE'S GRAVE

The world's fascination with Marilyn Monroe, the most famous blonde bombshell in Hollywood history, continuesdecades after her death. That fascination even carries over to Monroe's final resting place, which is in a hallway of above-ground crypts at the Pierce Brothers Westwood Village Memorial Park and Mortuary. While you're there, you can also find other luminaries like Truman Capote, Billy Wilder, Rodney Dangerfield, Jack Lemmon, and many others.

BARNSDALL ART PARK

In East Hollywood is a hidden away park that happens to be a Los Angeles Historic-Cultural Monument and National Historic Landmark that features the Hollyhock House, a Frank Lloyd Wright masterpiece. Named after Aline Barnsdall, an oil heiress who commis-sioned the Wright work in 1915, the park today is a destination for art, archi-tecture, and a city getaway. During summer months, the park hosts a Friday night

wine tasting event where Angeleno's can picnic on the lawn with glasses of chardonnay while watching the setting sun.

HOLLYWOOD FOREVER CEMETERY

The most famous celebrity burial ground around is without question the Hollywood Forever Cemetery. Built in 1899, the cemetery is home to Judy Garland, Bugsy Siegel, Cecil B. DeMille, and many others. There are tours of the space that last around two hours where you can discover lots of history and a few mysteries. The cemetery is also known for movie screenings and concerts.

SPADENA HOUSE

Otherwise known as the Witch's House in Beverly Hills, the Spadena House has an interesting history. First built on the Willat Studios lot in 1920, the house was physically

moved to its current ritzy location in 1924. The house is not open for tourists, but the fairy-tale like appearance is viewable from the street for on-lookers to snap pics. Movie buffs will also recognize it from a background shot in the film *Clueless*.

VIRGINIA ROBINSON GARDENS

As an heiress to the Robinson department store dynasty, Virginia Robinson lived on what is the oldest in-tact estate in Beverly Hills—dating back to 1911. The house and gardens cover 6.5 acres of immaculately landscaped flora with a distinct Italian villa vibe right out of Tuscany. The Beaux Arts style house includes a tennis court, pool house, and five separate gardens including a rose garden, Italian terrace, palm tree forest, and more.

Best Celebrity Hangouts

CAFÉ GRATITUDE LARCHMONT
Round out your L.A. vacation with a plant-based meal at local chain, Café Gratitude. For a celeb sighting, head to their Larchmont Blvd. location where Jake Gyllenhaal and Beyoncé, obligingly declare what they're grateful for before digging in.

THE HOLLYWOOD ROOSEVELT
The Hollywood Roosevelt is one of L.A.'s oldest hotels, and has hosted numerous celebrities and dignitaries in its Spanish Colonial Revival rooms. Set in the heart of Hollywood, it offers a convenient location as well as a number of watering holes, including Tropicana Pool & Café and The Spare Room. Incidentally, it's also one of the city's most haunted places, so if you don't spot a celeb, you may bump into a ghost.

PINZ BOWLING CENTER
For a bit of family-friendly fun, head to Pinz in Studio City, where bowling is more than just a game, it's also a neon- and black-light party. Every lane comes with an automated ordering system so you can overload on wings and fries without ever leaving your spot. Celebrities often pop in here for bowling night, from A-listers like Vin Diesel and Jessica Alba to performers like Bruno Mars and Missy Elliott.

THE GROVE
L.A. may be strewn with malls, but the Grove gets the top billing, for its collection of high-end shops and restaurants, its next-door neighbor, the Farmers Market and its celed shoppers: Lena Headey, Zendaya, and Mario Lopez.

NOBU MALIBU

If you've ever picked up a gossip magazine, you've undoubtedly seen photos of celebrities stepping out of the Malibu outpost of this celebrated restaurant franchise. It's a known A-list hotspot that's hosted everyone from Keanu Reeves to Kendall Jenner. Be warned, though: mingling with A-listers doesn't come cheap.

TOSCANA

Upscale Brentwood is home to many celebrities, and rustic trattoria Toscana is one of their neighborhood haunts. It may not be L.A.'s best Italian restaurant—for that, check out Jon & Vinny's —but for star sightings, it's your best bet. Jennifer Garner, Reese Witherspoon, and Heidi Klum have dined here.

CHATEAU MARMONT

The Chateau is possibly L.A.'s best-known celebrity haunt, making it your best bet to nonchalantly stumble into A-listers. Come for a classic L.A. brunch in the garden terrace or drop in the Hollywood-inspired cocktails. Just know: photos aren't allowed.

CATCH

Secure a table at the flora-cluttered Catch in West Hollywood and rub elbows with the likes of David Beckham and the Jenner-Kardashian clan. This eatery is as L.A. as you can get, with its al fresco setting, vegan and gluten-free offerings, and locally and sustainably grown ingredients.

CRAIG'S

A West Hollywood dining staple, Craig's plain façade provides a safe haven for the movie industry's most important names and well-known faces like John Legend and Chrissy Teigen. We're not going to lie: this joint is always busy, so you might not even get a table. It's a good thing the food is worth the effort.

RUNYON CANYON

Out of L.A.'s numerous beautiful hiking spots, Runyon Canyon gets the biggest share of celebrity regulars, probably because it's strategically tucked between the Hollywood Hills, where many stars live, and the Hollywood strip. It's also a great venue for getting some fresh air, not to mention an ideal spot to take panoramic sunset photos.

Historic Restaurants

COLE'S

There's a fight in Los Angeles over who created the French Dip sandwich. The first contender is Cole's, whose sign on the door says they're the originator of the salty, juicy, melt-in-your-mouth meats. The restaurant opened in 1908 and today is still going strong with dark lighting, delicious sandwiches, and a secret speakeasy called the Varnish hidden in the back.

PHILLIPE'S

Also opened in 1908, Phillipe's is the second restaurant to claim ownership of the French Dip. Owner Philippe Mathieu claims that the sandwich was invented in 1918 when he accidentally dropped the roll into a vat of hot jus and the customer said he didn't care. It was so good that he came back the next day for more. The French Dip sandwich was coined because of the dipping into the jus and because of Mathieu's French heritage, or possibly because the customer was French. No one actually knows, but their sandwiches are incredible.

THE MUSSO & FRANK GRILL

This classic steakhouse opened in 1919 by Frank Toulet, Joseph Musso, and French chef Jean Rue. The eatery quickly became a

hot spot for A-list guests like Charlie Chaplin, Gary Cooper, Marilyn Monroe, Elizabeth Taylor, and even F. Scott Fitzgerald, who allegedly proofread his novels in the booths. Today the restaurant is known for perfect martinis, red tux-wearing waiters, leather booths, and sizzling steaks.

ORIGINAL PANTRY CAFÉ
Opened in 1924 by Dewey Logan, this classic diner claims to have never closed in the entirety of its run and is currently owned by former L.A. mayor Richard Riordan. Open 24/7, the diner serves American food for breakfast, lunch, and dinner, and is known for cakes, pies, steaks, and chops. The cash-only establishment is also a Los Angeles historic cultural monument.

GREENBLATT'S DELI-RESTAURANT
In 1926, Herman Greenblatt opened his eponymous deli, which serves Jewish deli food, wine, and spirits. The restaurant claims to have the rarest roast beef in town—and they're probably right. The deli also boasts a famous clientele that included Marlon Brando, Lenny Bruce, Rita Hayworth, and John Belushi.

CANTER'S
Opened in 1931, Canter's is your classic Jewish deli. In front you can buy freshly baked breads and pastries, while the enormous restaurant offers everything from giant sandwiches to matzo ball soup 24 hours a day. In addition to the food, there's also the Kibbitz Room, which features live music and comedy throughout the week.

EL COYOTE
Blanche and George March opened El Coyote in 1931; they chose the name because the word is the same in English and Spanish. The family-friendly Mexican restaurant is one of the oldest in town and offers all the standard nachos, burritos, and enchiladas. If it's on the menu, make sure you get the Ostrich tacos— they're one of a kind.

PINK'S HOT DOGS
Since Paul and Betty Pink opened it in 1939, this ultra-famous hot dog stand has had lines around the block filled with Angelenos and tourists alike. Pink's is best known for their chili dogs as well as being open until 3 am on weekends.

Los Angeles with Kids

With seemingly endless sunny days, Angeleno kids almost never have to play indoors. There are a few things to keep in mind, however, when navigating the city with little ones: if possible, avoid the freeways by exploring no more than one neighborhood each day, and remember that you can never have too much sunscreen—L.A. parents don't leave home without the stuff.

Of course, the top reason many families come to the L.A. area is to visit Disneyland. Experience all the classic attractions that you may recall from your own childhood visit, such as the "It's a Small World" ride, a meet-and-greet with Tinkerbell, or a Mickey Mouse home tour, who, unlike less amenable celebrities, makes a daily appearance for fans. But there's plenty more to see and do.

HEAD UNDER THE SEA

Head down to the **Aquarium of the Pacific** in Long Beach to learn tons of interesting facts about the Pacific Ocean. On display are shimmering schools of fish, a swaying kelp forest, a shark lagoon featuring more than 150 varieties, and a tropical reef habitat filled with zebra sharks, porcupine puffers, and a large blue Napoleon wrasse.

COMMUNE WITH NATURE

Don't miss your chance to test-ride a high-wire bicycle or catch a film at the seven-story IMAX theater at the **California Science Center.** Just down the road is the **Natural History Museum,** where kids can explore everything from diamonds to its new dinosaur hall. In spring, don't miss the outdoor butterfly habitat, fittingly named the Pavilion of Wings, which makes way for the Spider Pavilion come fall.

WALK IN THE PARK

Griffith Park is the largest municipal park and urban wilderness area in the United States, and the kids will go wild for the pony rides and the classic 1926 merry-go-round. But the pièce de résistance is the Griffith Park and Southern Railroad, a circa-1940s miniature train that travels through an old Western town and a Native American village. Other highlights are the Los Angeles Zoo and the Griffith Observatory, an L.A. icon in its own right.

LEARN BY DOING

Little ones can pan for gold in a small creek, play Spider-Man on a weblike climber, or race around a trike track at the **Kidspace Children's Museum.** Indoor activities include a walk-through kaleidoscope, two climbing towers—one mimicking raindrops, the other modeled after a wisteria vine, a bug diner (think banana worm bread and roasted cricket pizza), and a contraption that lets kids generate their very own earthquake.

HIT THE BEACH

The best way to check out **Santa Monica Beach** is by renting bikes or roller skates at any one of the shacks on the Strand (a stretch of concrete boardwalk that snakes along the beach toward Venice). Some must-sees along the way: the roller dancers of Venice Beach, the bodybuilders of Muscle Beach, and the Santa Monica Pier, a 100-year-old structure that's home to a vintage 1920s carousel, an oversize Ferris wheel, and old-time amusement park games. After hitting the beach, drive over to the pedestrian-only Third Street Promenade to grab a bite and do some shopping.

Los Angeles Sports Action

Famed Dodgers sportscaster Vin Scully may have recently retired, but his name lives on: in 2016 Elysian Park Avenue officially became Vin Scully Avenue—just one example of how sports are deeply woven into L.A. culture. It's an understatement to say the city takes pride in its professional sports.

BASEBALL

Los Angeles Angels of Anaheim. The Angels often contend for the top slot in the Western Division of pro baseball's American League. ✉ *Angel Stadium of Anaheim, 2000 E. Gene Autry Way, Anaheim* ☎ *714/940–2000* ⊕ *www.angels-baseball.com.*

Los Angeles Dodgers. The Dodgers take on their National League rivals at one of major league baseball's most comfortable ballparks, Dodger Stadium. ✉ *Dodger Stadium, 1000 Elysian Park Ave., exit off I–110, Pasadena Fwy.* ☎ *323/224–1507* ⊕ *www.dodgers.com.*

BASKETBALL

Los Angeles Clippers. L.A.'s "other" pro basketball team, the Clippers, was formerly an easy ticket, but these days the club routinely sells out its home games. ✉ *Staples Center, 1111 S. Figueroa St.* ☎ *213/742–7100* ⊕ *www.nba.com/clippers.*

Los Angeles Lakers. The team of pro-basketball champions Magic, Kareem, Shaq, and Kobe has slipped in recent years, but thanks to LeBron's arrival, excitement has been renewed and seats are packed. ✉ *Staples Center, 1111 S. Figueroa St., Downtown* ☎ *310/426–6000* ⊕ *www.nba.com/lakers.*

Los Angeles Sparks. The women's pro basketball team has made it to the WNBA playoffs more than a dozen times in the past two decades. ✉ *Staples Center, 1111 S. Figueroa St.* ☎ *310/426–6031* ⊕ *www.wnba.com/sparks.*

University of California at Los Angeles. The University of California at Los Angeles Bruins play at Pauley Pavilion on the UCLA campus. ✉ *Pauley Pavilion, 405 Hilgard Ave.* ☎ *310/825–2101* ⊕ *www.uclabruins.collegesports.com.*

University of Southern California. The Trojans of the University of Southern California play at the Galen Center. ✉ *Galen Center, 3400 S. Figueroa St.* ☎ *213/740–4672* ⊕ *www.usctrojans.com.*

FOOTBALL

The Los Angeles Rams began playing home games at the L.A. Memorial Coliseum in 2016, and the Los Angeles Chargers joined them in town in 2018, though claiming the Dignity Health Sports Park as their homefield. Both will be calling the Los Angeles Stadium at Hollywood Park home sweet home starting in 2020.

UCLA Bruins. The UCLA Bruins pack 'em in at the Rose Bowl. ✉ *Rose Bowl, 1010 Rose Bowl, Pasadena* ☎ *626/577–3100* ⊕ *www.uclabruins.collegesports.com.*

USC Trojans. The USC Trojans play at the L.A. Memorial Coliseum, both a state and federal historic landmark. ✉ *L.A. Memorial Coliseum, 3939 S. Figueroa St., Downtown* ☎ *213/740–4672* ⊕ *www.usctrojans.collegesports.com.*

HOCKEY

Anaheim Ducks. The Anaheim Ducks push the puck at Honda Center. They became the first Southern California team to win the Stanley Cup, in 2007. ✉ *Honda Center, 2695 E. Katella Ave* ☎ *877/945–3946* ⊕ *www.nhl.com/ducks.*

L.A. Kings. The National Hockey League's L.A. Kings clinched the Stanley Cup for the first time in 2012, and in 2014 they won it again against the New York Rangers. ✉ *Staples Center, 1111 S. Figueroa St.* ☎ *213/742–7100* ⊕ *www.lakings.com.*

What to Read and Watch Before Your Trip

Movie: *Mulholland Drive*
Surreal, psychotic, and artsy, David Lynch's *Mulholland Drive* paints L.A. as a city of scary funhouse turns that blur the lines between reality and cuts from a movie. Such dichotomies exist as well in the two main characters: Betty (Naomi Watts), the blond midwesterner fresh to L.A. and full of dreams, and Rita, an amnesiac whose life seems to be shrouded in violence and mystery.

Movie: *Sunset Boulevard*
This 1950s Billy Wilder classic is a wild ride and entertaining glimpse into the film business and its eccentric characters. A has-been star and a young screenwriter hope to use each other in some way, while things get more complicated—proving that what happens behind the scenes in Hollywood isn't the same as what appears on the big screen.

Movie: *Chinatown*
In this classic crime noir, a young private eye (Jack Nicholson) in Depression-era Los Angeles gets in over his head with a client's case involving her husband's death and the city's sketchy water rights dealings. Incorporating fictionalized details of L.A.'s historic water wars, it's a tale of corruption and mystery.

Movie: *Tangerine*
Shot entirely with an iPhone camera, this indie film explores the streets of Hollywood with a close lens on a few characters. Recently out of prison, a transgender prostitute tries to track down her pimp and his new girlfriend with the help of a friend. It's hard to explain just how much light, humor, and beauty fills this film—you just have to see it for yourself.

Book: *Ask the Dust* **by John Fante**
Set in Los Angeles during the Great Depression, an Italian American writer lives in a seedy hotel in Bunker Hill and struggles with poverty, love, and creativity. Downtown L.A. is rendered well, and the character's relationship with Los Angeles—his love and hopes for the city—remains complicated.

Book: *Shanghai Girls* **by Lisa See**
Two sisters from Shanghai begin the novel as young women celebrated for their beauty in a sophisticated, international city—but all this works against them when they are forced into marriage by their father and must leave a now war-torn Shanghai for new life in L.A. Set in the late 1930s, at the brink of change and revolution, this novel mixes historical events, revolution, and culture clashes with themes about womanhood and friendship.

Book: *The Revolt of the Cockroach People* **by Oscar Zeta Acosta**
This story about Chicano radicalization in East Los Angeles is based on real events. The protagonist lawyer is based on Oscar Zeta Acosta himself, an author, activist, and lawyer/politician with his own fascinating life (and mysterious disappearance), and a key player in the movement.

Book: *Ham on Rye* **by Charles Bukowski**
America's favorite degenerate poet writes an off-the-cuff novel about growing up in L.A. during the mid-20th century as the child of German immigrants. As told through Henry Chinaski, the author's alter ego and antihero, the book starts with family violence, alcoholism, Model Ts, and orange trees, and segues into schoolyard bullying and some realist, gritty views on the America (and Southern California) of the times.

Chapter 2

TRAVEL SMART LOS ANGELES

Updated by
Paul Feinstein

★ **CAPITAL**
Sacramento

POPULATION
4 million in the city; 10 million
county-wide

LANGUAGE
English

CURRENCY
$ U.S. dollar

☎ **AREA CODE**
310, 323, 213, 424

⚠ **EMERGENCIES**
911

🚗 **DRIVING**
On the right

⚡ **ELECTRICITY**
120–240 v/60 cycles; plugs
have two or three rectangu-
lar prongs

🕐 **TIME**
Three hours behind New
York

🌐 **WEB RESOURCES**
discoverlosangeles.com;
lacity.org; fodors.com

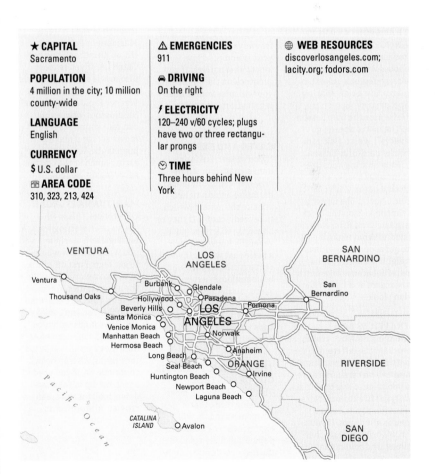

10 Things to Know Before You Go

THIS CITY IS BIG

Oh, you wanted to do Malibu and Disneyland on the same day? That's cute. Here's some perspective—that drive is 77 miles and, depending on traffic, can take more than three hours from end to end. Think about L.A. in chunks. There's the Westside, consisting of Malibu, Santa Monica, and Venice. The middle: Beverly Hills, West Hollywood, and Hollywood. The Eastside: Downtown, Silver Lake, and Pasadena. Stick to these chunks on individual days.

TRANSPORTATION IS ANNOYING

You have a lot of options, so choose wisely. You can rent a car, ride a bus, take the metro, use a ride-sharing app, or scoot. Lesson 1. Never ride the bus. Lesson 2. The metro doesn't go everywhere, so pick your routes carefully. Lesson 3. Ride-sharing apps are infinitely cheaper than taxis. Lesson 4. If you must, scoot. The newest transpo kids on the block are Lime and Bird, electric scooters that make it easy to get around individual neighborhoods. Just be careful because bike lanes are scarce and L.A. drivers don't look.

TRAFFIC IS BAD

Knowing how L.A. traffic works is the difference between a sweet vacation and hell on earth. Here are some rules to live by: First, only get in a car before 7 am, after 10 am, before 3 pm, or after 7 pm. If you MUST drive at any other times, find routes that don't involve L.A.'s maze of freeways. Side streets are your friends and give you lots of alternatives. If you get stuck on the 405 at 5:30, you will miss your dinner reservation.

PARKING IS COMPLI-CATED AND EXPENSIVE

If you've seen L.A.'s draconian signage, you know how confusing things can be. But to avoid a ticket, stick to the meters (which take credit cards). If they're blinking red/green, you'll generally know you're in a place that works. If you rent a car, hotel parking can be obnoxiously expensive. We're talking $40–$50 per night. To avoid all these pratfalls, use ride-sharing apps and save yourself the hassle.

THE HOMELESS CRISIS IS OUT OF CONTROL

This is probably the most shocking thing that newcomers to L.A. will experience. The homeless population has exploded in the last decade and rough estimates put it at 60,000 people on the streets. You'll see tents, you'll see cardboard signs, you'll see the sadness. It's a big problem, we know, we're working on it. Just don't be surprised and, most importantly, don't be rude. People are people, and some need more help than others.

CELEBRITIES LIVE HERE, TOO

If you want to see celebs, you need to know where to find them. But this isn't a safari—they're not animals—so be cool. If you want some guarantees, go to lunch at the Chateau Marmont or Polo Lounge. Hit up dinner at Craig's or Catch LA. If you're more into movie stuff than movie people, head over to the Warner Bros. and Universal Studios lots, where you can tour sound stages and movie sets and maybe, just maybe, see an A-lister eating lunch at the commissary—again, be cool.

MARIJUANA IS LEGAL

OK, stoners, this is what you've been waiting for. L.A. has legalized marijuana and you want to know where to get high. First off, think of the marijuana rules like the alcohol rules. You need to be 21. You can't consume in public. You can't smoke and drive (and really, you shouldn't). Fines can be as high (not a pun) as $250 just for driving with an open container. So, if you need a pick-me-up or take-me-down, look for the green crosses on storefronts.

THERE ARE A LOT OF BEACHES

No trip to L.A. would be complete without bumming out on the beaches. Whether you're a surfer, skater, or volleyball player, there's a beach for you. Malibu is worth hitting for the drive alone along PCH. But it's far away. Santa Monica and Venice are closer, though less serene. Head a little farther south and you'll get your top surf spots: Manhattan, Hermosa, and Redondo.

IT'S (USUALLY) HOT HERE

L.A. really only has two seasons: hot, and two months in January and February where it rains a bit. But this city is also a desert where temps can drop at night into the low 50s, so bring a jacket. Depending on where you stay, fluctuations in temperature can be a little extreme. The beaches are consistently 5-10 degrees cooler than Downtown, which can be 5-10 degrees cooler than the Valley. Yes, we're all weather wimps in L.A., but it's still good to know this stuff.

THIS IS A FOODIE'S PARADISE

New Yorkers can disagree all they want—L.A. is one of the best food cities in America. The food truck was practically invented here, and you'll find a rolling restaurant for any cuisine imaginable. Beyond the trucks, L.A. has dozens of farmers' markets and near-weekly food festivals celebrating the melting pot that is this city. Lastly, you'll find more celebrity chefs in L.A. than just about any other city as cheap(er) rents have ushered in an experimental wave of food not seen elsewhere. Whether it's tacos, Italian, Ethiopian, Korean, or burgers, L.A. is a primo city for any traveling foodie.

Getting Here

The Los Angeles metro area has more than 13 million residents, so be prepared to rent a car and fight for space on the freeway (especially at rush hour) to make your way along the array of destinations that span from the carefree beaches of the coastline to the glitz and glamour of Beverly Hills shops, the nightlife of Hollywood, and the film studio action of the Valley. It's worth it. Nowhere else in the country can you spot celebrities over breakfast or sunbathe on the beach and head to the slopes for skiing on the same day.

✈ Air Travel

Nonstop flights from New York to Los Angeles take about six hours; with the three-hour time change, you can leave JFK by 8 am and be in L.A. by 11 am. Some flights may require a midway stop, making the total excursion between 7½ and 8½ hours. Flight times are three hours from Dallas, four hours from Chicago, and 11½ hours from London.

AIRPORTS

The fourth-largest airport in the world in terms of passenger traffic, Los Angeles International Airport (LAX) is served by more than 65 major airlines. Because of heavy traffic around the airport (not to mention the city's extended rush hours), you should allow yourself plenty of extra time. All departures are from the upper level, while arrivals are on the lower level.

Several secondary airports serve the city. Hollywood Burbank Airport in Burbank is close to Downtown L.A., so it's definitely worth checking out. Long Beach Airport is equally convenient. Flights to Orange County's John Wayne Airport are often more expensive than those to the other secondary airports. Also check out L.A./Ontario International Airport.

Driving times from LAX to different parts of the city vary considerably: it will take you 20 minutes to get to Santa Monica, 30 minutes to Beverly Hills, and at least 45 minutes to Downtown L.A. In heavy traffic it can take much longer. From Hollywood Burbank Airport, it's 30 minutes to Downtown. Plan on at least 45 minutes for the drive from Long Beach Airport, and an hour from John Wayne Airport or L.A./Ontario International Airport.

GROUND TRANSPORTATION

If you're not renting a car, a taxi is the most convenient way to get to and from the airport. There's a flat rate between LAX and Downtown for $50.50. Getting Downtown from Hollywood Burbank Airport costs $40 to $50. Taxis to and from L.A./Ontario International Airport run on a meter and cost $60 and $70, depending on traffic. From Long Beach Airport, trips to Downtown L.A. are metered and cost roughly $72.

For two or three passengers, shuttles can be an economical option at $17 to $35. These big vans typically circle the airport, departing when they're full. Your travel time depends on how many other travelers are dropped off before you. At LAX, SuperShuttle allows walk-on shuttle passengers without prior reservations; if you're headed to the airport, call at least 24 hours in advance.

Operated by Los Angeles World Airports, FlyAway buses travel between LAX and Van Nuys, Westwood, La Brea, and Union Station in Downtown L.A. The cost is $8 to $10 and is payable only by credit or debit card. With departure at least every hour, buses run 24 hours a day.

Most Angelenos use ride-share apps like Lyft, which you can download to your smartphone. The app will estimate the cost before you accept the ride. A ride from the airport (drivers are permitted to pick you up at the departure terminals) to the Eastside could cost as much as $40-plus, or less if you pick up another passenger along the way.

FLIGHTS

Delta, United, Southwest, and American have the most nonstop flights to LAX. JetBlue and Alaska also have numerous daily flights to airports in and around Los Angeles.

🚌 Bus Travel

Inadequate public transportation has plagued L.A. for decades. That said, many local trips can be made, with time and patience, by buses run by the Los Angeles County Metropolitan Transit Authority. In certain cases—visiting the Getty Center, for instance, or Universal Studios—buses may be your best option. There's a special Dodger Stadium Express that shuttles passengers between Union Station and the world-famous ballpark for home games. It's free if you have a ticket in hand and saves you parking-related stress.

Metro Buses cost $1.75, plus 50¢ for each transfer to another bus or to the subway. A one-day pass costs $7, and a weekly pass is $25 for unlimited travel on all buses and trains. Passes are valid from Sunday through Saturday. For the fastest service, look for the red-and-white Metro Rapid buses; these stop less frequently and are able to extend green lights. There are 25 Metro Rapid routes, including along Wilshire and Vermont boulevards.

Other bus services make it possible to explore the entire metropolitan area. DASH minibuses cover six different circular routes in Hollywood, Mid-Wilshire, and Downtown. You pay 50¢ every time

you get on. The Santa Monica Municipal Bus Line, also known as the Big Blue Bus, is a pleasant and inexpensive way to move around the Westside. Trips cost $1.25. An express bus to and from Downtown L.A., run by Culver CityBus, costs $2.50. Transfers to Metro or Metro Rail are 50¢.

You can pay your fare in cash on MTA, Santa Monica, and Culver City buses, but you must have exact change. You can buy MTA TAP cards at Metro Rail stations, customer centers throughout the city, and some convenience and grocery stores.

🚗 Car Travel

If you're used to urban driving, you shouldn't have too much trouble navigating the streets of Los Angeles. If not, L.A. can be unnerving. However, the city has evolved with drivers in mind. Streets are wide and parking garages abound, so it's more car friendly than many older big cities.

If you get discombobulated while on the freeway, remember this rule of thumb: even-numbered freeways run east and west, odd-numbered freeways run north and south.

GASOLINE

As of this writing, gasoline costs around $3 a gallon. Most stations are self-service; the few remaining full-service stations are mostly in and around the Westside. There are plenty of stations everywhere. Most stay open late, and many are open 24 hours.

GETTING AROUND

There are plenty of identical or similarly named streets in L.A. (Beverly Boulevard and Beverly Drive, for example), so be as specific as you can when asking

Getting Here

directions or inputting into a map app. Expect sudden changes in addresses as streets pass through neighborhoods, then incorporated cities, then back into neighborhoods. This can be most bewildering on Robertson Boulevard, an otherwise useful north–south artery that, by crossing through L.A., West Hollywood, and Beverly Hills, dips in and out of several such numbering shifts in a matter of miles.

PARKING

Parking rules are strictly enforced in Los Angeles, so make sure you check for signs and read them carefully. Illegally parked cars are ticketed or towed quickly. Parking prices vary from 25¢ (in public lots and at meters) to $2 per half hour (in private lots). Downtown and Century City rates may be as high as $25 an hour.

Parking in Downtown L.A. can be tough, especially on weekdays. Try the garage at the FIG at 7th retail complex (⊠ 725 S. Figueroa St.), which is spacious, reasonably priced, and visitor friendly.

In Hollywood, the underground facility at the Hollywood & Highland shopping complex (⊠ 6801 Hollywood Blvd.) charges $3 for the first four hours with validation. In Beverly Hills, the first two hours are free at several lots on or around Rodeo Drive. The Westside Pavilion (⊠ 10800 Pico Blvd.) offers three hours of free parking at its garage.

At some shops, most restaurants, and hotels in Los Angeles, valet parking is virtually assumed. The cost is usually $6 to $16. Keep small bills on hand to tip the valets.

ROAD CONDITIONS

Beware of weekday rush-hour traffic, which is heaviest from 7 to 10 am and 3 to 7 pm. Go511.com and the Waze app offer real-time traffic information, and the California Highway Patrol has

a road-conditions hotline. To encourage carpooling, some crowded freeways reserve an express lane for cars carrying more than one passenger.

Parallel streets can often provide viable alternatives to jam-packed freeways, notably Sepulveda Boulevard for I–405; Venice and Washington boulevards for I–10 from Mid-Wilshire west to the beach; and Ventura Boulevard, Moorpark Street, or Riverside Drive for U.S. 101 through the San Fernando Valley.

ROADSIDE EMERGENCIES

For minor problems faced by motorists (running out of gas, blowing a tire, needing a tow to the nearest phone), California's Department of Transportation has a Metro Freeway Service Patrol. More than 145 tow trucks patrol the freeways offering free aid to stranded drivers. Reach them on your cell phone by calling 511.

If your car breaks down on an interstate, pull over onto the shoulder and call the state police from your cell phone or walk to the nearest emergency roadside phone. When calling for help, note your location according to the small green mileage markers posted along the highway.

RULES OF THE ROAD

Seat belts are required for all passengers in California, as is the use of federally approved car seats for children under nine or less than 4 feet, 9 inches tall. California law requires that drivers use hands-free devices when talking on cell phones. Texting and driving is illegal and results in a hefty fine.

The speed limit is 25 to 35 mph on city streets and 65 mph on freeways unless otherwise posted. Some towns, including Beverly Hills and Culver City, use cameras at traffic lights to reduce speeding. Speeding can earn you fines starting at $266. It is illegal to drive in California with a blood alcohol content of 0.08% or above (0.01% if you're under 21). There are strict penalties for first offenders. Checkpoints are set up on weekends and holidays across the county.

Parking infractions can result in penalties starting at $68. Having your vehicle towed and impounded will cost nearly $300 even if you pay up immediately, and more if you don't. LAX is notorious for handing out tickets to drivers circling its busy terminals; avoid the no-parking zones and keep loading or unloading to a minimum.

Turning right on red after a complete stop is legal unless otherwise posted. Many streets in Downtown L.A. are one-way, and a left turn from one one-way street onto another is allowed. On some major arteries, left turns are illegal during rush hour. Certain carpool lanes, designated by signage and a white diamond, are reserved for cars with more than one passenger. Freeway on-ramps often have stop-and-go signals to regulate the flow of traffic, but cars in high-occupancy-vehicle (HOV) lanes can pass the signal without stopping.

Keep in mind that pedestrians always have the right of way in California; not yielding to them, even if they're jaywalkers, may result in a $211 ticket.

CAR RENTAL

In Los Angeles, a car is a necessity. Keep in mind that you'll likely be spending a lot of time in it, and options like a plug for your cell phone could make a significant difference in your day-to-day comfort.

Major-chain rates in L.A. begin at $38 a day and $300 a week, plus sales tax and concession fees. Luxury vehicles start at $75 a day. Open-top convertibles are a popular choice for visitors wanting to make the most of the sun. Note that the major agencies offer services for

travelers with disabilities, such as hand controls, for little or no extra cost.

In California you must be 21 and have a valid credit card to rent a car. Some agencies won't rent to those under 25, and those that do may charge extra.

Ⓜ Metro/Public Transport

Metro Rail covers only a small part of L.A.'s vast expanse, but it's convenient, frequent, and inexpensive. Most popular with visitors is the underground Red Line, which runs from Downtown's Union Station through Mid-Wilshire, Hollywood, and Universal City on its way to North Hollywood, stopping at the most popular tourist destinations along the way.

The light-rail Green Line stretches from Redondo Beach to Norwalk, while the partially underground Blue Line travels from Downtown to the South Bay. The monorail-like Gold Line extends from Union Station to Pasadena and out to the deep San Gabriel Valley and Azusa. The Orange Line, a 14-mile bus corridor, connects the North Hollywood subway station with the western San Fernando Valley.

Most recently extended was the Expo Line, which connects Downtown to the Westside, and terminates in Santa Monica, two blocks from the Pacific Ocean.

Daily service is offered from about 4:30 am to 12:30 am, with departures every 5 to 15 minutes. On weekends trains run until 2 am. Buy tickets from station vending machines; fares are $1.75, or $7 for an all-day pass. Bicycles are allowed on Metro Rail trains at all times.

Getting Here

🚗 Ride-Sharing

Request a ride using apps like Lyft, and a driver will usually arrive within minutes. Fares increase during busy times, but it's often the most affordable option, especially for the convenience.

🚕 Taxi Travel

Instead of trying to hail a taxi on the street, phone one of the many taxi companies. The Curb Taxi app allows for online hailing of L.A. taxis. The metered rate is $2.70 per mile, plus a $2.85 per-fare charge. Taxi rides from LAX have an additional $4 surcharge. Be aware that distances are greater than they might appear on the map so fares add up quickly.

On the other end of the price spectrum, limousines come equipped with everything from full bars to night-club-style sound-and-light systems. Most charge by the hour, minimum hours sometimes required.

🚆 Train Travel

Downtown's Union Station is one of the great American railroad terminals. The interior includes comfortable seating, a restaurant, and several snack bars. As the city's rail hub, it's the place to catch an Amtrak, Metrolink commuter train, or the Red, Gold, or Purple lines. Among Amtrak's Southern California routes are 11 daily trips to San Diego and 6 to Santa Barbara. Amtrak's luxury *Coast Starlight* travels along the spectacular coastline from Seattle to Los Angeles in just a day and a half (though it's often a little late). The *Sunset Limited* arrives from New Orleans, and the *Southwest Chief* comes from Chicago.

Before You Go

Passport

American travelers never need a passport to travel domestically. Non-American travelers always need a valid passport to visit California.

🆔 Visa

For international travelers, a tourism visa is required for traveling to California and the rest of the United States.

✏️ Immunizations

No specific immunizations or vaccinations are required for visits to California.

💲 Customs and Duties

You're always allowed to bring goods of a certain value back home without having to pay any duty or import tax. But there's a limit on the amount of tobacco and liquor you can bring back duty free. If the total value of your goods is more than the duty-free limit, you'll have to pay a tax (most often a flat percentage) on the value of everything beyond that limit.

📅 When to Go

LOW SEASON $

Los Angeles's weather is so ideal that most locals shrug off the high cost of living as a "sunshine tax." But it does get chilly (read: highs in the 50s). January and February tend to be the coldest and rainiest months. However, occasionally the rain begins in December and ends in March.

SHOULDER SEASON $$

Springtime in Los Angeles is typically from mid-March to May, when the temperatures fluctuate between the low 70s and mid-80s. Nights tend to be in the 50s. Jacaranda trees bloom across the city and purple flowers litter the sidewalks. It's no cherry blossoms in Japan, but it's still pretty. September is usually the hottest and driest month. It's also when the Santa Ana winds begin—the hot "devil winds" that usher in fire season and fray everyone's nerves. They usually blow on out of here in December.

AWARDS SEASON $$$

Awards Season in Los Angeles can be mildly annoying. From January through February, L.A. hosts the Golden Globes, the Academy Awards, the Grammys (sometimes), and a slew of other ceremonies. This creates two problems: hotel prices tend to go up on the weekends of events, especially in Beverly Hills, West Hollywood, and Downtown; and traffic is even worse—Hollywood Boulevard is closed around Hollywood & Highland, the Oscars venue, for a week.

HIGH SEASON $$$$

The peak season runs from June through August. Beaches are packed every weekend, so plan to go early and expect traffic, especially en route to Malibu. June is usually cooler, especially in the mornings and evenings when the fog rolls in—they don't call it "June gloom" for nothing. But temperatures in July and August hover in the 80s and can spike to triple digits. The coasts are usually between 5 and 10 degrees cooler than Downtown.

Essentials

Dining

Los Angeles may be known for its beach living and celebrity-infused backdrop, but it was once a farm town. The hillsides were covered in citrus orchards and dairy farms, and agriculture was a major industry. Today, even as L.A. is urbanized, the city's culinary landscape has reembraced a local, sustainable, and seasonal philosophy at many levels—from fine dining to street snacks.

With a growing interest in farm-to-fork, the city's farmers' market scene has exploded, becoming popular at big-name restaurants and small eateries alike. In Hollywood and Santa Monica you can often find high-profile chefs scouring farm stands for fresh produce.

The status of the celebrity chef carries weight around this town. People follow the culinary zeitgeist with the same fervor as celebrity gossip. You can queue up with the hungry hordes at Nancy Silverton's **Mozza,** or try and snag a reservation to Ludo Lefebvre's ever-popular **Trois Mec** or David Chang's L.A. outpost, **Majordomo.**

Ethnic eats continue to be a backbone of the L.A. dining scene. People head to Koreatown for epic Korean cooking and late-night coffeehouses and to West L.A. for phenomenal sushi. Latin food is well represented in the city, making it tough to choose between Guatemalan eateries, Peruvian restaurants, nouveau Mexican bistros, and Tijuana-style taco trucks. With so many dining options, sometimes the best strategy is simply to drive and explore.

CHILDREN

Although it's unusual to see children in the dining rooms of L.A.'s most elite restaurants, dining with youngsters here does not have to mean culinary exile.

SMOKING

Smokers should keep in mind that California law forbids smoking in all enclosed areas, including bars.

RESERVATIONS

You'll be happy to hear it's getting easier to snag a desired reservation, but it's still a good idea to plan ahead. Some renowned restaurants are booked weeks or even months in advance. If that's the case, you can get lucky at the last minute if you're flexible—and friendly. Most restaurants keep a few tables open for walk-ins and VIPs. Show up for dinner early (6 pm) or late (after 9 pm) and politely inquire about any last-minute vacancies or cancellations. Try booking apps like Open Table and Resy. Most places, except small mom-and-pop establishments, provide valet parking at dinner for reasonable rates (often around $10, plus tip).

DINING HOURS

Despite its veneer of decadence, L.A. is not a particularly late-night city for eating. (The reenergized Hollywood dining scene is emerging as a notable exception.) The peak dinner times are from 7 to 9, and most restaurants won't take reservations after 10. Unless otherwise noted, the restaurants listed in this guide are open daily for lunch and dinner. Generally speaking, restaurants are closed either Sunday or Monday; a few are shuttered both days. Most places—even the upscale spots—are open for lunch on weekdays, since many Hollywood megadeals are conceived at that time.

WHAT TO WEAR

Dining out in Los Angeles tends to be a casual affair, and even at some of the most expensive restaurants you're likely to see customers in jeans (although this is not necessarily considered in good taste). It's extremely rare for L.A. restaurants to actually require a jacket and tie, but all of the city's more formal establishments appreciate a gentleman who dons a jacket—let your good judgment be your guide.

TIPPING AND TAXES

In most restaurants, tip the waiter 16%–20%. (To figure out a 20% tip quickly, just move the decimal point one place to the left on your total and double that amount.) Note that checks for parties of six or more sometimes include the tip already. Tip at least $1 per drink at the bar, and $1 for each coat checked. Never tip the maître d' unless you're out to impress your guests or expect to pay another visit soon. Also, be prepared for a sales tax of around 9.5% to appear on your bill.

PRICES

If you're watching your budget, be sure to ask the price of daily specials recited by the waiter. The charge for specials at some restaurants is noticeably out of line with the other prices on the menu. Beware of the $10 bottle of water; ask for tap water instead.

If you eat early or late, you may be able to take advantage of a prix-fixe deal not offered at peak hours. Most upscale restaurants are offering great lunch deals with special menus at cut-rate prices designed to give customers a true taste of the place.

Credit cards are accepted unless otherwise noted in the review. While many restaurants do accept credit cards, some smaller places accept only cash. If you plan to use a credit card it's a good idea to double-check its acceptability when making reservations or before sitting down to eat.

What It Costs			
$	$$	$$$	$$$$
RESTAURANTS			
under $14	$14–$22	$23–$31	over $31

🛏 Lodging

When it comes to finding a place to stay, travelers have never been more spoiled for choice than in today's Los Angeles. From luxurious digs in Beverly Hills and along the coast to budget boutiques in Hollywood, hotels are stepping up service, upgrading amenities, and trying all-new concepts, like upscale hostels and retro-chic motels. Hotels in Los Angeles today are more than just a place to rest your head; they're a key part of the experience.

RESERVATIONS

Hotel reservations are an absolute necessity when planning your trip to Los Angeles—although rooms are easier to come by these days. Competition for clients also means properties undergo frequent improvements, so when booking ask about any renovations, lest you get a room within earshot of construction. In this ever-changing city travelers can find themselves without amenities like room service or spa access if their hotel is upgrading.

SERVICES

Most hotels have air conditioning and flat-screen cable TV. Those in the moderate and expensive price ranges often have voice mail, coffeemakers, bathrobes, and hair dryers. Most also have high-speed Internet access in guest rooms, with a 24-hour use fee (though at a number of hotels, it's free). Wi-Fi is common even at budget properties. Southern California's emphasis on being

Where Should I Stay?

	Neighborhood Vibe	Pros	Cons
Downtown	High-rises, office towers, commercial districts, and cultural institutions, with a growing residential scene.	Affordable hotels within walking distance of art museums, concert halls, and the L.A. Live complex.	Homeless encampments, with some sketchy areas at night.
Hollywood	Historic theaters and the Walk of Fame; L.A.'s Time Square.	Heart of the city's nightlife and see-and-be-seen spots, from lively nightclubs to popular eateries.	Steep parking fees, tourist trap, often crowded.
Studio City, Universal City, and North Hollywood	Residential and suburban feel, with some commercial (strip-mall) spots.	Safe, family-friendly, affordable accommodations, plentiful dining options.	Requires a car to get anywhere, even to a nearby coffee shop.
Beverly Hills	Upscale—one of the city's most sought-after addresses, with classy and elegant hotels.	Great shopping, celeb spotting, numerous restaurants all near quiet residential areas.	Big bucks to stay, dine, park, and shop here; limited diversity.
Culver City	Businesses mixed with residential buildings; centrally located.	Easy access to all points on the Westside; pedestrian-friendly strip in Culver City.	Some strictly office areas; no beach or ocean views.
Bel Air, West Hollywood, Westwood	Coveted neighborhood for elite; boutique hotels abound in West Hollywood.	Close proximity to Getty Center; ambitious restaurants and fun night spots in West Hollywood.	Stuffy attitudes in Bel Air; spendy stays in West Hollywood.
LAX vicinity	Concentration of office towers and commercial buildings.	Convenient location near airport; incredibly affordable.	Little activity, dull nearby strip malls with restaurants and shopping.
Santa Monica and Malibu	Upscale beach towns with waterfront resorts and hip boutique properties.	Ocean breezes, super-safe, family friendly; walkable pockets with restaurants, cafés, and boutiques.	Some bars, but limited nightlife; steep prices for an ocean view.
Venice, Marina del Rey, Manhattan, Hermosa, Long Beach	Edgy, artsy in Venice; residential in Manhattan Beach; sailing and biking in Marina del Rey.	Diverse neighborhoods but close to the ocean without Malibu's spendiness. Long Beach airport is a great alternative to LAX.	Mostly residential in some pockets; traffic along Highway 1 means long driving times.
Pasadena	Residential with walkable strip of shops and cafés.	Charming small-town feel, family friendly, historic.	Removed from the Westside and beaches; lengthy driving time into the city.

in shape means most hotels have fitness facilities; if the one on-site is not to your liking, ask for a reference to a nearby sports club or gym.

STAYING WITH KIDS

From Disneyland to the beach cities, laid-back Los Angeles definitely has a reputation as a family-friendly destination. Resorts and hotels along the coast, in particular, attract plenty of beach-going family vacationers looking for sun and sand castles. Some properties provide such diversions as in-room movies, toys, and video games; others have suites with kitchenettes and fold-out sofa beds. Hotels often provide cribs, rollaway beds, and references for babysitting services, but make arrangements when booking the room, not when you arrive. *Properties that are especially kid-friendly are marked FAMILY throughout the chapter.*

PARKING

Exploring Los Angeles, a sprawling city of wide boulevards and five-lane freeways, requires a car. Though you might stroll Rodeo Drive on foot or amble along the Hollywood Walk of Fame, to get from one part of town to another, you'll need wheels. Thankfully, there's street parking in most areas (read signs carefully as some neighborhoods are by permit only), and many public parking lots are free for the first hour or two. Though a few hotels have free parking, most charge for the privilege, and some resorts only have valet parking, with fees as high as $50 per night.

PRICES

Tax rates for the area will add 10%–14% to your bill depending on where in Los Angeles County you stay; some hoteliers tack on energy, service, or occupancy surcharges—ask about customary charges when you book your room.

When looking for a hotel, don't write off the pricier establishments immediately. Price categories here are determined by "rack rates"—the list price of a hotel room—which are often higher than those you'll find online or by calling the hotel directly. Specials abound, particularly in Downtown on the weekends. Many hotels have packages that include breakfast, theater tickets, spa services, or luxury rental cars. Pricing is competitive, so always check with the hotel for current special offers.

When making reservations, don't forget to check the hotel's website for exclusive online specials.

What It Costs

	$	$$	$$$	$$$$
HOTELS	under $200	$200–$300	$301–$400	over $400

🍸 Nightlife

Los Angeles is not the city that never sleeps—instead it parties until 2 am (save for the secret after-hours parties at private clubs or warehouses) and wakes up to imbibe green juices and breakfast burritos as hangover cures or to sweat it out in a yoga class. Whether you plan to test your limit at historic establishments Downtown or take advantage of a cheap happy hour at a Hollywood dive, this city's nightlife has something for you.

A night out in Los Angeles can simultaneously surprise and impress. Seeing an unscheduled set by an A-list comedian at the stand-up comedy club, being talked into singing karaoke at the diviest place you've ever seen, dancing at a bar with no dance floor because, well, the DJ is

Essentials

just too good at his job—going out isn't always what you expect, but it certainly is never boring.

The focus of nightlife once centered on the Sunset Strip, with its multitude of bars, rock clubs, and dance spots, but more neighborhoods are competing with each other and forcing the nightlife scene to evolve. Although the Strip can be a worthwhile trip, other areas of the city are catching people's attention. Downtown Los Angeles, for instance, is a destination in its own right. Other areas foster more of a neighborhood vibe. Silver Lake and Los Feliz have both cultivated a relaxed environment.

So if you find yourself disappointed with a rude bouncer, or drinks that are too watery, or a cover charge that just isn't worth it, try again. Eventually you'll find that perfect place where each time is the best time. If not, at least you'll walk away with a good story.

🎭 Performing Arts

The art scene in Los Angeles extends beyond the screen and onto the stage. A place of artistic innovation and history, one can discover new and challenging theatrical works across L.A. stages, while the city still maintains a respect for tradition with its restored theaters and classic plays. See live music at impeccably designed amphitheaters like the Hollywood Bowl or listen in on captivating lectures by authors and directors at various intimate spaces. In homage to the city's roots as a filmmaking mecca, there are also retrospectives and rare screenings in movie theaters all over the city, often followed by Q&As with the cast.

L.A.'s art scene is varied and caters to all budgets and tastes. East West Players at

Item	Average Cost
Cup of Coffee	$3
Glass of Wine	$10
Beer	$8
Sandwich	$12
15-Minute Taxi Ride	$30
Museum Admission	$15

the David Henry Hwang Theatre focuses on Asian American–themed plays, and if an opera at the Dorothy Chandler Pavilion seems out of your price range, Actors' Gang in Culver City offers a free Shakespeare play in Media Park in the summer. The Independent Theatre Company hosts a free Shakespeare festival in Griffith Park, also during summer.

➕ Health

The air pollution in L.A. may affect sensitive people in different ways. When pollution levels are high, it's a good idea to plan a day indoors or on a windy beach. The sun can burn even on overcast days, and the dry heat can dehydrate, so wear hats, sunglasses, and sunblock, and carry water with you.

💲 Money

Although not inexpensive, costs in Los Angeles tend to be a bit lower than in New York or San Francisco. For instance, in a low-key local diner, a cup of coffee might cost around $3. In high-profile establishments, costs escalate; a cup of coffee in a trendy eatery can cost as much as $7.

Prices throughout this guide are given for adults. Reduced fees are almost always available for children, students, and senior citizens.

✚ Safety

Very minor earthquakes occur frequently in Southern California; most of the time they're so slight that you won't notice them. If you feel a stronger tremor, follow basic safety precautions. If you're indoors, take cover in a doorway or under a table or desk—whichever is closest. Protect your head with your arms. Stay clear of windows, mirrors, or anything that might fall from the walls. Do not use elevators. If you're in an open space, move away from buildings, trees, and power lines. If you're outdoors near buildings, duck into a doorway. If you're driving, pull over to the side of the road, avoiding overpasses, bridges, and power lines, and stay inside the car. Expect aftershocks, and take cover again if they are strong.

Of the Metro lines, the Red, Green, and Expo lines are the safest and are more regularly patrolled. The Blue Line can be sketchy after dark. Avoid riding in empty cars, and move with the crowd when going from the station to the street.

$ Taxes

The sales tax in L.A. is 9.5%, one of the highest in California. There's none on most groceries, but there is on newspapers and magazines. The tax on hotel rooms ranges from 13% to 15.5%. Food tax varies, but expect to pay around 9.5%.

💵 Tipping

The customary tip rate is 15%–20% for waiters, taxi drivers, hairdressers, and barbers. Bellhops and baggage handlers receive $1–$2 per bag; parking valets and hotel housekeepers are usually tipped $2–$3. Bartenders get about $1 per drink, but tip your mixologists like you would a waiter.

📍 Visitor Information

Discover Los Angeles, the official tourism site, has an annually updated general information packet that includes suggestions for entertainment, lodging, and dining and a list of special events. There are two visitor information centers, both accessible to Metro stops: the Hollywood & Highland Center and Union Station.

Contacts

✈ Air Travel

AIRPORT INFORMA-TION Hollywood Burbank Airport (*BUR*). ✉ *2627 N. Hollywood Way, near I–5 and U.S. 101, Burbank* ☎ *818/840–8840* ⊕ *www. hollywoodburbankair-port.com.* **John Wayne Airport** (*SNA*). ✉ *18601 Airport Way, Santa Ana* ☎ *949/252–5200* ⊕ *www. ocair.com.* **L.A./Ontario International Airport** (*ONT*). ✉ *E. Airport Dr., off I–10, Ontario* ☎ *909/544–5300* ⊕ *www.flyontario. com.* **Long Beach Airport** (*LGB*). ✉ *4100 Donald Douglas Dr., Long Beach* ☎ *562/570–2600* ⊕ *www. lgb.org.* **Los Angeles International Airport** (*LAX*). ✉ *1 World Way, off Hwy. 1* ☎ *855/463–5252* ⊕ *www. flylax.com.*

AIRPORT TRANS-PORTATION FlyAway. ☎ *866/435–9529* ⊕ *www. flylax.com/en/flyaway-bus.* **SuperShuttle.** ☎ *323/775–6600, 800/258–3826* ⊕ *www.supershuttle.com.*

🚌 Bus Travel

BUS INFORMATION Culver CityBus. ☎ *310/253–6510* ⊕ *www.culvercity.org.* **DASH.** ☎ *310/808–2273* ⊕ *www.ladottransit. com.* **Los Angeles County Metropolitan Transit Authority.** ☎ *323/466–3876* ⊕ *www.metro.net.* **Santa**

Monica Municipal Bus Line. ☎ *310/451–5444* ⊕ *www. bigbluebus.com.*

🚗 Car Travel

INFORMATION Caltrans Current Highway Conditions. ☎ *800/427–7623 for road conditions* ⊕ *www.dot. ca.gov.* **Go511.** ☎ *511* ⊕ *www.go511.com.*

EMERGENCY SERVICES Metro Freeway Service Patrol. ☎ *511 for break-downs* ⊕ *www.go511. com.*

AUTOMOBILE ASSOCIA-TIONS American Automo-bile Association (*AAA*). ☎ *800/400–4222* ⊕ *www. aaa.com.* **National Automo-bile Club.** ☎ *650/294–7000* ⊕ *www.thenac.com.*

Ⓜ Metro/ Public Transport

RAIL INFORMATION Los Angeles County Metro-politan Transit Authority. ☎ *213/922–6235* ⊕ *www. metro.net.*

🚕 Taxi Travel

LIMO COMPANIES Apex Limo. ☎ *818/788–5466, 877/427–1777 for 24-hr pickup* ⊕ *www.apexlimola. com.* **Dav El Chauffeured Transportation Network.** ☎ *800/672–7676* ⊕ *www.*

davelbostoncoach.com. **First Class Limousine Service.** ☎ *800/400–9771* ⊕ *www.first-classlimo. com.* **Wilshire Limousine Services.** ☎ *888/813–8420* ⊕ *www.wilshirelimousine. com.*

TAXI COMPANIES Beverly Hills Cab Co. ☎ *800/273–6611* ⊕ *www.beverlyhills-cabco.com.* **Independent Cab Co.** ☎ *800/521–8294* ⊕ *www.taxi4u.com.* **LA Checker Cab.** ☎ *800/300–5007* ⊕ *www.ineedtaxi. com.* **United Independent Taxi.** ☎ *800/822–8294, 323/207–8294 text to order taxi* ⊕ *www.united-taxi.com.* **Yellow Cab Los Angeles.** ☎ *424/222–2222* ⊕ *www.layellowcab.com.*

🚆 Train Travel

INFORMATION Amtrak. ☎ *800/872–7245* ⊕ *www. amtrak.com.* **Metrolink.** ☎ *800/371–5465* ⊕ *www. metrolinktrains.com.* **Union Station.** ✉ *800 N. Alam-eda St.* ☎ *213/683–6979* ⊕ *www.unionstationla. com.*

📍 Visitor Information

CONTACTS Discover Los Angeles. ☎ *213/624–7300, 800/228–2452* ⊕ *www. discoverlosangeles.com.*

Best Tours in Los Angeles

BUS TOURS

Guideline Tours offers sightseeing trips all around L.A., including Downtown, Universal Studios, and Hollywood. Starline Tours picks up passengers from the TCL Chinese Theatre and in Santa Monica for double-decker hop-on/off tours around town and operates tours to Disneyland, Universal Studios, and Six Flags Magic Mountain. The TMZ Celebrity Tour of reputed celebrity hot spots leaves from in front of the Hard Rock in Hollywood or The Grove.

CONTACTS Guideline Tours. ☎ 323/465–3004, 800/604–8433 ⊕ www.tourslosangeles.com. **Starline Tours.** ☎ 800/959–3131 ⊕ www.starlinetours.com. **TMZ Celebrity Tour.** ☎ 844/869–8687 ⊕ www.tmztour.com.

HELICOPTER TOURS

If you want an aerial tour, lift off with Orbic Air. Based at Hollywood Burbank Airport, the company has been flying its four-passenger helicopters for more than 25 years. It's $99 per person for the basic 15-minute Hollywood Sign tour.

CONTACTS Orbic Air. ☎ 818/561–4838 ⊕ www.orbicair.com.

SCOOTER TOURS

For an unusual perspective on L.A.'s attractions, you can take a tour of the city on a Segway electric scooter. The $89 Segwow tours might include the UCLA campus, Santa Monica, or Downtown. The guided rides last just over two hours.

CONTACTS Segwow. ☎ 310/358–5900 ⊕ www.segwow.com.

SPECIAL-INTEREST TOURS

With Architecture Tours L.A., you can zip all over the city in a comfortable minivan on a private tour with a historian. Rates start at $75 per person. Esotouric has an innovative take on the city; its varied weekend bus tours ($58 and up) explore historic architecture along Route 66 and the darker side of L.A. that Raymond Chandler revealed in books like *The Big Sleep* and *The Long Goodbye*.

Beverly Hills operates year-round trolley tours focused on art and architecture. They last 40 minutes and depart from 11 am to 4 pm every weekend throughout the year, as well as Tuesday to Friday in the summer. Tickets cost $5. Soak up the glow of classic neon signs from an open double-decker bus on tours offered by the Museum of Neon Art. They cost $55 and are offered May through September.

Take My Mother Please will arrange lively, thematic combination walking and driving tours. Rates start at $450 for up to three people for a half day.

CONTACTS Architecture Tours L.A. ☎ 323/464–7868 ⊕ www.architecture-toursla.com. **Beverly Hills Trolley Tours.** ✉ Dayton Way and Rodeo Dr., Beverly Hills ☎ 310/285–1128 ⊕ www.beverly-hills.org/exploring/trolleytours. **Esotouric.** ☎ 213/373–1947 ⊕ www.esotouric.com. **Neon Cruise.** ☎ 818/696–2149 ⊕ www.neonmona.org/neon-cruise. **Take My Mother Please.** ☎ 323/737–2200 ⊕ www.takemymotherplease.com.

WALKING TOURS

Red Line Tours offers daily one- and two-hour walking tours of behind-the-scenes Hollywood. Tours, which cost $25, are led by docents and include headsets to block out street noise. The Los Angeles Conservancy's 2½-hour-long walking tours ($10) cover the Downtown area.

CONTACTS Los Angeles Conservancy. ☎ 213/623–2489 ⊕ www.laconservancy.org. **Red Line Tours.** ✉ 6708 Hollywood Blvd. ☎ 323/402–1074 ⊕ www.redline-tours.com.

Continued on page 57

CRUISING THE SUNSET STRIP

For more than half a century, Hollywood's night owls have headed for the 1¾-mile stretch of Sunset Boulevard between Crescent Heights Boulevard on the east and Doheny Drive on the west, known as the Sunset Strip. The experience of driving it from end to end gives you a sampling of everything that makes L.A. what it is, with all its glamour and grit, and its history of those who rose fast and fell faster.

Left and top right, two views of Sunset Boulevard. Bottom right, Mel's Drive-in Diner.

In the 1930s and '40s, stars such as Errol Flynn and Rita Hayworth came for wild evenings of dancing and drinking at nightclubs like Trocadero, Ciro's, and Mocambo.

The Strip's image as Tinseltown's glamorous nighttime playground began to die in the '50s, and by the mid-'60s it was the center of L.A.'s raucous music-and-nightlife scene. Bands like the Doors and the Byrds played the Whisky a Go Go, and the city's counterculture clashed with police in the famous Sunset Strip curfew riots in the summer of 1966.

In the '70s, the Strip was all about glam rock, with David Bowie, T. Rex, and Queen hitting the venues. But this was when it began a decline that would last almost two decades, until it became a seedy section of the city where hookers hung out on every corner.

It's only been in the last decade that the Strip has seen a true revitalization, with new hotels, restaurants, and bars opening that have become haunts for celebs and A-listers. It retains its rough-and-tumble image in some sections but overall is a much classier spot to spend a night out.

A CLASSIC DRIVE THROUGH L.A.

Depending on the time of day, driving the Strip is a different experience. In the afternoon grab lunch at a hotel and hobnob with industry types. At night, drive with the top down and come to hear music, hit a club, or have cocktails at a rooftop bar. Either way, it's good to park the car and walk (yes, walk!).

WHERE TO EAT & DRINK

See and be seen at **Sky-bar at the Mondrian Hotel** (✉ 8440 Sunset Blvd. ☎ 323/848–6025), the luxe outdoor lounge and pool deck. The bar opens to the public at 8 pm daily. Come early to enjoy sweeping views of the city before turning your gaze inward to the beautiful people milling around. Go to **Greenblatt's Deli** (✉ 8017 Sunset Blvd. ☎ 323/656-0606) for some of the best roast beef you'll ever have. Around since 1926, this casual deli has free parking in the back, and you can order picnic basket dinners to take to the Hollywood Bowl.

Stop in for a burger and shake at **Mel's Drive-In** (✉ 8585 Sunset Blvd. ☎ 310/854–7201), open 24 hours a day. The iconic

TIPS FOR PARKING

Parking and traffic around the Strip can be tough on weekends. Although there's some parking on side streets, it may be worth it to park in a lot and pay $10-$25. Most of the hotels have garages as well.

Whisky a Go Go

The Roxy

The Chateau Marmont

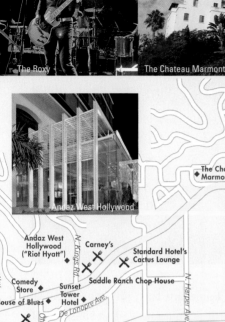

Andaz West Hollywood

The Chateau Marmont

Greenblatt's Deli

Sunset Blvd.

Andaz West Hollywood ("Riot Hyatt")

Carney's

Standard Hotel's Cactus Lounge

Comedy Store

Sunset Tower Hotel

Saddle Ranch Chop House

House of Blues

Skybar at the Mondrian Hotel

Fountain Ave.

1950s-inspired diner in the heart of the Strip is a fun place to people-watch, day or night.

For the city's best hot dogs, chili fries, and frozen chocolate-dipped bananas, head to **Carney's** (⌧ 8351 Sunset Blvd. ☎ 323/654-8300), a popular spot for a quick bite. You can't miss it—look for the yellow railcar.

SIGHTS TO SEE

The Chateau Marmont (⌧ 8221 West Sunset Boulevard). Greta Garbo

once called this castle-like hotel home. It's also where John Belushi died.

Comedy Store (⌧ 8433 Sunset Boulevard). David Letterman and Robin Williams rose to fame here.

Andaz West Hollywood ("Riot Hyatt") (⌧ 8401 Sunset Boulevard). Led Zeppelin, the Rolling Stones, and the Who stayed and played here when they hit town.

Rainbow Bar & Grill (⌧ 9015 Sunset Boulevard). Jimi Hendrix and

Bob Marley began their climb to the top of the charts here.

The Roxy (⌧ 9009 Sunset Boulevard). Neil Young was the opening act here in 1973; it's been a Strip anchor and front-runner in revitalization.

The Viper Room (⌧ 8852 Sunset Blvd.) This always popular, always booked venue was where River Phoenix OD'd in 1993.

Saddle Ranch Chop House (⌧ 8371 Sunset Boulevard). Originally the Thunder Roadhouse (co-owned by Dennis Hopper and Peter Fonda), this raucous steakhouse has a mechanical bull featured on many a TV show, including *Sex and the City*.

A DRIVE BEYOND THE STRIP

California's Pacific Coast Highway at dusk

There's more to see along Sunset Boulevard than just the Strip. For another classic L.A. drive, just before dusk, continue west on Sunset until you reach the Pacific Coast Highway (PCH) in Pacific Palisades, right along the ocean, and you'll understand how the boulevard got its name.

WHEN TO GO

Time it right so you can catch that famous L.A. sunset, or drive down Sunset Boulevard late morning after rush hour and arrive just in time for lunch at a waterfront restaurant or a picnic on the beach.

The PCH is also known for its fresh seafood shacks along the roadside. For a cocktail with a great view, try **Gladstone's 4 Fish** (✉ 17300 Pacific Coast Hwy.), where Sunset Boulevard hits the PCH.

TRIP TIPS

While it's hard to tear your eyes away from sites along the way, there are hairpin turns on the Boulevard, and driving can be a challenge. Stop-and-go traffic—especially along the Strip—means lots of fender benders, so be careful and keep a safe distance.

Sunset view from Gladstone's

Great Itineraries

The trick to having a decent quality of life in Los Angeles, claims one longtime Angeleno, is to live near where you work. The same adage holds true for visitors in that staying put in a single area of the city—being in a car for as short a time as possible—is a good rule of thumb. The best way to explore is one neighborhood at a time. Here are a few of our favorite itineraries to try.

Downtown Los Angeles

■ TIP→ **Best for fans of architecture, cuisine lovers, and bar hoppers.**

If you have a half day: Formerly an unwelcoming neighborhood dominated by the glass-and-steel office buildings of Bunker Hill on one side and the poverty and despair of Skid Row on the other, Downtown Los Angeles has staged a major comeback.

While the skyscrapers and tent cities still exist, there is also a middle ground that lures visitors with the promise of high art and historic architecture.

Don't miss the gems of Grand Avenue: the Walt Disney Concert Hall, the Broad Museum, and the Museum of Contemporary Art. At the concert hall, be sure to take the hour-long self-guided audio tour, which includes a walk through the venue's second-story hidden garden.

If you have a whole day: After feasting on culture, dine at the many stalls of Grand Central Market. Then Uber over to the art deco icon Union Station to admire the heavy wood-beam ceilings, leather-upholstered chairs, and inlaid marble floors.

Walk across Alameda Street to stroll past the shops and restaurants of L.A.'s historic Olvera Street, where you'll find traditional Mexican fare. Other eats can be found by venturing into Little Tokyo for a wide variety of Japanese cuisine or to Chinatown, especially for dim sum. Head back to the Historic Core for drinks. There's a large concentration of bars on Spring Street between 5th and 7th streets, and on 6th between Main and Los Angeles streets.

Hollywood

■ TIP→ **Best for first-timers to L.A. as well as film and music history buffs.**

If you have a half day: Tourists flock to Hollywood Boulevard to see old movie palaces such as TCL Chinese Theatre, where movie stars have left their mark, literally, in the concrete courtyard of the theater since 1927.

These days the theater's entrance is also graced by dozens of impersonators— from Marilyn Monroe to Spiderman— who are more than happy to pose for photos with visitors (they do expect to be paid, however).

Go to Hollywood & Highland Center for lunch, followed by a tour of the Kodak Theatre, which hosts the annual Academy Awards ceremony.

Wander the Walk of Fame, a 5-acre stretch of bronze stars embedded in pink terrazzo that lines Hollywood Boulevard, to pay homage to your favorite movie stars. Or visit the independent record store Amoeba Records for just about everything a music lover could want.

If you have a whole day: Some of the historic movie palaces, including TCL, still show films, but the real movie buffs should opt to see a movie at the ArcLight, a state-of-the-art theater on Sunset Boulevard that features gourmet food and reserved seating. Though all the theaters at the ArcLight are great, opt to see something

Great Itineraries

at the iconic Cinerama Dome. The ArcLight also boasts an in-house café bar that is perfect for a quick meal before a film or an après-show martini.

West Hollywood

■TIP→ **Best for trend-savvy shoppers, farmers' market foodies, and parents pushing strollers.**

If you have a half day: Thanks to its central location, West Hollywood is the ideal place to spend a couple of hours without committing an entire day—not that there isn't a day's worth of things to do in this neighborhood.

A shopping hub in its own right, West Hollywood lets visitors choose to stroll around the outdoor pedestrian area, The Grove, or the mammoth indoor Beverly Center. There are also countless small boutiques and specialty shops lining Beverly Boulevard, 3rd Street, and Melrose Avenue.

For lunch, grab a corned beef sandwich or some matzo ball soup at Canter's Delicatessen, a Los Angeles landmark since 1931, or head to the Farmers Market for a collection of ethnic food stalls and local products.

If you have a whole day: Tack Robertson Boulevard onto your shopping agenda to find boutiques ranging from Chanel to Kitson. Swing by the picket-fenced Ivy, a restaurant which had its celebrity heyday in the mid-aughts, but you still may see a star or two.

West Hollywood is known for its buzzing nightlife, so afterward choose from hundreds of small restaurants for dinner, then follow up with a drink from one of the area's many bars.

Beverly Hills and Mid-Wilshire

■TIP→ **Best for high-end shoppers, ladies who lunch, and contemporary art museum–goers.**

If you have a half day: Depending on how hardcore of a shopper you are, you can easily check out the boutiques of Beverly Hills in a couple of hours. In fact, with all of the designer flagships and tony department stores, it might be dangerous to spend too much time (translation: too much money) in this ritzy neighborhood.

Hit Rodeo Drive for all the runway names, such as Chanel, Christian Dior, Dolce & Gabbana, Fendi, Gucci, Prada, Valentino, and Versace.

Of course, not all the action is on Rodeo; don't forget to wander the side streets for more high fashion. The department stores—Barneys New York, Neiman Marcus, and Saks Fifth Avenue—are located nearby on Wilshire Boulevard. After you finish shopping, refuel with a dose of sugar at local dessert favorite Sprinkles Cupcakes.

If you have a whole day: After all that shopping, jump in the car to get some culture by heading east to the Miracle Mile in Mid-Wilshire, a stretch of Wilshire Boulevard that's home to the mammoth Los Angeles County Museum of Art, the Petersen Automotive Museum, and the Academy Museum of Motion Pictures. Depending on your preference of cuisine, have dinner in either Little Ethiopia or Koreatown.

Santa Monica and the Beaches

■ TIP➔ **Best for families with kids of all ages, sun worshippers and surfers, and anyone who likes cruising in a convertible.**

If you have a half day: With a couple of hours on your hands, it's a quick trip (if there's no traffic) to the beaches of Santa Monica or Venice. While they may not offer quite as much in the natural beauty department as their Malibu counterparts, they have plenty of sights of a different variety.

Don't miss the boardwalk vendors who hang out on Venice Beach or the street performers who frequent the Santa Monica Pier. Grab a snack at one of the beach-theme restaurants on the Strand. If you feel like a splurge, try the restaurant at Shutters on the Beach.

If you have a whole day: The ideal way to see Los Angeles's most beautiful beaches is to set aside an entire day for Malibu. Driving down the scenic Pacific Coast Highway is a treat in and of itself with sheer cliffs on one side of the road and ocean views on the other.

Topanga State Beach, Malibu Lagoon State Beach, and Malibu Surfrider Beach are all beautiful and popular spots to pass the day, but it's worth the extra drive time to see Point Dume State Beach, which is nestled away from the hustle and bustle of the highway.

Be sure to seek out the single-track trail that winds its way up a nearby coastal bluff revealing breathtaking views of Santa Monica Bay, the Malibu Coast, and Catalina Island. Stop for lunch at any of the seafood shacks that line PCH.

PASADENA

■ TIP➔ **Best for multigenerational groups, as well as art and architecture aficionados.**

If you have a half day: Aside from spending time poring over the massive collection of rare manuscripts and books at the Huntington Library, be sure to set aside a couple of hours for the Botanical Gardens to explore the more than a dozen themed areas, including authentic examples of both Japanese and Chinese gardens.

The Huntington has a beautiful outdoor café, as well as the Rose Garden Tea Room, where you can grab a tasty treat.

Another must-see museum is the Norton Simon Museum, with a collection that includes everything from ancient Asian art to 20th-century works.

If you have a whole day: Take a tour of Charles and Henry Greene's 1908 masterpiece, the Gamble House, followed by a trip to the Castle Green, the architects' Moorish Colonial and Spanish-style building.

Then, walk around in Old Town Pasadena, a revitalized shopping area with boutiques and eateries housed in historic buildings.

If you happen to be here during the once-a-month, massive Rose Bowl Flea Market, which takes over the Rose Bowl parking lot, you can browse around roughly 2,500 vendors' stalls.

Orange County and Catalina Island

■ TIP→ **Best for families traveling with young children and those who yearn for the great outdoors.**

If you have a half day: Head to one of the seemingly endless strings of beaches along this stretch of shoreline, extending from Long Beach to San Juan Capistrano. There's plenty to do besides sit in the sand: head to one of the fascinating aquariums, explore a nature preserve, or take in some impressive art at the area's surprisingly good museums.

Finding somewhere to eat won't be a problem, as this area is a major foodie destination. There are also plenty of reasonably priced family eateries.

If you have a whole day: If you're traveling with kids, you're going to end up at one of the classic theme parks, either Disneyland or Knott's Berry Farm. Grown-ups will be drawn to the natural beauty of Catalina Island. There's a tiny town with its fair share of attractions, but make sure you see the unspoiled coastline.

Chapter 3

SANTA MONICA AND THE BEACHES

Updated By
Candice Yacono

⊙ Sights	🍴 Restaurants	🛏 Hotels	🛍 Shopping	🍸 Nightlife
★★★☆☆	★★★★☆	★★★☆☆	★★★★☆	★★★☆☆

NEIGHBORHOOD SNAPSHOT

GREAT EXPERIENCES

Bike along the Strand. Spend the day on this 22-mile paved path, also known as the South Bay Bike Trail, which stretches from Santa Monica to Redondo Beach.

Watch the Sun Set over the Pacific in Malibu. Whether you watch it cliffside or parked on a beach blanket, the view will stay fixed in your mind as a trip highlight.

Spend the Day at Santa Monica Pier. See concerts here in the summer, or bring your family for a stroll during the day and enjoy classic fair food.

Catch the Mellow Vibe in Venice Beach. Walk along the canals, shop, and grab an all-organic lunch on Abbot Kinney, or watch tanned locals in tie-dye toting longboards.

Have a Bonfire at Dockweiler Beach. Bonfires are pretty much illegal in L.A., except for at Dockweiler. Pick up a grill and have a barbeque, or just toast marshmallows.

QUICK BITES

The Cow's End Cafe. Stop at this two-story locals' favorite for coffee and pastries, or choose from a long list of sandwiches for something more substantial. ⊠ *34 Washington Blvd.*

Mariasol Cocina Mexican. Soak up the atmosphere inside this fun-loving eatery at the very end of Santa Monica Pier. The menu's newly updated, but the fajitas still reign as the most popular item. ⊠ *401 Santa Monica Pier*

Venice Whaler. This beachfront bar has been the local watering hole for musicians like the Doors and the Beach Boys since 1944. It boasts an amazing view and serves tasty California pub food like fish tacos, pulled pork sliders, and avocado toast with a basic selection of beers. ⊠ *10 Washington Blvd.*

GETTING HERE

■ From Downtown, the easiest way to hit the coast is by taking the Santa Monica Freeway (I–10) due west. Once you reach the end of the freeway, I–10 runs into Pacific Coast Highway, or PCH. MTA buses run from Downtown along Pico, Olympic, Santa Monica, Sunset, and Wilshire boulevards to the coast. The Metro Expo Line runs to Downtown Santa Monica. Driving along the coast is a quintessential L.A. experience—so is sitting in beach traffic. Avoid driving to Malibu during rush hour when traffic along PCH moves at a snail's pace. Public parking is usually available at beaches, though fees can range anywhere from $8 to $20.

PLANNING YOUR TIME

■ If you've got time, break your coastal visit into two excursions: Santa Monica and Venice in one excursion, and Malibu in another. The best way to tour L.A.'s coastal communities is to park your car and walk, cycle, or skate along the bike path, known as the Strand. Late afternoon to sunset is the liveliest time on the Santa Monica Pier. Try to avoid the boardwalk, beach, and backstreets of Santa Monica and Venice at night, when the crowds dissipate.

L.A.'s beaches are an iconic and integral part of Southern California, and getting some sand on the floor of your car is a rite of passage. Hugging the Santa Monica Bay in an arch, the desirable communities of Malibu, Santa Monica, and Venice move from ultrarich to ultracasual to bohemian. Continuing south to L.A.'s three beach cities, Manhattan Beach, Hermosa, and Redondo, the scene shifts from posh to working class, but the sand remains the center of the action.

Santa Monica

This pedestrian-friendly little city, about 8.3 square miles, has a dynamic population of artists and writers, entertainment folks, educators, and retired people; its left-wing politics have earned it the nickname of the People's Republic of Santa Monica (just like Berkeley in Northern California). Mature trees, Mediterranean-style architecture, and strict zoning have helped create a sense of place often missing from L.A.'s residential neighborhoods, and its cooler, sometimes-foggy climate is another draw. Since it's a desirable neighborhood, real estate here isn't cheap.

⊙ Sights

Annenberg Community Beach House
POOL | This beachfront property was originally developed in the 1920s by William Randolph Hearst as a palatial private residence and a gathering spot for Hollywood's megastars. In 1947 it was converted into a members-only beach club; the state of California bought and renamed the club in 1959, but it took the earthquake of 2004 for the state to reconceive the property as a public place. With the help of the Annenberg Foundation, it reopened as a community beach house in 2009. Feel like a millionaire lounging by the pool on one of the beachside chairs, or lunch at the café while enjoying uninterrupted ocean views. The house's Beach=Culture event series includes a variety of classes (yoga, beach volleyball), readings, and exhibits; check

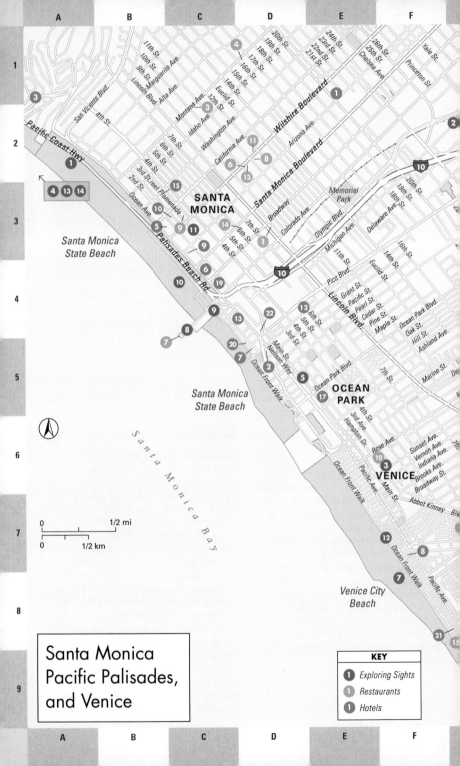

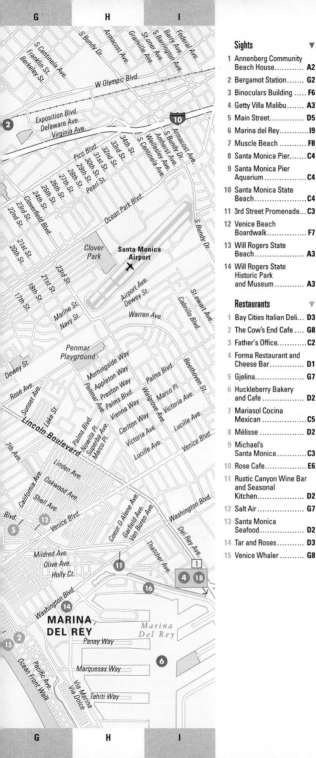

Sights ▼

1 Annenberg Community Beach House............ **A2**
2 Bergamot Station....... **G2**
3 Binoculars Building **F6**
4 Getty Villa Malibu...... **A3**
5 Main Street.............. **D5**
6 Marina del Rey........... **I9**
7 Muscle Beach **F8**
8 Santa Monica Pier....... **C4**
9 Santa Monica Pier Aquarium **C4**
10 Santa Monica State Beach **C4**
11 3rd Street Promenade... **C3**
12 Venice Beach Boardwalk................ **F7**
13 Will Rogers State Beach **A3**
14 Will Rogers State Historic Park and Museum **A3**

Restaurants ▼

1 Bay Cities Italian Deli... **D3**
2 The Cow's End Cafe **G8**
3 Father's Office............ **C2**
4 Forma Restaurant and Cheese Bar.............. **D1**
5 Gjelina.................... **G7**
6 Huckleberry Bakery and Cafe **D2**
7 Mariasol Cocina Mexican **C5**
8 Mélisse **D2**
9 Michael's Santa Monica **C3**
10 Rose Cafe................. **E6**
11 Rustic Canyon Wine Bar and Seasonal Kitchen................... **D2**
12 Salt Air **G7**
13 Santa Monica Seafood................. **D2**
14 Tar and Roses........... **D3**
15 Venice Whaler **G8**

Hotels ▼

1 The Ambrose............. **E1**
2 Bayside Hotel **D5**
3 Channel Road Inn....... **A1**
4 Custom Hotel.............. **I8**
5 Fairmont Miramar Hotel & Bungalows Santa Monica **C3**
6 The Georgian Hotel...... **C4**
7 Hotel Casa del Mar..... **D5**
8 Hotel Erwin **F7**
9 Hotel Shangri-La......... **C3**
10 Huntley Santa Monica Beach **C3**
11 The Kinney.............. **H7**
12 Le Méridien Delfina Santa Monica **D4**
13 Loews Santa Monica Beach Hotel **D4**
14 Marina del Rey Marriott.................. **G8**
15 Palihouse Santa Monica.................. **B3**
16 The Ritz-Carlton, Marina del Rey............ **I8**
17 Sea Shore Motel......... **E5**
18 Sheraton Gateway Los Angeles **I8**
19 Shore Hotel............... **C4**
20 Shutters on the Beach **C5**
21 Venice Beach House... **G8**
22 Viceroy Santa Monica **D4**

The three-block Third Street Promenade is great for shopping and is for pedestrians only

the website for the calendar. Hours are subject to change, so call to confirm hours and book in advance. Book a pool reservation online in advance if possible. ✉ 415 Pacific Coast Hwy., Santa Monica ☎ 310/458–4904 ⊕ www.annenberg-beachhouse.com ✇ Free; pool $10.

Bergamot Station

MUSEUM | Named after a stop on the Red Trolley line that once shuttled between Downtown and the Santa Monica Pier, Bergamot Station is now a depot for intriguing art. The industrial facades house more than 30 art galleries, shops, a café, and a museum. The galleries cover many kinds of media: photography, jewelry, and paintings from somber to lurid. ✉ 2525 Michigan Ave., Santa Monica ☎ 310/453–7535 ⊕ www.bergamot-station.com ⊘ Closed Sun. and Mon.

Main Street

COMMERCIAL CENTER | FAMILY | This thoroughfare is a great spot for star sightings or for strolling among the laid-back California crowd. Streets are lined with old-fashioned, colorful, and cozy boutiques that stock everything from high-end garments to bohemian favorites. There's also a standard crop of shopping mall outposts plus a good selection of casual restaurants and cafés. If you're in town on the last Saturday of the month, check out the sidewalk sale. ✉ Between Pacific St. and Rose Ave., and Santa Monica and Venice Blvds., Santa Monica ⊕ www.mainstreetsm. com.

Santa Monica Pier

AMUSEMENT PARK/WATER PARK | FAMILY | Souvenir shops, carnival games, arcades, eateries, an outdoor trapeze school, a small amusement park, and an aquarium all contribute to the festive atmosphere of this truncated pier at the foot of Colorado Boulevard below Palisades Park. The pier's trademark 46-horse Looff Carousel, built in 1922, has appeared in several films, including The Sting. The Soda Jerks ice cream fountain (named for the motion the attendant makes when pulling the machine's arm) inside the carousel building is a pier staple.

Free concerts are held on the pier in the summer. ✉ *Colorado Ave. and the ocean, Santa Monica* ☎ *310/458–8901* 🌐 *www.santamonicapier.org.*

Santa Monica Pier Aquarium

MARINA | FAMILY | Run by beach conservation group Heal the Bay, this live marine life menagerie contains more than 100 species of marine animals and plants, all found in Santa Monica Bay. The Dorothy Green Room features live and interactive exhibits about local watersheds and short educational films on the weekends. The Kid's Corner provides books, games, and a puppet show. Don't miss this chance to learn about the area's ecology and staggering evidence of how pollution is affecting ocean life. The aquarium can be tricky to find—look for it tucked under the eastern end of the Santa Monica Pier bridge along Ocean Front Walk. Follow the colorful seascape murals that cover the outside walls. **TIP→** Kids ages 12 and under receive free admission. ✉ *1600 Ocean Front Walk, Santa Monica* ☎ *310/393–6149* 🌐 *www.healthebay.org/aquarium* 🎟 *$5* ⏲ *Closed Mon.*

Santa Monica State Beach

BEACH—SIGHT | The first beach you'll hit after the Santa Monica Freeway (I–10) runs into the Pacific Coast Highway, wide and sandy Santa Monica is *the* place for sunning and socializing. Be prepared for a mob scene on summer weekends, when parking becomes an expensive ordeal. Swimming is fine (with the usual post-storm-pollution caveat); for surfing, go elsewhere. For a memorable view, climb up the stairway over PCH to Palisades Park, at the top of the bluffs. Free summer concerts are held on the pier on Thursday evening. **Amenities:** parking; lifeguards; toilets; food and drink; showers; water sports. **Best for:** partiers; sunset; surfing; swimming; walking. ✉ *1642 Promenade, PCH at California Incline, Santa Monica* ☎ *310/458–8573* 🌐 *www.smgov.net/portals/beach* 🎟 *Parking from $6.*

Third Street Promenade and Santa Monica Place

COMMERCIAL CENTER | Stretch your legs along this pedestrian-only, three-block stretch of 3rd Street, close to the Pacific, lined with jacaranda trees, ivy-topiary dinosaur fountains, strings of lights, and branches of nearly every major U.S. retail chain. Outdoor cafés, street vendors, movie theaters, and a rich nightlife make this a main gathering spot for locals, visitors, street musicians, and performance artists. Plan a night just to take it all in or take an afternoon for a long people-watching stroll. There's plenty of parking in city structures on the streets flanking the promenade. **Santa Monica Place,** at the south end of the promenade, is a sleek outdoor mall and foodie haven. Its three stories are home to Nordstrom, Louis Vuitton, Coach, and other upscale retailers. Don't miss the ocean views from the rooftop food court. ✉ *3rd St., between Colorado and Wilshire Blvds., Santa Monica* 🌐 *www.downtownsm.com.*

🍴 Restaurants

This idyllic seaside town is a hotbed of culinary activity, with a dynamic farmers' market that attracts chefs from all over Los Angeles and local restaurants that celebrate farm-to-table, seasonal dining.

Bay Cities Italian Deli

$ | | Part deli, part market, Bay Cities has been home to incredible Italian subs since 1925. This renowned counter-service spot is always crowded (best to order ahead), but monster subs run the gamut from the mighty meatball to the signature Godmother, made with prosciutto, ham, capicola, mortadella, Genoa salami, and provolone. **Known for:** market with rare imports; excellent service. [$] *Average main: $10* ✉ *1517 Lincoln Blvd., Santa Monica* ☎ *310/395–8279* 🌐 *www.baycitiesitaliandeli.com* ⏲ *Closed Mon.*

Father's Office

$ | **AMERICAN** | Distinguished by its vintage neon sign, this gastropub is famous for handcrafted beers and a brilliant signature burger. Topped with Gruyère and Maytag blue cheeses, arugula, caramelized onions, and applewood-smoked bacon compote, the Office Burger is a guilty pleasure worth waiting in line for, which is usually required. **Known for:** addictive sweet potato fries; strict no-substitutions policy; 36 craft beers on tap. [$] *Average main: $15* ✉ *1018 Montana Ave., Santa Monica* ☎ *310/736–2224* 🌐 *www.fathersoffice.com* 🕒 *No lunch weekdays.*

Forma Restaurant and Cheese Bar

$$ | **ITALIAN** | Pasta is served here *dalla forma,* meaning it's cooked, then dipped into a cheese wheel and stirred up before serving. Catering to a higher-end crowd, Forma specializes in cheeses, pastas, and pizzas. **Known for:** generous happy hour; fresh mozzarella knots; Roman-style crispy artichokes. [$] *Average main: $28* ✉ *1610 Montana Ave., Santa Monica* ☎ *424/231–2868* 🌐 *www.formarestaurant.com.*

Huckleberry Bakery and Cafe

$ | **AMERICAN** | **FAMILY** | Founded by Santa Monica natives, Huckleberry brings together the best ingredients from local farmers and growers to craft diner-style comfort food with a chic twist. The light, bright space is perfect for a quick brunch. **Known for:** from-scratch diner-style breakfast options; delectable pastries. [$] *Average main: $14* ✉ *1014 Wilshire Blvd., Santa Monica* ☎ *310/451–2311* 🌐 *www.huckleberrycafe.com.*

★ **Mélisse**

$$$$ | **FRENCH** | Chef-owner Josiah Citrin enhances his modern French cooking with seasonal California produce at this Santa Monica institution. The tasting menu might feature egg caviar with smoked lemon crème fraiche, wild Scottish red partridge with chocolate persimmons, or Kagoshima Wagyu beef rib eye. **Known for:** domestic and European cheese cart; contemporary/elegant decor. [$] *Average main: $145* ✉ *1104 Wilshire Blvd., Santa Monica* ☎ *310/395–0881* 🌐 *www.melisse.com* 🕒 *Closed Sun. and Mon. No lunch.*

Michael's Santa Monica

$$$ | **MODERN AMERICAN** | Michael's is a Santa Monica institution, and after a remodel and new chef and menu, its reputation is secure. The new American shared-plates menu runs the gamut from peruviana beans to branzino with pomegranate to sunchoke gnocchi. **Known for:** stunning patio; incredible cheesecake. [$] *Average main: $30* ✉ *1147 3rd St., Santa Monica* ☎ *310/451–0843* 🌐 *www.michaelssantamonica.com* 🕒 *Closed Sun. No lunch.*

★ **Rustic Canyon Wine Bar and Seasonal Kitchen**

$$$ | **MODERN AMERICAN** | A Santa Monica mainstay, the seasonally changing menu at this farm-to-table restaurant consistently upends norms. The homey, minimalist space offers sweeping views of Wilshire Boulevard, and on any given night the menu of California cuisine may include Channel Island rockfish with shelling beans and Sun Gold tomatoes, or buttered ricotta dumplings with golden chanterelles and Coolea cheese. **Known for:** never-ending wine list; knowledgeable staff. [$] *Average main: $35* ✉ *1119 Wilshire Blvd., Santa Monica* ☎ *310/393–7050* 🌐 *www.rusticcanyonwinebar.com.*

Santa Monica Seafood

$$ | **SEAFOOD** | **FAMILY** | A Southern California favorite, this Italian seafood haven has been serving up fresh fish since 1939. This freshness comes from its pedigree as the largest seafood distributor in the Southwest. **Known for:** deliciously seasoned rainbow trout; oyster bar; kids' meals. [$] *Average main: $20* ✉ *1000 Wilshire Blvd., Santa Monica* ☎ *310/393–5244* 🌐 *www.santamonicaseafood.com.*

Tar and Roses

$$$ | MODERN AMERICAN | This small and dimly lit romantic spot in Santa Monica is full of adventurous options, like octopus skewers and venison loin. The new American cuisine also features standouts like braised lamb belly with minted apple chutney and drool-worthy strawberry ricotta crostata with honeycomb ice cream for dessert. **Known for:** phenomenal oxtail dumplings; delicious hanger steak. $ *Average main: $30 ⊠ 602 Santa Monica Blvd., Santa Monica* ☏ *310/587–0700* ⊕ *www.tarandroses.com.*

 # Hotels

The Ambrose

$$$ | HOTEL | Tranquility pervades the airy, California Craftsman–style, four-story Ambrose, which blends right into its mostly residential Santa Monica neighborhood. **Pros:** "green" practices like nontoxic cleaners and recycling bins; partial ocean view. **Cons:** quiet, residential area of Santa Monica; parking fee ($27); not walking distance to beach. $ *Rooms from: $359 ⊠ 1255 20th St., Santa Monica* ☏ *310/315–1555, 877/262–7673* ⊕ *www.ambrosehotel.com* ⤶ *77 rooms* |◎| *Breakfast.*

Bayside Hotel

$$ | HOTEL | Tucked snugly into a narrow corner lot, the supremely casual Bayside's greatest asset is its prime spot directly across from the beach, within walkable blocks from the Third Street Promenade and Santa Monica Pier. **Pros:** cheaper weeknight stays; beach access and views. **Cons:** homeless encampments nearby; basic bedding; thin walls and street noise. $ *Rooms from: $249 ⊠ 2001 Ocean Ave., Santa Monica* ☏ *310/396–6000, 800/525–4447* ⊕ *baysidehotel.com* ⤶ *45 rooms* |◎| *No meals.*

★ Channel Road Inn

$$ | B&B/INN | A quaint surprise in Southern California, the Channel Road Inn is every bit the country retreat bed-and-breakfast lovers adore, with four-poster beds, fluffy duvets, and a cozy living room with a fireplace. **Pros:** free wine and hors d'oeuvres every evening; home-cooked breakfast included; meditative rose garden on-site. **Cons:** no pool; need a car to get around. $ *Rooms from: $225 ⊠ 219 W. Channel Rd., Santa Monica* ☏ *310/459–1920* ⊕ *www.channelroadinn.com* ⤶ *15 rooms* |◎| *Breakfast.*

Fairmont Miramar Hotel and Bungalows Santa Monica

$$$$ | HOTEL | A mammoth Moreton Bay fig tree dwarfs the main entrance of the 5-acre, beach-adjacent Santa Monica wellness retreat and lends its name to the inviting on-site Mediterranean-inspired restaurant, FIG, which focuses on local ingredients and frequently refreshes its menu. **Pros:** guests can play games on the heated patio; swanky open-air cocktail spot, the Bungalow, on-site; stay in retrofitted '20s and '40s bungalows. **Cons:** all this luxury comes at a big price. $ *Rooms from: $599 ⊠ 101 Wilshire Blvd., Santa Monica* ☏ *310/576–7777, 866/540–4470* ⊕ *www.fairmont.com/santamonica* ⤶ *334 rooms* |◎| *No meals.*

The Georgian Hotel

$$$$ | HOTEL | Driving by, you can't miss the Georgian: the art deco exterior is aqua, with ornate bronze grillwork and a charming oceanfront veranda. **Pros:** many ocean-view rooms; front terrace is a great people-watching spot; free Wi-Fi. **Cons:** $38 parking; some rooms have unremarkable views. $ *Rooms from: $409 ⊠ 1415 Ocean Ave., Santa Monica* ☏ *310/395–9945, 800/538–8147* ⊕ *www.georgianhotel.com* ⤶ *84 rooms* |◎| *No meals.*

Hotel Casa del Mar

$$$$ | HOTEL | In the 1920s it was a posh beach club catering to the city's elite; now the Casa del Mar is one of SoCal's most luxurious and pricey beachfront hotels with a heavenly lobby, three extravagant two-story penthouses, a

raised deck and pool, a newly reimagined spa, and an elegant ballroom facing the sand. **Pros:** excellent dining at Catch; modern amenities; lobby socializing; gorgeous beachfront rooms. **Cons:** no room balconies; without a doubt, one of L.A.'s priciest beach stays. $ *Rooms from: $700* ✉ *1910 Ocean Way, Santa Monica* ☎ *310/581–5533, 800/898–6999* ⊕ *www.hotelcasadelmar.com* ⤳ *129 rooms* |◎| *No meals.*

Hotel Shangri-La

$$$ | HOTEL | Across from Santa Monica's oceanfront Palisades Park, the 1939-built art deco, ocean-liner-inspired Hotel Shangri-La is now firmly in tune with the 21st century after a $30 million upgrade. **Pros:** sunken Jacuzzis in bathrooms; ONYX rooftop bar is the place to be; active pool scene in the summer. **Cons:** some rooms have tight, cruise-ship-like quarters; pricey parking rates ($49); some furnishings are a little tired. $ *Rooms from: $385* ✉ *301 Ocean Ave., Santa Monica* ☎ *310/394–2791* ⊕ *www.shangri-la-hotel.com* ⤳ *70 rooms* |◎| *No meals.*

Huntley Santa Monica Beach

$$$$ | HOTEL | This sleek, tech-savvy property was fully renovated in 2017 and 2018 with the Silicon Beach business traveler in mind. **Pros:** ocean views; fun social scene; great views (and drinks) at the Penthouse, the hotel's top-floor restaurant. **Cons:** no pool; Fodorites complain of noise from the restaurant and bar. $ *Rooms from: $459* ✉ *1111 2nd St., Santa Monica* ☎ *310/394–5454* ⊕ *www.thehuntleyhotel.com* ⤳ *204 rooms* |◎| *No meals.*

Le Meridien Delfina Santa Monica

$$$ | HOTEL | FAMILY | Not far from I–10 and four blocks from the new Expo Line, this hotel appeals to business travelers and jet-setting leisure travelers who fancy the sleek interiors, free self-parking, and close proximity to beaches and restaurants. **Pros:** casual and upscale eateries on property; retro designer touches; cabanas and pool on ground floor. **Cons:**

not as centrally located as some Santa Monica hotels; fee for Wi-Fi. $ *Rooms from: $319* ✉ *530 Pico Blvd., Santa Monica* ☎ *310/399–9344, 888/627–8532* ⊕ *www.lemeridiendelfina.com* ⤳ *310 rooms* |◎| *No meals.*

Loews Santa Monica Beach Hotel

$$$$ | HOTEL | FAMILY | Walk to the ocean side of the soaring atrium at this family- and pet-friendly hotel, and you feel like you're on a cruise ship: massive windows give way to the expansive sea below, sunny staff seems content to assist with your needs, and a massive photo screen behind reception intuits a sense of place. **Pros:** resort vibe with three restaurants; walk to beach; upgraded spa and fitness center. **Cons:** small pool; parking is pricey ($55). $ *Rooms from: $600* ✉ *1700 Ocean Ave., Santa Monica* ☎ *310/458–6700, 800/235–6397* ⊕ *www.loewshotels.com* ⤳ *347 rooms* |◎| *No meals.*

Palihouse Santa Monica

$$$ | HOTEL | Tucked in a posh residential area three blocks from the sea and lively Third Street Promenade, Palihouse Santa Monica caters to design-minded world travelers, with spacious rooms and suites decked out in whimsical antiques. **Pros:** Apple TV in rooms; walking distance to Santa Monica attractions; fully equipped kitchens. **Cons:** no pool; decor might not appeal to more traditional travelers; parking fee ($45). $ *Rooms from: $355* ✉ *1001 3rd St., Santa Monica* ☎ *310/394–1279* ⊕ *www.palihousesantamonica.com* ⤳ *38 rooms* |◎| *No meals.*

Sea Shore Motel

$ | HOTEL | On Santa Monica's busy Main Street, the Sea Shore is a charming throwback to Route 66 and to '60s-style, family-run roadside motels and is surrounded by an ultratrendy neighborhood. **Pros:** close to beach and restaurants; free Wi-Fi, parking, and use of beach equipment; popular rooftop deck and on-site restaurant, Amelia's. **Cons:** street noise; motel-style decor and beds. $ *Rooms from: $159* ✉ *2637 Main St.,*

Santa Monica ☎ *310/392–2787* 🌐 *www.seashoremotel.com* 🛏 *25 rooms* 🍴 *No meals.*

★ Shore Hotel

$$$$ | HOTEL | With views of the Santa Monica Pier, this hotel with a friendly staff offers eco-minded travelers stylish rooms with a modern design, just steps from the sand and sea. **Pros:** near beach and Third Street Promenade; rainfall showerheads; solar-heated pool and hot tub. **Cons:** expensive rooms and parking fees; fronting busy Ocean Avenue; some sharing a room may be wary of the see-through shower. [$] *Rooms from: $432* ✉ *1515 Ocean Ave., Santa Monica* ☎ *310/458–1515* 🌐 *shorehotel.com* 🛏 *164 rooms* 🍴 *No meals.*

★ Shutters on the Beach

$$$$ | HOTEL | FAMILY | Set right on the sand, this inn has become synonymous with staycations. **Pros:** built-in cabinets filled with art books and curios; rooms designed by Michael Smith; rooms come with whirlpool tub. **Cons:** have to pay for extras like beach chairs; very expensive. [$] *Rooms from: $675* ✉ *1 Pico Blvd., Santa Monica* ☎ *310/458–0030, 800/334–9000* 🌐 *www.shuttersonthebeach.com* 🛏 *198 rooms* 🍴 *No meals.*

Viceroy Santa Monica

$$$$ | HOTEL | Whimsy abounds at this stylized, airy seaside escape—just look at the porcelain dogs as lamp bases and Spode china plates mounted on the walls—yet the compact rooms, which all have French balconies and sexy mirrored walls, draw quite the upscale clientele. **Pros:** in-room aromatherapy products; chic lobby and poolside socializing; pedestrian-friendly area. **Cons:** super-pricey bar and dining; pool for dipping, not laps. [$] *Rooms from: $510* ✉ *1819 Ocean Ave., Santa Monica* ☎ *310/260–7500, 800/622–8711* 🌐 *www.viceroysantamonica.com* 🛏 *162 rooms* 🍴 *No meals.*

LOS ANGELES INTERNATIONAL AIRPORT

Custom Hotel

$ | HOTEL | Close enough to LAX to see the runways, the Custom Hotel is a playful and practical redo of a 12-story, mid-century modern tower by famed L.A. architect Welton Becket (of Hollywood's Capitol Records building and the Dorothy Chandler Pavilion). **Pros:** shuttle to LAX; close to beach and airport; socializing at poolside restaurant/lounge, Deck 33. **Cons:** at the desolate end of Lincoln Boulevard; thin walls; in need of updating. [$] *Rooms from: $183* ✉ *8639 Lincoln Blvd., Los Angeles International Airport* ☎ *310/645–0400, 877/287–8601* 🌐 *www.customhotel.com* 🛏 *250 rooms* 🍴 *No meals.*

Sheraton Gateway Los Angeles

$$ | HOTEL | LAX's swanky hotel just had some serious work done to its already sleek look, yet the appeal is in more than just the style; in-transit visitors love the 24-hour room service, pool and hot tub, fitness center, and airport shuttle, making this the perfect option for an early-morning flight. **Pros:** significantly lower weekend rates; free LAX shuttle; the on-site restaurant, Costero California Bar and Bistro, slings craft beer. **Cons:** convenient to airport but not much else. [$] *Rooms from: $279* ✉ *6101 W. Century Blvd., Los Angeles International Airport* ☎ *310/642–1111, 800/325–3535* 🌐 *www.sheratonlosangeles.com* 🛏 *803 rooms* 🍴 *No meals.*

Activities

Legends Beach Bike Tours

TOUR—SIGHT | Those who like a little history with their vacations should take a guided tour with Legends, part of Perry's Café and Rentals. A tour takes you through the unique enclaves of Santa Monica and Venice Beach, and you can learn their role in the history of surf and skate in Southern California. Bike tours are offered daily at 11 am, last two hours (plus one hour of free riding), and cost $69 per adult, $35 for kids under 12, and $60 for students with ID and seniors. ✉ *930 Palisades Beach Rd., Santa Monica* ☎ *310/939–0000* ⊕ *www.perryscafe. com.*

Trapeze School New York

PROMENADE | Get a different view of the energetic scene by taking a trapeze class right on the Santa Monica Pier. Launch off from a platform 23 feet high and sail above the crowds and waves. Beginners are welcome. Classes are held daily, but times vary, so check the website and make reservations in advance. ✉ *370 Santa Monica Pier, Santa Monica* ☎ *310/394–5800* ⊕ *www.trapezeschool. com.*

ⓨ Nightlife

In Santa Monica, the focus of nightlife shifts toward live music, historic dives, and any space that has a view of the ocean.

★ Chez Jay

BARS/PUBS | Around since 1959, this dive bar continues to be a well-loved place in Santa Monica. Everyone from the young to the old (including families) frequents this historical landmark. It's a charming place, from the well-worn booths with their red checkered tablecloths to the ship's wheel near the door. Be on the lookout for ongoing *Goliath* filmings, and consider the patio for private parties. ✉ *1657 Ocean Ave., Santa Monica* ☎ *310/395–1741* ⊕ *www.chezjays.com.*

The Galley

BARS/PUBS | Santa Monica's oldest restaurant and bar, the Galley has a consistent nautical theme inside and out: the boatlike exterior features wavy blue neon lights and porthole windows; inside, fishing nets and anchors adorn the walls, and the whole place is aglow with colorful string lights. Most patrons tend to crowd the center bar, with the more dinner-oriented folks frequenting

the booths. Prices are a good deal during "most hours" and a steal during "happy hours." ✉ *2442 Main St., Santa Monica* ☎ *310/452–1934.*

Harvelle's

MUSIC CLUBS | The focus of this bar and music club is on jazz, blues, and soul. The club is small, with an even smaller checkerboard dance floor. Reserve tables in advance at this Westside establishment; order a martini off the Deadly Sins menu, and catch a Toledo burlesque show on Sunday night. ✉ *1432 4th St., Santa Monica* ☎ *310/395–1676* ⊕ *www. harvelles.com.*

UnUrban Coffee House

CAFES—NIGHTLIFE | Looking for a real neighborhood experience, with mismatched furniture and undiscovered talent? This is the place to enjoy a laid-back evening of entertainment by local performers (and good espresso drinks and organic pastries). The music and poetry open-mic nights attract interesting and talented folks, and the musical showcase draws a random mix of musicians. There's no cover to get in, but it typically costs $5 to participate in the open mics. ✉ *3301 Pico Blvd., at Urban Ave., Santa Monica* ☎ *310/315–0056* ⊕ *www.unurban.com.*

ⓣ Performing Arts

Nuart

FILM | Foreign, indie, documentaries, classics, recent releases, Oscar short-film screenings—there's not much the Nuart doesn't show. Midnight showings, like the long-running *Rocky Horror Picture Show* with a live "shadow cast" on Saturday nights, continue to bring in locals. Q&A sessions with directors and actors also happen here frequently. ✉ *11272 Santa Monica Blvd., West L.A.* ☎ *310/473–8530* ⊕ *www.landmarktheatres.com/los-angeles/nuart-theatre.*

Santa Monica Playhouse

THEATER | FAMILY | Housing three theaters, this venue brings a number of original plays, touring companies, poetry readings, spoken word events, and revival shows to the stage. The Family Theatre Musical Matinee Series features family-friendly reworked classic plays. A number of educational programs and workshops are available for all ages. ✉ *1211 4th St., Santa Monica* ☎ *310/394–9779* ⊕ *www.santamonicaplayhouse.com.*

🛍 Shopping

The breezy beachside communities of Santa Monica and Venice are ideal for leisurely shopping. Scores of tourists (and many locals) gravitate to the Third Street Promenade, a popular pedestrians-only shopping area that's within walking range of the beach and historic Santa Monica Pier. But there's more to the area than trendy chain stores; there's also a treasure trove of vintage goods and antiques to be found on Main Street and Ocean Park Boulevard, and Montana Avenue is home to retailers specializing in indie and artisanal wares.

In Venice, Abbot Kinney Boulevard is abuzz with spots to shop for chic clothing, accessories, and housewares—including plenty of upscale outposts. The strip also has some of the city's best eateries, so it's easy to kill two birds with one stone. Nearby Lincoln and Rose avenues have also gained retail momentum in recent years, with many emerging brands choosing the area to open their first-ever storefronts. For those looking for the next big thing, this just might be the place to find it.

The Acorn Store

TOYS | FAMILY | Remember when toys didn't require computer programming? This old-fashioned shop (for ages 10 and under) sparks children's imaginations with dress-up clothes, picture books, and hand-painted wooden toys by brands like Poan and Haba. ✉ *1220 5th St., near Wilshire Blvd., Santa Monica* ☎ *310/451–5845* ⊕ *www.theacornstore.com.*

Lady Chocolatt

FOOD/CANDY | This is the shop where chocolate dreams are made. The purveyor of the finest Belgian chocolate in all of Los Angeles, Lady Chocolatt is the perfect answer to the age-old question "What should we buy for our loved one's birthday, anniversary, baby shower, celebration, etc.?" The ornate display case is filled with dark chocolate truffles, hazelnut pralines, Grand Marnier ganaches, and so much more. Post up for a late-afternoon espresso and let your chocolate dreams wander. ✉ *12008 Wilshire Blvd., Santa Monica* ☎ *310/442–2245* ⊕ *www. chocolatt.com.*

Limonaia

GIFTS/SOUVENIRS | This charming and cozy neighborhood boutique has something for every kind of gift recipient. Ben's Garden goods (pillows, coasters, trays, etc.) decorated with inspirational words, lovely cards for all occasions, beaded jewelry, cookbooks, and an extensive puzzle selection are just a few things shoppers can find here. ✉ *1325 Montana Ave., Santa Monica* ☎ *310/458–1858* ⊕ *www. shoplimonaia.com.*

Parking Tips ⦿

Parking in Santa Monica is next to impossible on Wednesday, when some streets are blocked off for the Farmers Market, but there are several parking structures with free one-to-two-hour parking.

There are several well-marked, free (for two hours) parking lots throughout the core shopping area around Beverly Hills.

The Getty Villa: a gorgeous setting for a spectacular collection of ancient art

Planet Blue
CLOTHING | The beachy bohemian style is the focus at this small local chain, with an abundance of jeans, breezy dresses, turquoise jewelry, bikinis, and other SoCal staples. ✉ *800 14th St., Santa Monica* ☎ *310/394–0135* ⊕ *www.shopplanetblue. com.*

Third Street Promenade
SHOPPING CENTERS/MALLS | There is no shortage of spots to shop everything from sporting goods to trendy fashions on this pedestrian-friendly strip. Outposts here are mainly of the chain variety, and in between splurging on books, clothing, sneakers, and more, shoppers can pop into one of the many eateries to stay satiated or even catch a movie at one of the theaters. Additionally, the chef-approved Farmers Market takes over twice a week, and with the beach just a few steps away, the destination is a quintessential California stop. ✉ *3rd St., between Broadway and Wilshire Blvd., Santa Monica.*

Wasteland
CLOTHING | This vintage emporium, a block from the Third Street Promenade, sells gently used items for both women and men. You'll find everything from wide-lapel polyester shirts to last year's Michael Kors bag. There is also a location on Ventura Boulevard. ✉ *1330 4th St., between Arizona Ave. and Santa Monica Blvd., Santa Monica* ☎ *310/395–2620* ⊕ *www.shopwasteland.com.*

Pacific Palisades

Stunning ocean views, glamorous homes, and dusty canyons define this affluent area snug between Santa Monica and Malibu. Although there is a downtown village of sorts south of Sunset Boulevard, natural terrain is the main draw here, luring visitors to hiking trails or the Palisades' winding roads.

◉ Sights

★ Getty Villa Malibu

HOUSE | Feeding off the cultures of ancient Rome, Greece, and Etruria, the villa exhibits astounding antiquities, though on a first visit even they take a backseat to their environment. This megamansion sits on some of the most valuable coastal property in the world. Modeled after the Villa dei Papiri in Herculaneum, a Roman estate owned by Julius Caesar's father-in-law that was covered in ash when Mount Vesuvius erupted, the Getty Villa includes beautifully manicured gardens, reflecting pools, and statuary. The structures blend thoughtfully into the rolling terrain and significantly improve the public spaces, such as the new outdoor amphitheater, gift store, café, and entry arcade. Talks, concerts, and educational programs are offered at an indoor theater. ■TIP→ **An advance timed entry ticket is required for admission. Tickets are free and may be ordered from the museum's website or by phone.** ✉ 17985 Pacific Coast Hwy., Pacific Palisades ☎ 310/440–7300 ⊕ www.getty. edu ⛫ Free, tickets required; parking $15 ⊘ Closed Tues.

Will Rogers State Beach

BEACH—SIGHT | This clean, sandy, 3-mile beach, with a dozen volleyball nets, gymnastics equipment, and a playground for kids, is an all-around favorite. The surf is gentle, perfect for swimmers and beginning surfers. However, it's best to avoid the beach after a storm, when untreated water flows from storm drains into the sea. **Amenities:** parking; lifeguards; toilets; food and drink; showers. **Best for:** sunset; swimming; walking. ✉ 17700 PCH, 2 miles north of Santa Monica Pier, Pacific Palisades ☎ 310/305–9503 ⊕ www.parks. ca.gov ⛫ parking $15.

Will Rogers State Historic Park and Museum

HISTORIC SITE | A humorist, actor, and rambling cowboy, Will Rogers lived on this site in the 1920s and 1930s. His ranch house, a folksy blend of Navajo rugs and Mission-style furniture, has become a museum of Rogers memorabilia. A short film shown in the visitor center highlights Rogers's roping technique and homey words of wisdom. Open for docent-led tours Thursdays through Sundays, the ranch house features Rogers's stuffed practice calf and the high ceiling he raised so he could practice his famed roping style indoors.

Rogers was a polo enthusiast, and in the 1930s his front-yard polo field attracted such friends as Douglas Fairbanks Sr. for weekend games. Today the park's broad lawns are excellent for picnicking, and there are miles of eucalyptus-lined trails for hiking, as well as a horseback riding concession. Free weekend games are scheduled from May through October, weather permitting.

Also part of the park is **Inspiration Point Trail.** Who knows how many of Will Rogers's famed witticisms came to him while he and his wife hiked or rode horses along this trail from their ranch? The point is on a detour off the lovely 2-mile loop, which you can join near the riding stables beyond the parking lot. The panorama is one of L.A.'s widest and most wow-inducing, from the peaks of the San Gabriel Mountains in the east and the Oz-like cluster of downtown skyscrapers to Catalina Island looming off the coast to the southwest. If you're looking for a longer trip, the top of the loop meets up with the 65-mile Backbone Trail, which connects to Topanga State Park. ✉ 1501 Will Rogers State Park Rd., Pacific Palisades ☎ 310/454–8212 ⊕ www.parks. ca.gov/?page_id=626 ⛫ Free; parking $12.

Venice

From the resident musicians and roving hippies of the boardwalk to the hipster boutiques and farm-to-table cafés of Abbot Kinney Boulevard, Venice is not easily defined—which is what makes this creative-minded neighborhood so fun to explore.

Considering all of the dreamers who flock here today, it makes sense that Venice was a turn-of-the-20th-century fantasy that never quite came to be. Abbot Kinney, a wealthy Los Angeles businessman, envisioned this little piece of real estate as a romantic replica of Venice, Italy. He developed an incredible 16 miles of canals, floated gondolas on them, and built scaled-down versions of the Doge's Palace and other Venetian landmarks. Some canals were rebuilt in 1996, but they don't reflect the old-world connection quite as well as they could.

Ever since Kinney first planned his project, it was plagued by ongoing engineering problems and drifted into disrepair. Today only a few small canals and bridges remain. On nearby **Abbot Kinney Boulevard** there's a wealth of fashion, design, and home decor shops and chic cafés—plus great people-watching.

◉ Sights

Binoculars Building
BUILDING | Frank Gehry is known around the world for his architectural master-pieces. In L.A. alone he's responsible for multiple houses and buildings like the Gehry Residence, Loyola Law School, and Walt Disney Hall. But one of his most interesting creations is the Binoculars Building, a quirky Venice spot that is exactly as advertised—a giant set of binoculars. The project was originally designed for the Chiat/Day advertising agency and today is home to Google's main L.A. office. ⊠ *340 Main St., Venice.*

Marina del Rey
MARINA | Just south of Venice, this condo-laden, chain restaurant–lined development is a good place to grab brunch (but watch for price gougers), walk, or ride bikes along the waterfront. A number of places, such as **Hornblower Cruises and Events** in Fisherman's Village, rent boats for romantic dinner or party cruises around the marina. There are a few man-made beaches, but you're better off hitting the larger (and cleaner) beaches up the coast. ⊠ *Fisherman's Village, 13755 Fiji Way, Los Angeles* ☏ ⊕ *www.hornblower.com/port/category/mdr+diningcruises.*

Muscle Beach
LOCAL INTEREST | Bronzed young men bench-pressing five girls at once, weight lifters doing tricks on the sand—the Muscle Beach facility fired up the country's imagination from the get-go. There are actually two spots known as Muscle Beach. The original Muscle Beach, just south of the Santa Monica Pier, is where bodybuilders Jack LaLanne and Vic and Armand Tanny used to work out in the 1950s. When it was closed in 1959, the bodybuilders moved south along the beach to Venice, to a city-run facility known as "the Pen," and the Venice Beach spot inherited the Muscle Beach moniker. The spot is probably best known now as a place where a young Arnold Schwarzenegger first came to flex his muscles in the late '60s and began his rise to fame. The area now hosts a variety of sports and gymnastics events and the occasional "beach babe" beauty contests that always draw a crowd. But stop by any time during daylight for an eye-popping array of beefcakes (and would-be beefcakes). ⊠ *1800 Ocean Front Walk, Venice* ⊕ *www.musclebeach.net.*

Venice Beach Boardwalk
MARINA | The surf and sand of Venice are fine, but the main attraction here is the boardwalk scene, which is a cosmos all

The boardwalk of Venice Beach

its own. Go on weekend afternoons for the best people-watching experience. You can also swim, fish, surf, and skateboard, or play racquetball, handball, shuffleboard, and basketball (the boardwalk is the site of hotly contested pickup games). You can rent a bike or in-line skates and hit the Strand bike path, then pull up a seat at a sidewalk café and watch the action unfold. ⊠ *1800 Ocean Front Walk, west of Pacific Ave., Venice* 🕿 *310/392–4687* ⊕ *www.venicebeach. com.*

 Restaurants

A bit rough around the edges, this urban beach town is home to many of L.A.'s artists, skaters, and surfers. The dining scene continues to grow but remains true to its cool and casual roots.

The Cow's End Cafe

$ | **CAFÉ** | Stop at this two-story locals' favorite for coffee and pastries, or choose from a long list of sandwiches for something more substantial. Sit out front and watch the crowds drifting in off the beach, or get cozy upstairs in one of the comfortable reading chairs. **Known for:** coffee; pastries; sandwiches. $ *Average main: $5* ⊠ *34 Washington Blvd., Venice* 🕿 *310/574–1080* ⊕ *www.thecowsendcafe.com.*

Gjelina

$$ | **AMERICAN** | Gjelina comes alive the minute you walk through the rustic wooden door and into a softly lit dining room with long communal tables. The menu is seasonal, with outstanding small plates, charcuterie, pastas, and pizza. **Known for:** lively crowd on the patio; late-night menu; inventive pizzas and salads. $ *Average main: $20* ⊠ *1429 Abbot Kinney Blvd., Venice* 🕿 *310/450–1429* ⊕ *www. gjelina.com.*

Rose Cafe

$$ | **MODERN AMERICAN** | **FAMILY** | This indoor-outdoor restaurant has served Venice for decades but constantly reinvents itself, serving mouthwatering California cuisines with multiple patios, a full bar, and a bakery. Creative types loiter for the

Wi-Fi and sip espressos, while young families gather out back to nibble on yellowtail crudo and crispy brussels sprouts. **Known for:** sophisticated but unpretentious vibe; location in the heart of Venice; being L.A. in a nutshell. [$] *Average main: $25* ✉ *220 Rose Ave., Venice* ☎ *310/399–0711* 🌐 *www.rosecafevenice.com.*

Salt Air

$$$ | **SEAFOOD** | A white marlin is camouflaged by the stark white walls in this hip Venice seafood spot on trendy Abbot Kinney Boulevard. Groups and daters pop in for brunch, lunch, or dinner to shuck oysters by the dozen or enjoy tender grilled octopus by the tentacle. **Known for:** killer brunch options on the patio; daily specials determined by freshest catch. [$] *Average main: $30* ✉ *1616 Abbot Kinney Blvd., Venice* ☎ *310/396–9333* 🌐 *www.saltairvenice.com.*

Venice Whaler

$$ | **AMERICAN** | This beachfront bar that's been the local watering hole for musicians like the Doors and the Beach Boys since 1944 boasts an amazing view and serves tasty California pub food like fish tacos, pulled pork sliders, and avocado toast with a basic selection of beers. Be prepared for rowdy crowds of sports fans and beachgoers at happy hour and on weekends. **Known for:** rock-n-roll history; pub food; brunch. [$] *Average main: $15* ✉ *10 W. Washington Blvd., Venice* ☎ *310/821–8737* 🌐 *www.venicewhaler.com.*

Hotels

Hotel Erwin

$$$ | **HOTEL** | A boutique hotel a block off the Venice Beach Boardwalk, the newly renovated Erwin will make you feel like a hipper version of yourself. **Pros:** dining emphasizes fresh ingredients; playful design in guest rooms; free Wi-Fi. **Cons:** some rooms face a noisy alley; no pool. [$] *Rooms from: $369* ✉ *1697 Pacific Ave., Venice* ☎ *310/452–1111, 800/786–7789* 🌐 *www.hotelerwin.com* 🛏 *119 rooms* 🍴 *No meals.*

★ **The Kinney**

$$ | **HOTEL** | Walking distance to Venice Beach and Abbot Kinney's artsy commercial strip, this playful new hotel announces itself boldly with wall murals by Melissa Scrivner before you even enter the lobby. **Pros:** affordable, artistic rooms; Ping-Pong area; Jacuzzi bar. **Cons:** valet parking is a must ($15). [$] *Rooms from: $239* ✉ *737 Washington Blvd., Venice* ☎ *310/821–4455* 🌐 *www.thekinneyvenicebeach.com* 🛏 *68 rooms* 🍴 *No meals.*

Venice Beach House

$$ | **HOTEL** | A vestige of Venice's founding days, the newly renovated Venice Beach House drips with beachy cottage chic and California history; think piles of fluffy Parachute linens, dark leather Chesterfield sofas, and nubby rugs. **Pros:** historic home with many charms; heavenly breakfast options; great budget options. **Cons:** privacy and noise issues; parking $25; cancellation penalties if cancelled less than a week in advance. [$] *Rooms from: $230* ✉ *15 30th Ave., Venice* ☎ *310/823–1966* 🌐 *www.venicebeachhouse.com* 🛏 *9 rooms* 🍴 *Breakfast.*

Nightlife

The Brig

BARS/PUBS | This charming bar has its pluses (interesting drinks, talented DJs) and minuses (ugh, parking) but is worth a look if you're in the area. There's always a food truck around, and the bar's fine with you bringing in outside food. ✉ *1515 Abbot Kinney Blvd., Venice* ☎ *310/399–7537* 🌐 *www.thebrig.com.*

The Otheroom

BARS/PUBS | With a focus on hard-to-find craft beers and fine wines, this bar has become a favorite local hangout. The space is welcoming, especially with its large front windows thrown open on particularly gorgeous days. The bar doesn't serve food but allows patrons to bring their own—a wise decision, given the number of food trucks in the area. ⊠ *1201 Abbot Kinney Blvd., Venice* ☎ *310/396–6230* ⊕ *www.theotheroom. net.*

🛍 Shopping

Christy Dawn

CLOTHING | The fact that designer/store owner (and occasional model) Christy Dawn is a native Californian shows in her modern bohemian dresses, rompers, separates, and outwear. Effortless with a decidedly feminine feel, the line is created using exclusively deadstock fabric (for less of an environmental impact) and made locally. Her Venice storefront also features many other sustainable goods, including organic and biodynamic chocolates by Zenbunni, vintage jeans, French work shirts, accessories, and vegan sneakers. ⊠ *1930 Lincoln Blvd., Venice* ☎ *310/450–7860* ⊕ *www.christydawn. com.*

Coutula

CLOTHING | Owner Carrie Hauman of Coutula (a portmanteau of "Couture LA") travels around the globe to hand-select the clothing, accessories, jewelry, and home furnishings sold in her light-filled, airy Abbot Kinney 1930s cottage. Nab anything from a $10 bracelet to a $6,000 necklace here, along with floaty sundresses that look much more expensive than they are, handmade Cut n Paste leather handbags, and bliss-inducing Tyler candles. ⊠ *1204 Abbot Kinney Blvd., Venice* ☎ *310/581–8010* ⊕ *www.coutula. com.*

General Store

GIFTS/SOUVENIRS | Right at home in the beachy, bohemian neighborhood, this well-curated shop is a decidedly contemporary take on the concept of general stores. The very definition of "California cool," General Store offers beauty and bath products loaded with organic natural ingredients, handmade ceramics, linen tea towels, and a spot-on selection of art books. Featuring an impressive number of local makers and designers, the boutique also sells modern, minimal clothing and has a kids' section that will wow even the hippest moms and dads. ⊠ *1801 Lincoln Blvd., Venice* ☎ *310/751– 6393* ⊕ *www.shop-generalstore.com.*

Heist

CLOTHING | Owner Nilou Ghodsi has admitted that she stocks her Westside shop like an extension of her own closet, which in her case means keeping the focus on modern-yet-classic pieces as opposed to trendy ones. The airy boutique offers elegantly edgy separates from American designers like Nili Lotan and Ulla Johnson, as well as from hard-to-find French and Italian designers. ⊠ *1100 Abbot Kinney Blvd., Venice* ☎ *310/450–6531* ⊕ *www.shopheist.com.*

LCD

CLOTHING | Anyone who's looking to get a leg up on the hottest new designers will want to make this Lincoln Boulevard boutique a stop on their Venice shopping spree. The clean, modern space features cool, contemporary clothing by the likes of Ryan Roche, Sandy Liang, and Assembly New York, plus beauty loot from Verso, bags and eyewear from beloved local labels, and so much more for fashion followers to fawn over. ⊠ *1919 S. Lincoln Blvd., Venice* ☎ *424/500–2552* ⊕ *www. shoplcd.co.*

Strange Invisible Perfumes

PERFUME/COSMETICS | Finding your signature fragrance at this sleek Abbot Kinney boutique won't come cheap, but perfumer Alexandra Balahoutis takes creating her scents as seriously as a seasoned winemaker—and they're just as nuanced as a well-balanced glass of vino. Essences for the perfumes are organic, wild crafted, biodynamic, and bottled locally. Highlights from SI's core collection include the cacao-spiked Dimanche and leathery Black Rosette. ⊠ *1138 Abbot*

Continued on page 83

ALONG
THE STRAND
L.A.'S COASTAL
BIKE PATH

Cycling along the Strand

Venice Beach graffiti

On the Waterfront Cafe

Santa Monica Beach

Venice Beach café

When L.A. wants to get out and play by the water, people hit the Strand for the afternoon. This paved 22-mile path hugs the coastline and loops through tourist-packed stretches and sleepy beach towns. Quirky cafés, loads of souvenir stands, a family-packed amusement park on a pier, and spots for gazing at the Pacific are just a few things to see along the way.

The path extends from Santa Monica's Will Rogers State Beach to Torrance County Beach in South Redondo. It's primarily flat—aside from a few hills you encounter as you head toward Playa del Rey—and it's a terrific way for people of all fitness levels to experience L.A.'s beaches not far from Hollywood or Beverly Hills. You can explore at your own pace.

The hardest part of the journey isn't tackling the path itself—it's trying to get through it all without being distracted by the surrounding activity. With colorful graffitied murals, surfers and sailboats, weightlifters and tattoo parlors, local characters in carnivalesque costumes, volleyball games and skateboarders, there are almost too many things to busy youself with.

Santa Monica amusement park

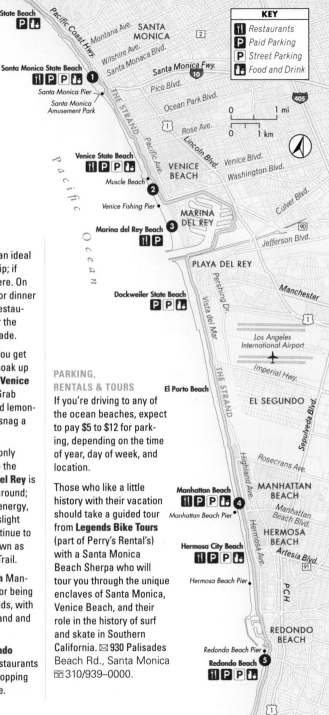

GETTING HERE AND AROUND

ITINERARY BASICS

❶ Santa Monica is an ideal place to start your trip; if you're biking, rent here. On the way back, stop for dinner at one of the many restaurants along and near the Third Street Promenade.

Take a break when you get to Venice Beach to soak up the scene on the **❷ Venice Ocean Boardwalk**. Grab some fresh-squeezed lemonade from a stand or snag a table at a café.

If you're dedicating only a half-day to explore the Strand, **❸ Marina del Rey** is a good spot to turn around; with more time and energy, follow signs for the slight detour here and continue to the second half, known as the South Bay Bike Trail.

❹ Manhattan Beach Manhattan Beach wins for being one of the best for kids, with its wide stretch of sand and good swimming.

The pier at **❺ Redondo Beach**, lined with restaurants and shops, makes stopping here well worthwhile.

PARKING, RENTALS & TOURS

If you're driving to any of the ocean beaches, expect to pay $5 to $12 for parking, depending on the time of year, day of week, and location.

Those who like a little history with their vacation should take a guided tour from **Legends Bike Tours** (part of Perry's Rental's) with a Santa Monica Beach Sherpa who will tour you through the unique enclaves of Santa Monica, Venice Beach, and their role in the history of surf and skate in Southern California. ✉ 930 Palisades Beach Rd., Santa Monica ☎ 310/939–0000.

Kinney Blvd., Venice ☎ 310/314–1505 ⊕ www.siperfumes.com.

Activities

Venice Skatepark

CITY PARK | Watch skateboarders displaying a wide range of ability levels as they careen around this concrete park, situated between the beach and the boardwalk in Venice. There's also an impressive crew of disco roller skaters, and drum circles that gravitate toward the middle of the boardwalk. ⊠ *1800 Ocean Front Walk, off E. Market St., Venice* ⊕ *www. veniceskatepark.com.*

Malibu

North of Santa Monica, up the Pacific Coast Highway, past rockslides, roller-bladers, and cliffside estates, Malibu is home to blockbuster names like Spielberg, Hanks, and Streisand. This ecologically fragile 23-mile stretch of coastline is a world of its own, with its slopes slipping dramatically into the ocean. But Malibu is constantly reinventing itself, and the devastating 2018 Woolsey Fire has forced it to reinvent once more.

In the public imagination Malibu is synonymous with beaches and wealth—but in the past couple of years there's been some friction between these two signature elements. Some property owners, such as billionaire music producer David Geffen, have come under attack for blocking public access to the beaches in front of their homes. All beaches are technically public, though; if you stay below the mean high-tide mark you're in the clear.

◉ Sights

Adamson House and Malibu Lagoon Museum

MUSEUM | With spectacular views of Surfrider Beach and lush garden grounds, this Moorish Spanish–style house epitomizes all the reasons to live in Malibu. It was built in 1929 by the Rindge family, who owned much of the Malibu area in the early part of the 20th century. The Rindges had an enviable Malibu lifestyle, decades before the area was trendy. In the 1920s, Malibu was quite isolated; in fact all visitors and some of the supplies arrived by boat at the nearby Malibu Pier. (The town becomes isolated today whenever rockslides close the highway.) The house, covered with magnificent tile work in rich blues, greens, yellows, and oranges from the now-defunct Malibu Potteries, is right on the beach—high chain link fences keep out curious beachgoers. Even an outside dog bathtub near the servants' door is a tiled gem. Docent-led tours provide insights on family life here as well as the history of Malibu and its real estate. Signs posted around the grounds outside direct you on a self-guided tour, but you can't go inside the house without a guide. Guided tours take place on Friday and Saturday at 11 am. There's pay parking in the adjacent county lot or in the lot at PCH and Cross Creek Road. ⊠ *23200 Pacific Coast Hwy., Malibu* ☎ *310/456–8432* ⊕ *www.adamsonhouse.org* ⊠ *$7* ⊙ *Check website for closing times.*

Dan Blocker Beach (*Corral Beach*)

BEACH—SIGHT | The narrow stretch of fine sand and rocks here make this little beach great for walking, light swimming, kayaking, and scuba diving. Clustered boulders create cozy spots for couples and picnickers, and because of the limited parking available along PCH, it's rarely crowded. Originally owned by the star of the *Bonanza* TV series, the beach was donated to the state after Blocker (who played Hoss) died in 1972. Locals

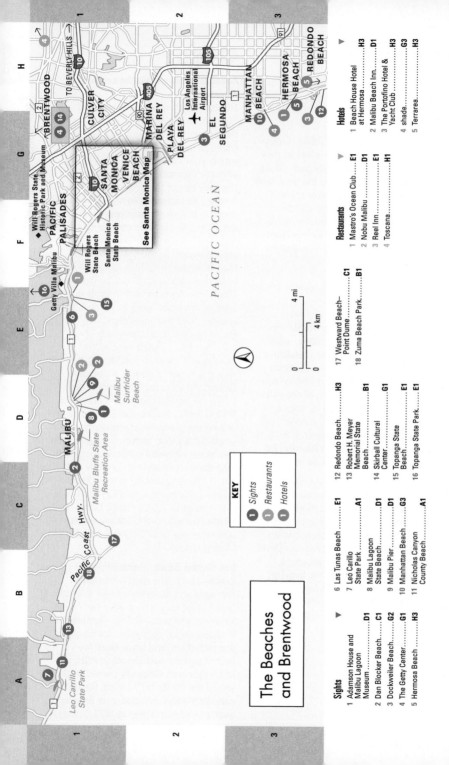

The Beaches and Brentwood

KEY

1 Sights
1 Restaurants
1 Hotels

Sights ►

1 Adamson House and
  Malibu Lagoon
  Museum D1
2 Dan Blocker Beach C1
3 Dockweiler Beach G2
4 The Getty Center G1
5 Hermosa Beach H3

6 Las Tunas Beach E1
7 Leo Carrillo
  State Park A1
8 Malibu Lagoon
  State Beach D1
9 Malibu Pier D1
10 Manhattan Beach G3
11 Nicholas Canyon
   County Beach A1

12 Redondo Beach H3
13 Robert H. Meyer
   Memorial State
   Beach B1
14 Skirball Cultural
   Center G1
15 Topanga State
   Beach E1
16 Topanga State Park E1

17 Westward Beach–
   Point Dume C1
18 Zuma Beach Park B1

Restaurants ►

1 Mastro's Ocean Club E1
2 Nobu Malibu D1
3 Reel Inn E1
4 Toscana H1

Hotels ►

1 Beach House Hotel
  at Hermosa H3
2 Malibu Beach Inn D1
3 The Portofino Hotel &
  Yacht Club H3
4 shade G3
5 Terrarea H3

PACIFIC OCEAN

0 ___ 4 km
0 ___ 4 mi

still know this as Corral Beach. From the parking lot, walk a short distance up PCH in either direction to access the beach. **Amenities:** lifeguards; toilets. **Best for:** solitude; walking; swimming; snorkeling. ⊠ *26000 Pacific Coast Hwy., at Corral Canyon Rd., Malibu* ☎ *310/305–9503* ⊕ *beaches.lacounty.gov/ dan-blocker-beach.*

Las Tunas Beach

BEACH—SIGHT | This small beach, the southernmost in Malibu, is known for its groins (metal gates constructed in 1929 to protect against erosion) and has good swimming, diving, and fishing conditions and a rocky coastline that wraps elegantly around the Pacific Coast Highway. Watch out for high tides. **Amenities:** lifeguards; food and drink. **Best for:** solitude; swimming. ⊠ *19444 Pacific Coast Hwy., Malibu* ☎ *310/305–9545* ⊕ *beaches. lacounty.gov/las-tunas-beach.*

Leo Carrillo State Park

BEACH—SIGHT | FAMILY | On the very edge of Ventura County, this narrow beach is better for exploring than for sunning or swimming (watch that strong undertow!). If you do plan to swim, stay north of lifeguard towers 2, 4, and 5, but be sure to ask lifeguards about water conditions when you arrive. On your own or with a ranger, venture down at low tide to examine the tide pools among the rocks. Sequit Point, a promontory dividing the northwest and southeast halves of the beach, creates secret coves, sea tunnels, and boulders on which you can perch and fish. Generally, anglers stick to the northwest end of the beach; experienced surfers brave the rocks to the southeast. Campgrounds are set back from the beach; campsites must be reserved well in advance. Tide pools make this a great place for exploration. **Amenities**: parking; lifeguards (seasonally); toilets; showers. **Best for:** sunset; surfing; swimming; walking; windsurfing. ⊠ *35000 Pacific Coast*

Hwy., Malibu ☎ *310/457–8143* ⊕ *parks. ca.gov/?page_id=616.*

Malibu Lagoon State Beach

BEACH—SIGHT | Bird watchers, take note: in this 5-acre marshy area near Malibu Beach Inn you can spot egrets, blue herons, avocets, and gulls. (You need to stay on the boardwalks so as not to disturb their habitats.) The path leads out to a rocky stretch of Surfrider Beach and makes for a pleasant stroll. The sand is soft, clean, and white, and you're also likely to spot a variety of marine life. Look for the signs to help identify these sometimes exotic-looking creatures. The lagoon is particularly enjoyable in the early morning and at sunset—and even more so now, thanks to a restoration effort that improved the lagoon's scent. The parking lot has limited hours, but street-side parking is usually available at off-peak times. Close by are shops and a theater. **Amenities:** parking (fee); lifeguards; toilets; showers. **Best for:** sunset; walking. ⊠ *23200 Pacific Coast Hwy., Malibu* ☎ *310/457–8143* ⊕ *www.parks. ca.gov* 🚗 *Parking $12.*

Malibu Pier

MARINA | FAMILY | This 780-foot fishing dock is a great place to drink in the sunset, take in some coastal views, or watch local fishermen reel up a catch. Some tours also leave from here. A pier has jutted out here since the early 1900s; storms destroyed the last one in 1995, and it was rebuilt in 2001. The pier's landing was damaged in 2011 and has required repair. Over the years, private developers have worked with the state to refurbish the pier, which now yields a gift shop, water-sport rentals, and a wonderful farm-to-table restaurant with stunning views and locations at both ends of the pier. ⊠ *Pacific Coast Hwy. at Cross Creek Rd., Malibu* ⊕ *www.malibupier.com.*

Nicholas Canyon County Beach

BEACH—SIGHT | Sandier and less private than most of the rocky beaches surrounding it, this little beach is great for picnics. You can sit at a picnic table high up on a bluff overlooking the ocean or cast out a fishing line. Surfers call it Zero Beach because the waves take the shape of a hollow tube when winter swells peel off the reef. This site also hosts a 4-acre traditional Chumash village, which replicates a day in the life of the Native American Chumash people, including their homes, canoes, handicrafts, and ceremonies. Request a guided tour in advance. **Amenities:** parking (fee); lifeguards; toilets; showers. **Best for:** solitude; surfing; walking; windsurfing. ⊠ *33805 Pacific Coast Hwy., Malibu* ☎ *310/305–9503.*

★ Robert H. Meyer Memorial State Beach

BEACH—SIGHT | Part of Malibu's most beautiful coastal area, this beach is made up of three minibeaches—El Pescador, La Piedra, and El Matador—each with the same spectacular view. Scramble down the steps to the rocky coves via steep, steep stairways; all food and water needs to be toted in, as there are no services. Portable toilets at the trailhead are the only restrooms. "El Mat" has a series of caves, Piedra some nifty rock formations, and Pescador a secluded feel, but they're all picturesque and fairly private. ⚠ **Keep track of the incoming tide so you won't get trapped between those otherwise scenic boulders. Amenities:** parking (fee); toilets. **Best for:** snorkeling; solitude; sunset; surfing; walking; windsurfing. ⊠ *32350, 32700, and 32900 Pacific Coast Hwy., Malibu* ☎ *818/880–0363* ⊕ *http://parks. ca.gov/?page_id=633.*

Topanga State Beach

BEACH—SIGHT | The beginning of miles of public beach, Topanga has good surfing at the western end, the mouth of the canyon. Close to a busy section of PCH and rather narrow, the beach here is more lively, as groups of teenagers often zip over Topanga Canyon Boulevard from the Valley. There are swing sets on-site, as well as spots for fishing. **Amenities:** parking (fee); lifeguards; toilets; food and

drink; showers. **Best for:** surfing. ⊠ *18700 block of Pacific Coast Hwy., Malibu* ☎ *310/305–9503* ⊕ *beaches.lacounty.gov/ topanga-beach.*

Topanga State Park

NATIONAL/STATE PARK | This is another way into Santa Monica, via the Trippet Ranch entrance, which gives you several options: a ½-mile nature loop, a 7-mile round-trip excursion to the Parker Mesa Overlook—breathtaking on a clear day—or a 10-mile trek to the Will Rogers park. (Exit U.S. 101 onto Topanga Canyon Boulevard in Woodland Hills and head south until you can turn left onto Entrada; if going north on PCH, turn onto Topanga Canyon Boulevard—a bit past Sunset Boulevard—and go north until you can turn right onto Entrada.) ⊠ *20829 Entrada Rd., Malibu* ☎ *310/574–2488* ⊕ *www. parks.ca.gov/?page_id=629* 🚗 *Parking $10.*

Westward Beach–Point Dume

BEACH—SIGHT | Go tide pooling, fishing, snorkeling, or bird-watching (prime time is late winter to early spring). Hike to the top of the sandstone cliffs at Point Dume to whale-watch—their migrations can be seen between December and April—and take in dramatic coastal views. Westward is a favorite surfing beach, but the steep surf isn't for novices. The Sunset restaurant is between Westward and Point Dume (at 6800 Westward Beach Road). Bring your own food, since the nearest concession is a long hike away. **Amenities:** parking (fee); lifeguards; toilets; food and drink; showers. **Best for:** surfing; walking. ⊠ *71030 Westward Beach Rd., Malibu* ☎ *310/305–9503* 🚗 *Parking $14.*

Zuma Beach Park

BEACH—SIGHT | This 2-mile stretch of white sand, usually dotted with tanning teenagers, has it all, from fishing and kitesurfing to swings and volleyball courts. Beachgoers looking for quiet or privacy should head elsewhere. Stay alert in the water: the surf is rough and inconsistent. **Amenities:** parking; lifeguards;

toilets; food and drink; showers. **Best for:** partiers; sunset; swimming; walking. ✉ *30000 Pacific Coast Hwy., Malibu* ☎ *310/305–9522* 🌐 *www.zuma-beach.com* 🎫 *Parking $10.*

🍴 Restaurants

The beauty of the coastline makes every meal here taste like the best you've ever had. Here you'll find quaint family spots and extravagant hot spots.

Mastro's Ocean Club

$$$$ | STEAKHOUSE | This steak house not only features the best views of the beach, it's also a great place to scope out A-listers. You may be paying for the ambience, but mouthwatering steaks, Dungeness crab, and lobster mashed potatoes just seem to taste better when the ocean is nipping at your feet. **Known for:** lively weekend brunch; live jazz nightly; reservations needed in advance. [$] *Average main: $50* ✉ *18412 Pacific Coast Hwy., Malibu* ☎ *310/454–4357* 🌐 *www.mastrosrestaurants.com.*

Nobu Malibu

$$$ | JAPANESE | At famous chef-restaurateur Nobu Matsuhisa's coastal outpost, super-chic clientele sails in for morsels of the world's finest fish. It's hard not to be seduced by the oceanfront property, and stellar sushi and ingenious specialties match the upscale setting. **Known for:** exotic fish; toro with truffle teriyaki; bento box Valrhona chocolate soufflé. [$] *Average main: $35* ✉ *22706 Pacific Coast Hwy., Malibu* ☎ *310/317–9140* 🌐 *www.noburestaurants.com.*

Reel Inn

$ | SEAFOOD | FAMILY | Long wooden tables and booths are often filled with fish-loving families chowing down on mahimahi sandwiches and freshly caught swordfish. Get in line and choose your fish and sides, then nab a table. **Known for:** easy-to-miss spot on PCH; fresh catches. [$] *Average main: $17* ✉ *18661 Pacific Coast Hwy., Malibu* ☎ *310/456–8221* 🌐 *www.reelinnmalibu.com.*

🛏 Hotels

Malibu Beach Inn

$$$$ | B&B/INN | Set right on exclusive Carbon Beach, Malibu's hideaway for the super-rich remains the room to nab along the coast, with an ultrachic new look thanks to designer Waldo Fernandez, and an upscale restaurant and wine bar perched over the Pacific. **Pros:** see the ocean from your private balcony; wine list curated by sommelier Laurie Sutton; world-class chocolate chip cookies at reception. **Cons:** billionaire's travel budget required; some in-room noise from PCH; no pool, gym, or hot tub—but with the ocean a step away, who cares?. [$] *Rooms from: $749* ✉ *22878 Pacific Coast Hwy., Malibu* ☎ *310/456–6444* 🌐 *www.malibubeachinn.com* 🛏 *47 rooms* 🍴 *No meals.*

🍸 Nightlife

Duke's Barefoot Bar

BARS/PUBS | FAMILY | With a clear view of the horizon from almost everywhere, a sunset drink at Duke's Barefoot Bar is how many beachgoers like to end their day. The entertainment is in keeping with the bar's theme, with Hawaiian dancers as well as live music on Friday night by Hawaiian artists. The menu features island favorites like *poke* tacos, macadamia-crusted fish, and kalua pork and a Sunday brunch buffet from 10 to 2. Just don't expect beach-bum prices, unless you stop by the happy hour weekday events like Taco Tuesday ($3 fish, kalua pork, or grilled chicken tacos, along with $3 beer). ✉ *21150 Pacific Coast Hwy., Malibu* ☎ *310/317–0777* 🌐 *www.dukesmalibu.com.*

Moonshadows

BARS/PUBS | This newly renovated outdoor lounge attracts customers with its modern look and views of the ocean. Think dark woods, cabana-style draperies, and ambient lighting in the Blue Lounge. DJs are constantly spinning lounge music in the background, and there's never a cover charge. Try the new lobster roll and dessert lineup. This restaurant maintains some amount of notoriety as the establishment frequented by Mel Gibson just before his infamous 2006 arrest. ⊠ *20356 Pacific Coast Hwy., Malibu* ☎ *310/456–3010* ⊕ *www.moonshadows-malibu.com.*

🎭 Performing Arts

Will Geer Theatricum Botanicum

THEATER | FAMILY | This open-air theater puts on classic as well as new and relevant plays from June to October, along with several off-season events and Family Fundays. The gardens have sitting areas for picnics before the show and they encourage you to "Play and Stay" in the Topanga area by pairing your theater experience with a hike in the local hills or a trip to one of the area's unique restaurants beforehand; the company also hosts dinner (and a show) on certain nights. ■TIP→ **Select weekends are great for families, with special shows performed with children in mind.** ⊠ *1419 N. Topanga Canyon Blvd., Topanga* ☎ *310/455–3723* ⊕ *www.theatricum.com.*

🛍 Shopping

MALLS AND SHOPPING CENTERS

Malibu Country Mart

SHOPPING CENTERS/MALLS | Have the quintessential beachside shopping experience complete with browsing designer clothing (Morgane le Fay, Ron Herman, or Madison) and eclectic California housewares and gifts (Burro), picking up body-boosting wellness goodies at Sunlife Organics, and finishing the day off with dinner at iconic eatery Mr. Chow. If you can squeeze in a workout, there's a Pure Barre and 5 Point Yoga to choose from, plus tarot readings at

metaphysical outpost Malibu Shaman, and Eastern medicine treatments at Malibu Acupuncture. Then reward yourself for your good health habits by stopping at fan-favorite Italian gelateria Grom's Malibu outpost for out-of-this-world fresh pistachio or *gianduia* (chocolate hazelnut) gelato. ⊠ *3835 Cross Creek Rd., Malibu* ☎ *310/456–7300* ⊕ *www.malibucountry-mart.com.*

Malibu Lumber Yard

SHOPPING CENTERS/MALLS | Emblematic Malibu lifestyle stores in this shopping complex include James Perse, Maxfield, and too-chic Intermix. The playground and alfresco dining area make this an ideal weekend destination for families. ⊠ *3939 Cross Creek Rd., Malibu* ⊕ *www.themalibulumberyard.com.*

El Segundo

Just south of LAX, you'll find this quaint, sleepy beach community. Originally an oil town—Standard Oil set up its second refinery in El Segundo (hence the name, which means "the second" in Spanish)—now it's full of families, out wandering the cute residential streets.

👁 Sights

Dockweiler Beach

BEACH—SIGHT | Is there a dreamier way to top off your day at the beach than a bonfire at twilight? In L.A., where beach bonfires are largely illegal, you can have that along Dockweiler's 3.7-mile stretch. Here, lighting up isn't just permitted, it's practically encouraged, thanks to fire pits peppered throughout. It's probably for this reason that the beach is almost always a scene where young twenty- and thirtysomethings are roasting jumbo marshmallows on long, makeshift skewers as they guzzle beer in red cups. ⊠ *12001 Vista Del Mar, Playa del Rey* ☎ *310/322–4951.*

Nightlife

Purple Orchid

BARS/PUBS | This is a dive bar. If you don't like dive bars, you won't like this place. But if you do happen to like them, you won't feel mere affection for the Purple Orchid, but love. This is also a tiki bar, though the tiki drinks are mainly sipped by those who are new to the joint. If you want to drink like the regulars, go for a beer or a gin and tonic. ✉ *221 Richmond St., El Segundo* ☎ *310/322–5829.*

Manhattan Beach

Chic boutiques, multimillion-dollar homes, and some of the best restaurants in Los Angeles dot the hilly downtown streets of this tiny community. While the glamour and exclusivity are palpable, with attractive residents making deals over cocktails, this is still a beach town. Annual volleyball and surfing tournaments, crisp ocean breezes, and a very clean walking and biking path invite all visitors.

Sights

Manhattan Beach

BEACH—SIGHT | A wide, sandy strip with good swimming and rows of volleyball courts, Manhattan Beach is the preferred destination of muscled, tanned young professionals and dedicated bikini watchers. There are also such amenities as a bike path, a playground, a bait shop, fishing equipment for rent, and a sizable fishing pier. It's also the perfect place to unwind during a long layover at LAX. **Amenities:** parking (fee); lifeguards; toilets; food and drink; showers. **Best for:** swimming; walking. ✉ *Manhattan Beach Blvd. at N. Ocean Dr., Manhattan Beach* ☎ *310/372–2166* 🌐 *beaches.lacounty.gov/manhattan-beach* 🅿 *Metered parking; long- and short-term lots.*

Hotels

shade

$$$$ | **HOTEL** | Super-contemporary design makes this hotel, rooftop pool, and Skydeck feel like an adults-only playground, and it's just a short walk to the shoreline, the local pier, and Manhattan Beach's lively downtown. **Pros:** fun freebies like cake pops and bike use; passes to Equinox gym; cool amenities like "chromatherapy" lighting and in-room martini shaker. **Cons:** sharp-edged furniture; recommended for adults or older kids only; small dipping pool. [$] *Rooms from: $449* ✉ *1221 N. Valley Dr., Manhattan Beach* ☎ *310/546–4995, 866/742–3377* 🌐 *www.shadehotel.com* 🔑 *38 rooms* 🍴 *Breakfast.*

Hermosa Beach

This energetic beach city boasts some of the priciest real estate in the country. But down by the sand, the vibe is decidedly casual, with plenty of pubs and ambling young couples. Volleyball courts line the wide beach, drawing many amateur and pro tournaments. The walkable 330-yard pier features dramatic views of the coastline winding southward.

Sights

Hermosa Beach

BEACH—SIGHT | South of Manhattan Beach, Hermosa Beach has all the amenities of its neighbor but attracts a rowdier crowd. Swimming takes a backseat to the volleyball games and parties on the pier and bustling boardwalk, but the water here is consistently clean and inviting. **Amenities:** parking (fee); lifeguards; toilets; food and drink; showers. **Best for:** partiers; surfing; swimming. ✉ *1201 The Strand, Hermosa Ave. at 33rd St., Hermosa Beach* ☎ *310/372–2166* 🌐 *beaches.lacounty.gov/hermosa-beach/* 🅿 *Parking* *(metered) at 11th St. and Hermosa Ave., and 13th St. and Hermosa Ave.*

Hotels

★ Beach House Hotel at Hermosa
$$$ | **HOTEL** | **FAMILY** | Bordering the Strand (SoCal's famous bike path on the beach), Beach House looks like a New England sea cottage from a century ago but has contemporary amenities in its bright studio suites. **Pros:** in-room massages available; enjoy delicious muffins and coffee (and more) in the breakfast room; oceanfront rooms and sunset views. **Cons:** noise from the busy Strand, especially on weekends; no pool; continental breakfast only. [$] *Rooms from: $349* ✉ *1300 The Strand, Hermosa Beach* ☎ *310/374–3001, 888/895–4559* 🌐 *www.beach-house.com* 🛏 *96 suites* 🍴 *Breakfast.*

Nightlife

Abigaile Restaurant and Brewery/Alta House
BREWPUBS/BEER GARDENS | Originally a church and then a Black Flag punk band rehearsal space, the building hosting Abigaile has a long history of the sacred and the profane. This is reflected in the cheeky brewery and gastropub's decor (think pew seating, an altar bar, and graffitied walls) and an incredibly diverse, globally inspired new American menu by chef Tin Vuong, which includes smoked pork confit "pop tarts," a Medjool date and kale salad, and the Buddha Belly Feast for vegans. Abigaile also churns out a wide range of ales from its in-house copper brewing system, which serves as the bar's backdrop. Upstairs, the newly renovated Alta House lounge (with a shared kitchen) is the place for sunset cocktails, boasting ocean views, comfortable seating, and a DJ. ✉ *1301 Manhattan Ave., Hermosa Beach* ☎ *310/798–8227* 🌐 *abigailerestaurant.com.*

Lighthouse Cafe
BARS/PUBS | Featured in *La La Land*, the 2016 musical set in Los Angeles, this onetime jazz bistro now offers a wide range of live entertainment, adding salsa, country, reggae, and karaoke (either backed by a DJ or a live band, depending on when you go) to the repertoire. There's a $5 cover charge on Friday and Saturday after 9 pm, and brunch and live music all day on weekends. Check out the happy hour specials ($5 food and drinks). ✉ *30 Pier Ave., Hermosa Beach* ☎ *310/376–9833* 🌐 *www.thelighthouse-cafe.net.*

Redondo Beach

With its worn-in pier and cozy beach, Redondo is a refreshingly unglamorous counterpoint to neighboring beach cities. This was the first port in Los Angeles County in the early 1890s, before business shifted south to San Pedro Harbor, and the community still retains a working-class persona. The best way to soak up the scene these days is with a stroll along the sprawling pier, which features shops, casual restaurants, a live fish market, and fantastic sunset views.

Hotels

The Portofino Hotel & Yacht Club
$$$ | **HOTEL** | **FAMILY** | Open your balcony door and listen to the calls of seabirds and sea lions from ocean- and channel-side rooms (earplugs are provided for humbugs); marina-side rooms overlook sailboats and docks. **Pros:** bike or walk to beach from the hotel's private peninsula; excellent Baleen restaurant overlooking the harbor. **Cons:** higher rates in summer and for ocean-view rooms; restaurant may be noisy due to the adjacent bar; some areas could do with a refresh. [$] *Rooms from: $369* ✉ *260 Portofino Way, Redondo Beach* ☎ *310/379–8481,*

800/468–4292 ⊕ *www.hotelportofino. com* ⌖ *166 rooms* ○ *No meals.*

RANCHO PALOS VERDES
★ Terranea
$$$$ | **RESORT** | **FAMILY** | The Pacific Ocean and Catalina Island are within view at Terranea, L.A.'s only full-service ocean-front resort straddling 102 terraced acres at land's end on the scenic Palos Verdes Peninsula. Its location gives it the feel of a retreat. **Pros:** kid-friendly amenities and pool slide; blissful oceanfront spa; four saline pools and hot tubs. **Cons:** pricey on-site dining; with resort fee and parking, this luxury becomes very expensive. $ *Rooms from: $475* ⊠ *100 Terranea Way, Rancho Palos Verdes* ☎ *310/265– 2800* ⊕ *www.terranea.com* ⌖ *582 rooms* ○ *No meals.*

◉ Sights

Redondo Beach
BEACH—SIGHT | The pier here marks the starting point of this wide, busy beach along a heavily developed shoreline community. Restaurants and shops flourish along the pier, excursion boats and privately owned crafts depart from launching ramps, and a reef formed by a sunken ship creates prime fishing and snorkeling conditions. If you're adventurous, you might try to kayak out to the buoys and hobnob with pelicans and sea lions. A series of free rock and jazz concerts takes place at the pier every summer. **Amenities:** parking; lifeguards; food and drink; toilets; showers; water sports. **Best for:** snorkeling; sunset; swimming; walking. ⊠ *Torrance Blvd. at Catalina Ave., Redondo Beach* ☎ *310/372–2166* ⊕ *www.redondopier.com.*

Brentwood

This wealthy residential enclave west of Beverly Hills is home to the world-class Getty Center.

◉ Sights

★ The Getty Center
MUSEUM | **FAMILY** | With its curving walls and isolated hilltop perch, the Getty Center resembles a pristine fortified city of its own. You may have been lured there by the beautiful views of Los Angeles—on a clear day stretching all the way to the Pacific Ocean—but the amazing architecture, uncommon gardens, and fascinating art collections will be more than enough to capture and hold your attention. When the sun is out, the complex's rough-cut travertine marble skin seems to soak up the light.

Getting to the center involves a bit of anticipatory lead-up. At the base of the hill, a pavilion disguises the underground parking structure. From there you either walk or take a smooth, computer-driven tram up the steep slope, checking out the Bel Air estates across the humming 405 freeway. The five pavilions that house the museum surround a central courtyard and are bridged by walkways. From the courtyard, plazas, and walkways, you can survey the city from the San Gabriel Mountains to the ocean.

In a ravine separating the museum and the Getty Research Institute, conceptual artist Robert Irwin created the playful Central Garden in stark contrast to Richard Meier's mathematical architectural geometry. The garden's design is what Hollywood feuds are made of: Meier couldn't control Irwin's vision, and the two men sniped at each other during construction, with Irwin stirring the pot with every loose twist his garden path took. The result is a refreshing garden walk whose focal point is an azalea maze (some insist the Mickey Mouse shape is on purpose) in a reflecting pool.

Inside the pavilions are the galleries for the permanent collections of European paintings, drawings, sculpture, illuminated manuscripts, and decorative arts, as well as world-class temporary exhibitions and photographs gathered internationally. The Getty's collection of French furniture and decorative arts, especially from the early years of Louis XIV (1643–1715) to the end of the reign of Louis XVI (1774–92), is renowned for its quality and condition; you can even see a pair of completely reconstructed salons. In the paintings galleries, a computerized system of louvered skylights allows natural light to filter in, creating a closer approximation of the conditions in which the artists painted. Notable among the paintings are Rembrandt's *The Abduction of Europa,* Van Gogh's *Irises,* Monet's *Wheatstack, Snow Effects,* and *Morning,* and James Ensor's *Christ's Entry into Brussels.*

If you want to start with a quick overview, pick up the brochure in the entrance hall that guides you to collection highlights. There's also an instructive audio tour (free, but you have to leave your ID) with commentaries by art historians and other experts. Art information rooms with multimedia computer stations contain more details about the collections. The Getty also presents lectures, films, concerts, art workshops, and special programs for kids, families, and all-around culture lovers. The complex includes an upscale restaurant and downstairs cafeteria with panoramic window views. There are also outdoor coffee carts. ■ TIP→ **On-site parking is subject to availability and can fill up by midday on holidays and in the summer, so try to come early in the day or after lunch.** A tram takes you from the street-level entrance to the top of the hill. Public buses (Metro Rapid Line 734) also serve the center and link to the Expo Rail extension. ✉ *1200 Getty Center Dr., Brentwood* ☎ *310/440–7300* 🌐 *www.getty.edu* 🎟 *Free; parking $15* 🕒 *Closed Mon.*

Skirball Cultural Center

MUSEUM | The mission of this Jewish cultural institution in the beautiful Santa Monica Mountains is to explore the connections "between 4,000 years of Jewish heritage and the vitality of American democratic ideals." The extraordinary museum, featuring exhibits like *Visions and Values: Jewish Life from Antiquity to America,* has a massive collection of Judaica—the third largest in the world. A big draw is the Noah's Ark interactive exhibition, where children are invited to recreate the famous tale using their own imagination. ✉ *2701 N. Sepulveda Blvd., north of Brentwood, Los Angeles* ☎ *310/440–4500* 🌐 *www.skirball.org* 🎟 *$12; free Thurs.* 🕒 *Closed Mon.*

🍴 Restaurants

Toscana

$$$ | **ITALIAN** | This rustic trattoria along San Vicente is a favorite celebrity haunt. Expect elevated sensory offerings, from its cozy atmosphere to its mouthwatering Tuscan fare and excellent wine list. **Known for:** excellent wine list; white truffles; celeb-spotting. [$] *Average main: $35* ✉ *11633 San Vicente Blvd., Brentwood* ☎ *310/820–2448* 🌐 *www.toscanabrentwood.com.*

🛍 Shopping

Brentwood Country Mart

SHOPPING CENTERS/MALLS | FAMILY | Among the dozens of stores within this family-friendly faux country market are Goop (Gwyneth Paltrow's lifestyle brand's gorgeous first brick-and-mortar store), Turpan (for luxury home goods), James Perse (for laid-back cotton knits), Jenni Kayne (for a curated mix of modern clothing, housewares, and gifts), and Malia Mills (for American-made swimwear separates). Grab a chicken basket at Reddi Chick and chow down on the open-air patio. ✉ *225 26th St., at San Vicente Blvd., Brentwood* ☎ *310/451–9877* ⊕ *www.brentwoodcountrymart.com.*

Chapter 4

BEVERLY HILLS, WEST HOLLYWOOD, AND THE WESTSIDE

Updated By
Paul Feinstein

⦿ Sights	🍴 Restaurants	🛏 Hotels	🛍 Shopping	🍸 Nightlife
★★★★☆	★★★★☆	★★★★☆	★★★★★	★★★☆☆

NEIGHBORHOOD SNAPSHOT

TOP EXPERIENCES

■ **Shop on Rodeo:** Even if it's window-shopping, it's a one-of-a-kind experience to watch the parade of diamonds, couture gowns, and Ferraris being fetishized.

■ **Wander the Grove and feast at the Farmers Market :** Visit for a shopping respite or to take in and appreciate the Farmers Market's 75-year-old history and atmosphere.

■ **Drive down Sunset Boulevard to the Ocean:** The quintessential Los Angeles experience, it's best to start at La Cienega headed west on Sunset, which will take you through the Sunset Strip. Now may be a good time to test-drive that convertible.

■ **Experience the '60s, '70s, and '80s all over again:** To truly experience the L.A. music scene of decades past, wander into the venues where everyone from the Doors to Guns N' Roses used to pay: the Troubadour, the Whisky A Go Go, and the Rainbow Bar and Grill.

QUICK BITES

Milk Bar LA. This place is so popular that lines often spill out the door and onto the sidewalk. Suffer through them for the crack pie and cereal-milk soft serve. ⊠ *7150 Melrose Ave.*

Nate 'n' Al. A longtime refuge from California's lean cuisine, Nate 'n' Al serves up steaming pastrami, matzo ball soup, and potato latkes. ⊠ *414 N. Beverly Dr.*

Urth Caffé Melrose. Join the beautiful people at this ultratrendy cafe and refuel on organic coffee and tea with a range of health-conscious sandwiches, salads, and juices. ⊠ *8565 Melrose Ave.*

GETTING HERE

■ All main west–east roads will get you toward Beverly Hills and West Hollywood. Santa Monica Boulevard is the easiest. It starts in Santa Monica, heads into Beverly Hills, and then diverts northeast and wanders into West Hollywood, before heading due east again. But traffic can be a nightmare, as it can be for L.A.'s main artery, Wilshire Boulevard, which also hits Beverly Hills. Try Pico or Olympic Boulevard, which both run roughly parallel a bit farther south.

■ In Beverly Hills, you can park your car in one of several municipal lots (often free for the first hour or two), and spend as long as you like strolling along Rodeo Drive. For street parking, bring quarters for the meter, or pay with a credit card. Parking on residential streets is often by permit only.

PLANNING YOUR TIME

■ Let's be honest—you're here to shop and do lunch. And this can easily take a whole day. Start out wandering the various shops along Rodeo Drive, before heading out to The Grove and the adjacent Farmers Market, where you can sit down for lunch or grab a quick bite. After, wander Melrose Avenue, which is also full of shopping and eating. In the evening, hit up West Hollywood for trendy eats and drinks.

The rumors are true: Beverly Hills delivers on a dramatic, cinematic scale of wealth and excess. A known celebrity haunt, come here to daydream or to live like the rich and famous for a day. Window-shop or splurge at tony stores, and keep an eye out for filming locales; just walking around here will make you feel like you're on a movie set.

Beverly Hills

⊙ Sights

When visiting Beverly Hills for the first time, many people head for the boutiques and restaurants that line the palm tree–fringed sidewalks of **Rodeo Drive.** People tend to stroll, not rush. Shopping ranges from the accessible and familiar (Pottery Barn) to the unique, expensive, and architecturally stunning (Prada).

Fox Plaza

BUILDING | Towering over the 20th Century Fox studio lot in Century City is Fox Plaza, a 34-story skyscraper where former president Ronald Reagan once had an office. Savvy screen watchers will undoubtedly know it by its more famous name—Nakatomi Plaza. Starring in the blockbusting juggernaut *Die Hard ,* the building is shot at, blown apart, and set on fire as Bruce Willis takes down a German terrorist cell. You should know—this is just an office building, so there's not a whole lot to do but look at it. ⊠ *2121 Avenue of the Stars, Century City.*

Gagosian Gallery

ART GALLERIES—ARTS | This contemporary art gallery, owned and directed by the legendary Larry Gagosian, features cutting-edge artists in a minimalist-styled space. It's free to enter, exhibits rotate every six weeks, and the gallery has displayed everyone from Richard Avedon and Takashi Murakami to Frank Gehry and Jeff Koons. During Oscar season the gallery is known for its celeb-filled openings. ⊠ *456 N. Camden Dr., Beverly Hills* ☎ *310/271–9400* ⊕ *www.gagosian.com.*

Greystone Mansion

HOUSE | Built in 1928, this stunning mansion resides in a discreet residential part of Beverly Hills, surrounded by 18 acres of manicured grounds that are open to the public. The historic house was built by oil magnate Ned Doheny (inspiration for the Daniel Day-Lewis character in *There Will Be Blood*) and has been featured in a number of films like *The Big Lebowski* , *Spider-Man, The Social Network,* and *X-Men.* Park rangers offer tours for $20 where you can gawk at the 46,000-square-foot estate with bowling alley, secret panels for liquor, and even a screening room. ⊠ *905 Loma*

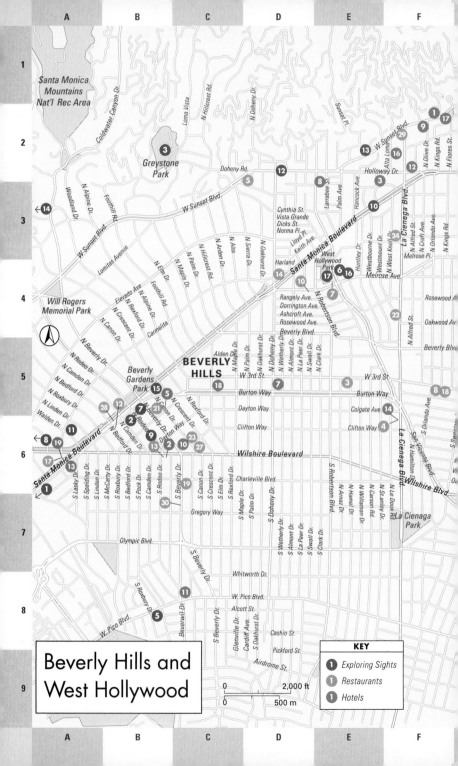

Beverly Hills and West Hollywood

KEY

- 1 Exploring Sights
- 1 Restaurants
- 1 Hotels

Santa Monica Mountains Nat'l Rec Area

Greystone Park

Will Rogers Memorial Park

Beverly Gardens Park

BEVERLY HILLS

West Hollywood Park

La Cienega Park

0 — 2,000 ft
0 — 500 m

Sights ▼

1 Fox Plaza................. A6
2 Gagosian Gallery B6
3 Greystone Mansion B2
4 Melrose Avenue G4
5 Museum of
   Tolerance B8
6 Pacific Design Center... E4
7 The Paley Center
   for Media B6
8 Pierce Brothers
   Westwood Village
   Memorial Park
   & Mortuary A6
9 Rodeo Drive B6
10 Santa Monica
   Boulevard............... E3
11 Spadena House........ A6
12 Sunset Boulevard.... D2
13 Sunset Plaza E2
14 Virginia Robinson
   Gardens................. A3
15 Wallis Annenberg
   Center for the
   Performing Arts........ B5
16 West Hollywood
   Design District E4
17 West Hollywood
   Library................... E4

Restaurants ▼

1 Angelini Osteria.......... I5
2 Animal.................... H4
3 A.O.C..................... E5
4 The Bazaar by
   José Andrés............. F6
5 BOA Steakhouse D2
6 Canter's H4
7 Catch LA E4
8 Cleo...................... F5
9 Connie and Ted's........ G2
10 Craig's.................. D4
11 Crossroads G4
12 Crustacean B6
13 CUT...................... C6
14 Dan Tana's.............. D4
15 El Coyote
   Mexican Food........... I5
16 Greenblatt's Deli G1
17 Jean-Georges
   Beverly Hills........... A6
18 Joan's on Third.......... F5
19 Maude C6
20 Milk Bar LA.............. I4
21 Nate 'n' Al B5
22 The Nice Guy........... F4
23 Nozawa Bar............. C6
24 Petite Taqueria F3
25 Petty Cash Taqueria..... I5
26 Republique I7
27 Spago Beverly Hills..... C6

28 Sprinkles Cupcakes B6
29 Tesse.................... F2
30 Urth Caffé Melrose C7

Hotels ▼

1 ANdAZ West
   Hollywood F2
2 Beverly Wilshire,
   A Four Seasons Hotel... C6
3 Chamberlain............. E3
4 Chateau Marmont...... G1
5 The Crescent
   Beverly Hills............. C6
6 Farmer's Daughter
   Hotel..................... H5
7 Four Seasons Hotel
   Los Angeles At
   Beverly Hills............. D5
8 The London West
   Hollywood at
   Beverly Hills............. E3
9 Mondrian
   Los Angeles F2
10 Montage
   Beverly Hills............. C6
11 Mr. C Beverly Hills...... C8
12 Palihouse West
   Hollywood F2
13 The Peninsula
   Beverly Hills............. A6
14 SLS Hotel
   Beverly Hills............. F6
15 The Standard........... G2
16 Sunset Marquis
   Hotel & Villas........... F2
17 Sunset Tower Hotel..... F2
18 Viceroy L'Ermitage
   Beverly Hills............. C5
19 Waldorf Astoria
   Beverly Hills............. A6

Window-shop and gawk at celebs at the famous and upscale Rodeo Drive.

Vista Dr., Beverly Hills ☎ 310/285–6830 ⊕ www.beverlyhills.org/exploring/ greystonemansiongardens/?NFR=1.

Museum of Tolerance

MUSEUM | FAMILY | This museum unflinchingly confronts bigotry and racism. One of the most affecting sections covers the Holocaust, with film footage of deportations and concentration camps. Upon entering, you are issued a "passport" bearing the name of a child whose life was dramatically changed by the Nazis; as you go through the exhibit, you learn the fate of that child. An exhibit called *Anne: The Life and Legacy of Anne Frank* brings her story to life through immersive environments, multimedia presentations, and interesting artifacts. Simon Wiesenthal's Vienna office is set exactly as the famous "Nazi hunter" had it while conducting his research that brought more than 1,000 war criminals to justice.

Interactive exhibits include the Millennium Machine, which engages visitors in finding solutions to human rights abuses around the world; Globalhate.com, which examines hate on the Internet by exposing problematic sites via touch-screen computer terminals; and the Point of View Diner, a re-creation of a 1950s diner that "serves" a menu of controversial topics on video jukeboxes.

■**TIP**→ **Plan to spend at least three hours touring the museum; making a reservation is especially recommended for Friday, Sunday, and holiday visits.** ⊠ *9786 W. Pico Blvd., south of Beverly Hills, Los Angeles* ☎ *310/772–2505 for reservations* ⊕ *www.museumoftolerance.com* ☑ *From $16* ⊗ *Closed Sat.*

The Paley Center for Media

LIBRARY | Famed architect Richard Meier designed this sleek stone-and-glass building that holds a world-class collection of television and radio programs. You can search for more than 180,000 of them, spanning eight decades, on an easy-to-use computer. Want to watch a disco-infused, late-1970s episode of *Sesame Street*? It's here, along with award shows, radio serials, and hundreds of TV sitcoms. Visits are free, but memberships also have their privileges with early and discounted ticket access to public programs that feature lectures, screenings, and premieres of upcoming TV shows. In addition to their robust calendar, the center also has rotating exhibits with historical prints, movie and TV memorabilia, and more. ■TIP→ **Free parking is available in the lot off Santa Monica Boulevard.** ✉ *465 N. Beverly Dr., Beverly Hills* ☎ *310/786–1000* ⊕ *www. paleycenter.org* ⌚ *Free* ☾ *Closed Mon. and Tues.*

Pierce Brothers Westwood Village Memorial Park and Mortuary

CEMETERY | The who's who of the dearly departed can all be found at this peaceful, though unremarkable, cemetery. Notable residents include Marilyn Monroe and Joe DiMaggio; authors Truman Capote, Ray Bradbury, and Jackie Collins; actors Natalie Wood, Rodney Dangerfield, Farrah Fawcett, Jack Lemmon, and Dean Martin; and directors Billy Wilder and John Cassavetes. ✉ *1218 Glendon Ave., Westwood.*

Rodeo Drive

NEIGHBORHOOD | The ultimate shopping indulgence, Rodeo Drive is one of L.A.'s bona fide tourist attractions. The art of window-shopping (and reenacting your *Pretty Woman* fantasies) is prime among the retail elite: Tiffany & Co., Gucci, Jimmy Choo, Valentino, Harry Winston, Prada—you get the picture. Near the southern end of Rodeo Drive is Via Rodeo, a curvy cobblestone street designed to resemble a European shopping area and the perfect backdrop to pose for your Instagram feed. To give your feet a rest, free trolley tours depart from the southeast corner of Rodeo Drive and Dayton Way from 11:30 to 4:30. They're a terrific way to get an overview of the neighborhood. ✉ *Rodeo Dr., Beverly Hills* ⊕ *www.rodeodrive-bh.com.*

Spadena House

BUILDING | Otherwise known as the Witch's House in Beverly Hills, the Spadena House has an interesting history. First built on the Willat Studios lot in 1920, the house was physically moved to its current ritzy location in 1924. The house is not open for tourists, but the fairy-tale-like appearance is viewable from the street for onlookers to snap pics. Movie buffs will also recognize it from a background shot in the film *Clueless.* ✉ *516 Walden Dr., Beverly Hills.*

Virginia Robinson Gardens

GARDEN | As an heiress to the Robinson department store dynasty, Virginia Robinson lived on what is the oldest intact estate in Beverly Hills—dating back to 1911. The house and gardens cover 6.5 acres of immaculately landscaped flora with a distinct Italian villa vibe right out of Tuscany. The beaux arts–style house includes a tennis court, pool house, and five separate gardens including a rose garden, Italian terrace, palm tree forest, and more. ✉ *1008 Elden Way, Beverly Hills* ☎ *310/550–2068* ⊕ *www.robinsongardens.org* ☾ *Closed Sun. and Mon.*

Wallis Annenberg Center for the Performing Arts

THEATER | Located in the heart of Beverly Hills, the Wallis Annenberg Center for the Performing Arts opened its doors in 2013. A breath of fresh air, this complex is centered on the 1934 Italianate-style Beverly Hills Post Office. The interior is gorgeous, with eight Depression-era murals painted by California artist Charles Kassler depicting laborers and artisans. There's a new building holding the 500-seat Bram Goldsmith Theater and the 150-seat Lovelace Studio Theater. Affordable parking is available underneath the space. ✉ *9390 N. Santa Monica Blvd., Beverly Hills* ☎ *310/746–4000* ⊕ *www.thewallis.org.*

🍴 Restaurants

Dining in the 90210 is always an elegant experience, especially when you're leaving your car with the valet at one of the hot new restaurants along Wilshire

The Annenberg Space for Photography

Boulevard. But meals here don't always break the bank; there are plenty of casual and affordable eateries here worth a visit.

The Bazaar by José Andrés

$$$$ | SPANISH | Spanish celebrity chef José Andrés has conquered L.A. with this colorful and opulent Beverly Hills spot, which features a bar stocked with liquid nitrogen and a super-flashy patisserie. Pore over a menu of items like Spanish tapas (with a twist) and "liquid" olives (created using a technique called spherification). **Known for:** molecular gastronomy; foie gras cotton candy. $ *Average main: $65 ⊠ SLS Hotel at Beverly Hills, 465 S. La Cienega Blvd., Beverly Hills ☎ 310/246–5555 ⊕ slshotels.com/ beverlyhills/bazaar ⊘ No lunch.*

Crustacean

$$$ | VIETNAMESE | Crustacean, the Euro-Vietnamese fusion gem in the heart of Beverly Hills, received a $10 million makeover in 2018. You can still walk on water above exotic fish, but now you can see the kitchen preparing your perfect garlic noodles through a glass window.

Known for: sake-simmered dishes; colossal tiger prawns; no-grease garlic noodles. $ *Average main: $36 ⊠ 468 N. Bedford Dr., Beverly Hills ☎ 310/205–8990 ⊕ crustaceanbh.com ⊘ Closed Mon. No lunch weekends.*

CUT

$$$$ | STEAKHOUSE | In a true collision of artistic titans, celebrity chef Wolfgang Puck presents his take on steak houses in a space designed by Getty Center architect Richard Meier. Playful dishes like bone-marrow flan take center stage, while dry-age and seared hunks of Nebraskan sirloin prove the Austrian-born chef understands America's love affair with beef. **Known for:** decadent dark chocolate soufflé; "Louis" cocktail. $ *Average main: $40 ⊠ Beverly Wilshire (a Four Seasons Hotel), 9500 Wilshire Blvd., Beverly Hills ☎ 310/275–5200 ⊕ www.wolfgang-puck.com ⊘ Closed Sun. No lunch.*

Jean-Georges Beverly Hills

$$$$ | FRENCH FUSION | Fine dining is hard to come by in L.A. (even in Beverly Hills), so when it's actually done well, it's

worth applauding. World-famous chef Jean-Georges Vongerichten's elaborate menu inside the Waldorf Astoria isn't just fine dining, it's a tasting wonderland filled with delights like toasted egg yolk and caviar, honey-nut squash ravioli, and Wagyu rib eyes from a wood-burning grill. **Known for:** fine-dining daters; endless wine lists. $ *Average main: $50* ⊠ *Waldorf Astoria Beverly Hills, 9850 Wilshire Blvd., Beverly Hills* ☎ *310/860–6566* ⊕ *www.jean-georges.com.*

Maude

$$$$ | INTERNATIONAL | Maude is a much-needed addition to the Beverly Hills dining scene as it bucks a traditional tried-and-true menu for a tasting explosion that changes four times a year (we'd say seasonally, but it's L.A.). Helmed by celeb chef Curtis Stone, the cuisine ranges from Spanish and Italian influences to French and coastal Californian. **Known for:** titillating tasting menus; intimate dining. $ *Average main: $185* ⊠ *212 S. Beverly Dr., Beverly Hills* ☎ *310/859–3418* ⊕ *www.mauderestaurant.com* ⊗ *Closed Sun. and Mon.*

Nate 'n' Al

$ | DELI | A longtime refuge from California's lean cuisine, Nate 'n' Al serves up steaming pastrami, matzo ball soup, and potato latkes. Media and entertainment insiders like newsman Larry King have been seen kibbitzing at this old-time East Coast–style establishment. **Known for:** matzo ball soup; killer pastrami; Larry King. $ *Average main: $15* ⊠ *414 N. Beverly Dr., Beverly Hills* ☎ *310/274–0101* ⊕ *www.natenal.com.*

Nozawa Bar

$$$$ | JAPANESE | Tucked into the back of Sugarfish (a popular sushi chain) in the middle of Beverly Hills, this secret *omakase* (chef's choice) sushi spot has only 10 seats, where master chef Osamu Fujita slices up the freshest cuts of raw fish from a 20-course tasting menu. If you ever wanted to get a one-on-one with a culinary wizard, this is your chance

as you sit a foot away from the chef while he prepares your perfect portions. **Known for:** omakase sushi; Japanese jellyfish; bluefin tuna hand rolls. $ *Average main: $175* ⊠ *212 N. Canon Dr., Beverly Hills* ☎ *424/216–6158* ⊕ *www.nozawabar.com.*

★ Spago Beverly Hills

$$$ | MODERN AMERICAN | Wolfgang Puck's flagship restaurant is a modern L.A. classic. Spago centers on a buzzing redbrick outdoor courtyard (with retractable roof) shaded by 100-year-old olive trees, and a daily-changing menu that offers dishes like smoked salmon pizza or off-menu schnitzel. **Known for:** great people-watching; off-menu schnitzel; sizzling smoked salmon pizza. $ *Average main: $35* ⊠ *176 N. Canon Dr., Beverly Hills* ☎ *310/385–0880* ⊕ *www.wolfgangpuck.com* ⊗ *No lunch Sun. or Mon.*

 ## Hotels

Beverly Wilshire, a Four Seasons Hotel

$$$$ | HOTEL | Built in 1928, this Rodeo Drive–adjacent hotel is part Italian Renaissance (with elegant details like crystal chandeliers) and part contemporary. **Pros:** complimentary car service; Wolfgang Puck restaurant on-site; first-rate spa. **Cons:** small lobby; valet parking is expensive. $ *Rooms from: $545* ⊠ *9500 Wilshire Blvd., Beverly Hills* ☎ *310/275–5200, 800/427–4354* ⊕ *www.fourseasons.com/beverlywilshire* ⋧ *395 rooms* ⦿| *No meals.*

★ The Crescent Beverly Hills

$$ | HOTEL | Built in 1927 as a dorm for silent-film actors, the Crescent is now a fanciful boutique hotel with a great location—within the Beverly Hills shopping triangle—and with an even better price (for the area). **Pros:** indoor/outdoor fireplace; lively on-site restaurant, Crescent Bar and Terrace; economic room available for $148. **Cons:** resort fee is $30 and not optional; no elevator. $ *Rooms from: $245* ⊠ *403 N. Crescent Dr., Beverly Hills*

Did You Know?

Beverly Hills became a haven for the stars during the Roaring '20s, when Charlie Chaplin, Rudolph Valentino, and dozens of other film luminaries built mansions here. Today it remains one of Southern California's most coveted addresses.

☎ 310/247–0505 🌐 www.crescentbh.com 🛏 35 rooms 🍴 Free Breakfast.

Four Seasons Hotel, Los Angeles at Beverly Hills

$$$$ | **HOTEL** | High hedges and patio gardens make this hotel a secluded retreat that even the hum of traffic can't permeate—one reason it's a favorite of Hollywood's elite, whom you might spot at the pool and espresso bar. **Pros:** tropical terrace with pool; high-end Italian eatery, Culina, on-site; great massages and nail salon. **Cons:** Hollywood scene in bar and restaurant means rarefied prices. [$] *Rooms from: $500 ✉ 300 S. Doheny Dr., Beverly Hills ☎ 310/273–2222, 800/332–3442 🌐 www.fourseasons.com/losangeles 🛏 285 rooms 🍴 No meals.*

★ **Montage Beverly Hills**

$$$$ | **HOTEL** | **FAMILY** | The nine-story, Mediterranean-style palazzo is dedicated to welcoming those who relish luxury, providing classic style and exemplary service. **Pros:** secret whiskey bar tucked upstairs; Gornick and Drucker barbershop on-site; obliging, highly trained staff; lots of activities and amenities for kids. **Cons:** the hefty tab for all this finery. [$] *Rooms from: $550 ✉ 225 N. Canon Dr., Beverly Hills ☎ 310/860–7800, 855/691–1162 🌐 www.montagebeverlyhills.com/beverlyhills 🛏 201 rooms 🍴 No meals.*

Mr. C Beverly Hills

$$ | **HOTEL** | An Italian getaway in the middle of Los Angeles, Mr. C Beverly Hills of the famed Cipriani family welcomes guests to their European home. **Pros:** free shuttle to Beverly Hills shops; classic Italian restaurant and bar; live music Saturday. **Cons:** not directly in prime Beverly Hills; not great views of Beverly Hills are often 15% extra. [$] *Rooms from: $300 ✉ 1224 Beverwil Dr., Beverly Hills ☎ 877/334–5623 🌐 https://mrcbeverlyhills.com 🛏 138 rooms 🍴 No meals.*

★ **Peninsula Beverly Hills**

$$$$ | **HOTEL** | This French Riviera–style palace overflowing with antiques and art is a favorite of boldface names, but visitors consistently describe a stay here as near perfect. **Pros:** 24-hour check-in/check-out policy; sunny pool area with cabanas; complimentary Rolls-Royce takes you to nearby Beverly Hills. **Cons:** very expensive; room decor might feel too ornate for some. [$] *Rooms from: $600 ✉ 9882 S. Santa Monica Blvd., Beverly Hills ☎ 310/551–2888, 800/462–7899 🌐 www.peninsula.com/en/beverly-hills/5-star-luxury-hotel-beverly-hills 🛏 195 rooms 🍴 No meals.*

SLS Hotel Beverly Hills

$$$ | **HOTEL** | From the sleek, Philippe Starck–designed lobby and lounge with fireplaces, hidden nooks, and a communal table, to poolside cabanas with DVD players, this hotel offers a cushy, dreamlike stay. **Pros:** on-property cuisine masterminded by José Andrés; free shuttle to nearby Beverly Hills; dreamy Ciel spa. **Cons:** standard rooms are compact; pricey dining and parking; on a busy intersection outside of Beverly Hills. [$] *Rooms from: $365 ✉ 465 S. La Cienega Blvd., Beverly Hills ☎ 310/247–0400 🌐 slshotels.com/beverlyhills 🛏 297 rooms 🍴 No meals.*

★ **Viceroy L'Ermitage Beverly Hills**

$$$$ | **HOTEL** | This all-suite hotel is the picture of luxury: French doors open to a mini balcony with views of the Hollywood sign; inside rooms you'll find soaking tubs and oversize bath towels, and they even have fully curated packages for your pet. **Pros:** traditional French cuisine at Avec Nous on-site; free shuttle service with 2-mile radius; all suite rooms. **Cons:** small spa and pool; very expensive; a bit of a trek to the Beverly Hills shopping. [$] *Rooms from: $495 ✉ 9291 Burton Way, Beverly Hills ☎ 310/278–3344 🌐 www.viceroyhotelsandresorts.com/en/beverlyhills 🛏 116 rooms 🍴 No meals.*

Waldorf Astoria Beverly Hills

$$$$ | **HOTEL** | The new belle of Beverly Hills, this Pierre-Yves Rochon–designed five-star property impresses with a top-notch spa, rooftop pool with VIP

cabanas, a restaurant program created by Jean-Georges Vongerichten, and state-of-the-art amenities. **Pros:** impeccable service; free shuttle with 5-mile radius; La Prairie Spa. **Cons:** one of L.A.'s priciest rooms; on the busy corner of Wilshire and Santa Monica; cheap toilet paper. [$] *Rooms from: $815* ✉ *9850 Wilshire Blvd., Beverly Hills* ☎ *310/860–6666* 🌐 *www.waldorfastoriabeverlyhills.com* 🛏 *170 rooms* 🍴 *No meals.*

Shopping

Agent Provocateur
CLOTHING | Garter belts, corsets, and pasties—oh my! Shoppers will find a playful mix of naughty and nice at this Beverly Hills outpost of the beloved lingerie brand. Yes, the boudoir items here range from lovely and lacy (slinky slips and plunging bras) to downright racy (handcuffs and body chains), but everything in the shop is without question beautifully made, which makes it a desirable shopping destination even for the shy set. ✉ *242 N. Rodeo Dr., Beverly Hills* ☎ *310/888–0050* 🌐 *www.agent-provocateur.com.*

AllSaints Spitalfields
CLOTHING | The British store invaded Robertson Boulevard, bringing with it a rock-and-roll edge mixed with a dash of Downton Abbey. Look for leather biker jackets, tough shoes, edgy prints, and long sweaters and cardigans, which, worn correctly, let them know you're with the band. ✉ *100 N. Robertson Blvd., Beverly Hills* ☎ *310/432–8484* 🌐 *www.us.allsaints.com.*

Alo Yoga
CLOTHING | In a city that takes its yoga seriously, it only makes sense that this locally designed activewear brand would take its very first Los Angeles storefront to the next level. For Alo Yoga's flagship, that means an 8,000-square-foot space complete with an organic coffee bar, kombucha on tap, and a rooftop deck that hosts daily sweat-and-stretch sessions. As for the clothing, the model-favorite line offers stylish leggings, sports bras, tanks, and more pieces that look as cool outside the fitness studio as they do during downward dog. ✉ *370 N. Canon Dr., Beverly Hills* ☎ *310/295–1860* 🌐 *www.aloyoga.com.*

Anto Distinctive Shirtmaker
CLOTHING | A who's who of Hollywood's leading men, including Ryan Gosling and Tom Cruise, have been wearing Anto's bespoke shirts both on- and offscreen since 1955. An expertly tailored, customized shirt from this iconic showroom is decidedly an investment piece (you'll need to make an appointment for that service ahead of time), but you can also shop ready-made ties and button-downs here if you're just dropping by. If you know your measurements, take a look at their website, where you can build custom shirts from scratch. ✉ *258 N. Beverly Dr., Beverly Hills* ☎ *310/278–4500* 🌐 *www.antoshirt.com* 🕒 *Closed Sun.*

Barneys New York
DEPARTMENT STORES | This is truly an impressive one-stop shop for high fashion. Deal hunters will appreciate the co-op section, which introduces indie designers before they make it big. Shop for beauty products, shoes, and accessories on the first floor, then wind your way up the staircase for couture. Keep your eyes peeled for fabulous and/or famous folks spearing salads at Fred's on the top floor. ✉ *9570 Wilshire Blvd., Beverly Hills* ☎ *310/276–4400* 🌐 *www.barneys.com.*

Bijan
CLOTHING | The House of Bijan is hard to miss with its trademark canary yellow Bugatti or Rolls-Royce always parked right out front. Inside, a Mediterranean palazzo welcomes high-end menswear shoppers into what is billed as the most expensive store in the world (by appointment only, of course). Some of the famous clientele includes George W. Bush, Bill Clinton, Barack Obama,

and, infamously, Paul Manafort. ⊠ *420 N. Rodeo Dr., Beverly Hills* ☏ *310/273–6544* ⊕ *bijan.com.*

Cartier

JEWELRY/ACCESSORIES | Cartier has a bridal collection to sigh for in its chandeliered and respectfully hushed showroom, along with more playful pieces (chunky, diamond-encrusted panther cocktail rings, for example), watches, and accessories. The stop itself feels like the ultimate playground for A-list clientele, complete with a red-carpeted spiral staircase. ⊠ *370 N. Rodeo Dr., Beverly Hills* ☏ *310/275–4272* ⊕ *www.cartier.com.*

Céline

CLOTHING | Under designer Hedi Slimane's creative direction, the Parisian brand has entered a new chapter. At the Beverly Hills brick-and-mortar, fashion lovers looking for French Cool Girl clothing will love the selection of the label's leather handbags, heels, and chic ready-to-wear clothing. ⊠ *319 N. Rodeo Dr., Beverly Hills* ☏ *310/888–0120* ⊕ *www.celine.com.*

Chanel

CLOTHING | Fans of the French luxury retailer will be happy to find that the Beverly Hills flagship store stocks the brand's trademark pieces, like quilted leather bags, tweed jackets, and jewelry designed with the signature double C logo. Beyond those essentials are plenty of other pieces from Chanel's ready-to-wear collection. ⊠ *400 N. Rodeo Dr., Beverly Hills* ☏ *310/278–5500* ⊕ *www.chanel.com.*

Gearys of Beverly Hills

GIFTS/SOUVENIRS | Since 1930, this has been the ultimate destination for those seeking the most exquisite fine china, crystal, silver, and jewelry, mostly from classic sources like Christofle, Baccarat, and Waterford. No wonder it's a favorite for registries of the rich and famous. ⊠ *351 N. Beverly Dr., Beverly Hills* ☏ *310/273–4741* ⊕ *www.gearys.com.*

Harry Winston

JEWELRY/ACCESSORIES | Perhaps the most locally famous jeweler is Harry Winston, *the* source for Oscar-night jewelry. The three-level space, with a bronze sculptural facade, velvet-panel walls, private salons, and a rooftop patio, is as glamorous as the gems. ⊠ *310 N. Rodeo Dr., Beverly Hills* ☏ *800/988–4110* ⊕ *www.harrywinston.com.*

Jimmy Choo

SHOES/LUGGAGE/LEATHER GOODS | This footwear designer is practically synonymous with flat-out sexy, sky-high stilettos. But there's also plenty more eye candy for fashionistas within the Rodeo Drive location's posh, monochromatic interior. ⊠ *240 N. Rodeo Dr., Beverly Hills* ☏ *310/860–9045* ⊕ *www.jimmychoo.com.*

Louis Vuitton

JEWELRY/ACCESSORIES | Holding court on a prominent corner, Louis Vuitton carries its sought-after monogram (the ultimate symbol of luxury for many) on all manner of accessories and leather goods. ⊠ *295 N. Rodeo Dr., Beverly Hills* ☏ *310/859–0457* ⊕ *www.louisvuitton.com.*

Neiman Marcus

DEPARTMENT STORES | Luxury shopping at its finest, this couture salon frequently trots out designer trunk shows, and most locals go right for the shoe department, which features high-end footwear favorites like Giuseppe Zanotti and Christian Louboutin. A café on the third floor keeps your blood sugar high during multiple wardrobe changes, while a bar on the fourth is for celebrating those perfect finds with a glass of champagne. ⊠ *9700 Wilshire Blvd., Beverly Hills* ☏ *310/550–5900* ⊕ *www.neimanmarcus.com.*

Prada

CLOTHING | Prada's Rodeo Drive haven sits inside the incredibly cool Rem Koolhaas–designed Italian showcase space, which features 20-foot-wide staircases and funhouse curves. ⊠ *343 N. Rodeo Dr.,*

Beverly Hills ☎ 310/278–8661 ⊕ www. prada.com.

Saint Laurent

CLOTHING | Celebrities with the coolest, edgiest styles know they can head to the slick storefront to score the label's signature pieces, like moto jackets, skinny jeans, and platform pumps. A men's store with equally rock star–worthy clothing and accessories is just down the street. ⊠ 326 N. Rodeo Dr., Beverly Hills ☎ 310/271–5051 ⊕ www.ysl.com.

Taschen

BOOKS/STATIONERY | Philippe Starck designed the Taschen space to evoke a cool 1920s Parisian salon—a perfect showcase for the publisher's design-forward coffee-table books about architecture, travel, culture, and photography. A suspended glass cube gallery in back hosts art exhibits and features limited-edition books. ⊠ 354 N. Beverly Dr., Beverly Hills ☎ 310/274–4300 ⊕ www. taschen.com.

Tiffany & Co.

JEWELRY/ACCESSORIES | Who can resist a gift that comes in those iconic blue boxes? Discover three floors of classic and contemporary jewelry (including plenty of sparklers perfect for popping the question) as well as watches, crystal, and china. ⊠ 210 N. Rodeo Dr., Beverly Hills ☎ 310/273–8880 ⊕ www.tiffany.com.

Versace

CLOTHING | With its columned facade, temple dome ceiling, and recherché design, this is just the place for a dramatic red-carpet gown, bold bags, sunglasses, and accessories. It also stocks sleek menswear for fashion-forward fellows. ⊠ 248 N. Rodeo Dr., Beverly Hills ☎ 310/205–3921 ⊕ us.versace.com.

West Hollywood

West Hollywood is not a place to see things (like museums or movie studios) as much as it is a place to do things—like go to a nightclub, eat at a world-famous restaurant, or attend an art gallery opening. Since the end of Prohibition, the **Sunset Strip** has been Hollywood's nighttime playground, where stars headed to such glamorous nightclubs as the Trocadero, the Mocambo, and Ciro's. It's still going strong, with crowds still filing into well-established spots like Whisky A Go Go and paparazzi staking out the members-only Soho House. But hedonism isn't all that drives West Hollywood. Also thriving is an important interior design and art gallery trade exemplified by the Cesar Pelli–designed **Pacific Design Center.**

West Hollywood has emerged as one of the most progressive cities in Southern California. It's also one of the most gay-friendly cities anywhere, with a large LGBTQ community. Its annual Gay Pride Parade is one of the largest in the nation, drawing tens of thousands of participants each June.

The historic **Farmers Market** and **The Grove** shopping mall are both great places to people-watch over breakfast.

◉ Sights

Los Angeles Museum of the Holocaust

MUSEUM | A museum dedicated solely to the Holocaust, it uses its extensive collections of photos and artifacts as well as award-winning audio tours and interactive tools to evoke European Jewish life in the 20th century. The mission is to commemorate the lives of those who perished and those who survived the Holocaust. The building is itself a marvel, having won two awards from the American Institute of Architects. Every Sunday, the museum hosts talks given by Holocaust survivors, while other

Did You Know?

Rodeo Drive is the main drag of the chic shopping district bordered by Santa Monica Boulevard, Wilshire Boulevard, and Beverly Drive.

events include a lecture series, educational programs, and concerts. ⊠ *100 The Grove Dr., Los Angeles* ☎ *323/651–3704* ⊕ *www.lamoth.org* ☞ *Free.*

Melrose Avenue

NEIGHBORHOOD | Melrose Avenue is a tale of two streets. West of Fairfax Avenue is a haven of high-end boutique shopping, chichi restaurants, and avant-garde galleries. To the east of Fairfax is much grittier, where street style is more in vogue, with sneaker stores, head shops, fast casual food, and vintage boutiques. Fans of *Melrose Place* will be excited to learn that the eponymous street actually exists and is home to upscale shops and restaurants. Instagram junkies will recognize a number of photo hot spots like the shockingly pink Paul Smith store or graffitied angel wings along numerous storefronts. ⊠ *Melrose Ave., West Hollywood.*

Pacific Design Center

MARKET | World-renowned architect Cesar Pelli's original vision for the Pacific Design Center was three buildings that together housed designer showrooms, office buildings, parking, and more—a sleek shrine to design. These architecturally intriguing buildings were built years apart: the building sheathed in blue glass (known as the Blue Whale) opened in 1975; the green building opened in 1988. The final "Red" building opened in 2013, completing Pelli's grand vision many years later. All together the 1.6-million-square-foot complex covers more than 14 acres, housing more than 100 design showrooms as well as 2,200 interior product lines. You'll also find restaurants such as Red Seven by Wolfgang Puck, the Silverscreen movie theater, and an outpost of the Museum of Contemporary Art. ⊠ *8687 Melrose Ave., West Hollywood* ☎ *310/657–0800* ⊕ *www. pacificdesigncenter.com.*

Santa Monica Boulevard

NEIGHBORHOOD | From La Cienega Boulevard in the east to Doheny Drive in the west, Santa Monica Boulevard is the commercial core of West Hollywood's gay community, with restaurants and cafés, bars and clubs, bookstores and galleries, and other establishments catering largely to the LGBTQ scene. Twice a year—during June's L.A. Pride and on Halloween—the boulevard becomes an open-air festival. ⊠ *Santa Monica Blvd., between La Cienega Blvd. and Doheny Dr., West Hollywood* ⊕ *weho.org.*

Sunset Boulevard

NEIGHBORHOOD | One of the most fabled avenues in the world, Sunset Boulevard began humbly enough in the 18th century as a route from El Pueblo de Los Angeles to the Pacific Ocean. Today, as it passes through West Hollywood, it becomes the sexy and seductive Sunset Strip, where rock and roll had its heyday and cocktail bars charge a premium for the views. It slips quietly into the tony environs of Beverly Hills and Bel Air, twisting and winding past gated estates and undulating vistas. ⊠ *Sunset Blvd., West Hollywood* ⊕ *www.weho.org.*

Sunset Plaza

NEIGHBORHOOD | With a profusion of sidewalk cafés, Sunset Plaza is one of the best people-watching spots in town. Sunny weekends reach the highest pitch, when people flock to this stretch of Sunset Boulevard for brunch or lunch and to browse in the trendy shops that offer a range of price points. There's free parking in the lot behind the shops. ⊠ *8623 Sunset Blvd., West Hollywood* ⊕ *www. sunsetplaza.com.*

West Hollywood Design District

STORE/MALL | More than 200 businesses—art galleries, antiques shops, fashion outlets (including Rag & Bone and Christian Louboutin), and interior design stores—are found in the design district. There are also about 30 restaurants, including the famous paparazzi magnet, the Ivy. All are clustered within walking distance of each other—rare for L.A. ⊠ *Melrose Ave. and Robertson and Beverly Blvds., West Hollywood*

☎ *310/289–2534* 🌐 *westhollywood-designdistrict.com.*

West Hollywood Library

LIBRARY | Across from the Pacific Design Center, this library, designed by architects Steve Johnson and James Favaro in 2011, is a welcome addition to the city. Replete with floor-to-ceiling glass, a modern and airy interior, a huge mural by Shepard Fairey, and other art by Kenny Scharf and Retna, this three-story building and the adjoining park are a great place to take a break from your tour of the city. They also have an impressive LGBT book collection. There's inexpensive parking and a café below. ✉ *625 N. San Vicente Blvd., West Hollywood* ☎ *310/652–5340* 🌐 *lacountylibrary.org/west-hollywood-library.*

🍴 Restaurants

Lively, stylish, and surrounded by the best restaurants and nightlife in Los Angeles, WeHo (as locals call it) is a magnet for celebrity sightings. There are great bakeries, well-regarded burger joints, and upscale bars serving couture cocktails.

★ **Angelini Osteria**

$$$$ | **ITALIAN** | Despite its modest, rather congested dining room, this is one of L.A.'s most celebrated Italian restaurants. The keys are chef-owner Gino Angelini's consistently impressive dishes, like whole branzino, *tagliolini al limone,* veal chop *alla* Milanese, as well as lasagna oozing with *besciamella* (Italian béchamel sauce). **Known for:** large Italian wine selection; bold flavors; savory pastas. [$] *Average main: $40* ✉ *7313 Beverly Blvd., West Hollywood* ☎ *323/297–0070* 🌐 *www.angeliniosteria.com* 🕒 *No lunch weekends.*

Animal

$$$ | **AMERICAN** | Owned by Jon Shook and Vinny Dotolo of *Iron Chef* fame, this oft-packed James Beard Award–winning restaurant offers shareable plates with a focus on meat. Highlights include barbecue pork belly sandwiches, poutine with oxtail gravy, and foie gras *loco moco* (a hamburger topped with foie gras, quail egg, and Spam). **Known for:** bacon-chocolate crunch bar; reputation as a must for foodies; being carnivore heaven. [$] *Average main: $30* ✉ *435 N. Fairfax Ave., Fairfax District* ☎ *323/782–9225* 🌐 *www.animalrestaurant.com* 🕒 *No lunch.*

A.O.C.

$$ | **MEDITERRANEAN** | An acronym for Appellation d'Origine Contrôlée, the regulatory system that ensures the quality of local wines and cheeses in France, A.O.C. upholds this standard of excellence from shared plates to perfect wine pairings in its stunning exposed-brick and vine-laden courtyard. Try the Spanish fried chicken; wood-oven brioche with prosciutto, Gruyère, and egg; or *arroz negro* (black rice) with squid. **Known for:** amazing cocktail hour; quaint outdoor courtyard; fireplaces indoors. [$] *Average main: $25* ✉ *8700 W. 3rd St., West Hollywood* ☎ *310/859–9859* 🌐 *www.aocwinebar.com.*

BOA Steakhouse

$$$$ | **STEAKHOUSE** | The ultimate in steakhouse dining, this sceney spot on the border of West Hollywood and Beverly Hills is an indoor/outdoor gem with perfectly prepared cuts of prime rib. Every night has a packed crowd of well-heeled carnivores looking to flirt at the back-lit bar or devour slabs of sizzling steak. **Known for:** sizzling steaks; sceney bar; table-side Caesar. [$] *Average main: $50* ✉ *9200 Sunset Blvd., Suite 650, West Hollywood* ☎ *310/278–2050* 🌐 *www.innovativedining.com/restaurants/boa* 🕒 *No lunch weekends.*

Canter's

$ | **DELI** | **FAMILY** | This granddaddy of L.A. delicatessens (it opened in 1931) cures its own corned beef and pastrami and features delectable desserts from the in-house bakery. It's not the best (or friendliest) deli in town, but it's a classic. **Known for:** location adjacent to Kibitz Room bar; plenty of seating and short wait times. $ *Average main: $12* ✉ *419 N. Fairfax Ave., Fairfax District* ☎ *323/651–2030* ⊕ *www.cantersdeli. com.*

Catch LA

$$$$ | ASIAN FUSION | Boasting the best see-and-be-seen crowd in West Hollywood, this rooftop restaurant also has some of the best views. As you enter through a pergola, you'll find an extremely good-looking crowd of well-heeled diners and drinkers flirting at the large bar or getting cozy in the teal brushed leather booths. **Known for:** celeb sightings; rooftop views; crab tempura. $ *Average main: $40* ✉ *8715 Melrose Ave., West Hollywood* ☎ *323/347–6060* ⊕ *catchrestaurants.com/catchla* ⊙ *No brunch weekdays.*

Cleo

$$$ | MEDITERRANEAN | A Mediterranean wave is sweeping through L.A. and one of the better spots for small plates of hummus, baba ghanoush, and skillet *halloumi* (grilling cheese) is along West 3rd Street. You'll recognize the restaurant at the base of the Orlando Hotel by the glistening silver ball hanging over the open patio in front. **Known for:** shared plates; harissa tuna; sceney atmosphere. $ *Average main: $35* ✉ *8384 W. 3rd St., West Hollywood* ☎ *323/579–1600* ⊕ *www.sbe.com/restaurants.*

Connie and Ted's

$$ | SEAFOOD | Inspired by the classic clam, oyster, and fish houses of New England, this beautiful space (the roof is arched like a wave) is occupied by a well-heeled crowd dipping fried calamari or spooning up Jo's wicked-good chowda. Lobster rolls are insanely good, and you can never go wrong with the catch of the day. **Known for:** buttery lobster rolls; catch of the day. $ *Average main: $28* ✉ *8171 Santa Monica Blvd., West Hollywood* ☎ *323/848–2722* ⊕ *www.connieandteds.*

com ⊙ *No brunch or lunch Mon. and Tues.*

Craig's

$$$ | AMERICAN | Behind the unremarkable facade is an uber-trendy—yet decidedly old-school—den of American cuisine that doubles as a safe haven for the movie industry's most important names and well-known faces. We're not going to lie: this joint is always busy so you might not even get a table and reservations are hard to come by. **Known for:** celebrities; chick Parm; strong drinks. $ *Average main: $32* ✉ *8826 Melrose Ave, West Hollywood* ☎ *310/276–1900* ⊕ *craigs.la.*

★ Crossroads

$$ | VEGETARIAN | From its famous Impossible Burger (you can't believe it's not meat) to its spicy meatball pizza (again, not meat), Crossroads's level of plant-based inventiveness knows no bounds. The space itself is dimly lit, with red leather booths and a full bar illuminating its A-list clientele. **Known for:** high-end plant-based cuisine; full bar; A-list clientele. $ *Average main: $24* ✉ *8284 Melrose Ave., West Hollywood* ☎ *323/782–9245* ⊕ *www.crossroadskitchen.com.*

Dan Tana's

$$$ | ITALIAN | If you're looking for an Italian vibe straight out of *Goodfellas* , your search ends here. Checkered tablecloths cover the tightly packed tables as Hollywood players dine on the city's best chicken and veal Parm, and down Scotches by the finger. **Known for:** elbow-room-only bar; lively atmosphere; celeb spotting. $ *Average main: $35* ✉ *9071 Santa Monica Blvd., West Hollywood* ☎ *310/275–9444* ⊕ *www.dantanasrestaurant.com.*

★ El Coyote Mexican Food

$ | MEXICAN | FAMILY | Open since 1931, this landmark spot is perfect for those on a budget or anyone after an authentic Mexican meal. The traditional fare is decadent and delicious; the margaritas are sweetened to perfection. **Known for:**

affordable, quality cuisine; festive atmosphere; being an L.A. staple. $ *Average main: $14* ✉ *7312 Beverly Blvd., Fairfax* ☎ *323/939–2255* ⊕ *www.elcoyotecafe. com.*

Greenblatt's Deli

$ | DELI | In 1926, Herman Greenblatt opened his eponymous deli which serves Jewish deli food, wine, and spirits. The restaurant claims to have the rarest roast beef in town—and they're probably right. **Known for:** matzo ball soup; pastrami sandwiches; old-school vibe. $ *Average main: $18* ✉ *8017 Sunset Blvd., West Hollywood* ☎ *323/656–0606* ⊕ *www. greenblattsdeli.com.*

Joan's on Third

$ | CAFÉ | FAMILY | Part restaurant, part bakery, part market, Joan's on Third has a little bit of everything. This roadside French-style café caters to families, the occasional local celebrity, and lovers of all things wholesome. **Known for:** crispy baguettes; fresh pastries; long lines. $ *Average main: $16* ✉ *8350 W. 3rd St., West Hollywood* ☎ *323/655–2285* ⊕ *www.joansonthird.com.*

Milk Bar LA

$ | BAKERY | This place is so popular that lines often spill out the door and onto the sidewalk. The Milk Bar pie (formely the crack pie) and cereal-milk soft serve are favorites, but you can also take classes with owner Christina Tosi to become your own baking master. **Known for:** Milk Bar pie; cereal milk soft serve; long lines. $ *Average main: $6* ✉ *7150 Melrose Ave., West Hollywood* ☎ *213/341–8423* ⊕ *milkbarstore.com* ▭ *No credit cards.*

The Nice Guy

$$ | ITALIAN | This dark and brooding Italian restaurant sits discretely on La Cienega Boulevard and hides one of the cooler scenes in L.A. A favorite among privacy-minded celebs (there's a no-photo policy), the Nice Guy is known for its cavatelli *alla* vodka and mouthwatering chicken Parm. **Known for:** mouthwatering

pastas; see-and-be-seen crowd. $ *Average main: $25* ✉ *401 N. La Cienega Blvd., West Hollywood* ☎ *310/360–9500* ⊕ *www.theniceguyla.com.*

Petite Taqueria

$$ | MODERN MEXICAN | A dark, upscale, and super-lively restaurant, Petite Taqueria has a Día de los Muertos vibe with gothic art and melted candles. The food and service are much brighter, however, as exciting takes on Mexican classics slide down smoothly. **Known for:** inventive Mexican food; original cocktails; lively vibe. $ *Average main: $25* ✉ *755 N. La Cienega Blvd., West Hollywood* ☎ *310/855–7223* ⊕ *petitetaqueria.com* ☽ *Closed Sun.*

Petty Cash Taqueria

$ | MODERN MEXICAN | A boisterous vibe permeates PCT as groups of twenty- and thirtysomethings feast on fresh guacamole under the graffitied walls. There are 10 or so tacos on the ever-changing menu, from grilled octopus and Baja fish to pork belly and shrimp. **Known for:** house-made tortillas; delicious mezcal cocktails. $ *Average main: $15* ✉ *7360 Beverly Blvd., West Hollywood* ☎ *323/933–5300* ⊕ *www.pettycash-taqueria.com* ☽ *No lunch Mon.–Thurs.*

★ Republique

$$$ | FRENCH | FAMILY | This stunning expansive space, originally built for Charlie Chaplin back in the 1920s, serves French delicacies for breakfast, lunch, and dinner every day of the week. The scent of homemade croissants wafts through the building in the morning; steak frites can be enjoyed at night. **Known for:** classics like escargot; unbeatable pastries. $ *Average main: $35* ✉ *624 S. La Brea Ave., West Hollywood* ☎ *310/362–6115* ⊕ *www.republiquela.com.*

Tesse

$$$ | FRENCH FUSION | Jaws will drop upon entering this new French hot spot in West Hollywood. The interior design is a marvel with sloping wood ceilings, lush

leather banquettes, angled mirrors, and an open kitchen. **Known for:** duck leg confit; stunning interior design;. $ *Average main: $35* ✉ *8500 Sunset Blvd., Suite B, West Hollywood* ☎ *310/360–3866* ⊕ *www.tesserestaurant.com/tesse-restaurant.*

Urth Caffé Melrose

$. | AMERICAN | The ultratrendy Urth Caffé is full of beautiful people refueling on organic coffee and tea with a range of health-conscious sandwiches, salads, and juices. The outdoor patio is a great place to take in the scene or spot celebrities. **Known for:** healthy eats; organic coffee and tea; celeb spotting. $ *Average main: $10* ✉ *8565 Melrose Ave., West Hollywood* ☎ *310/659–0628* ⊕ *www.urthcaffe.com.*

🛏 Hotels

ANdAZ West Hollywood

$$ | HOTEL | On the north side of the Sunset Strip, the ANdAZ is Hyatt's fun younger sister, catering to hipsters, techies, and rock stars lounging in the lobby as "hosts" check them in via tablets (there's no front desk). **Pros:** fridge stocked with healthy drinks and snacks; ambitious hotel dining and bar concepts; gym overlooks Sunset Boulevard. **Cons:** traffic congestion impedes access; Sunset Strip is wildly popular on weekends and holidays; expensive parking ($44). $ *Rooms from: $299* ✉ *8401 Sunset Blvd., West Hollywood* ☎ *323/656–1234, 800/233–1234* ⊕ *www.andaz.com* ⤵ *239 rooms* ⦿ *No meals.*

Chamberlain

$$ | HOTEL | On a leafy residential side street, the Chamberlain is steps from Santa Monica Boulevard and close to the Sunset Strip, bringing in fashionable young professionals and 24-hour party people looking to roam West Hollywood. **Pros:** excellent guests-only dining room and bar; suites come with fireplace and balcony; 24-hour fitness center. **Cons:**

compact bathrooms; uphill climb to the Sunset Strip. $ *Rooms from: $249* ✉ *1000 Westmount Dr., West Hollywood* ☎ *310/657–7400, 800/201–9652* ⊕ *www.chamberlainwesthollywood.com* ⤵ *114 suites* ⦿ *No meals.*

Chateau Marmont

$$$$ | HOTEL | Built in 1929 as a luxury apartment complex, the Chateau is now one of the most unique see-and-be-seen hotel hot spots in all of L.A. A remarkably good-looking, young, and super-creative crowd of artists, writers, actors, and photographers roams about this historic haunt. **Pros:** private; exclusive; beautiful pool. **Cons:** some may find it pretentious; service can be spotty; some of the rooms are underwhelming. $ *Rooms from: $450* ✉ *8221 Sunset Blvd., West Hollywood* ☎ *323/656–1010* ⊕ *www.chateaumarmont.com.*

★ Farmer's Daughter Hotel

$$ | HOTEL | A favorite of *Price Is Right* and *Dancing with the Stars* hopefuls (both TV shows tape at the CBS studios nearby), this hotel has a tongue-in-cheek country style with a hopping Sunday brunch and a little pool accented by giant rubber duckies and a living wall. **Pros:** bikes for rent; daily yoga; book lending library. **Cons:** shaded pool; no bathtubs; restaurant is just okay. $ *Rooms from: $200* ✉ *115 S. Fairfax Ave., Fairfax District* ☎ *323/937–3930, 800/334–1658* ⊕ *www.farmersdaughterhotel.com* ⤵ *65 rooms* ⦿ *No meals.*

The London West Hollywood at Beverly Hills

$$$ | HOTEL | Cosmopolitan and chic, especially after the recent multimillion-dollar renovation, the London West Hollywood is known for its large suites, rooftop pool with citywide views, and luxury touches throughout. **Pros:** state-of-the-art fitness center; chef Anthony Keene oversees dining program; 110-seat screening room. **Cons:** too refined for kids to be comfortable; lower floors have mundane views. $ *Rooms from: $350* ✉ *1020 N. San Vicente Blvd., West Hollywood*

☎ *310/854–1111* 🌐 *www.thelondonwest-hollywood.com* 🛏 *226 suites* 🍴 *No meals.*

Mondrian Los Angeles

$$$ | **HOTEL** | The Mondrian has a city club feel; socializing begins in the lobby bar and lounge and extends from the Ivory on Sunset restaurant to the scenic patio and pool, where you can listen to music underwater, and the lively Skybar. **Pros:** acclaimed Skybar on property; Benjamin Noriega-Ortiz guest room design; double-paned windows keep out noise. **Cons:** pricy valet parking only ($44); late-night party scene; no free Wi-Fi. [$] *Rooms from: $300* ✉ *8440 Sunset Blvd., West Hollywood* ☎ *323/650–8999, 800/606–6090* 🌐 *www.mondrianhotel.com* 🛏 *237 rooms* 🍴 *No meals.*

Palihouse West Hollywood

$$ | **HOTEL** | Inside an unassuming condo complex just off West Hollywood's main drag, you'll find DJs spinning tunes on the ground floor and a gorgeous collection of assorted suites with fully equipped kitchens upstairs. **Pros:** fun scene at lobby bar; eclectic design; kitchens in all rooms. **Cons:** lobby can be loud in the evenings; no pool. [$] *Rooms from: $280* ✉ *8465 Holloway Dr., West Hollywood* ☎ *323/656–4100* 🌐 *www.palihousewesthollywood.com* 🛏 *36 suites* 🍴 *No meals.*

The Standard

$$ | **HOTEL** | Hotelier André Balazs created this kitschy Sunset Strip hotel out of a former retirement home, and a '70s aesthetic abounds with pop art, shag carpets, and suede sectionals in the lobby, and beanbag chairs, surfboard tables, and Warhol poppy-print curtains in the rooms. **Pros:** late-night dining on-site; choose-your-own checkout time; secret nightclub, mmhmmm. **Cons:** for partying more than for resting; staff can be aloof. [$] *Rooms from: $250* ✉ *8300 Sunset Blvd., West Hollywood* ☎ *323/650–9090* 🌐 *www.standardhotels.com* 🛏 *139 rooms* 🍴 *No meals.*

★ **Sunset Marquis Hotel and Villas**

$$$ | **HOTEL** | If you're in town to cut your new hit single, you'll appreciate this near-the-Strip hidden retreat in the heart of WeHo, with two on-site recording studios. **Pros:** favorite among rock stars; 53 villas with lavish extras; exclusive Bar 1200. **Cons:** rooms can feel dark; small balconies. [$] *Rooms from: $365* ✉ *1200 N. Alta Loma Rd., West Hollywood* ☎ *310/657–1333, 800/858–9758* 🌐 *www.sunsetmarquis.com* 🛏 *154 rooms* 🍴 *No meals.*

Sunset Tower Hotel

$$$$ | **HOTEL** | A 1929 art deco landmark once known as the Argyle, this boutique hotel on the Sunset Strip brings out as many locals as it does tourists. **Pros:** incredible city views; Tower Bar, a favorite of Hollywood's elite; exclusive spa favored by locals. **Cons:** wedged into the Strip, so the driveway is a challenge; small standard rooms; parts of the hotel feel dated. [$] *Rooms from: $400* ✉ *8358 Sunset Blvd., West Hollywood* ☎ *323/654–7100, 800/225–2637* 🌐 *www.sunsettowerhotel.com* 🛏 *83 rooms* 🍴 *No meals.*

Nightlife

Gay or straight, head to West Hollywood if you're looking for a party-loving crowd. This town has plenty of bars and clubs within walking distance, so you can hop around easily. Santa Monica Boulevard has everything from low-key sports bars to trendy clubs with raised dancing platforms.

The Abbey

BARS/PUBS | The Abbey in West Hollywood is one of the most famous gay bars in the world. And rightfully so. Seven days a week, a mixed and very good-looking crowd comes to eat, drink, dance, and flirt. Creative cocktails are whipped up by buff bartenders with a bevy of themed nights and parties each day. A generous happy hour runs 4–7 pm on weekdays and until 9 on Friday with $8 apps and $6 cocktails. ✉ *692 N. Robertson Blvd., West Hollywood* ☎ *310/289–8410* ⊕ *www.theabbeyweho.com.*

Barney's Beanery

BARS/PUBS | Open since 1920, Barney's Beanery is an iconic spot that drew legendary regulars Janis Joplin and Jim Morrison (among others) to its doorstep. There's an extensive menu, but all anyone talks about is the famous chili and the list of more than 85 beers. There are plenty of distractions, including three pool tables, a foosball table, and arcade games. ✉ *8447 Santa Monica Blvd., West Hollywood* ☎ *323/654–2287* ⊕ *www.barneysbeanery.com.*

Comedy Store

COMEDY CLUBS | Three stages give seasoned and unseasoned comedians a place to perform and try out new material, with big-name performers dropping by just for fun. The front bar along Sunset Boulevard is a popular hangout after or between shows, oftentimes with that night's comedians mingling with fans. ✉ *8433 Sunset Blvd., West Hollywood* ☎ *323/650–6268* ⊕ *www.thecomedystore.com.*

Delilah

THEMED ENTERTAINMENT | Reservations are definitely required for this swanky, New York–style space in West Hollywood. Waiters in white coats serve a mix of upscale American cuisine, but the true reason to come happens a little later when live jazz and burlesque dancers turn the night into a sultry singles scene that's visited by the who's who of Hollywood celebrity royalty. ✉ *7969 Santa Monica Blvd., West Hollywood* ☎ *323/745–0600* ⊕ *www.delilahla.com.*

★ El Rey Theater

MUSIC CLUBS | This former Art Deco movie house from the 1930s has been given a second life as a live music venue. Legends and rising stars grace the stage of El Rey. The Pixies and Ringo Starr

have both stopped here while on tour. ✉ *5515 Wilshire Blvd., West Hollywood* ☎ *323/936–6400* ⊕ *www.theelrey.com.*

Employees Only

BARS/PUBS | If you're looking for the best cocktail program in L.A., you'll find it at Employees Only. This very chic spot is a sister of the New York original and is consistently awarded worldwide for its delicious drinks. At this iteration, there are various themed nights with burlesque on Saturday and sporadic live music. In the back is a speakeasy called Harry's, which is a more intimate space where you can get up close and personal with the master barkeeps to tailor you the perfect drink. ✉ *7953 Santa Monica Blvd., West Hollywood* ☎ *323/536–9045* ⊕ *www.employeesonlyla.com.*

Jones

BARS/PUBS | Italian food and serious cocktails are the mainstays at Jones. Whiskey is a popular choice for the classic cocktails, but the bartenders also do up martinis properly (read: strong). The Beggar's Banquet is their version of happy hour (10 pm to 2 am, Sunday through Thursday), with specials on drinks and pizza. ✉ *7205 Santa Monica Blvd., West Hollywood* ☎ *323/850–1726* ⊕ *www.joneshollywood.com.*

Laugh Factory

COMEDY CLUBS | Top stand-up comics appear at this Sunset Boulevard mainstay, often working out the kinks in new material in advance of national tours. Stars such as Whitney Cummings and Tim Allen sometimes drop by unannounced, and themed nights like Midnight Madness and Chocolate Sundaes are extremely popular, with comics performing more daring sets. ✉ *8001 W. Sunset Blvd., West Hollywood* ☎ *323/656–1336* ⊕ *www.laughfactory.com* ✑ *$17.*

Rage

DANCE CLUBS | The various events at this gay bar and dance club draw different crowds—show queens for Broadway musical sing-alongs on Mondays, drag queens (and more show queens) on themed nights, half-nude chiseled-bodied men most nights, as well as Latin Saturdays and Starboy Sundays. There's lots of eye candy, even more so on weekends. ⊠ *8911 Santa Monica Blvd., West Hollywood* ☎ *310/652-7055* ⊕ *www. ragenightclub.com.*

Rainbow Bar and Grill

BARS/PUBS | Its location next door to a long-running music venue, the Roxy, helped cement this bar and restaurant's status as a legendary watering hole for musicians (as well as their entourages and groupies). The Who, Guns N' Roses, Poison, Kiss, and many others have all passed through the doors. Expect a $5–$10 cover, but you'll get the money back in drink tickets or a food discount. ⊠ *9015 W. Sunset Blvd., West Hollywood* ☎ *310/278–4232* ⊕ *www.rainbowbarand-grill.com.*

Skybar

BARS/PUBS | This beautiful poolside bar is well worth a visit, but it can be a hassle to get into if you're not staying at the hotel, on the guest list, or know someone who can pull strings. The drinks are on the pricier side, but in this part of town that's to be expected, and the views might just make it all worthwhile. ⊠ *Hotel Mondrian, 8440 Sunset Blvd., West Hollywood* ☎ *323/848–6025* ⊕ *www.mondrianhotel.com.*

The Standard

BARS/PUBS | Weekend pool parties in the summer are downright notorious at the Standard Hollywood. Party on the pool deck with DJs, or hear acoustic sets in the Cactus Lodge on Wednesday evenings. Check the calendar for special events like film screenings. ⊠ *The Standard Hollywood, 8300 Sunset Blvd., West Hollywood* ☎ *323/650–9090* ⊕ *www. standardhotels.com.*

The Troubadour

MUSIC CLUBS | The intimate vibe of the Troubadour helps make this club a favorite with music fans. Around since 1957, this venue has a storied past where legends like Elton John and James Taylor have graced the stage. These days, the eclectic lineup is still attracting crowds, with the focus mostly on rock, indie, and folk music. Those looking for drinks can imbibe to their heart's content at the adjacent bar. ⊠ *9081 Santa Monica Blvd., West Hollywood* ⊕ *www.troubadour. com.*

Whisky A Go Go

MUSIC CLUBS | The hard-core metal and rock scene is alive and well at the legendary Whisky A Go Go (the full name includes the prefix "World Famous"), where Janis Joplin, Led Zeppelin, Alice Cooper, Van Halen, the Doors (they were the house band for a short stint), and Frank Zappa have all played. On the Strip for more than five decades, the club books both underground acts and huge names in rock. ⊠ *8901 Sunset Blvd., West Hollywood* ☎ *310/652–4202* ⊕ *www.whiskyagogo.com.*

⬤ Shopping

West Hollywood is prime shopping real estate. And as they say with real estate, it's all about location, location, location. Here you can find art, design, and antiques stores, clothing boutiques for the ladies-who-lunch set, mega music stores, and specialty book vendors.

Melrose Avenue, for instance, is part bohemian-punk shopping district (from North Highland to Sweetzer) and part upscale art and design mecca (upper Melrose Avenue and Melrose Place). Discerning locals and celebs haunt the posh boutiques around Sunset Plaza (Sunset Boulevard at Sunset Plaza Drive), on Robertson Boulevard (between Beverly Boulevard and 3rd Street), and along upper Melrose Avenue.

The huge, blue Pacific Design Center, on Melrose at San Vicente Boulevard, is the focal point for this neighborhood's art- and interior design–related stores, including many on nearby Beverly Boulevard. The Beverly–La Brea neighborhood also claims a number of trendy clothing stores. Perched between Beverly Hills and West Hollywood, 3rd Street (between La Cienega Boulevard and Fairfax Avenue) is a magnet for small, friendly designer boutiques.

Melrose Place, not to be confused with the cheaper and trendier Melrose Avenue, is an in-the-know haven to savvy Los Angeles fashionistas and a charming anecdote to the city's addiction to strip malls and mega shopping centers. This three-block-long strip, east of La Cienega and a block north of Melrose Avenue, lacks the pretentiousness of Rodeo. Reminiscent of the best of West Village shopping in New York, here haute couture meets pedestrian-friendly, tree-lined walkways.

Finally, the Fairfax District, along Fairfax Avenue below Melrose Avenue, encompasses the flamboyant, historic Farmers Market at Fairfax Avenue and 3rd Street, and the adjacent shopping extravaganza, The Grove; and some excellent galleries around Museum Row at Fairfax Avenue and Wilshire Boulevard.

★ **American Rag Cie**

CLOTHING | Half the store features new clothing from established and emerging labels, while the other side is stocked with well-preserved vintage clothing organized by color and style. You'll also find plenty of shoes and accessories being picked over by the hippest of Angelenos. ✉ 150 S. La Brea Ave., West Hollywood ☎ 323/935–3154 ⊕ american-rag.com.

Blackman Cruz

ANTIQUES/COLLECTIBLES | Not your grandmother's antiques shop, David Cruz and Adam Blackman's celebrity-loved shopping destination is known for selecting beautifully offbeat pieces (there's no shortage of ceremonial masks and animal figurines at any given time) as well as fine European and Asian furniture from the 18th to the mid-20th century. ✉ 836 N. Highland Ave., West Hollywood ☎ 323/466–8600 ⊕ www.blackmancruz.com ⊗ Closed Sun.

Book Soup

BOOKS/STATIONERY | One of the best independent bookstores in the country, Book Soup has been serving Angelenos since 1975. Given its Hollywood pedigree, it's especially deep in books about film, music, art, and photography. Fringe benefits include an international newsstand, a bargain-book section, and author readings several times a week. ✉ 8818 Sunset Blvd., West Hollywood ☎ 310/659–3110 ⊕ www.booksoup.com.

Boot Star

SHOES/LUGGAGE/LEATHER GOODS | This huge selection of Western-style boots is heaven for urban cowboys and cowgirls. You can find materials ranging from calfskin to alligator, and most boots are handmade in Mexico and Texas. Custom sizing is available for a guaranteed perfect fit. ✉ 8493 Sunset Blvd., West Hollywood ☎ 323/650–0475 ⊕ www.facebook.com/pg/westernboots.

Christian Louboutin

SHOES/LUGGAGE/LEATHER GOODS | You'll find more than the French designer's signature red-soled stilettos—coveted by the city's label-loving ladies—at this Robertson Boulevard outpost; chic leather handbags, sparkly sneakers, and even the brand's beauty line are just as worthy of a peek inside the store. Across the street male fashion aficionados can pick up dress shoes, embellished high-tops, and the lusted-after loafers. ✉ 657 N. Robertson Blvd., West Hollywood ☎ 310/247–9300 ⊕ www.christianlouboutin.com.

Decades

CLOTHING | A-listers scour these racks for dresses to wear during awards season. Owner Cameron Silver's stellar selection includes dresses by Pucci and Ossie Clark and bags by Hermès. On the street level, Decades Two resells contemporary designer and couture clothing and accessories. ⊠ 8214 Melrose Ave., West Hollywood ☎ 323/655–1960 ⊕ www. shopdecadesinc.com.

★ Fred Segal

CLOTHING | One of the most well-known boutiques in all of Los Angeles, Fred Segal is a fashion design mecca that has been clothing the rich, famous, and their acolytes since the 1960s. Since moving from its original location on Melrose, the new flagship store sits atop Sunset Blvd. with more than 21,000 square feet of space that showcases innovative brands and high-end threads. Inside is also Tesse Café and Bakery, which offers fashionistas some fast casual fare as they peruse the merchandise. ⊠ 8500 Sunset Blvd., West Hollywood ☎ 310/432-0560 ⊕ www.fredsegal.com.

Heath Ceramics

CERAMICS/GLASSWARE | This loftlike outpost of the beloved Sausalito-based ceramics company stocks everything from the Coupe Line (created by founder Edith Heath herself in the 1940s) to glass tumblers hand blown in West Virginia. Also look for table linens, bud vases, and specialty foods like artisanal jams from Pasadena. ⊠ 7525 Beverly Blvd., West Hollywood ☎ 323/965–0800 ⊕ www. heathceramics.com.

H. Lorenzo

CLOTHING | Funky, high-end designer clothes (Ann Demeulemeester, Walid, and Comme des Garcons, to name a few) attract a young Hollywood crowd that doesn't mind paying top dollar for such fresh finds. Next door, H. Men provides equally hot styles for guys. ⊠ 8660 Sunset Blvd., West Hollywood ☎ 310/659–1432 ⊕ shop.hlorenzo.com.

Isabel Marant

CLOTHING | Even before falling for the French designer's effortlessly cool clothing, footwear, and bags (think Paris meets Los Angeles), shoppers will already be enamored of the lush location on fashionable Melrose Place. Inside, the model-favorite destination has a modern rustic vibe, but the outside is a plant paradise, loaded with cacti and succulents. ⊠ 8454 Melrose Pl., West Hollywood ☎ 323/651–1493 ⊕ www.isabelmarant. com.

Jonathan Adler

HOUSEHOLD ITEMS/FURNITURE | For fans of the whimsical NYC-based designer, this West Coast flagship store is the place to be. Mid-century and country-club styles get retooled in playful pottery, cheeky pillows, and graphic textiles. ⊠ 8125 Melrose Ave., West Hollywood ☎ 323/658–8390 ⊕ www.jonathanadler.com.

★ Maxfield

CLOTHING | This modern concrete structure is one of L.A.'s most desirable destinations for ultimate high fashion. The space is stocked with sleek offerings from Givenchy, Saint Laurent, Valentino, and Rick Owens, plus occasional pop-ups by fashion's labels-of-the-moment. For serious shoppers (or gawkers) only. ⊠ 8825 Melrose Ave., West Hollywood ☎ 310/274–8800 ⊕ www.maxfieldla.com.

Melrose Trading Post

OUTDOOR/FLEA/GREEN MARKETS | Hollywood denizens love this hip market, where you're likely to find recycled rock T-shirts or some vinyl to complete your collection in addition to antique furniture and quirky arts and crafts. Live music and fresh munchies entertain vintage hunters and collectors. The market is held 9 to 5 every Sunday—rain or shine—in Fairfax High School's parking lot and admission is $5. ⊠ Fairfax Blvd. and Melrose Ave., West Hollywood ☎ 323/655–7679 ⊕ www. melrosetradingpost.org.

OK

GIFTS/SOUVENIRS | An uber-gift shop, OK stocks the classy (such as Scandinavian stemware and vintage phones) and specializes in architecture and design books. There's also a second Silver Lake location. ✉ *8303 W. 3rd St., West Hollywood* ☎ *323/653–3501* ⊕ *okthestore.com.*

Paul Smith

CLOTHING | You can't miss the massive, minimalist pink box that houses Paul Smith's fantastical collection of clothing, boots, hats, luggage, and objets d'art (seriously, there will be hordes of Instagrammers shooting selfies in front of the bright facade). Photos and art line the walls above shelves of books on pop culture, art, and Hollywood. As for the clothing here, expect the British brand's signature playfully preppy style, with vibrant colors and whimsical patterns mixed in with well-tailored closet staples. ✉ *8221 Melrose Ave., West Hollywood* ☎ *323/951–4800* ⊕ *www.paulsmith.com/uk.*

Reformation

CLOTHING | Local trendsetters flock here for the sexy, easy-to-wear silhouettes of Reformation's dresses (including a totally affordable bridal line), jumpsuits, and separates—it's a welcome bonus that the pieces here are sustainably manufactured using recycled materials. ✉ *8000 Melrose Ave., West Hollywood* ☎ *323/852–0005* ⊕ *www.thereformation.com.*

Restoration Hardware

HOUSEHOLD ITEMS/FURNITURE | With 40,000 square feet, this iteration of Restoration Hardware is a beacon for shoppers looking for a curated collection of furniture, rugs, lighting, textiles, bathware, and more. The stunning shop also has an outdoor rooftop park and conservatory with wicker furniture, hanging lights, tea candles, and epic views of the Hollywood Hills. ✉ *8564 Melrose Ave., West Hollywood* ☎ *310/652–0323* ⊕ *www.restorationhardware.com/content/category.jsp?context=WestHollywood.*

Supreme

SHOES/LUGGAGE/LEATHER GOODS | The L.A. location for NYC's premier street-wear brand regularly sees crowds of sneakerheads and skaters, who know that this is the place to get the freshest urban gear around. When new merchandise drops in, lines can easily wrap around the block—but getting your hands on the goods (namely shoes, shirts, outerwear, hats, and backpacks) before anyone else just might be worth the trouble. ✉ *439 N. Fairfax Ave., Beverly–La Brea* ☎ *323/655–6205* ⊕ *www.supremenewyork.com.*

The Way We Wore

CLOTHING | Beyond the over-the-top vintage store furnishings, you'll find one of the city's best selections of well-cared-for and one-of-a-kind items, with a focus on sequins and beads. Upstairs, couture from Halston, Dior, and Chanel can cost up to $20,000. ✉ *334 S. La Brea Ave., West Hollywood* ☎ *323/937–0878* ⊕ *www.thewaywewore.com.*

MALLS AND SHOPPING CENTERS

Beverly Center

SHOPPING CENTERS/MALLS | Having gone through a massive renovation in 2018, this eight-level shopping center is home to luxury retailers like Bloomingdale's, Henri Bendel, and Dolce & Gabbana but also offers plenty of outposts for more affordable brands including Aldo, H&M, and Uniqlo. The refurb also introduced a bevy of great dining options like Farmhouse, a seed-to-table spot with amazing pizzas; Eggslut, an extraordinarily popular breakfast joint; and Yardbird, a fried-chicken lovers' favorite, plus many, many more. ✉ *8500 Beverly Blvd., West Hollywood* ☎ *310/854–0070* ⊕ *www.beverlycenter.com.*

The Grove

OUTDOOR/FLEA/GREEN MARKETS | Come to this popular outdoor mall for familiar names like Apple, Nike, and Nordstrom; stay for the central fountain with "dancing" water and light shows, people-watching from the trolley, and, during the holiday season, artificial snowfall and a winter wonderland. Feel-good pop blasting over the loudspeakers aims to boost your mood while you spend, and a giant cineplex gives shoppers a needed break with the latest box office blockbusters. The adjacent Farmers Market offers dozens of freshly farmed food stalls and tons of great restaurants. ⊠ *189 The Grove Dr., West Hollywood* ☎ *323/900–8080* ⊕ *www.thegrovela. com.*

Chapter 5

HOLLYWOOD AND THE STUDIOS

Updated by
Michelle Rae Uy

Sights
★★★★★

Restaurants
★★★★☆

Hotels
★★★★★

Shopping
★★★☆☆

Nightlife
★★★★☆

NEIGHBORHOOD SNAPSHOT

GREAT EXPERIENCES

■ **See the Studios:** Catch a glimpse of movie magic in action at Paramount Pictures, Warner Bros. Studios, and Universal Studios Hollywood.

■ **Walk in Famous Footsteps:** Outside the TCL Chinese Theatre are footprints of more than 200 of the silver screen's biggest stars. The Hollywood Walk of Fame has stars honoring more than 2,500 of the entertainment industry's most famous on its sidewalks.

■ **Picnic at the Hollywood Bowl:** Even if you don't get tickets for a show, stop at this L.A. landmark just north of Hollywood Boulevard for a great outdoor meal.

■ **Check Out the Best Hollywood Memorabilia:** The Hollywood Museum has an incredible collection of Tinseltown's most glamorous costumes, photos, and more.

QUICK BITES

25 Degrees. Proudly serving its signature burgers, fries, and shakes, 25 Degrees has one of the best burgers in town. Located in the Roosevelt Hotel, the round-the-clock eatery exudes a bit of the old Hollywood glamour while putting a modern spin on the classic burger joint. ⊠ *7000 Hollywood Blvd.*

Pig 'n Whistle. During Hollywood's heyday, the Pig 'n Whistle was the place to stop for a bite before or after seeing a movie in the neighboring Egyptian Theatre. You can expect overstuffed booths, dramatic paneled ceilings, and attentive service. ⊠ *6714 Hollywood Blvd.*

Pink's Hot Dogs. Pink's is more than just an institution, it's a beloved family-run joint that serves an amazing hot dog. The chili dogs are the main draw and the lines are very long. ⊠ *709 N. La Brea Ave.*

GETTING HERE

■ Traffic jams on the Hollywood Freeway (U.S. 101/Highway 170), San Diego Freeway (I–405), and Ventura Freeway (U.S. 101/Highway 134) can make for lengthy trips to or from the Valley. The best way to get from Hollywood to Burbank is to skip the freeways and take Hollywood Boulevard to Cahuenga Boulevard heading north, and take a right on Barham Boulevard straight into Burbank. The Metro's Red Line subway makes two stops in the heart of Hollywood: the Hollywood/Vine Station and the Hollywood/Highland Station. This is the easiest way to get to the Valley or to Downtown L.A.

PLANNING YOUR TIME

■ Plan to spend several hours exploring central Hollywood, where you can see the TCL Chinese Theatre and the Walk of Fame. Hollywood Boulevard can be a little seedy, so families might prefer a daytime walk. Later in the evening, you can return to Hollywood for a movie at El Capitan or the ArcLight, or a concert at the Hollywood Bowl. Expect to spend most of a day at Universal Studios Hollywood and CityWalk; studio tours at Paramount and Warner Bros. last up to two hours.

The Tinseltown mythology of Los Angeles was born in Hollywood, still one of the city's largest and most vibrant neighborhoods. In the Hollywood Hills to the north of Franklin Avenue sit some of the most marvelous mansions the moguls ever built; in the flats below Sunset and Santa Monica boulevards are the classic Hollywood bungalows where studio workers once resided.

Reputation aside, though, it's mostly a workaday neighborhood without the glitz and glamour of places like Beverly Hills. The only major studio still located in Hollywood is Paramount; Warner Bros., Disney, and Universal Studios Hollywood are to the north in Burbank and Universal City.

Of course, the notion of Hollywood as a center of the entertainment industry can be expanded to include more than one neighborhood: to the north is Studio City, a thriving strip at the base of the Hollywood Hills, which is home to many smaller film companies; Universal City, where you'll find Universal Studios Hollywood; and Burbank, home to several major studios. North Hollywood, a suburban enclave that's actually in the San Fernando Valley, has its own thriving arts district. Los Feliz, to the east, is where you'll find Griffith Park and the trendy Vermont Avenue area where you can shop, browse for books, or catch a movie at the independent theater. Even farther east you'll find the arty havens of Silver Lake and Echo Park.

Hollywood

Sure, Hollywood's top attractions are a bit touristy—but if it's your first time, you should at least make a brief stop here. Be sure to check out the Hollywood Walk of Fame and catch a movie in one of the neighborhood's opulent movie palaces, such as the TCL Chinese Theatre or El Capitan.

Like Downtown L.A., Hollywood continues to undergo a transformation designed to lure a hip, younger crowd and big money back into the fold. New sleek clubs and restaurants seem to pop up every month drawing in celebrities, scenesters, and starry-eyed newcomers to create a colorful nighttime landscape (and some parking headaches).

Many daytime attractions can be found on foot around the home of the Academy Awards at the **Dolby Theatre,** part of the Hollywood & Highland entertainment complex. The adjacent **TCL Chinese Theatre** delivers silver-screen magic with its iconic facade and ornate interiors from a

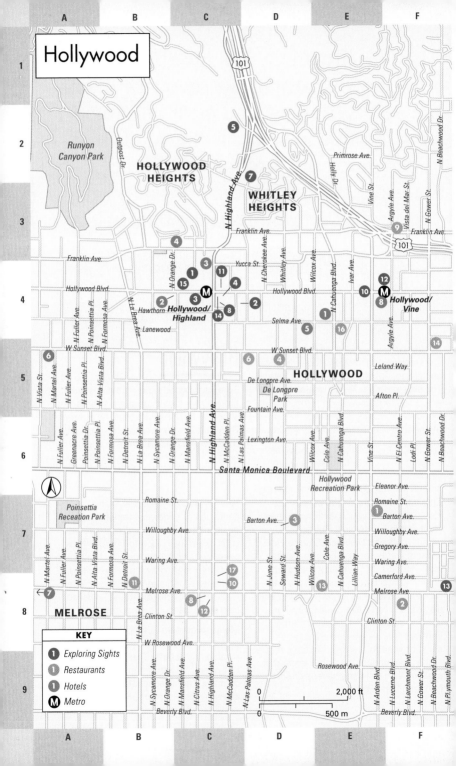

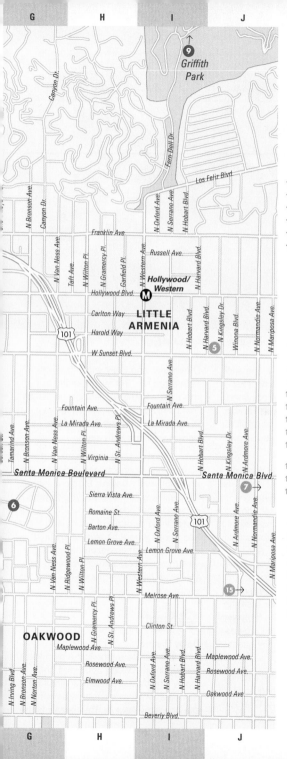

Sights ▼

1	Dolby Theatre	C4
2	Egyptian Theatre	D4
3	El Capitan Theatre	C4
4	Guinness World Records Museum	C4
5	Hollywood Bowl Museum	C2
6	Hollywood Forever Cemetery	G7
7	Hollywood Heritage Museum	D2
8	Hollywood Museum	C4
9	Hollywood Sign	I1
10	Hollywood Walk of Fame	E4
11	Hollywood Wax Museum	C4
12	Pantages Theatre	F4
13	Paramount Pictures	F8
14	Ripley's Believe It or Not!	C4
15	TCL Chinese Theatre	C4

Restaurants ▼

1	Cactus Taqueria #1	E7
2	Café Gratitude	F8
3	Grub	D7
4	Gwen	D5
5	Jitlada	J5
6	Luv2Eat Thai Bistro	D5
7	Marouch	J6
8	Osteria Mozza	C8
9	Papilles Bistro	F3
10	Petit Trois	C8
11	Pink's Hot Dogs	B8
12	Pizzeria Mozza	C8
13	Providence	E8
14	Roscoe's House of Chicken 'n Waffles	F5
15	Sqirl	J8
16	Stout	E4
17	Trois Mec	C7

Hotels ▼

1	Dream Hollywood	E4
2	Hollywood Roosevelt Hotel	B4
3	Loews Hollywood	C4
4	Magic Castle Hotel	C3
5	Mama Shelter	D4
6	Moment Hotel	A5
7	Palihotel	A8
8	W Hollywood	E4

There are more than 2,500 stars honored on the Hollywood Walk of Fame

bygone era. A shining example of a successful Hollywood revival can be seen and experienced just across Hollywood Boulevard at the 1926 **El Capitan Theatre,** which offers live stage shows and a Wurlitzer organ concert before select movie engagements.

Walk the renowned **Hollywood Walk of Fame** to find your favorite celebrities, and you can encounter derelict diversions literally screaming for your attention (and dollar), numerous panhandlers, and an occasional costumed superhero not sanctioned by Marvel Comics. At Sunset and Vine, a developer-interpreted revival with sushi, stars, and swank condos promises to continue the ongoing renovations of the area. In summer, visit the crown jewel of Hollywood, the **Hollywood Bowl,** which features shows by the Los Angeles Philharmonic and many guest stars.

The San Fernando Valley is only a couple of miles north of the Hollywood Bowl, yet some say it's worlds away. Over the hill from the notably trendier areas of

Downtown and Hollywood, "the Valley" gets a bad rap. But all snickering aside, this area is home to many of the places that have made Los Angeles famous: **Disney Studios, Warner Bros. Studios,** and **Universal Studios Hollywood.**

For newcomers, it's hard to resist the allure of the sound stages and back lots of Tinseltown's studios. Studio tours are the best way for mere mortals to get close to where celebs work. Most tours last at least a couple of hours, and allow you to see where hit television shows are filmed, spot actors on the lot, and visit movie sound stages—some directors even permit visitors on the set while shooting.

◉ Sights

Dolby Theatre

ARTS VENUE | More than just a prominent fixture on Hollywood Boulevard, the Dolby Theatre has a few accolades under its belt as well, most notably as home to the Academy Awards. The theater is the blend of the traditional and the modern, where an exquisite classical design inspired by the grand opera houses of Europe meets a state-of-the-art sound and technical system for an immersive, theatrical experience. Watch a concert or a show here to experience it fully, but before you do, take a tour for an informative, behind-the-scenes look and to step into the VIP lounge where celebrities rub elbows on the big night. ✉ *6801 Hollywood Blvd., Hollywood* ☎ *323/308–6300* ⊕ *www.dolbytheatre.com* 🎟 *Tour $22.*

Egyptian Theatre

ARTS VENUE | Built by Sid Grauman, who also constructed the TCL Chinese Theatre, this Hollywood Boulevard movie house is famed not only for its Egyptian theme, complete with hieroglyphs and carvings, but for being the venue of Hollywood's first-ever movie premiere. Currently, it hosts many of the American Cinematheque's classic film screenings. ✉ *6712 Hollywood Blvd., Hollywood* ☎ *323/466–3456* ⊕ *www.american-cinemathequecalendar.com* ☞ *Check website for tickets.*

El Capitan Theatre

ARTS VENUE | A classic movie palace built in 1926 and Los Angeles's first home of spoken drama, the El Capitan Theatre boasts two different architectural styles—the Spanish Colonial look of its facade and storm lobby, and the East Indian Revival style of its interior. Having survived several transformations, it has been restored to almost exactly how it looked in 1926 when Disney bought it in the 1980s. The theater is the grand venue for all Disney movie premieres, during which movie fans can watch celebrities walk the red carpet on Hollywood Boulevard. On a regular day, pop in to watch a movie, as they always have something special in store for their showings. ✉ *6838 Hollywood Blvd., Hollywood* ☎ *800/347–6396* ⊕ *elcapitantheatre.com.*

Guinness World Records Museum

MUSEUM | While there are several Guinness World Records Museum locations across the globe, popping into the location in Hollywood is a fun, little side trip of the record-breaking, albeit kitschy, kind. Besides its weird and interactive exhibits like those of the most tattooed lad and the world's heaviest man, it's also chock full of informative details and trivia, not to mention Hollywood-themed and movie-related facts. ✉ *6764 Hollywood Blvd., Hollywood* ☎ *323/463–6433* ⊕ *www.guinnessmuseumhollywood.com* 🎟 *$21.*

Hollywood Bowl Museum

MUSEUM | Originally the tearoom for the Hollywood Bowl, this unassuming, two-story museum not only recounts the history of one of L.A.'s most renowned landmarks, but also commemorates some of the major and unforgettable performances that have taken place here. While the second floor mostly touts temporary exhibits, the first floor boasts permanent displays, a few of which are interactive. A quick visit to this museum is a definite must whether you're a musicophile or you're coming to see a performance at the Hollywood Bowl. ✉ *2301 N. Highland Ave., Hollywood* ☎ *323/850–2058* ⊕ *www.hollywoodbowl.com/visit/hollywood-bowl-museum* 🎟 *Free* ⊙ *Closed Mon. in summer; closed Sat.–Mon. during off-season.*

Hollywood Forever Cemetery

ARTS VENUE | One of the many things that makes this cemetery in the middle of Hollywood so fascinating is the fact that it's the final resting place of many of the Hollywood greats, from directors like Cecil B. DeMille and actors like Douglas Fairbanks and Judy Garland to musicians like Johnny Ramone. Beyond its famous residents, however, the Hollywood Forever Cemetery is also frequented for its serene grounds peppered with intricately designed tombstones, not to mention by cinephiles in the summer and fall

Take a tour of this classic Hollywood studio

months for the outdoor movie screenings that take place under the stars on the Fairbanks Lawn. If you're looking for both tourist and local experiences while in town, this sight lets you tick off both in one visit. ✉ *6000 Santa Monica Blvd., Hollywood* ☎ *323/469–1181* ⊕ *www.hollywoodforever.com* ✉ *Free; check online for film screenings.*

Hollywood Heritage Museum

MUSEUM | This unassuming building across from the Hollywood Bowl is a treasure trove of memorabilia from the earliest days of Hollywood filmmaking, including a thorough look back at Cecil B. DeMille's starry career. Large sections of the original stone statues from *The Ten Commandments* lay like fallen giants among smaller items in glass cases around the perimeter of this modest museum. A documentary tracking Hollywood's golden era is worth taking in.

The building itself is the restored Lasky-DeMille Barn, designated a California State Historic Landmark in 1956. ✉ *2100 N. Highland Ave., Hollywood*

☎ *323/874–4005* ⊕ *www.hollywoodheritage.org* ✉ *$7* ⊙ *Closed weekdays.*

★ **Hollywood Museum**

MUSEUM | Don't let its kitschy facade turn you off. The Hollywood Museum, nestled at the busy intersection of Hollywood and Highland, is worth it, especially for film aficionados. A museum deserving of its name, it boasts an impressive collection of exhibits from the moviemaking world, spanning several film genres and eras. Start in its pink, art deco lobby where the Max Factor exhibit pays tribute to the cosmetics company's pivotal role in Hollywood, make your way to the dark basement, where the industry's penchant for the macabre is on full display, and wrap up your visit by admiring Hollywood's most famous costumes and set props on the top floor. ✉ *1660 N. Highland Ave., at Hollywood Blvd., Hollywood* ☎ *323/464–7776* ⊕ *www.thehollywoodmuseum.com* ✉ *$15* ⊙ *Closed Mon. and Tues.*

Hollywood Sign

MEMORIAL | With letters 50 feet tall, Hollywood's trademark sign can be spotted from miles away. The icon, which originally read "Hollywoodland," was erected in the Hollywood Hills in 1923 to advertise a segregated housing development and was outfitted with 4,000 light bulbs. In 1949 the "land" portion of the sign was taken down. By 1973 the sign had earned landmark status, but because the letters were made of wood, its longevity came into question. A makeover project was launched and the letters were auctioned off (rocker Alice Cooper bought an "O" and singing cowboy Gene Autry sponsored an "L") to make way for a new sign made of sheet metal. Inevitably, the sign has drawn pranksters who have altered it over the years, albeit temporarily, to spell out "Hollyweed" (in the 1970s, to push for more lenient marijuana laws), "Go Navy" (before a Rose Bowl game), and "Perotwood" (during businessman Ross Perot's 1992 presidential bid). A fence and surveillance equipment have since been installed to deter intruders, but another vandal managed to pull the "Hollyweed" prank once again in 2017 after Californians voted to make recreational use of marijuana legal statewide. △ **Use caution if driving up to the sign on residential streets; many cars speed around the blind corners.** ✉ *Griffith Park, Mt. Lee Dr., Hollywood* ⊕ *www.hollywoodsign.org.*

Hollywood Walk of Fame

ARTS VENUE | Along Hollywood Boulevard (and part of Vine Street) runs a trail of affirmations for entertainment-industry overachievers. On this mile-long stretch of sidewalk, inspired by the concrete handprints in front of TCL Chinese Theatre, names are embossed in brass, each at the center of a pink star embedded in dark gray terrazzo. They're not all screen deities; many stars commemorate people who worked in a technical field, such as sound or lighting. The first eight stars were unveiled in 1960 at the northwest corner of Highland Avenue and Hollywood Boulevard: Olive Borden, Ronald Colman, Louise Fazenda, Preston Foster, Burt Lancaster, Edward Sedgwick, Ernest Torrence, and Joanne Woodward (some of these names have stood the test of time better than others). Since then, more than 2,000 others have been immortalized, though that honor doesn't come cheap—upon selection by a special committee, the personality in question (or more likely his or her movie studio or record company) pays about $30,000 for the privilege. To aid you in spotting celebrities you're looking for, stars are identified by one of five icons: a motion-picture camera, a radio microphone, a television set, a record, or a theatrical mask. ✉ *Hollywood Blvd. and Vine St., Hollywood* ☎ *323/469–8311* ⊕ *www.walkoffame.com.*

Hollywood Wax Museum

MUSEUM | If a walk through Hollywood hasn't yielded any star-spotting, head over to this venerable icon of a museum, which has been open continuously since 1965. Get up close and personal with your favorite celebrity and experience recreated scenes from classic films, such as Katharine Hepburn and Humphrey Bogart in *The African Queen* or Tom Hanks in *Forrest Gump ,* as well as the figures from the *Wizard of Oz.* There's an homage to Heath Ledger in *The Dark Knight,* alongside older icons such as John Wayne and Charlie Chaplin. Be sure to walk the red carpet with the latest Oscar stars and, if you're so inclined, creep along the dimly lit "horror chamber" where scenes from popular films of fright are reconstructed. The effect is heightened at night when fewer visitors are around. ✉ *6767 Hollywood Blvd., Hollywood* ☎ *323/462–5991* ⊕ *www. hollywoodwaxmuseum.com* 💲 *$23.*

Pantages Theatre

ARTS VENUE | Besides being home to the Academy Awards for a decade in the '50s, this stunning art deco–style theater near Hollywood and Vine has been playing host to many of the musical theater world's biggest and greatest productions, from the classics like *Cats*, *West Side Story*, and *Phantom of the Opera* to modern hits like *Hamilton* and *Wicked*. During your Los Angeles jaunt, see a show or two in order to really experience its splendor. While guided tours are not being offered to the public, an annual open house is available to season pass holders for an exclusive and informative tour of the theater and its history. ⊠ *6233 Hollywood Blvd., Hollywood* ☎ *323/468–1770* ⊕ *www.hollywoodpantages.com.*

★ **Paramount Pictures**

FILM STUDIO | With a history dating to the early 1920s, the Paramount lot was home to some of Hollywood's most luminous stars, including Mary Pickford, Rudolph Valentino, Mae West, Marlene Dietrich, and Bing Crosby. Director Cecil B. DeMille's base of operations for decades, Paramount offers probably the most authentic studio tour, giving you a real sense of the film industry's history. This is the only major studio from film's golden age left in Hollywood—all the others are in Burbank, Universal City, or Culver City.

Memorable movies and TV shows with scenes shot here include *Sunset Boulevard, Forrest Gump*, and *Titanic*. Many of the *Star Trek* movies and TV series were shot entirely or in part here, and several seasons of *I Love Lucy* were shot on the portion of the lot Paramount acquired in 1967 from Lucille Ball. You can take a 2-hour studio tour or a 4½-hour VIP tour, led by guides who walk and trolley you around the back lots. As well as gleaning some gossipy history, you'll spot the sets of TV and film shoots in progress. Reserve ahead for tours, which are for those ages 10 and up. ■ TIP→ **You can be part of the audience for live TV tapings (tickets are free), but you must book ahead.** ⊠ *5515 Melrose Ave., Hollywood*

☎ *323/956–1777* ⊕ *www.paramountstudiotour.com* ☎ *From $58.*

Ripley's Believe It or Not

MUSEUM | The ticket prices may be a bit steep for these slightly faded relics of the bizarre and sometimes creepy, but where else can you see a bikini made of human hair, a sculpture of Marilyn Monroe made of shredded money, and animal freaks of nature? Whether you believe it or not, it's fun to marvel at the museum's wacky curiosities. ⊠ *6780 Hollywood Blvd., Hollywood* ☎ *323/466–6335* ⊕ *www.ripleys.com/hollywood* ☎ *$25.*

TCL Chinese Theatre

ARTS VENUE | The stylized Chinese pagodas and temples of the former Grauman's Chinese Theatre have become a shrine both to stardom and the combination of glamour and flamboyance that inspire the phrase "only in Hollywood." Although you have to buy a movie ticket to appreciate the interior trappings, the courtyard is open to the public. The main theater itself is worth visiting, if only to see a film in the same setting as hundreds of celebrities who have attended big premieres here.

And then, of course, outside in front are the oh-so-famous cement hand- and footprints. This tradition is said to have begun at the theater's opening in 1927, with the premiere of Cecil B. DeMille's *King of Kings,* when actress Norma Talmadge just happened to step in wet cement. Now more than 160 celebrities have contributed imprints for posterity, including some oddball specimens, such as casts of Whoopi Goldberg's dreadlocks. ⊠ *6925 Hollywood Blvd., Hollywood* ☎ *323/461–3331* ⊕ *www.tclchinesetheatres.com* ☎ *Tour $18.*

🍴 Restaurants

Hollywood has two faces; while it's a hub for tourists who come here to take photos along the Hollywood Walk of Fame, it is still in touch with its irreverent rock-and-roll roots. The result is a complex dining scene made up of cheap fast food, upscale eateries, and provocative hot spots helmed by celebrity chefs.

Cactus Taqueria #1

$ | **MEXICAN** | **FAMILY** | A humble taco shack on the side of the road, Cactus offers up $2 tacos with all types of meat you could imagine, even beef tongue. They also have carne asada and chicken for the less adventurous. **Known for:** California burritos; super fries; street-style tacos. [$] *Average main: $11* ✉ *950 Vine St., Hollywood* ☎ *323/464–5865* 🌐 *www.cactustaqueriainc.com.*

Café Gratitude

$ | **VEGETARIAN** | **FAMILY** | Of L.A.'s long list of vegan restaurants, this is among the best, with luscious dishes that are also social media worthy. But it's more than just gourmet, plant-based dining—Café Gratitude is also about leading a sustainable lifestyle full of positivity and (obviously) gratitude. **Known for:** vegan fare; the Mucho Mexican Bowl; pressed juices. [$] *Average main: $16* ✉ *639 N. Larchmont Blvd., Hollywood* ☎ *323/580–6383* 🌐 *www.cafegratitude.com.*

Grub

$ | **CONTEMPORARY** | **FAMILY** | The name Grub perfectly captures the kind of good, hearty, comforting American food that you'll feast on at this flower-adorned, 1920s Hollywood spot off Santa Monica Boulevard. It prides itself on adding quirky twists to its otherwise familiar plates, but not so much as to lose what makes it great in the first place. **Known for:** croissant French toast with raspberry butter; brunch; outdoor seating. [$] *Average main: $14* ✉ *911 Seward St., Hollywood* ☎ *323/461–3663* 🌐 *www.grub-la.com.*

★ **Gwen**

$$$$ | **STEAKHOUSE** | Upscale carnivores: this is your heaven. A fine-dining restaurant that serves impossibly exquisite dishes in a copper-and-marble setting. **Known for:** steak; duck fat potatoes; house-cured meats. [$] *Average main: $50* ✉ *6600 Sunset Blvd., Hollywood* ☎ *323/946–7513* 🌐 *www.gwenla.com/butcher-shop-about.html.*

Jitlada

$$$ | **THAI** | Los Angeles is known for wonderful holes-in-the-wall tucked inside tiny strip malls, and family-owned Jitlada is exhibit A. It's churned out delicious, spicy, southern Thai dishes since 2006. **Known for:** coco mango salad; the very spicy khua kling phat lung; huge menu. [$] *Average main: $25* ✉ *5233 W. Sunset Blvd., Hollywood* ☎ *323/667–9809* 🌐 *www.jitladala.wordpress.com* ⏲ *Closed Mon.*

Luv2Eat Thai Bistro

$ | **THAI** | **FAMILY** | When it comes to Thai food, at least in Los Angeles, it's usually a rule of thumb that the more ordinary a place looks, the better the food. Such is the case of Luv2Eat Thai Bistro, whose kitschy name and food court furnishings hardly hint at the outstanding traditional Thai dishes it serves. **Known for:** crying tiger; jade noodles; northern Thai sausage. [$] *Average main: $12* ✉ *6660 W. Sunset Blvd. Unit P, Hollywood* ☎ *323/498–5835* 🌐 *www.luv2eatthai.com.*

Marouch

$$ | **LEBANESE** | Part of L.A.'s appeal is its eclectic gastronomy scene that boasts a medley of authentic cuisines from all over the world. Just take Marouch, where you can sample traditional Lebanese and Armenian plates prepared just the way they're made 7,500 miles away. Here, Chef Sossi Brady has honed that art of creating comforting dishes that will make you feel at home whether you're in Hollywood, Beirut, or Yerevan. **Known for:** hummus; wood-burning-oven-baked pita bread; shawarma. [$] *Average main: $20* ✉ *4905 Santa Monica Blvd., Hollywood* ☎ *323/662–9325* 🌐 *marouchrestaurant.com.*

Did You Know?

At the top of the Capitol Records Tower, a blinking light spells out "Hollywood" in Morse code.

★ Osteria Mozza

$$ | **ITALIAN** | How close do you think you can get to divinity? At chef Nancy Silverton's passion project–slash–culinary masterpiece, you'll come pretty damn close after sampling a few of its celestial dishes. **Known for:** ricotta and egg ravioli; all-Italian wine; artisanal spirits. $ *Average main: $30* ✉ *6602 Melrose Ave., Hollywood* ☎ *323/297–0100* ⊕ *osteria-mozza.com.*

Papilles Bistro

$$$ | **FRENCH** | This underrated French bistro boasting a stunning prix-fixe menu on Franklin Avenue seems a bit out of place in its strip mall location, what with unremarkable neighbors like a dry cleaner, a supermart, and a doughnut shop. But that little detail is hardly a reflection on Papilles's cozy ambience, impeccable service, and modern take on traditional French fare. **Known for:** local ingredients; great wine selection. $ *Average main: $38* ✉ *6221 Franklin Ave., Hollywood* ☎ *323/871–2026* ⊕ *www.papillesla.com.*

Petit Trois

$$$ | **MODERN AMERICAN** | Located next door to its sister restaurant Trois Mec, Petit Trois features the same kind of modest, you'll-hardly-notice-it's-there exterior and a small, packed-like-sardines interior—one that you're likely to have to wait in line to get into. But trust us when we say that it's worth it. **Known for:** steak tartare; Big Mec double cheeseburger; bar dining. $ *Average main: $30* ✉ *718 N. Highland Ave., Hollywood* ☎ *323/468–8916* ⊕ *petittrois.com.*

★ Pink's Hot Dogs

$ | **HOT DOG** | **FAMILY** | Since 1939, Angelenos and tourists alike have been lining up at this roadside hot dog stand. But Pink's is more than just an institution, it's a beloved family-run joint that serves a damn good hot dog. **Known for:** the Brando Dog; late-night dining; chili fries. $ *Average main: $6* ✉ *709 N. La Brea Ave., Hollywood* ☎ *323/931–4223* ⊕ *www.pinkshollywood.com.*

Pizzeria Mozza

$$ | **ITALIAN** | Chef Nancy Silverton, of Osteria Mozza, own this upscale pizza and antipasto eatery. The pies—thin-crusted delights with golden, blistered edges—are more Campania than California and are served piping hot daily. **Known for:** late-night eats; goat cheese, leek, scallion, garlic, and bacon pizza; family friendliness. $ *Average main: $20* ✉ *641 N. Highland Ave., Hollywood* ☎ *323/297–0101* ⊕ *www.pizzeriamozza.com.*

★ Providence

$$$$ | **SEAFOOD** | This is widely considered one of the best seafood restaurants in the country, and chef-owner Michael Cimarusti elevates sustainably driven fine dining to an art form. The elegant space is the perfect spot to sample exquisite seafood with the chef's signature application of French technique, traditional American themes, and Asian accents. **Known for:** seafood; immaculate presentation; excellent wine list. $ *Average main: $120* ✉ *5955 Melrose Ave., Hollywood* ☎ *323/460–4170* ⊕ *www.providencela.com* ☾ *No lunch Mon.–Thurs. and weekends.*

Roscoe's House of Chicken and Waffles

$ | **SOUTHERN** | **FAMILY** | Roscoe's is *the* place for down-home southern cooking in Southern California. Just ask the patrons who drive from all over L.A. for bargain-priced fried chicken and waffles. The name of this casual eatery honors a late-night combo popularized in Harlem jazz clubs. **Known for:** chicken and waffles; soul food; eggs with cheese and onions. $ *Average main: $15* ✉ *1514 N. Gower St., Hollywood* ☎ *323/466–7453* ⊕ *www.roscoeschickenandwaffles.com.*

Sqirl

$ | **CAFÉ** | Sitting on the fringe of East Hollywood where L.A.'s most touristy neighborhood transitions into the city's hippest zip code, it's hardly a surprise that Sqirl is every bit as trendy as Silver Lake—from the beautiful twenty- and thirtysomethings that frequent it to the vegan and gluten-free options the café has on hand. But don't let that tidbit turn you off—its worldly breakfast menu is just the ticket to sustain you for a busy day ahead. **Known for:** crispy rice salad; breakfast all day; sorrel-pesto rice. [$] *Average main: $12* ✉ *720 N. Virgil Ave. Suite 4, Hollywood* ☎ *323/284–8147* 🌐 *www.sqirlla.com.*

Stout
$ | **BURGER** | Stout is more than just about beer. Though it does have an excellent craft beer selection and a practically legendary happy hour, this pub-style joint also prides itself on its heavenly burgers, house-made sauces, and (this being Los Angeles) a decent selection of vegetarian and vegan options. **Known for:** Stout protein-style burgers; secret menu; extensive beer list. [$] *Average main: $13* ✉ *1544 N. Cahuenga Blvd., Hollywood* ☎ *323/469–3801* 🌐 *www.stoutburgersandbeers.com.*

Trois Mec
$$$$ | **FRENCH** | What happens when you combine fine dining and a French speakeasy? You get Trois Mec. **Known for:** unique storefront; tasting menu; prebooked reservations. [$] *Average main: $85* ✉ *716 N. Highland Ave., Hollywood* 🌐 *www.troismec.com* 🕒 *Closed Sun. and Mon.*

Hotels

Dream Hollywood
$$ | **HOTEL** | Drawing from the city's color palette of blues, whites, and oranges, this mid-century modern hotel is certainly dreamy, with a rooftop pool and floor-to-ceiling windows in guest rooms displaying epic views of Hollywood. **Pros:** 24-hour room service; some rooms include private balcony; bath amenities from C.O. Bigelow. **Cons:** pricey; surrounding area can be sketchy at night. [$] *Rooms from: $300* ✉ *6417 Selma Ave., Hollywood* ☎ *323/844–6417* 🌐 *www.dreamhotels.com/hollywood/default-en.html* 🛏 *178 rooms* 🍴 *No meals.*

★ **Hollywood Roosevelt Hotel**
$$$$ | **HOTEL** | Poolside cabana rooms are adorned with cowskin rugs and marble bathrooms, while rooms in the main building accentuate the property's history at this party-centric hotel in the heart of Hollywood. **Pros:** Spare Room bowling alley on-site; pool is a popular weekend hangout; great burgers at the on-site 25 Degrees restaurant. **Cons:** reports of noise and staff attitude; stiff parking fees ($42). [$] *Rooms from: $419* ✉ *7000 Hollywood Blvd., Hollywood* ☎ *323/466–7000, 800/950–7667* 🌐 *www.hollywoodroosevelt.com* 🛏 *353 rooms* 🍴 *No meals.*

Loews Hollywood
$$$ | **HOTEL** | **FAMILY** | Part of the massive Hollywood & Highland shopping, dining, and entertainment complex, the 20-story Loews is at the center of Hollywood's action but manages to deliver a quiet night's sleep. **Pros:** large rooms with contemporary furniture; free Wi-Fi; Red Line Metro station adjacent. **Cons:** corporate feeling; very touristy; pricey parking ($50). [$] *Rooms from: $349* ✉ *1755 N. Highland Ave., Hollywood* ☎ *323/856–1200, 800/769–4774* 🌐 *www.loewshotels.com/en/hollywood-hotel* 🛏 *628 rooms* 🍴 *No meals.*

★ **Magic Castle Hotel**
$ | **HOTEL** | **FAMILY** | Guests at the hotel can secure advance dinner reservations and attend magic shows at the Magic Castle, a private club in a 1908 mansion next door for magicians and their admirers. **Pros:** heated pool; near Hollywood & Highland; lush patio. **Cons:** strict dress code; no elevator; highly trafficked street. [$] *Rooms from: $199* ✉ *7025 Franklin Ave., Hollywood* ☎ *323/851–0800, 800/741–4915* 🌐 *magiccastlehotel.com* 🛏 *43 rooms* 🍴 *Breakfast.*

Local Chains Worth Indulging In 🍴

It's said that the drive-in burger joint was invented in L.A., probably to meet the demands of an ever-mobile car culture. Burger aficionados line up at all hours outside **In-N-Out Burger** (🌐 *www.in-n-out.com, multiple locations*), still a family-owned operation whose terrific made-to-order burgers are revered by Angelenos. Visitors may recognize the chain as the infamous spot where Paris Hilton got nabbed for drunk driving, but locals are more concerned with getting their burger fix off the "secret" menu, with variations like "Animal Style" (mustard-grilled patty with grilled onions and extra spread), a "4 x 4" (four burger patties and four cheese slices, for big eaters), or the bunless "Protein Style" that comes wrapped in a bib of lettuce. Go online for a list of every "secret" menu item.

Tommy's is best known for its delightfully sloppy chili burger. Visit its no-frills original location (✉ *2575 Beverly Blvd., Los Angeles* ☎ *213/389–9060*)—a culinary landmark. For rotisserie chicken that will make you forget the Colonel altogether, head to **Zankou Chicken** (✉ *5065 Sunset Blvd., Hollywood* ☎ *323/665–7845* 🌐 *www.zankouchicken.com*), a small chain noted for its golden crispy-skinned birds, potent garlic sauce, and Armenian specialties. One-of-a-kind-sausage lovers will appreciate **Wurstküche** (✉ *800 E. 3rd St., Downtown* ☎ *213/687–4444* 🌐 *www.jerrysfamous-deli.com*), where the menu includes items like rattlesnake and rabbit or pheasant with *herbes de Provence*, while health nuts will devour the cuisine at **Lemonade** (✉ *9001 Beverly Blvd., West Hollywood* ☎ *310/247–2500* 🌐 *www.senorfish.net*), which is known for its seasonally driven menu, pulled straight from L.A.'s farmers' markets.

★ Mama Shelter

$ | **HOTEL** | Even locals are just catching on to Hollywood's sexiest new property, complete with a rooftop bar populated with beautiful people lounging on love seats, simple affordable rooms with quirky amenities like Bert and Ernie masks, and a down-home lobby restaurant that serves a mean Korean-style burrito. **Pros:** delicious food and cocktails on the property; affordable rooms don't skimp on style; foosball in lobby. **Cons:** spare and small rooms; creaky elevators. [$] *Rooms from: $159* ✉ *6500 Selma Ave., Hollywood* ☎ *323/785–6666* 🌐 *www.mamashelter.com/en/los-angeles* 🛏 *70 rooms* 🍴 *No meals.*

Moment Hotel

$ | **HOTEL** | Hollywood's best-value property housed in a former motor inn caters to young partygoers, who breeze in and out of the lobby (which doubles as a bar and breakfast lounge). **Pros:** suite comes with private balcony; on-site 24-hour room service ordered via in-room tablets; free Wi-Fi. **Cons:** street noise; not the safest neighborhood for walking at night. [$] *Rooms from: $180* ✉ *7370 Sunset Blvd., Hollywood* ☎ *323/822–5030* 🌐 *themomenthotel.com* 🛏 *39 rooms* 🍴 *No meals.*

★ Palihotel

$ | **HOTEL** | Catering to young and hip budget travelers who crave style over space, this design-centric boutique property on Melrose Avenue is in the heart of Hollywood's best shopping and dining, including hot spot Hart and the Hunter. **Pros:** funky aesthetic; sweet-corn hush puppies at the Hart and the Hunter restaurant are delish; fantastic location in a walkable neighborhood. **Cons:** small rooms; congested lobby; decor might not appeal to everyone. [$] *Rooms from: $190* ✉ *7950 Melrose Ave., Hollywood* ☎ *323/272–4588* 🌐 *www.pali-hotel.com* 🛏 *33 rooms* 🍴 *No meals.*

W Hollywood

$$$$ | HOTEL | This centrally located, ultra-modernly lit location is outfitted for the wired traveler and features a rooftop pool deck and popular on-site bars, like the Station Hollywood and the mod Living Room lobby bar. **Pros:** Metro stop outside the front door; comes with in-room party necessities, from ice to cocktail glasses; comfy beds with petal-soft duvets. **Cons:** small pool; pricey dining and valet parking; in noisy part of Hollywood. [$] *Rooms from: $659* ✉ *6250 Hollywood Blvd., Hollywood* ☎ *323/798–1300, 888/625–4955* 🌐 *www.whotels.com/hollywood* 🛏 *305 rooms* 🍴 *No meals.*

Activities

Bronson Canyon

HIKING/WALKING | Bronson Canyon—or more popularly, Bronson Caves—is one of L.A.'s most famous filming locations, especially for western and sci-fi flicks. This section of Griffith Park, easily accessible through a trail that's less than half a mile, is a great place to visit whether you're a film buff or an exercise junkie. ✉ *3200 Canyon Dr., Hollywood.*

Runyon Canyon Trail and Park

HIKING/WALKING | Is Runyon Canyon the city's most famous trail? To the world, it just might be, what with so many A-listers frequenting it. Many folks visiting L.A. take the trail specifically for celebrity spotting. But, if that's not something you're into, this accessible trail right in the middle of Hollywood is also a good place to hike, run, see the Hollywood sign, photograph the city skyline, or simply get a bit of fresh air. If you just happen to run into a famous face, well that's just the cherry on the cake. ✉ *2000 N. Fuller Ave., Hollywood* ☎ *805/370–2301* 🌐 *www.nps.gov/samo/planyourvisit/runyoncanyon.htm.*

Nightlife

Hollywood is no longer just a tourist magnet. With the renewed interest in discovering Hollywood history, this area is once again a nightlife destination for locals and visitors alike. Its blend of glitz and grime is reflected here in the after-hours scene.

Avalon

MUSIC CLUBS | This multitasking art deco venue offers both live music and club nights. The killer sound system, cavernous space, and multiple bars make it a perfect venue for both. The club is best known for its DJs, who often spin well past the 2 am cutoff for drinks. The crowd can be a mixed bag, depending on the night, but if you're looking to dance, you likely won't be disappointed. Upstairs is **Bardot,** which hosts a free Monday night showcase of up-and-coming artists called School Night!, curated by KCRW DJ Chris Douridas, that's always a good time. ✉ *1735 Vine St., Hollywood* ☎ *323/462–8900* 🌐 *www.avalonhollywood.com.*

Birds

BARS/PUBS | They call it your neighborhood bar, because even if you don't live in the neighborhood you'll feel at home at this Alfred Hitchcock–themed eatery. Located in Franklin Village, a block-long stretch of bars, cafés, and bookstores, come here for pub food or a cheap poultry-centric dinner. Weekend nights mean cheap beer and well drinks, crowds spilling onto the streets, and a few rounds of oversized Jenga. Right next to the UCB Theatre, you're likely to see a few comedians grabbing a drink here after their shows. ✉ *5925 Franklin Ave., Hollywood* ☎ *323/465–0175* 🌐 *www.birdshollywood.com.*

Blue Palms Brewhouse

BREWPUBS/BEER GARDENS | Even if gastropubs are not your thing, it's still worth checking out this casual joint on Hollywood and Gower if only to get some grub after a concert at the Fonda Theatre or for the great rotating collection of more than 20 draft beers and incredible food. ⌧ *6124 Hollywood Blvd., Hollywood* ☎ *323/464–2337* ⊕ *www. bluepalmsbrewhouse.com.*

Boardner's

BARS/PUBS | Priding itself as one of the last remaining neighborhood bars in Los Angeles's ever-evolving bar scene, Boardner's has maintained its no-nonsense vibe after more than 70 years. Leave your self-importance at the door, order ice-cold beer and mac and cheese, and keep an eye out for any weird apparitions—this place is known to be one of the most haunted spots in the city. ⌧ *1652 N. Cherokee Ave., Hollywood* ☎ *323/462–9621* ⊕ *www.boardners.com.*

The Brickyard Pub

BARS/PUBS | The beer selection is endless with more than 100 options that will appease even the most discerning drinker. Sitting a couple blocks off Hollywood Boulevard, the Brickyard Pub has a more local feel, as well as a cool assortment of diversions: pool tables, shuffleboards, and steel-tip darts. ⌧ *1810 N. Wilcox Ave., Hollywood* ☎ *323/465–6356* ⊕ *www.brickyardnoho.com.*

Burgundy Room

BARS/PUBS | Around since 1919, Burgundy Room attracts a fiercely loyal crowd of locals, as well as the occasional wandering tourists. The bar is supposedly haunted (check out the Ouija boards toward the back), but that just adds to its charm. Its rock-and-roll vibe, strong drinks, and people-watching opportunities make this a worthy detour on any night out on the town. ⌧ *1621 N. Cahuenga Blvd., Hollywood* ☎ *323/465–7530.*

The Cat and Fiddle

BARS/PUBS | While shuttered for two years in the mid-2010s, the Cat and Fiddle is once again going strong at its new, patioed location, continuing a tradition started in 1982 by Londoner Kim Gardner and his wife, Paula. For those wanting to just grab a pint and a savory pie or to satisfy their inner anglophile, this pub is the perfect spot. ⌧ *742 N. Highland Ave., Hollywood* ☎ *323/468–3800* ⊕ *www. thecatandfiddle.com.*

★ Dirty Laundry

BARS/PUBS | Tucked away in a basement on the quiet Hudson Avenue, Dirty Laundry is a former speakeasy turned proper cocktail bar with live music and DJs spinning both fresh and throwback music, not to mention jazz-inspired details. There's beer on hand, but here, cocktails are king. ⌧ *1725 Hudson Ave., Hollywood* ☎ *323/462–6531.*

The Fonda Theatre

MUSIC CLUBS | Right on the edge of the Walk of Fame, this historic venue was one of the area's first theaters when it opened in the 1920s. The Spanish Colonial–style theater now hosts some of the biggest names in indie music, but don't expect any major acts on the calendar. Drinks are pricey—so grab a cocktail on Hollywood Boulevard before the show—as is parking, which will cost you at least $20 in the adjacent lot. ⌧ *6126 Hollywood Blvd., Hollywood* ☎ *323/464–6269* ⊕ *www.fondatheatre.com.*

Frolic Room

BARS/PUBS | Once frequented by one of L.A.'s most famous sons, Charles Bukowski, the Frolic Room was also owned at one point by Howard Hughes and has served as a filming location for period flicks like *L.A. Confidential.* Despite its impressive history, its down-to-earth atmosphere and proximity to the Pantages makes it the perfect place to start off your night. ⌧ *6245 Hollywood Blvd., Hollywood* ☎ *323/462–5890.*

★ Good Times at Davey Wayne's

BARS/PUBS | It's a fridge; it's a door; it's the entrance to Davey Wayne's, a bar and lounge that pulls out all the stops to transport you back in time to the '70s. The interior is your living room; the outside is an ongoing backyard barbecue with all of your friends. Except, wait, I don't recognize anyone … who invited all these drunk people to my house?! Come early to beat the crowds or be prepared to get up close and personal with your neighbors. ⊠ *1611 N. El Centro Ave., Hollywood* ☎ *323/962–3804* ⊕ *www. goodtimesatdaveywaynes.com.*

Harvard and Stone

MUSIC CLUBS | An interior that's one part industrial, one part mid-century modern, and one part ski lodge plays witness to the coolest live music this side of the city and some of the most exquisite cocktails you'll ever guzzle in your life. Of course, if live music isn't exactly your thing, there are also dark, quiet corners where you can enjoy your drinks in peace. ⊠ *5221 Hollywood Blvd., Hollywood* ☎ *747/231– 0699* ⊕ *harvardandstone.com.*

Hotel Cafe

MUSIC CLUBS | This intimate venue caters to fans of folk, indie rock, and music on the softer side. With red velvet backdrops, hard wood furnishings, and the occasional celebrity surprise performance—notably John Mayer—musicophiles will not only be very happy but will receive a respite from the ordinary Hollywood experience. ⊠ *1623½ N. Cahuenga Blvd., Hollywood* ☎ *323/461–2040* ⊕ *www.hotelcafe.com.*

The Know Where Bar

BARS/PUBS | Think 1930s art deco decor, friendly bartenders, classic and delicious cocktails, and then toss in a whole lot of curated vinyl. The Know Where Bar is not only the kind of place that allows great conversations, but it also has excellent themed nights focusing on mezcal, martinis, and more. ⊠ *5634 Hollywood Blvd.,* *Hollywood* ☎ *323/871–4108* ⊕ *theknow- wherebar.com.*

★ Musso and Frank Grill

BARS/PUBS | FAMILY | The prim and proper vibe of this old-school steak house won't appeal to those looking for a raucous night out; instead, its appeal lies in its history and sturdy drinks. Established a century ago, its dark wood decor, red tuxedo–clad waiters, and highly skilled bartenders can easily shuttle you back to its Hollywood heyday when Marilyn Monroe, F. Scott Fitzgerald, and Greta Garbo once hung around and sipped martinis. ⊠ *6667 Hollywood Blvd., Hollywood* ☎ *323/467–7788* ⊕ *www.mussoand-frank.com.*

No Vacancy

BARS/PUBS | Though at first glance, No Vacancy might boast an air of exclusivity and pretentiousness, its relaxed interiors and welcoming staff will almost instantly make you feel like you're at a house party. You know, the kind with burlesque shows, tightrope performances, a speakeasy secret entrance, and mixologists who can pretty much whip up any drink your heart desires. ⊠ *1727 N. Hudson Ave., Hollywood* ☎ *323/465–1902* ⊕ *www.novacancyla.com.*

The Parker Room

BARS/PUBS | Everything about the Parker Room, from its kitchen and cocktails menu to its live music, is jazz inspired. It's an homage to the location's history and its significant role in the city's burgeoning jazz scene in the mid to late '40s. Come and enjoy your jazz-named cocktails on Tuesday night when the resident live jazz band is playing. ⊠ *1358 Vine St., Hollywood* ☎ *323/745–0041* ⊕ *theparkerroom.com.*

The Pikey

BARS/PUBS | There's something comforting about this Sunset Boulevard spot— perhaps it's the charming, British-inspired look; the hearty, home-style British fare; or that cozy pub atmosphere. Whatever it is, the Pikey will tempt both anglophiles and brown-liquor lovers, not to mention fans of craft beer. ✉ *7617 W. Sunset Blvd., Hollywood* ☎ *323/850–5400* ⊕ *thepikeyla.com.*

Pour Vous

DANCE CLUBS | It feels like you might run into F. Scott and Zelda Fitzgerald while at Pour Vous. After all, this Melrose Avenue cocktail lounge is inspired by Paris at the height of the '20s Jazz Age, from the beaux arts design elements to the black-and-white movies playing out back, where a repurposed train car offers quiet, romantic corners. Soak up those cocktails with a Nutella crepe made fresh out back. ✉ *5574 Melrose Ave., Hollywood* ☎ *323/871–8699* ⊕ *pourvousla.com.*

Sassafras Saloon

BARS/PUBS | Put on your dancing shoes (or your cowboy boots) and step back in time. The Sassafras boasts not only an oddly cozy, western atmosphere but plenty of opportunities to strut your moves on the dance floor. Indulge in exquisite craft mezcal, whiskey, and tequila cocktails for some liquid courage before you salsa the night away. ✉ *1233 N. Vine St., Hollywood* ☎ *323/467–2800* ⊕ *www.sassafrassaloon.com.*

The Spare Room

PIANO BARS/LOUNGES | While your typical Hollywood crowd might be a permanent fixture at this Hollywood Roosevelt cocktail bar, it's still worth a visit for its luscious cocktails, hearty fare, and collection of classic board games. It can get a little too crowded, especially on the weekends, but if you come early, you should be able to admire its art deco appeal and perhaps enjoy a game at one of its two vintage bowling lanes. ✉ *7000 Hollywood Blvd., Hollywood* ☎ *323/769– 7296* ⊕ *www.spareroomhollywood.com.*

Three Clubs

BARS/PUBS | Cocktail bars are a dime a dozen in Hollywood, but there's something about this Vine Street joint that makes patrons keep coming back for more. Maybe it's the down-to-earth attitude, delicious no-frills cocktails, and the fact that a taco stand serving greasy grub is right next door. Come to see one of the burlesque or comedy shows for a full experience. ✉ *1123 Vine St., Hollywood* ☎ *323/462–6441* ⊕ *www. threeclubs.com.*

Tropicana Pool and Cafe

BARS/PUBS | There are a few reasons to spend a bit of time at the Hollywood Roosevelt, and one of them is the Tropicana Pool and Cafe. Despite being set in the middle of Hollywood's mad dash, this surprisingly serene oasis is where California fare meets refreshing tropical cocktails. Though mostly restricted to hotel guests, visitors are welcome at discretion to take advantage of its bar and kitchen service. ✉ *Hollywood Roosevelt Hotel, 7000 Hollywood Blvd., Hollywood* ☎ *323/466–7000* ⊕ *www.thehollywoodroosevelt.com/about/food-drink/ tropicana-pool-cafe.*

★ Upright Citizens Brigade

COMEDY CLUBS | The L.A. offshoot of New York's famous troupe continues its tradition of sketch comedy and improv with weekly shows like "Facebook," where the audience's online profiles are mined for material, and "ASSSSCAT," an improv show with rotating comedians including Zach Woods (*Silicon Valley*) and Matt Walsh (*Veep*). Arrive early as space is limited. A second theater on Sunset Boulevard opened in 2014. ✉ *5919 Franklin Ave., Hollywood* ☎ *323/908–8702* ⊕ *ucbtheatre.com.*

The Woods

PIANO BARS/LOUNGES | Don't let the forest fairy-tale vibe—one that'll make you think that a woodsman has fallen in love with a tree nymph and then went on to open a bar—or the baffling strip mall location fool you. When the occasion calls for it, this little dive bar knows how to throw a party and show you a good time with the simple concoction of jukebox music, DJ spins, and signature drinks. ✉ *1533 N. La Brea Ave., Hollywood* ☎ *323/463–7777* ⊕ *www.vintagebargroup.com/the-woods. php.*

🎭 Performing Arts

★ ArcLight

FILM | This big multiplex includes the historic Cinerama Dome, that impossible-to-miss golf ball–looking structure on Sunset Boulevard, which was built in 1963. Like many L.A. theaters, the ArcLight has assigned seating (you will be asked to select seats when purchasing tickets). The complex is a one-stop shop with a parking garage, shopping area, restaurant, and in-house bar. The events calendar is worth paying attention to, as directors and actors often drop by to chat with audiences. Amy Adams and Samuel L. Jackson, for example, have both made time for postscreening Q&As. Movies here can be pricey, but the theater shows just about every new release. ■TIP➔ **Evening shows on the weekend feature "21+" shows, during which moviegoers can bring alcoholic beverages into the screening rooms.** ✉ *6360 Sunset Blvd., Hollywood* ☎ *323/615–2550* ⊕ *www. arclightcinemas.com.*

El Capitan Theatre

FILM | FAMILY | The theater packs in as much preshow entertainment as it can, such as an immersive light-and-projection show before movies such as *Beauty and the Beast.* There's also an on-site organ player to entertain folks as they find their seats. VIP tickets are available and include reserved seating, popcorn, and a drink. ✉ *6838 Hollywood Blvd., Hollywood* ☎ *800/347–6396* ⊕ *elcapitan-theatre.com.*

★ Hollywood Bowl

CONCERTS | For those seeking a quintessential Los Angeles experience, a concert on a summer night at the Bowl, the city's iconic outdoor venue, is unsurpassed. The Bowl has presented world-class performers since it opened in 1920. The L.A. Philharmonic plays here from June to September; its performances and other events draw large crowds. Parking is limited near the venue, but there are additional remote parking locations serviced by shuttles. You can bring food and drink to any event, which Angelenos often do, though you can only bring alcohol when the L.A. Phil is performing. (Bars sell alcohol at all events, and there are dining options.) It's wise to bring a jacket even if daytime temperatures have been warm—the Bowl can get quite chilly at night. ■TIP➔ **Visitors can sometimes watch the L.A. Phil practice for free, usually on a weekday; call ahead for times.** ✉ *2301 Highland Ave., Hollywood* ☎ *323/850–2000* ⊕ *www.hollywoodbowl. com.*

Pantages Theatre

THEATER | For the grand-scale theatrics of a Broadway show, such as *Hamilton* and *The Book of Mormon,* the 2,703-seat Pantages Theatre (the last theater built by Greek American vaudeville producer Alexander Pantages) lights up Hollywood Boulevard on show nights, when lines of excited patrons extend down the block. ✉ *6233 Hollywood Blvd., Hollywood* ☎ *323/468–1770* ⊕ *www.hollywoodpan-tages.com.*

Ricardo Montalban Theatre

THEATER | Live stage and musical performances on the main stage aside, the Montalban has plenty to offer performing arts fans including small film festivals, comedy shows, and outdoor movie screenings on its rooftop. A movie-watching experience here, complete with noise-canceling headphones and comfy blankets, is a quintessentially L.A. experience. ✉ *1615 Vine St., Hollywood* ☎ *323/461–6999* ⊕ *www.themontalban. com.*

🛍 Shopping

Browsing Hollywood Boulevard, you'll find a mixed bag of offerings including lingerie, movie memorabilia, souvenir, and wig shops, while the crowd-heavy Hollywood & Highland complex is home to more familiar retailers and eateries.

Outside the main drag, Hollywood has a few other pockets for picking up high-end goods, including La Brea Avenue, where you'll find a handful of design-happy shops. Take a leisurely stroll as you browse upscale clothing, antiques, and furniture stores.

★ Amoeba Records

MUSIC STORES | Touted as the "World's Largest Independent Record Store," Amoeba is a playground for music lovers, with a knowledgeable staff and a focus on local artists. Catch free in-store appearances and signings by artists and bands that play sold-out shows at venues down the road. There's a massive and eclectic collection of vinyl records, CDs, and cassette tapes, not to mention VHS tapes, DVDs, and Blu-Ray discs. It's a paradise for both music and movie lovers. ⊠ 6400 W. Sunset Blvd., at Cahuenga Blvd., Hollywood ☎ 323/245–6400 ⊕ www.amoeba.com.

Hollywood & Highland Center

SHOPPING CENTERS/MALLS | If you're on the hunt for unique boutiques, look elsewhere. However, if you prefer the biggest mall retail chains America has to offer, Hollywood & Highland is a great spot for a shopping spree. The design of the complex pays tribute to the city's film legacy, with a grand staircase leading up to a pair of three-story-tall stucco elephants, a nod to the 1916 movie *Intolerance*. Pause at the entrance arch, called Babylon Court, which frames a picture-perfect view of the Hollywood sign. This place is a huge tourist magnet, so don't expect to mingle with the locals. ⊠ 6801 Hollywood Blvd., at Highland Ave., Hollywood

☎ 323/467–6412 ⊕ www.hollywoodandhighland.com.

Hollywood Farmers' Market

OUTDOOR/FLEA/GREEN MARKETS | Among L.A.'s many farmers' markets, the Hollywood Farmers' Market is one of the most well known. This family-friendly, open-air market, which has been around for almost 30 years, is also the city's largest with more than 150 local producers and farmers touting their seasonal yields every Sunday. Start your day right and stop by to shop organic, locally grown produce, see live music, and sample some delicious California fare. ⊠ Hollywood ⊹ Ivar Ave. and Selma Ave., between Hollywood Blvd. and Sunset Blvd. ☎ 323/463–3171 ⊕ www.hollywoodfarmersmarket.net.

Jet Rag

CLOTHING | While Jet Rag is a go-to for Halloween costumes and TV/film wardrobes, it's also on local vintage lovers' radars for sought-after items, like perfectly worn boots and leather jackets, denim cutoffs, and colorful cat-eye sunnies. The store takes its reasonable prices one step further on Sunday with an all-day parking lot sale where everything goes for $1; just be prepared to dig for the real finds. ⊠ 825 N. La Brea Ave., Hollywood ☎ 323/939–0528.

Larry Edmunds Bookshop

BOOKS/STATIONERY | Cinephiles have long descended upon this iconic 70-plus-year-old shop that in addition to stocking tons of texts about motion picture history offers film fans the opportunity to pick up scripts, posters, and photographs from Hollywood's Golden Era to the present. ⊠ 6644 Hollywood Blvd., Hollywood ☎ 323/463–3273 ⊕ www.larryedmunds.com.

The Record Parlour

MUSIC STORES | Vinyl records and music memorabilia abound in this hip yet modest record store–slash–music lover magnet that also touts vintage audio gear and retro jukeboxes. A visit here is usually a multihour affair, one that involves more than just browsing through display cases, digging through wooden carts of used vinyls, and playing your picks at the listening station. ⊠ *6408 Selma Ave., Hollywood* ☎ *323/464–7757* ⊕ *therecordparlour.com.*

Space 15 Twenty

SHOPPING CENTERS/MALLS | Trendy retailer Urban Outfitters' first concept store caters to creatives by combining a shopping experience with a cultural one by way of an adjacent space that regularly hosts art exhibitions, pop-ups featuring local makers, and other interactive events. The structure also houses popular eatery Umami Burger, a skate shop, an acclaimed hair salon, and more. ⊠ *1520 N. Cahuenga Blvd., Hollywood* ☎ *323/465–1893* ⊕ *www.space15twenty. com.*

Studio City

Ventura Boulevard, the famed commercial strip, cuts through the lively neighborhood of Studio City. This area, located west of Universal City, is home to several smaller film and TV studios.

🍴 Restaurants

The dining scene here continues to grow as restaurateurs realize how many locals are looking for stylish and swanky places to eat. Japanese, Mexican, and Italian eateries can all be found in this dynamic city.

Firefly

$$$ | AMERICAN | One minute you're in an old library quickly converted into a lounge, the next you're in the cabana of a modest country club. True, Firefly looks like it's in the middle of an identity crisis—is it posh or rustic, old-fashioned or modern? **Known for:** prix-fixe and à la carte dining; reputation as a date spot; seasonal fare. Ⓢ *Average main: $30* ⊠ *11720 Ventura Blvd., Studio City* ☎ *818/762–1833* ⊕ *www.fireflystudiocity. com.*

Good Neighbor Restaurant

$ | DINER | Its walls may be heavy with framed photographs of film and TV stars, and folks from the biz might regularly grace its tables, but this Studio City diner is every bit as down-to-earth as your next-door neighbor, even after 40-some years. It gets pretty busy from the Universal City crowd, but a plateful of that home cooking is worth the wait; or if you're in a mad dash, grab a caffeine or fruit smoothie fix from the Neighbarista. **Known for:** omelet; cottage fries; breakfast food. Ⓢ *Average main: $13* ⊠ *3701 Cahuenga Blvd., Studio City* ☎ *818/457–6050* ⊕ *goodneighborrestaurant.com.*

Hot Stone Slow Food from Korea

$ | KOREAN FUSION | FAMILY | Hot Stone Slow Food might sound more like the title of an indie band rather than a legitimate restaurant, but trust that this spot on Ventura is indeed the perfect place to partake in L.A.'s massive Korean gastronomy scene. There'll be no cooking your own meats over a hot grill here; but you may be creating your own bibimbap. **Known for:** Hot Stone bibimbap or dupbap; Hot Stone BBQ; dak kang jung. Ⓢ *Average main: $8* ⊠ *12265 Ventura Blvd., Suite 102, Studio City* ☎ *818/358–4223* ⊕ *hotstone.net* ☾ *Closed Mon.*

Mantee Café

$ | LEBANESE | Family-owned, charm-exuding Mantee Café is the neighborhood's go-to spot for authentic Lebanese and Armenian dishes, which are typically enjoyed by regulars under a canopy of patio umbrellas in its sun-dappled, flower-filled backyard. **Known for:** Mantee "Traditional"; family-style dining; outdoor seating. Ⓢ *Average main: $19* ⊠ *10962 Ventura Blvd., Studio City* ☎ *818/761–6565* ⊕ *www.manteecafe.com* ☾ *Closed Mon.*

Miceli's

$$ | PIZZA | FAMILY | If the charming, Italian square–inspired interior doesn't turn you into a sappy mush, then Miceli's musical servers serenading you with Italian opera will. Universal City might not be the most romantic place in L.A., but one romantic dinner at this restaurant might make you feel like you're in a Hollywood version of Rome. **Known for:** pizza; specialty pastas; singing servers. $ *Average main: $21* ⌧ *3655 Cahuenga Blvd. W, Studio City* ☎ *323/851–3344* ⊕ *www.micelisrestaurant.com.*

Hotels

Sportsmen's Lodge

$$ | HOTEL | FAMILY | This sprawling five-story hotel, a San Fernando Valley landmark just a short jaunt over the Hollywood Hills, has an updated contemporary look highlighted by the Olympic-size pool and summer patio with an outdoor bar. **Pros:** close to Ventura Boulevard restaurants; free shuttle to Universal Hollywood; quiet garden-view rooms worth asking for. **Cons:** pricey daily self-parking fee ($18); a distance from the city. $ *Rooms from: $249* ⌧ *12825 Ventura Blvd., Studio City* ☎ *818/769–4700, 800/821–8511* ⊕ *www.sportsmenslodge.com* ⌁ *190 rooms* ⦿ *No meals.*

Nightlife

Baked Potato

MUSIC CLUBS | Baked Potato might be a strange name to give a world-famous jazz club that's been holding performances of well-known acts (Allan Holdsworth and Michael Landau) under its roof since the '70s, but it only takes a quick peek at the menu to understand. Twenty-four different types of baked potatoes dominate its otherwise short menu, each of which come with sour cream, butter, and salad to offset all that carb intake. ⌧ *3787 Cahuenga Blvd., Studio City* ☎ *818/980–1615* ⊕ *www.thebakedpotato.com.*

The Fox and Hounds

BARS/PUBS | With bangers and mash, fish-and-chips, and shepherd's pie rolling out of the kitchen and 16 imported draft beers being poured into glasses, this pub is as British as can get—even if footie matches share screen time with the NFL and NBA. Anglophiles will keep coming back. ⌧ *11100 Ventura Blvd., Studio City* ☎ *818/763–7837* ⊕ *thefoxandhounds. com.*

Pinz Bowling Alley

BOWLING | "Bowl. Eat. Drink. Repeat" might be this bowling alley's motto, but thanks to its neon-slash-backlit lanes—each fully equipped with a touch-screen food and drink ordering system—and its very own arcade, Pinz is more than just your typical bowling experience. A few A-list names are among its loyal clientele, but you don't visit for celebrity sightings; all bells and whistles aside, it's a proper bowling alley and you come here to bowl. ⌧ *12655 Ventura Blvd., Studio City* ☎ *818/769–7600* ⊕ *pinzla.com.*

The Rendition Room

PIANO BARS/LOUNGES | A speakeasy cocktail lounge seems a little out of place in Studio City, especially on a middle-of-the-road commercial strip paved with quaint boutique stores, but the Rendition Room makes it work. It's a member's club with pretty laid-back rules about letting nonmembers in—so long as there's room, of course. Even as a tourist, you, too, can sample the Rendition's exciting cocktails, crafted by talented mixologists. ⌧ *4349 Tujunga Ave., Studio City* ☎ *818/769–0905* ⊕ *therenditionroom.wildapricot.org.*

Universal City

Although it has its own zip code and subway station, Universal City, over the hill from Hollywood, is simply the name for the unincorporated area of Los Angeles where Universal Studios Hollywood and CityWalk are located.

Sights

Universal Studios Hollywood

AMUSEMENT PARK/WATER PARK | FAMILY | A theme park with classic attractions like roller coasters and thrill rides, Universal Studios also provides a tour of some beloved television and movie sets. A favorite attraction is the tram tour, during which you can duck from King Kong; see the airplane wreckage of *War of the Worlds*; ride along with the cast of the *Fast and the Furious*; and get chills looking at the house from *Psycho*. ■ **TIP→ The tram ride is usually the best place to begin your visit, because the lines become longer as the day goes on.**

Most attractions are designed to give you a thrill in one form or another, including the thrilling Revenge of the Mummy and immersive rides like the 4D Simpsons Ride, where you can actually smell Maggie Simpson's baby powder. The Wizarding World of Harry Potter, however, is the crown jewel of the park, featuring magical rides, pints of frozen butterbeer, and enough merchandise to drain you wallet faster than you can shout "Expecto Patronum." If you're in town in October, stop by for Halloween Horror Nights, featuring mazes full of monsters, murderers, and jump scares.

Geared more toward adults, CityWalk is a separate venue run by Universal Studios, where you'll find shops, restaurants, nightclubs, and movie theaters. ✉ *100 Universal City Plaza, Universal City* ☎ *800/864–8377* 🌐 *www.universalstudioshollywood.com* 🎟 *$99.*

Restaurants

Café Sierra

$$$ | SEAFOOD | FAMILY | Don't let the fact that this airy Californian and pan-Asian spot is located inside a Hilton Hotel scare you; Café Sierra has a drool-worthy seafood and prime rib buffet. Lunching here can be a splurge, but it's worth every penny. **Known for:** champagne brunch; Alaskan king crab; live jazz music. [$] *Average main: $30* ✉ *555 Universal Hollywood Dr., Universal City* ☎ *818/824–4237* 🌐 *www.cafesierrahilton.com.*

Dongpo

$ | SICHUAN | FAMILY | Upmarket regional Chinese cuisine chain Meizhou Dongpo tries its hand at bringing its modern take on authentic Sichuanese cuisine with Dongpo Kitchen, and it's exactly what the CityWalk needed to up its dining game. This bright, contemporary-meets-traditional Chinese restaurant serves delightful, affordable fare right in the middle of a sea of tourists. **Known for:** Dongpo roast duck; Sichuan dumplings; kung pao chicken. [$] *Average main: $19* ✉ *1000 Universal Studios Blvd. V103, Universal City* ☎ *818/358–3272* 🌐 *www.citywalkhollywood.com.*

Three Broomsticks/Hog's Head

$ | BRITISH | FAMILY | While theme-park food is notoriously bad, the Three Broomsticks and Hog's Head, both at the Wizarding World of Harry Potter, are exceptions. Yes, you have to go into the park itself to grab a bite, but if you happen to be here (which, let's be honest, is probably the only reason you're in Universal City), you should wander in and feast on large helpings of traditional British fare and gulp down frozen butterbeer. **Known for:** fish-and-chips; spareribs platter; British pub. [$] *Average main: $15* ✉ *Universal Studios Hollywood, 100 Universal City Plaza, Universal City* ☎ *800/864–8377* 🌐 *www.universalstudioshollywood.com.*

Wasabi at CityWalk

$ | SUSHI | FAMILY | CityWalk is hardly the epicenter of dining in Los Angeles, but Wasabi is an enjoyable way to transport yourself to Japan. Dine on deliciously creative takes on traditional dishes under the light of traditional Japanese lamps. **Known for:** specialty rolls; beef rib eye teriyaki; garlic edamame. [$] *Average main: $16* ✉ *1000 Universal City Dr.,*

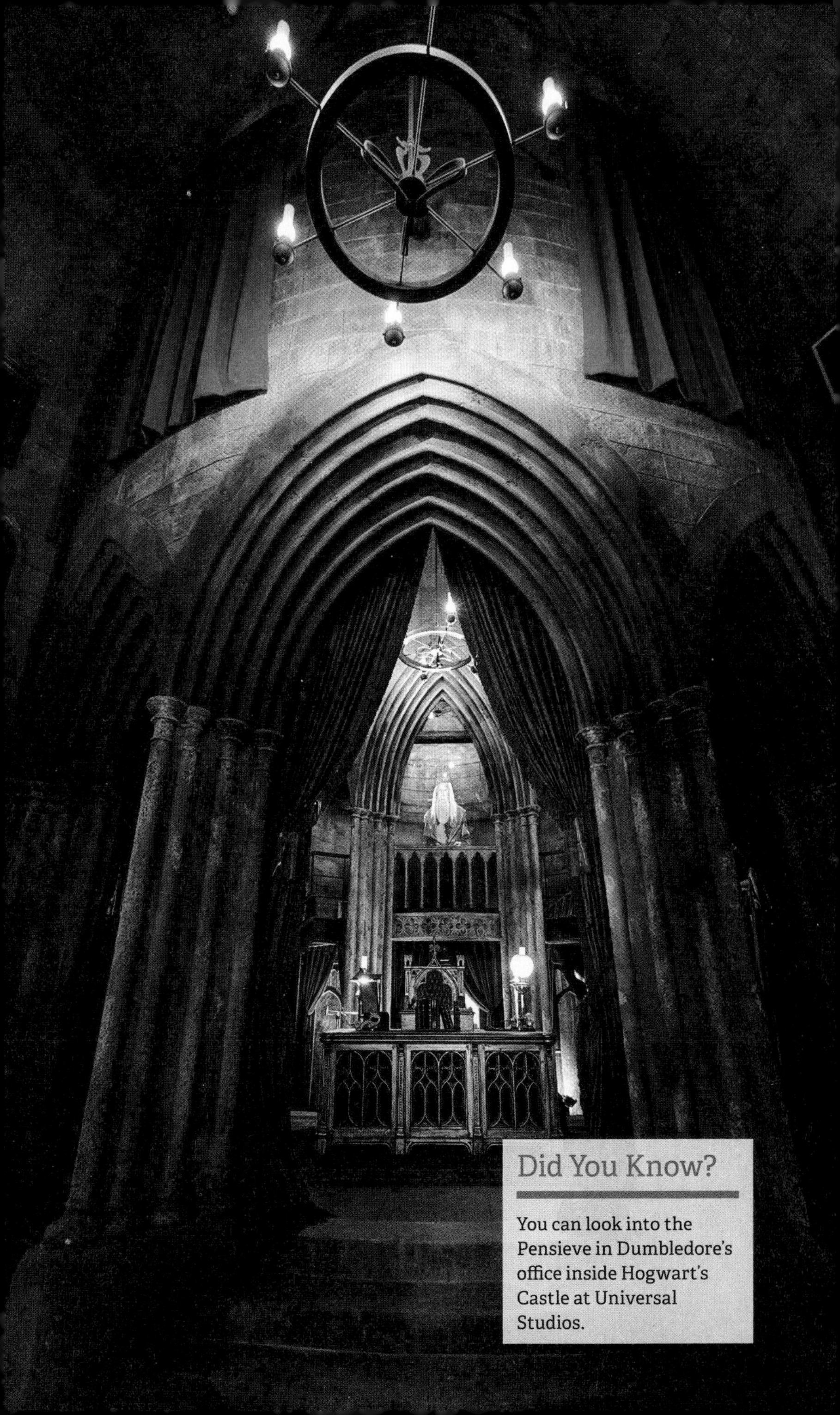

Did You Know?

You can look into the Pensieve in Dumbledore's office inside Hogwart's Castle at Universal Studios.

Suite 112, Universal City ☎ *818/763–8813* 🌐 *www.wasabiatcitywalk.com.*

🛏 Hotels

Sheraton Universal

$$ | HOTEL | FAMILY | With large meeting spaces and a knowledgeable staff, this Sheraton buzzes year-round with business travelers and families, providing easy access to the free shuttle that takes guests to adjacent Universal Studios and CityWalk. **Pros:** pool area with cabanas and bar; oversize desks and office chairs in room. **Cons:** average in-house restaurant; touristy. [$] *Rooms from: $299* ✉ *333 Universal Hollywood Dr., Universal City* ☎ *818/980–1212, 888/627–7184* 🌐 *www.sheratonuniversal.com* 🛏 *457 rooms* 🍴 *No meals.*

Burbank

Johnny Carson, host of *The Tonight Show,* used to ironically refer to downtown Burbank as "beautiful," but it's since become one of the area's most desirable suburbs. It's also home to Warner Bros. Studios, Disney Studios, and NBC Studios and to Bob Hope Airport (BUR), one of the two major airports serving L.A.

👁 Sights

Warner Bros. Studios

FILM STUDIO | You don't need to be a big film nerd to appreciate a visit to the Warner Bros. Studios, where you can pretend to be your favorite TV or movie characters, whether at a working replica of Central Perk from *Friends* or at a sorting ceremony from Harry Potter. You'll also visit backlots and sound stages to see how the magic is made.

If you're looking for an authentic behind-the-scenes look at how films and TV shows are made, head to this major studio center, one of the world's busiest. After a short film on the studio's movies and TV shows, hop aboard a tram for a ride through the sets and sound stages of such favorites as *Casablanca* and *Rebel Without a Cause.* You'll see the bungalows where Marlon Brando, Bette Davis, and other icons relaxed between shots, and the current production offices for Clint Eastwood and George Clooney. You might even spot a celeb or see a shoot in action—tours change from day to day depending on the productions taking place on the lot.

✉ *3400 W. Riverside Dr., Burbank* ☎ *818/977–8687* 🌐 *www.wbstudiotour.com* 🎟 *From $65.*

🍴 Restaurants

Home to movie and television studios, there's a quiet sophistication to this part of town. Great restaurants are tucked away in strip malls and side streets.

Bea Bea's

$ | DINER | Just because Bea Bea's is a no-nonsense kind of place, it doesn't mean the food isn't special. This diner serves breakfast food that is about as close to extraordinary as the most important meal of the day can be. **Known for:** large selection of pancakes and French toast; Happy Mornings; friendly staff. [$] *Average main: $12* ✉ *353 N. Pass Ave., Burbank* ☎ *818/846–2327* 🌐 *www.beabeas.com.*

Centanni Trattoria

$$ | ITALIAN | In a city full of adventurous restaurants touting new takes on traditional dishes and swanking about with bells and whistles and stunning interiors, a run-of-the-mill-looking place like Centanni Tratorria might never make it onto the radar. But what this authentic Italian spot lacks in swagger, it more than makes up for in delicious home cooking. **Known for:** homemade pasta; panini; seafood. [$] *Average main: $20* ✉ *117 N. Victory Blvd., Burbank* ☎ *818/561–4643* 🌐 *www.centannivenice.com.*

Los Amigos

$ | MEXICAN | FAMILY | If you're in the mood for good old-fashioned fun coupled with hearty Mexican fare and delicious margaritas, then you'll want to consider Los Amigos, whose legendary fruity margaritas alone are worth the drive. Pair those with something from the Platillos Mexicanos menu on karaoke night, and you're guaranteed a good time until the wee hours of the night. **Known for:** molcajete; guacamole; signature cocktails. $ *Average main: $18* ✉ *2825 W. Olive Ave., Burbank* ☎ *818/842–3700* ⊕ *www. losamigosbarandgrill.com.*

Pablito's Kitchen

$ | PERUVIAN | Those familiar with Peruvian cuisine know of its Chinese and Japanese influences, and Pablito's Kitchen, which grew from a food truck to this brick-and-mortar spot in Burbank, explores that fascinating intermingling with its *saltados, chuafas,* and sushi rolls. The legendary food truck is long gone, but the restaurant is here to stay. **Known for:** lomo saltado; chicharrón sandwich; delivery. $ *Average main: $18* ✉ *3803 W. Burbank Blvd., Burbank* ☎ *818/859–7755* ⊕ *pablitoskitchen.com.*

Porto's Bakery

$ | CUBAN | FAMILY | Waiting in line at Porto's is as much a part of the experience as is indulging in a roasted pork sandwich or a chocolate-dipped croissant. This Cuban bakery and café has been an L.A. staple for more than 50 years, often bustling during lunch. **Known for:** counter service; potato balls; roasted pork sandwiches. $ *Average main: $8* ✉ *3614 W. Magnolia Blvd., Burbank* ☎ *818/846–9100* ⊕ *www.portosbakery.com.*

Hotels

Hotel Amarano Burbank

$$ | HOTEL | Close to Burbank's TV and movie studios, the smartly designed Amarano feels like a Beverly Hills boutique hotel, complete with 24-hour room service, a homey on-site restaurant and lounge, and spiffy rooms. **Pros:** fireplace, cocktails, and tapas in lobby; penthouse with private gym; saltwater pool. **Cons:** street noise. $ *Rooms from: $269* ✉ *322 N. Pass Ave., Burbank* ☎ *818/842–8887, 888/956–1900* ⊕ *www.hotelamarano. com* ⤴ *98 rooms, 34 suites* ⦿ *No meals.*

Nightlife

Flappers Comedy Club

COMEDY CLUBS | Even though this live comedy club doesn't exactly have as long a history as others in town (it opened in 2010), it's attracted an impressive list of big names like Jerry Seinfeld, Maria Bamford, and Adam Sandler thanks to its Celebrity Drop-In Tuesdays. The food and drinks are good though not great, but you're here for the laughs not the grub. ✉ *102 E. Magnolia Blvd., Burbank* ☎ *818/845–9721* ⊕ *www.flapperscomedy.com.*

The Park Bar and Grill

BARS/PUBS | Though it has all the makings of your average sports bar—the 30-plus beer selection, menu of nibblers and sandwiches, and a number of TVs displaying different games—the Park Bar and Grill does have a few saving graces. This no-frills joint holds comedy shows and poker nights as well as live music. ✉ *2007 W. Burbank Blvd., Burbank* ☎ *818/557–6561* ⊕ *www.theparkbarandgrill.com.*

The Snug

BARS/PUBS | If you think that Magnolia Boulevard's the Snug is your typical Irish pub, think again. This neighborhood watering hole, which has a wide selection of whiskey, 28 draft and bottled beers, and cocktails, plays host to a number of events throughout the year, from holiday parties to chili cook-offs and trivia nights, not to mention a $3 happy hour on weekdays. ✉ *4108 W. Magnolia Blvd., Burbank* ☎ *818/557-0018* ⊕ *www. thesnugburbank.com.*

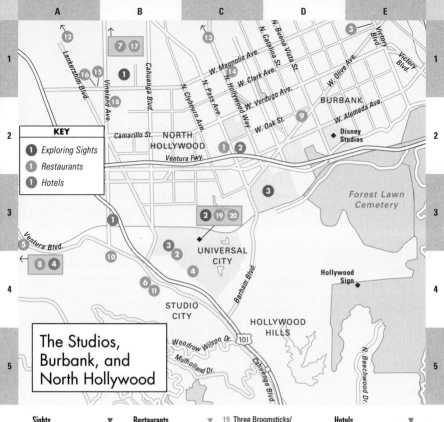

The Studios, Burbank, and North Hollywood

KEY

- 1 Exploring Sights
- 1 Restaurants
- 1 Hotels

Sights ▼

1 NoHo Arts District...... **B1**
2 Universal Studios Hollywood **C3**
3 Warner Bros. Studios................... **D3**

Restaurants ▼

1 Bea Bea's................. **C2**
2 Cafe Sierra **B4**
3 Centanni Trattoria........ **E1**
4 Dongpo.................... **C4**
5 Firefly.................... **A3**
6 Good Neighbor Restaurant.............. **B4**
7 Hayat's Kitchen **B1**
8 Hot Stone Slow Food From Korea........ **A4**
9 Los Amigos.............. **D2**
10 Mantee Café **B4**
11 Miceli's.................. **B4**
12 Mofongo's **A1**
13 Pablito's Kitchen......... **C1**
14 Porto's Bakery **C1**
15 Rodini Park **A1**
16 Spumante Restaurant.............. **A1**
17 The Swingin Door Texas BBQ.............. **B1**
18 TeaPop.................. **B2**

19 Three Broomsticks/ Hog's Head **C3**
20 Wasabi at CityWalk...... **C3**

Hotels ▼

1 The Garland **B3**
2 Hotel Amarano Burbank................... **C2**
3 Sheraton Universal..... **B3**
4 Sportsmen's Lodge **A4**

Laurel Canyon and Mulholland Drive ◉

The hills that separate Hollywood from the Valley are more than a symbolic dividing line between the city slickers and the suburbanites; they have a community in their own right and a reputation as a hideaway for celebrities and wealthy creatives.

The 2002 movie *Laurel Canyon* showed the lifestyle of one kind of Canyon dweller—freethinking entertainment industry movers and shakers seeking peaceful refuge in their tree-shaded homes. By day they're churning out business deals and working on projects; by night they're living it up with private parties high above the bustle of the city streets. Landslides can cause road closures in Laurel Canyon, so do some research beforehand.

Drive through Laurel Canyon and you'll pass estates and party pads dating back to the silent film era. If you have time to cruise Mulholland Drive, expect breathtaking views that show the city's serene side.

🛍 Shopping

It's not a major shopping destination, but Burbank has some offbeat shops that are well worth exploring. Given its close proximity to some major studios, the area has a few hidden gems for finding postproduction castaways, like mint-condition designer and vintage clothing.

Magnolia Park Vintage

SHOPPING NEIGHBORHOODS | Melrose Avenue might be Los Angeles's most well-known vintage shopping destination, but to many locals, especially those on the Eastside, Burbank's Magnolia Park is, in many ways, better. Spanning several blocks around Magnolia Avenue, this revitalized section blends convenience, plenty of vintage, thrift, and antique shopping opportunities and has that laid-back small-town vibe that Melrose lacks. Great dining spots and excellent coffee shops abound, as well as foot and nail spas for a bit of pampering. ✉ *W. Magnolia Blvd., between N. Niagara and N. Avon St., Burbank* ⊕ *www.visitmagnoliapark.com.*

North Hollywood

Originally called Lankershim after the family of ranchers and farmers who first settled here, this area took the name North Hollywood in the 1920s to capitalize on the popularity of the city just over the hill to the south. Today, the large and bustling neighborhood serves as the terminus of the Metro Red Line subway, around which the NoHo Arts District thrives.

◉ Sights

NoHo Arts District

NEIGHBORHOOD | In only a few years, North Hollywood's performance arts hub has grown from the residential home of aspiring actors who frequent a few small theaters and several chain restaurants to a completely revitalized district that boasts its own, albeit small, collection of new coffee shops and restaurants, bars serving up craft beer, and colorful street art. ✉ *Lankershim and Magnolia Blvds., North Hollywood* ⊕ *www.nohoartsdistrict.com.*

🍴 Restaurants

Hayat's Kitchen
$ | **LEBANESE** | Sit down to a table piled high with assorted hot and cold mezes, baba ghanoush, garlic fries, falafel, and kabobs piled on a bed of rice. It's there right in front of you and it's so very good. **Known for:** hummus with meat; appetizers; free dessert. [$] *Average main: $16* ✉ *11009 Burbank Blvd., Suite 117, North Hollywood* ☎ *818/761–4656.*

Mofongo's
$$ | **PUERTO RICAN** | Mofongo's small storefront represents one of the best and only venues to get authentic Puerto Rican food in L.A. Stop by and try the namesake dish (a delectable mash of fried plantains), but stay for the *pasteles* (cakes) and *rellenos de papa* (stuffed potatoes). **Known for:** mofongo de lechon (fried plantains with pork); Puerto Rican food; flan de queso (cream cheese flan). [$] *Average main: $20* ✉ *5757 Lankershim Blvd., North Hollywood* ☎ *818/754–1051* 🌐 *www.mofongosrestaurant.com.*

Rodini Park
$ | **MEDITERRANEAN** | Nestled in the heart of the NoHo Arts District amid newly minted high-rises, Rodini Park's "build your own" concept and highly rated house-made pastries make it the place to go for a quick, fresh, and delicious take on Greek cuisine. Between the multiple protein, topping, and sauce offerings, it offers something for all palates. **Known for:** chicken shawarma; baklava cheesecake; Mount Olympus sauce. [$] *Average main: $10* ✉ *11049 Magnolia Blvd., North Hollywood* ☎ *818/358–4802* 🌐 *www.rodinipark.com.*

Spumante Restaurant
$ | **ITALIAN** | The family-owned Spumante Restaurant harkens back to old-school trattorias with its traditional menu, floor-to-ceiling shelves of wine, white tablecloth settings, and excellent service. Not only are the trappings great, but the prices are reasonable and the food plenty good, too. **Known for:** lobster ravioli; excellent service; mustard chicken. [$] *Average main: $15* ✉ *11049 Magnolia Blvd., Suite 7, North Hollywood* ☎ *818/508–7716* 🌐 *www.spumanterestaurant.com* 🕓 *Closed Sun.*

The Swingin Door Texas BBQ
$$ | **BARBECUE** | **FAMILY** | Los Angeles is not known for barbecue so when a place like the Swingin Door does it right, it's worth taking note. Take a gander around and you'll see the smokers slowly cooking all that meaty goodness, ready to be enjoyed on plastic-covered tables and doused with so many different hot sauces (which you can buy to take home). **Known for:** Texas BBQ; baby back ribs; assorted hot sauces. [$] *Average main: $25* ✉ *11018 Vanowen St., North Hollywood* ☎ *818/763–8996* 🌐 *bbqnorthhollywood.wixsite.com/swingindoor* 🕓 *Closed Mon.*

TeaPop
$ | **CAFÉ** | At first glance, TeaPop may seem to be doing too many things at once, but this tea-centric café, with its art gallery–slash–industrial modern interior and picturesque patio, is a perfect spot to not only study or take a breather, but also to catch pop-up events like comedy nights and workshops. Don't let the hipster vibes turn you off—the service is fantastic and the drinks delicious. **Known for:** vintage milk tea; bubble tea; loose-leaf tea. [$] *Average main: $4* ✉ *5050 Vineland Ave., North Hollywood* ☎ *323/927–0330* 🌐 *teapopla.com.*

🛏 Hotels

The Garland
$$$ | **HOTEL** | **FAMILY** | The Garland is the Valley's cool kid with a Hollywood pedigree. **Pros:** large pool and play area; private balcony or patio in each room; the Front Yard restaurant is a local fave

for brunch. **Cons:** close to the freeway; bar and restaurant close early. $ *Rooms from: $309* ✉ *4222 Vineland Ave., North Hollywood* ☎ *818/980–8000, 800/238–3759* ⊕ *www.beverlygarland.com* ↪ *255 rooms* ☺ *No meals.*

▼ Nightlife

California Institute of Abnormal Arts
MUSIC CLUBS | What do a mummified clown, an alley full of Chinese red lanterns, and a collection of sideshow memorabilia have in common? They can all be found in the California Institute of Abnormal Arts, or CIA for short. This is a bar that proudly showcases the freak side of L.A., from the wonderfully bonkers decor to the utterly bizarre performances that often frequent its stage. ✉ *11334 Burbank Ave., North Hollywood* ☎ *818/221–8065.*

Catcher in the Rye
PIANO BARS/LOUNGES | Catcher in the Rye's theme is not specific to Holden Caulfield but rather to literature. Other odes to fictional greats can be found name-checked on the menu, including Huck Finn and Jay Gatsby. Should you have forgotten your book at home, check one out from the bar's bookshelf, or if reading's not your thing (you're in the wrong bar, pal), you can grab a board game instead. ✉ *10550 Riverside Dr., North Hollywood* ☎ *818/853–7835* ⊕ *www.catcherbar.com.*

The Fifth
BARS/PUBS | Sometimes all you need is a solid dive bar and the Fifth fits the bill. Pool table? Check. Vintage arcade games? Check. Most importantly, cheap drinks? Absolutely. ✉ *4821 Whitsett Ave., North Hollywood* ☎ *818/856–8006* ⊕ *www.vintagebargroup.com/the-fifth.php.*

The Other Door
BARS/PUBS | The Other Door occupies a strange space, somewhere between a steampunk-themed bar, a dive bar, and a music venue with a varied calendar featuring live music, karaoke, and silent disco. It also has a pool table and a vintage photo booth on hand, in case all these diversions aren't enough to distract you. ✉ *10437 Burbank Blvd., North Hollywood* ☎ *818/508–7008* ⊕ *theotherdoorbar.com.*

🛍 Shopping

Blastoff Comics
BOOKS/STATIONERY | Blastoff rises above L.A.'s collection of fantastic comic book stores. This is a wonderland for the serious collector, especially those looking to dive deep into vintage and rare comics. New comics are also on offer and a friendly, knowledgeable staff makes this a must-visit for any comic fan. ✉ *5118 Lankershim Blvd., North Hollywood* ☎ *323/980–2665* ⊕ *www.blastoffcomics.com.*

Circus Liquor
CONVENIENCE/GENERAL STORES | You might ask yourself, "Why is Fodor's advising me to go to a liquor store in the Valley?" And this is a very good question. After all, this is just a liquor store. Well, go here for the 'Gram. There's a 32-foot neon clown sign outside, which was already L.A. famous but was made even more so by being featured in *Clueless*. And, while here, you might as well pick up some booze. ✉ *5600 Vineland Ave., North Hollywood* ☎ *818/769–1500.*

The Iliad Book Shop
BOOKS/STATIONERY | For 30 years, Iliad not only has been selling used books but has been a set piece on a number of TV shows and movies, including *Lethal Weapon 3*. But with a collection of 125,000 books of all genres, including a solid selection of graphic novels, it's worth a visit just to peruse the aisles and find that next favorite novel. ✉ *5400 Cahuenga Blvd., North Hollywood* ☎ *818/509–2665* ⊕ *www.iliadbooks.com.*

Midcenturyla

HOUSEHOLD ITEMS/FURNITURE | The idea of going to Los Angeles to buy furniture may sound nuts, but go ahead, indulge your inner designer at Midcenturyla, a curated furniture store brimming with custom and vintage mid-century modern desks, sofas, and more. ⊠ *5333 Cahuenga Blvd., North Hollywood* ☎ *818/509–3050* ⊕ *midcenturyla.com.*

Chapter 6

MID-WILSHIRE AND KOREATOWN

Updated by
Paul Feinstein

◉ Sights	🍴 Restaurants	🛏 Hotels	🛍 Shopping	🍸 Nightlife
★★★★☆	★★★★☆	★★☆☆☆	★★☆☆☆	★★★★★

NEIGHBORHOOD SNAPSHOT

GREAT EXPERIENCES

■ **Get Cultured on Miracle Mile:** Check out Museum Row, which includes LACMA, the Petersen Automotive Museum, the new Academy Museum of Motion Pictures, and the La Brea Tar Pits.

■ **Relax at Korean Spas:** Whisk yourself away to Seoul at one of several spas in Koreatown, where you can get your scrub on or just lounge away the hours in pools and saunas.

■ **Dine on Global Cuisine:** Eat Oaxacan food at Guelaguetza, feast on Korean BBQ at Kobawoo House, or chow down on Ethiopian at Meals by Genet.

■ **Find the Party:** Hit up the summer pool scene inside the trendy Line Hotel or wander into the Wiltern for a night of live music.

QUICK BITES

Kogi Taqueria. Roy Choi's L.A. food truck set up a brick-and-mortar for those who don't want to hunt down that glorious moving van of deliciousness (which you can also find by checking out the weekly schedule at kogibbq.com). ⊠ *3500 Overland Ave., #100*

Merkato. A wholly authentic Ethiopian experience, serving classics like spongy injera bread, spicy beef, and grilled fish. ⊠ *1036 1/2 S. Fairfax Ave.*

Sky's Gourmet Tacos. You'll find some of the spiciest and most succulent tacos in L.A. at Sky's. They also dish out steaming breakfast tacos and have an enormous vegan and vegetarian menu. ⊠ *5303 Pico Blvd.*

GETTING HERE

■ Mid-Wilshire and Koreatown are in the middle of the city, meaning there isn't direct freeway access. Main thoroughfares include Wilshire, Olympic, and Pico boulevards, but to avoid traffic, try using 6th Street. Luckily, there is also direct Metro access that runs across both neighborhoods with stops at LACMA (opening 2019) on the Westside all the way to Wilshire/Vermont on the Eastside. However you get here, remember: parking can be challenging. Side streets are heavily regulated and meters are scarce. There are some public lots, particularly in Miracle Mile, but often it's valet all the way.

PLANNING YOUR TIME

■ Take a full day to tour the Petersen Automotive, LACMA, the La Brea Tar Pits, and the Academy Museum of Motion Pictures. They're all next to each other, making travel between them easy, but check out museum websites for the most up-to-date closing days and times. LACMA is closed Wednesday. Many others close on Monday. Koreatown is the perfect evening spot to grab dinner and drinks and, schedule permitting, a show at the Wiltern. If you're planning on going to a Korean spa, set aside half a day.

While they're two distinctly different neighborhoods, Mid-Wilshire and Koreatown sit side by side and offer Angelenos some of the most interesting sights, sounds, and bites in the city.

Mid-Wilshire is broadly known for its wide variety of museums, but there's also a strip called Little Ethiopia, where you can find incredible cuisine. Koreatown, meanwhile, is a haven for Seoul food (pun intended) but also an area with multiethnic dining nuggets that hit the top of many restaurant lists. Once your stomach is sated, check out a Korean spa, where scrubbing and pampering can close out a perfectly long day.

Mid-Wilshire and Miracle Mile

The 1½-mile strip of Wilshire Boulevard between La Brea and Fairfax avenues was bought up by developers in the 1920s, and they created a commercial district that catered to automobile traffic. Nobody thought the venture could be successful, so the burgeoning strip became known as Miracle Mile. It was the world's first linear downtown, with building designs incorporating wide store windows to attract attention from passing cars. As L.A.'s art deco buildings have come to be appreciated, preserved, and restored over the years, the area's exemplary architecture is a highlight. The surrounding Mid-Wilshire area encompassing Miracle Mile includes the notable **Petersen Automotive Museum,** which got a $90 million upgrade in 2015. Clad in steel ribbons, it sits as a beacon on the Mid-Wilshire section of Museum Row.

◉ Sights

Craft and Folk Art Museum

MUSEUM | This small but important cultural landmark pioneered support for traditional folk arts. The two-story space has a global outlook, embracing social movements and long-established trends. It mounts rotating exhibitions where you might see anything from costumes of carnival celebrations around the world to handmade quilts. The courtyard area is a tranquil space often used for opening receptions. The ground-level gift shop stocks a unique collection of handcrafts, jewelry, ceramics, books, and textiles. The museum also hosts myriad events from craft workshops and lectures to glassblowing and printmaking. ⊠ *5814 Wilshire Blvd., Mid-Wilshire* ☏ *323/937–4230* ⊕ *www.cafam.org* ☏ *$9* ⊙ *Closed Mon.*

La Brea Tar Pits Museum

NATURE SITE | FAMILY | Show your kids where Ice Age fossils come from by taking them to the stickiest park in town. The area formed when deposits of oil rose to the earth's surface, collected in shallow pools, and coagulated into asphalt. In the early 20th century geologists discovered that all that goo contained the largest collection of Pleistocene (Ice Age) fossils ever found at one location: more than 600 species of birds, mammals, plants, reptiles, and insects. Roughly 100 tons of fossil bones have been removed in excavations during the last 100 years, making this one of the

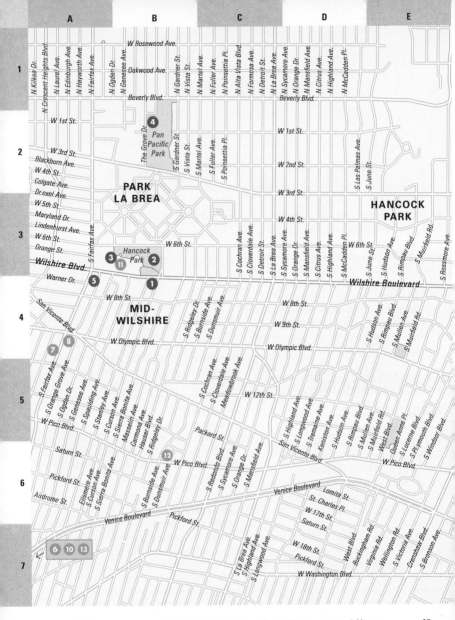

Sights ▼

1 Craft and Folk Art Museum **B4**
2 La Brea Tar Pits Museum **B3**
3 Los Angeles County Museum of Art (LACMA) **A3**
4 Los Angeles Museum of the Holocaust **B2**
5 Petersen Automotive Museum **A4**

Restaurants ▼

1 The Boiling Crab **I4**
2 Cassell's Hamburgers **I3**
3 Guelaguetza **I5**
4 Here's Looking At You **H3**
5 Kobawoo House **J4**
6 Margot **A7**
7 Meals By Genet **A4**
8 Merkato Ethiopian Restaurant & Market **A4**
9 Monty's Good Burger **H3**
10 n/naka **A7**
11 Ray's & Stark Bar **B3**

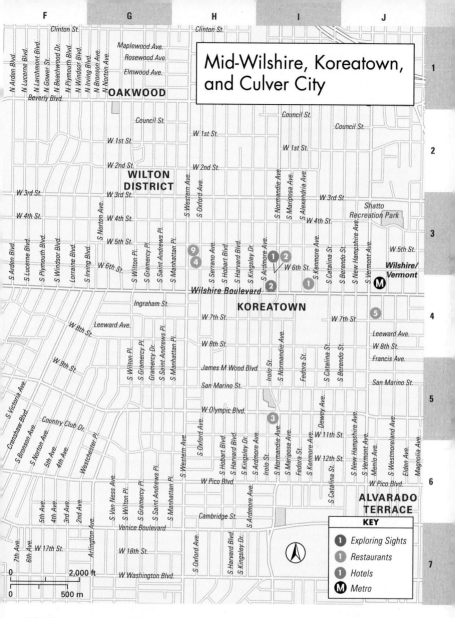

Mid-Wilshire, Koreatown, and Culver City

OAKWOOD

WILTON DISTRICT

KOREATOWN

Shatto Recreation Park

Wilshire/Vermont

ALVARADO TERRACE

Wilshire Boulevard

KEY

- 🟦 Exploring Sights
- 🟢 Restaurants
- 🟥 Hotels
- Ⓜ Metro

0 — 2,000 ft
0 — 500 m

12 Sky's Gourmet
Tacos **B6**

13 Vespertine **A7**

Hotels ▼

1 Hotel Normandie **I3**

2 The Line **I4**

world's most famous fossil sites. You can see most of the pits through chain link fences, and the new Excavator Tour gets you as close as possible to the action.

Pit 91 and Project 23 are ongoing excavation projects; tours are offered, and you can volunteer to help with the excavations in the summer. Several pits are scattered around Hancock Park and the surrounding neighborhood; construction in the area has often had to accommodate them, and in nearby streets and along sidewalks, little bits of tar occasionally ooze up. The museum displays fossils from the tar pits and has a glass-walled laboratory that allows visitors to view paleontologists and volunteers as they work on specimens. ■TIP→ **Museum admission is free for L.A. County residents weekdays 3–5 pm.** ⊠ *5801 Wilshire Blvd., Miracle Mile* ☎ *323/857–6300* ⊕ *www. tarpits.org* 🎫 *$15; free 1st Tues. of every month (except July and Aug.) and every Tues. in Sept.*

★ Los Angeles County Museum of Art (LACMA)

MUSEUM | Los Angeles has a truly fabulous museum culture and everything that it stands for can be epitomized by the massive, eclectic, and ever-changing Los Angeles County Museum of Art. Opened at its current location in 1965, today the museum boasts the largest collection of art in the western United States with more than 135,000 pieces from 6,000 years of history across multiple buildings atop over 20 acres. Highlights include the *Urban Light* sculpture by Chris Burden (an Instagram favorite), *Levitated Mass* by Michael Heizer, and prominent works by Frida Kahlo, Wassily Kandinsky, Henri Matisse, and Claude Monet. With an illustrative permanent collection to go along with an ever-rotating array of temporary exhibits, film screenings, educational programs, and more, the museum is a beacon of culture that stands alone in the middle of the city.

■TIP→ **Temporary exhibitions sometimes require tickets purchased in advance.** ⊠ *5905 Wilshire Blvd., Miracle Mile* ☎ *323/857–6000* ⊕ *www.lacma.org* 🎫 *$20* ⊗ *Closed Wed.*

Petersen Automotive Museum

MUSEUM | FAMILY | L.A. is a mecca for car lovers, which explains the popularity of this museum with a collection of more than 300 automobiles and other motorized vehicles. But you don't have to be a gearhead to appreciate the Petersen; there's plenty of fascinating history here for all to enjoy. Learn how Los Angeles grew up around its freeways, how cars evolve from the design phase to the production line, and how automobiles have influenced film and television. To see how the vehicles, many of them quite rare, are preserved and maintained, take the 90-minute tour of the basement-level Vault (young kids aren't permitted in the Vault, but they'll find plenty to keep them occupied throughout the museum). ⊠ *6060 Wilshire Blvd., Mid-Wilshire* ☎ *323/964–6331* ⊕ *www.petersen.org* 🎫 *From $16.*

🍽 Restaurants

★ Meals by Genet

$$ | ETHIOPIAN | In a tucked-away stretch along Fairfax Avenue is Little Ethiopia, where Angelenos of all stripes flock for the African country's signatures like *tibs*, *wat*, and *kitfo*. And while there is a plethora of Ethiopian options, no one does the cuisine justice quite like Meals by Genet. **Known for:** authentic Ethiopian cuisine; jovial atmosphere; unreal tibs. 🟤 *Average main: $20* ⊠ *1053 S. Fairfax Ave., Mid-Wilshire* ☎ *323/938–9304* ⊕ *www.mealsbygenetla.com* ⊗ *Closed Mon.–Wed.*

Merkato Ethiopian Restaurant and Market

$ | ETHIOPIAN | For a wholly authentic Ethiopian experience, you can't really go wrong with Merkato. Not only does it serve the classics like spongy injera

Chris Burden's iconic *Urban Light* sculpture sits at the entrance to LACMA

bread, spicy beef, and grilled fish, but there's also a market where you can buy Ethiopian ingredients to make your own mouthwatering cuisine at home. **Known for:** authentic Ethiopian cuisine; market products; friendly staff. [$] *Average main: $15* ✉ *1036 1/2 S. Fairfax Ave., Mid-Wilshire* ☎ *323/935–1775.*

Ray's and Stark Bar

$$ | **AMERICAN** | Whether you want to fill up before perusing L.A.'s best art galleries or simply grab a drink to soak in the priceless sculptures at the LACMA, Ray's and Stark Bar is the perfect complement to any museumgoer's experience. Situated just outside the main entrance of the museum, the restaurant/bar offers a variety of Americana cuisine like pizza, burgers, and pastas. **Known for:** happy hour; brunch; signature cocktails. [$] *Average main: $20* ✉ *5905 Wilshire Blvd., Miracle Mile* ☎ *323/857–6180* 🌐 *www.patinagroup.com/rays-and-stark-bar* 🕒 *Closed Wed.*

Sky's Gourmet Tacos

$ | **MEXICAN** | If you're searching for some of the spiciest and most succulent tacos in L.A., look no further than Sky's. This quaint taco joint offers up beef, chicken, turkey, seafood, and vegan options that will leave your mouth on fire and your belly full in all the best ways possible. **Known for:** tacos; spices; jovial atmosphere. [$] *Average main: $10* ✉ *5303 Pico Blvd., Mid-Wilshire* ☎ *323/932–6253* 🌐 *www.skysgourmettacos.com.*

Koreatown

Despite its name, Koreatown is one of the most eclectic neighborhoods in all of Los Angeles. Obviously, you can find drool-worthy Korean restaurants, but there are also gems like the Oaxacan eatery Guelaguetza; the Hawaiian/Asian hybrid Here's Looking at You; and the vegan burger joint Monty's Good Burger. Combine the food with the amazingness of the Korean spas and the incredible nightlife, and you'll find a mix of everything that makes L.A. great.

🍴 Restaurants

Home to the largest and densest Korean population outside of Korea, Koreatown is also an ethnically diverse neighborhood. While Korean cuisine is ubiquitous here, like in most of L.A., you can find incredible Asian fusion and even classic burger joints.

The Boiling Crab

$$ | SEAFOOD | FAMILY | Put on your bib and prepare to get messy, because this crab shack is not for stodgy eaters. Choices of blue, Dungeness, snow, king, and southern king, are brought out in plastic bags where you can rip, tear, twist, and yank the meaty goodness out of their shells. **Known for:** giant crab legs; unfussy environment; long lines. $ *Average main: $20* ⊠ *3377 Wilshire Blvd., Suite 115, Koreatown* ☎ *213/389–2722* ⊕ *www.theboilingcrab.com* ☉ *Lunch on weekends only* Ⓜ *Wilshire/Normandie Station.*

Cassell's Hamburgers

$ | DINER | FAMILY | Since 1948, Cassell's has been grilling up some of the city's best burgers and remains on just about every top burger list in town. The simple diner features barstools, a dozen or so tables, and large windows looking out onto the street. **Known for:** perfectly cooked burgers and fries; no-frills dining; late-night eats. $ *Average main: $10* ⊠ *3600 W. 6th St., Koreatown* ☎ *213/387–5502* ⊕ *www.cassellshamburgers.com* Ⓜ *Wilshire/Normandie Station.*

Guelaguetza

$ | MEXICAN | FAMILY | A classic L.A. Mexican eatery, Guelaguetza serves the complex but not overpoweringly spicy cooking of Oaxaca, one of Mexico's most renowned culinary capitals. Inside, you'll find a largely Spanish-speaking clientele bobbing their heads to nightly jazz and marimba while wolfing down the restaurant's specialty: the moles. **Known for:** salsa-covered chorizo; chili-marinated pork; family-owned restaurant. $ *Average main: $15* ⊠ *3014 W. Olympic Blvd., Koreatown* ☎ *213/427–0608* ⊕ *www.ilovemole.com.*

★ Here's Looking At You

$$ | ECLECTIC | Hawaiian and Asian-inspired dishes can be found on this menu featuring veggie, meat, poultry, and seafood. The environment is eclectic, as is the food, with signature dishes like blood cake with duck egg and pork belly with *nam jim.* **Known for:** pie; exceptional cocktails; inventive dishes. $ *Average main: $25* ⊠ *3901 W. 6th St., Koreatown* ☎ *213/568–3573* ⊕ *www.hereslookingatyoula.com.*

Kobawoo House

$ | KOREAN | FAMILY | Nestled into a dingy strip mall, this Korean powerhouse is given away by the lines of locals waiting outside. Once inside, scents of grilled meats and kimchi immediately fill your nostrils. **Known for:** kalbi beef; long lines; cheap eats. $ *Average main: $17* ⊠ *698 S. Vermont Ave., Koreatown* ☎ *213/389–7300* ⊕ *www.kobawoola.com* Ⓜ *Wilshire/Vermont.*

Monty's Good Burger

$ | BURGER | A 100% plant-based establishment in Koreatown shouldn't be a thing that works. But Monty's Good Burger has the neighborhood fooled, as its Impossible Burger makes believers out of the most devout carnivores. **Known for:** plant-based burgers; epic shakes; perfect tots. $ *Average main: $11* ⊠ *516 S. Western Ave., Koreatown* ☎ *909/259–0652* ⊕ *montysgoodburger.com* Ⓜ *Wilshire/Western Station.*

🛏 Hotels

Hotel Normandie

$ | HOTEL | Originally built in 1926, this Renaissance Revival gem has been renovated to today's standards and is now a hip and not-so-pricey spot to post up in the ever-booming center of Koreatown.

Sawtelle Boulevard's Little Osaka

The four blocks on Sawtelle Boulevard between Olympic Boulevard and Missouri Avenue are filled with predominantly Japanese specialty stores, restaurants, and plant nurseries. A trip here makes for an interesting, out-of-the-ordinary jaunt from either Westwood or Santa Monica.

In the 1920s, after a wave of Japanese immigrants arrived in L.A., Sawtelle began to resemble an authentic Japanese main street rather than a touristy Little Tokyo. Although most establishments remain Japanese, the area also encompasses Chinese, Taiwanese, and Malaysian businesses.

To reach Sawtelle from Westwood, head south on Westwood Boulevard, turn right on Santa Monica Boulevard, and take a left on Sawtelle. There's plenty of metered street parking, plus minimall lots near Olympic Boulevard.

Hide Sushi. Some of the best sushi spots in Los Angeles are the most hidden and most discreet and come with zero fanfare. Hide (pronounced hee-day) in Little Osaka is one of those restaurants. **Known for:** counter sushi; fresh fish; quiet atmosphere. ✉ *2040 Sawtelle Blvd., West L.A.* ☎ *310/477-7242* 🕓 *Closed Mon.* 💳 *No credit cards.*

Hurry Curry of Tokyo. For traditionalists, there are few places in Los Angeles that can match the authenticity of Hurry Curry. Set inside a minimall in the bustling stretch of Little Osaka, Hurry Curry dishes out steaming plates of chicken cutlets, braised beef, and pork doused in gravy-like *katsu* curry sauce. **Known for:** specialty Japanese curries; cheap prices; casual setting. ✉ *2131 Sawtelle Blvd., West L.A.* ☎ *310/473-1640* 🌐 *www.hurrycurryoftokyo.com.*

Nijiya Market. If you're looking for an authentic Japanese supermarket, you'll find everything you could ever want at Nijiya. Inside, you'll discover fresh fish for make-it-at-home sushi, baked Japanese delicacies, daily-made take-away bento boxes, and every Japanese candy treat imaginable. On weekends, there is a giant skillet set up outside the entrance where employees fry up sizzling and savory *okonomiyaki* (Japanese pancake). ✉ *2130 Sawtelle Blvd, #105, West L.A.* ☎ *310/575-3300* 🌐 *www.nijiya.com.*

Tsujita L.A. Artisan Noodles. Ramen lovers have no shortage of choices across Los Angeles, but if you want the best, head over to this Little Osaka hot spot. Lines typically bend around the corner as hungry Angelenos drive from far and wide to have Tsujita's signature *tsukemen* (a type of ramen where the noodles are served to the side of the broth and you dip each bite individually). **Known for:** tsukemen; ramen; long lines. ✉ *2057 Sawtelle Blvd., West L.A.* ☎ *310/231-7373.*

Pros: free wine happy hour; complimentary breakfast; cheap prices. **Cons:** feels dated; tiny bathrooms. [$] *Rooms from: $190* ✉ *605 Normandie Ave., Koreatown* ☎ *213/388-8138* 🌐 *www.hotelnormandiela.com* 🛏 *92 rooms.*

The Line

$$ | HOTEL | This boutique hotel pays homage to its Koreatown address with dynamic dining concepts and a hidden karaoke speakeasy. **Pros:** on-site bikes to explore the area; cheery staff; houses the Houston Brothers' '80s-themed bar. **Cons:**

expensive parking; lobby club crowds public spaces; far from parts of the city you may want to explore. $ *Rooms from: $250* ⊠ *3515 Wilshire Blvd., Koreatown* ☎ *213/381–7411* ⊕ *www.thelinehotel. com* ⇌ *384 rooms* ○○ *No meals* Ⓜ *Wilshire/Normandie Station.*

Nightlife

Known primarily for its boundless Korean barbecue spots and karaoke, this off-the-beaten-path segment of Central L.A. is also home to unique must-visit bars.

Dan Sung Sa

BARS/PUBS | Step through the curtained entrance and back in time to 1970s Korea at Dan Sung Sa, which gained wider popularity after Anthony Bourdain paid a visit. At this quirky time-capsule bar, wood-block menus feature roughly 100 small eats. You'll see much that looks familiar, but fortune favors the bold. Take a chance on corn cheese, or try the *makgeolli*: a boozy Korean rice drink you sip from a bowl. It pairs perfectly with good conversation and snacking all night long. ⊠ *3317 W. 6th St., Koreatown* ☎ *213/487–9100* Ⓜ *Wilshire/Vermont Station.*

★ HMS Bounty

BARS/PUBS | This super-kitschy nautical-themed bar in the heart of Koreatown offers drink specials and food at prices that will make you swoon. Make sure you speak to the grandmotherly Korean bartender—introduce yourself once and she'll never forget your name and order. ⊠ *3357 Wilshire Blvd., Koreatown* ☎ *213/385–7275* ⊕ *www.thehmsbounty. com* Ⓜ *Wilshire/Normandy Station.*

The Prince

BARS/PUBS | *Mad Men* and *New Girl* both had multiple scenes filmed in this Old Hollywood relic, which dates back to the early 1900s. The Prince is trimmed with vintage fabric wallpaper and bedecked with a stately mahogany bar; the grand piano waits in the wings. Squire lamps punctuate red leather booths where you can enjoy Korean fare and standard cocktails, wine, and beer. Whatever you do, get the deep-fried chicken. ⊠ *3198 W. 7th St., Koreatown* ☎ *213/389–1586* ⊕ *www.facebook.com/ The-Prince-Restaurant-257833677577910* Ⓜ *Wilshire/Vermont Station.*

Performing Arts

Wiltern Theater

CONCERTS | Built in 1931, this historical art deco landmark, named for its location at the intersection of Wilshire Boulevard and Western Avenue, serves mainly as a space for music (it's a top destination for touring musicians), but other live entertainment can be seen here as well, including comedy and dance. The main floor is standing room only for most shows, but there are some seating areas available if desired. ⊠ *3790 Wilshire Blvd., Los Angeles* ☎ *213/388–1400* ⊕ *www. wiltern.com* Ⓜ *Wilshire/Western Station.*

Shopping

Aroma Spa

SPA/BEAUTY | It's not difficult to find amazing spa experiences throughout Koreatown. Most places will offer up standard scrubs, hot and cold baths, dry and wet saunas, and more. Aroma takes things to another level as the spa is just the centerpiece of an entire entertainment complex. Spa services include all the traditional treatments, but when you're done getting pampered, the rest of the facility includes a gym, a swimming pool, restaurants, and a state-of-the-art golf driving range. ⊠ *3680 Wilshire Blvd., Koreatown* ☎ *213/387–2111* ⊕ *www. aromaresort.com.*

Wi Spa

SPA/BEAUTY | Koreatown is filled with endless spa experiences, but there are a few that rise above the rest. Wi Spa is a 24/7 wonderland of treatments that includes hot and cold baths, unique sauna rooms, and floors for men, women, or co-ed family spa fun. Signature sauna rooms

Culver City: The Heart of Screenland 🎬

Culver City. Located about halfway between Hollywood and the coast, Culver City has a glamorous history of its own. The area boasts two film studios, Sony (formerly MGM) Studios and the Culver Studios. Culver City itself has seen revitalization in recent years as visitors discover the charming district of the area's "downtown." Metro's new Expo Line has a Culver City Station stop, making it an easy subway and light rail trip from Hollywood or Downtown Los Angeles.

The Culver Hotel is in the heart of Culver City, and the surrounding area is loaded with shops, cafés, the art deco–style **Pacific Theatre** Culver Stadium 12 (310/559–2416), and a vibrant art gallery scene. ⊠ 9770 Culver Blvd., Culver City ⊕ www. culvercity.org.

Culver Hotel. In the heart of Culver City is the Culver Hotel, built in 1924 and now preserved as a historical landmark; it will catch your eye with its old-world glory and lobby entrance with its sweeping dark wood and high ceiling that's a seductive as the many classic film stars that took up residency here over the years, including Greta Garbo, Joan Crawford, John Wayne, Clark Gable, Buster Keaton, Ronald Reagan, and cast members from Wizard of Oz and Gone with the Wind as they filmed in the nearby studio. ⊠ 9400 Culver Blvd., Culver City ☎ 310/838–7963 ⊕ www. culverhotel.com.

Culver Studios. The Culver Studios are best known as the location where Gone with the Wind was filmed in addition to classics including Citizen Kane and the Desilu Productions TV hits of the '50s–'60s, including The Andy Griffith Show, Lassie, and Batman. Amazon Studio currently occupies the space and is further developing it. This studio currently does not offer tours to the public. ⊠ 9336 W. Washington Blvd., Culver City ☎ 310/202–1234 ⊕ www. theculverstudios.com.

Museum of Jurassic Technology. One museum with its own unique spin is the Museum of Jurassic Technology, with an oddball assortment of natural (and partly fictional) "art" pieces such as fruit stone carvings, theater models, string figures, finds from mobile home parks, and a tribute room filled with paintings of dogs from the Soviet Space Program, all housed in a low-lighted haunted house–style atmosphere that makes you feel as if the Addams Family butler will come to greet you at any moment. ⊠ 9341 Venice Blvd., Culver City ☎ 310/836–6131 ⊕ www.mjt.org 🖾 $8.

Sony Pictures Studios. Sony Pictures Studios (former the MGM studios), where movie magic from Wizard of Oz to Spiderman was made, offers two-hour walking tours ($50, reservation required) to dive into their rich TV and blockbuster film history. If game shows are your thing, you can also be a part of the studio audience for Jeopardy! or Wheel of Fortune. ⊠ 10202 W. Washington, Culver City ☎ 310/244–8687, 800/482–9840 ⊕ www. sonypicturesstudios.com 🖾 Tours $38.

vary from intense 231-degree thermotherapy to salt-enriched stations and specialty clay imported from Korea. Just remember, Korean spas are not for the shy at heart—you will be nude, you will get scrubbed, and you will feel like a million bucks after. ✉ *2700 Wilshire Blvd., Koreatown* ☎ *213/487–2700* 🌐 *www.wispausa.com.*

Culver City

🍴 Restaurants

Sandwiched between some of L.A.'s coolest neighborhoods, Culver City has spent the past few years forming its own identity. A place for adventurous eaters, here you can find cuisines spanning the globe.

Margot

$$ | MEDITERRANEAN | Boasting one of the most stunning rooftops in L.A., Margot is a fresh face and hopping hot spot for the Culver City dining and drinking scene. The expansive space gives off a Moroccan Casbah vibe with just as many hints of Southern California for good measure. **Known for:** fresh fish; epic views; fun happy hour. [$] *Average main: $25* ✉ *8820 Washington Blvd. , #301, Culver City* ☎ *310/643–5853* 🌐 *www.margot.la.*

★ n/naka

$$$$ | JAPANESE | *Chef's Table* star Niki Nakayama helms this *omakase* (chef-selected) fine-dining establishment. Small and intimate, any given night will feature sashimi with *kanpachi*, sea bass with *uni* butter, or Myazaki Wagyu beef. **Known for:** three-hour meals; excellent sake pairings. [$] *Average main: $185* ✉ *3455 Overland Ave., Culver City* ☎ *310/836–6252* 🌐 *www.n-naka.com* 🕒 *Closed Sun. and Mon.*

Vespertine

$$$$ | AMERICAN | Vespertine isn't a restaurant. It's a multisensory event. **Known for:** elaborate tasting menu; modern design; unique everything. [$] *Average main: $250* ✉ *3599 Hayden Ave., Culver City* ☎ *323/320–4023* 🌐 *vespertine.la* 🕒 *Closed Sun. and Mon.*

Chapter 7

DOWNTOWN LOS ANGELES

Updated by
Paul Feinstein

👁 Sights	🍴 Restaurants	🛏 Hotels	🛍 Shopping	🍸 Nightlife
★★★★★	★★★★★	★★★★☆	★★★☆☆	★★★★★

NEIGHBORHOOD SNAPSHOT

GREAT EXPERIENCES

■ **Visit Frank Gehry's Disney Concert Hall.** Be wowed by the genius architecture and grab tickets for an L.A. Phil performance led by Gustavo Dudamel.

■ **See a Lakers or Clippers Game.** Catch the action at the Staples Center and possibly rub elbows with stars like Jack Nicholson and Leo DiCaprio.

■ **Take a Historic Walking Tour.** The L.A. Conservancy offers several tours, such as of Olvera Street, where you can see traditional Mexican culture and shop for goods. If you're into the seedier side, Esotouric showcases the down-and-out history of old L.A.

■ **Peruse the Last Bookstore.** This is not only one of the best bookstores in Los Angeles, it's also one of the most fantastical. Peruse the endless collection of rare and used books and LPs downstairs, then go upstairs into a labyrinth of oddities.

■ **Have a Cocktail in Old L.A.** Downtown is great for drinking and even better for drinking in the history. Some of the city's oldest buildings have been converted into glorious hotels with excellent bars, like the NoMad or the Freehand, while other drinking halls have been around for more than a century, like the Golden Gopher.

QUICK BITES

Cole's. One of the oldest restaurants in L.A., Cole's also lays (disputed) claim to being the originator of the French dip. There's not a lot on the menu, but what they serve is made beautifully. ⊠ *118 E. 6th St.*

Philippe the Original. The other (disputed) originator of the French dip. Bottom line—when in Downtown and in want of a quick bite, eat a French dip. ⊠ *1001 N. Alameda St.*

Grand Central Market. Don't want a French dip? You have plenty of options here. A palace of food stalls that's so overwhelming, it's almost impossible to choose a meal. But to narrow it down, try either Ramen Hood at stall C-2 or Sticky Rice at stall C-5. ⊠ *317 S. Broadway*

GETTING HERE

■ **Driving Strategy.** The good news is that freeways 5, 101, 110, and 10 all get you there; the bad news is that the traffic can delay your travels. If you're coming from the Hollywood area, skip the freeways altogether and take Sunset Boulevard, which turns into César Chávez Boulevard. If you're coming from LAX, take the 105 Eeast to the 110 North. Be warned: parking can be very expensive. It's better to rideshare or take the Metro.

PLANNING YOUR TIME

■ Visit weekdays during the day, when the area is bustling and restaurants are open for lunch. The streets are packed weekend nights, and wait times can be long at restaurants and bars. Weekday evenings tend to be much quieter and it's easy to get find yourself a table or a barstool. Seeing everything in one day is possible, but it's best to spread it out over two. Plan your visits around specific areas you can walk to in one circuit.

If there's one thing Angelenos love, it's a makeover, and city planners have put the wheels in motion for a dramatic revitalization. Downtown is both glamorous and gritty and is an example of Los Angeles's complexity as a whole. There's a dizzying variety of experiences not to be missed here if you're curious about the artistic, historic, ethnic, or sports-loving sides of L.A.

Downtown Los Angeles isn't just one neighborhood: it's a cluster of pedestrian-friendly enclaves where you can sample an eclectic mix of flavors, wander through world-class museums, and enjoy great live performances or sports events.

As you venture into the different neighborhoods of Downtown—**Chinatown, Little Tokyo,** and **El Pueblo de Los Angeles**—take advantage of the tastes, sounds, and sights. Eat roast duck in Chinatown, red bean cakes in Little Tokyo, or pickled cactus on Olvera Street. Spend time browsing at the **Grand Central Market,** where stalls are filled with colorful locally grown produce and homemade treats such as tamales and olive bread. The market recently received a makeover, and is now offering everything from Texan barbecue to Thai-style chicken over rice. For art lovers, the **Geffen Contemporary at MOCA** has one of the most important modern and contemporary art collections, and those who are fans of architecture should make a point to see another Gehry creation, the **Walt Disney Concert Hall,** or the massive,

geometrically designed **Cathedral of Our Lady for the Angels.**

To see the glory of Broadway's golden years, look up above the storefront signs, and you'll find the marvelous architecture and theater marquees of the majestic buildings they reside in. From the late 19th century to the 1950s—before malls and freeways—**Broadway** glittered with the finest shops and the highest number of luxurious theaters in the world, making it a rich, cultural haven. Though it remains the main road through Downtown's **Historic Core,** the area has changed dramatically over the years. Though it once exclusively housed businesses catering to mostly Mexican and Central American immigrants, there are now trendy pockets for shopping and dining. However, you can still find the classic experience of mariachi and *banda* music blaring from electronics-store speakers between 1st and 9th streets, street-food vendors hawking sliced papaya sprinkled with chili powder, and fancy dresses for a girl's *quinceañera* (15th birthday).

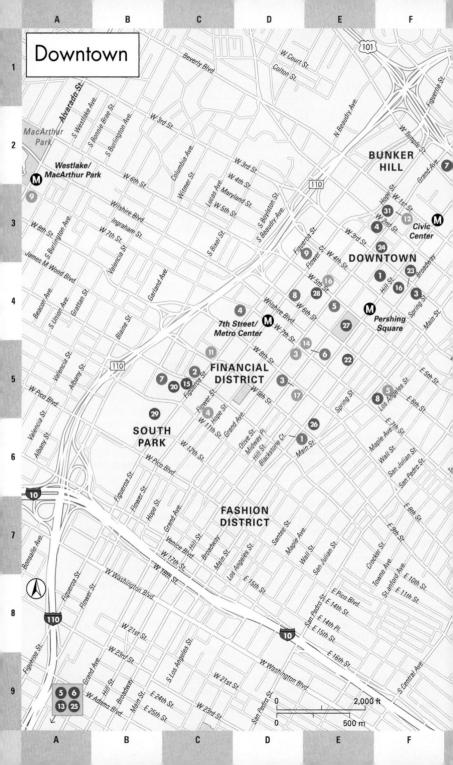

Sights ▼

1 Angels Flight Railway ... **F4**
2 Avila Adobe **H2**
3 Bradbury Building **F4**
4 The Broad Museum **F3**
5 California African
American Museum..... **A9**
6 California Science
Center................... **A9**
7 Cathedral of Our Lady
of the Angels **G2**
8 The Cecil Hotel.......... **F5**
9 Chinatown **H1**
10 Chinese American
Museum **H3**
11 City Hall of
Los Angeles **G3**
12 El Pueblo de
Los Angeles **H3**
13 Exposition Park **A9**
14 Geffen Contemporary
at MOCA **H4**
15 GRAMMY Museum...... **C5**
16 Grand Central Market... **F4**
17 Italian Hall Building..... **H2**
18 Japanese American
Cultural and Community
Center................... **G4**
19 Japanese American
National Museum....... **H4**
20 L.A. Live **C5**
21 Little Tokyo.............. **G4**
22 Los Angeles Theatre **E5**
23 Million Dollar Theater... **F4**
24 MOCA Grand Avenue.... **F3**
25 Natural History
Museum of
Los Angeles County **A9**
26 Orpheum Theatre........ **E6**
27 Pershing Square......... **E4**
28 Richard J. Riordan
Central Library **E4**
29 Staples Center **B5**
30 Union Station............ **H3**
31 Walt Disney
Concert Hall **F3**

Restaurants ▼

1 Bavel **I6**
2 Bestia **I8**
3 Bottega Louie **D5**
4 Broken Spanish.......... **C5**
5 Cole's French Dip **F5**
6 The Factory Kitchen **H6**
7 Guerrilla Tacos........... **I7**
8 Howlin' Ray's............ **H2**
9 Langer's Delicatesen-
Restaurant............... **A3**
10 majordōmo **H1**
11 The Original
Pantry Cafe.............. **C5**
12 Patina **F3**
13 Philippe the Original ... **H2**
14 Q Sushi.................... **E5**
15 Redbird................... **G4**
16 71Above................... **E4**
17 Shibumi **D5**
18 Sushi Gen................ **H5**

Hotels ▼

1 Ace Hotel Downtown
Los Angeles **D6**
2 Figueroa Hotel **C5**
3 Freehand
Los Angeles **D5**
4 InterContinental Los
Angeles Downtown **D4**
5 Millennium Biltmore
Hotel...................... **E4**
6 The NoMad Hotel........ **E5**
7 The Ritz-Carlton,
Los Angeles **B5**
8 The Standard,
Downtown LA............ **D4**
9 Westin Bonaventure
Hotel & Suites........... **E3**

Tulips by Jeff Koons at the Broad Museum

◉ Sights

★ Angels Flight Railway

HISTORIC SITE | The turn-of-the-20th-century funicular, dubbed "the shortest railway in the world," operated between 1901 and 1969, when it was dismantled to make room for an urban renewal project. Almost 30 years later, Angels Flight returned with its original orange-and-black wooden cable cars hauling travelers up a 298-foot incline from Hill Street to the fountain-filled Watercourt at California Plaza. Your reward is a stellar view of the neighborhood. Tickets are $1 each way, but you can buy a souvenir round-trip ticket for $2 if you want something to take home with you. ⊠ *351 S. Hill St., between 3rd and 4th Sts., Downtown* ☎ *213/626–1901* ⊕ *www.angelsflight.org.*

Avila Adobe

HOUSE | Built as a private home for cattle rancher Francisco Avila in 1818, this museum preserves 7 of what were originally 18 rooms in the city's oldest standing residence. This graceful structure features 3-foot-thick walls made of adobe brick over cottonwood timbers, a traditional interior courtyard, and 1840s-era furnishings that bring to life an era when the city was still part of Mexico. The museum is open daily from 9 to 4 and the complex is a California Historical Landmark. ⊠ *10 Olvera St., Downtown* ☎ *213/485–6855* ⊕ *www. elpueblo.lacity.org.*

Bradbury Building

BUILDING | Stunning wrought-iron railings, ornate plaster moldings, pink marble staircases, a birdcage elevator, and a sky-lighted atrium that rises almost 50 feet—it's easy to see why the Bradbury Building leaves visitors awestruck. Designed in 1893 by a novice architect who drew his inspiration from a science-fiction story and a conversation with his dead brother via Ouija board, the office building was originally the site of turn-of-the-20th-century sweatshops, but now it houses a variety of businesses. Scenes from *Blade Runner* and *Chinatown* were filmed here, which means there's often a barrage of tourists snapping photos. Visits are limited to the lobby and the first-floor landing. ■TIP→ **Historic Downtown walking tours hosted by the L.A. Conservancy cost $15 and include the Bradbury Building.** ✉ *304 S. Broadway, Downtown* ☎ *213/626–1893* ⊕ *www.laconservancy.org/locations/bradbury-building* Ⓜ *Pershing Square Station.*

★ The Broad Museum

MUSEUM | The talk of Los Angeles's art world when it opened in 2015, this museum in an intriguing, honeycomb-looking building was created by philanthropists Eli and Edythe Broad (rhymes with "road") to showcase their stunning private collection of contemporary art, amassed over five decades and still growing. With upward of 2,000 pieces by more than 200 artists, the collection has in-depth representations of the work of such prominent names as Jean Michel Basquiat, Jeff Koons, Ed Ruscha, Cindy Sherman, Cy Twombly, Kara Walker, and Christopher Wool. The "veil and vault" design of the main building integrates gallery space and storage space (visitors can glimpse the latter through a window in the stairwell): the veil refers to the fiberglass, concrete, and steel exterior; the vault is the concrete base. Temporary exhibits and works from the permanent collection are arranged in the small first-floor rooms and in the more expansive third floor of the museum, so you can explore everything in a few hours. Next door to the Broad is a small plaza with olive trees and seating, as well as the museum restaurant, Otium. Admission to the museum is free, but book timed tickets in advance to guarantee entry. ✉ *221 S. Grand Ave., Downtown* ☎ *213/232–6200* ⊕ *www.thebroad.org* ✆ *Free* ☾ *Closed Mon.*

California African American Museum

MUSEUM | With more than 4,500 historical artifacts, this museum showcases contemporary art of the African diaspora. Artists represented here include Betye Saar, Charles Haywood, and June Edmonds.

The museum has a research library with more than 6,000 books available for public use. ■TIP→ **If possible, visit on a Sunday, when there's almost always a diverse lineup of speakers and performances.** ✉ *600 State Dr., Exposition Park* ☎ *213/744–2084* ⊕ *www.caamuseum.org* ✆ *Free; parking $12* ☾ *Closed Mon.* Ⓜ *Expo/Vermont Station.*

California Science Center

MUSEUM | FAMILY | You're bound to see excited kids running up to the dozens of interactive exhibits here that illustrate the prevalence of science in everyday life. Clustered in different "worlds," the center keeps young guests busy for hours. They can design their own buildings and learn how to make them earthquake-proof; watch Tess, the dramatic 50-foot animatronic star of the exhibit *Body Works,* demonstrate how the body's organs work together; and ride a bike across a trapeze wire three stories high in the air. One of the exhibits in the Air and Space section shows how astronauts Pete Conrad and Dick Gordon made it to outer space in the Gemini 11 capsule in 1966; also here is NASA's massive space shuttle *Endeavor,* located in the Samuel Oschin Pavilion, for which a timed ticket is needed to visit. The IMAX theater screens science-related large-format films. ✉ *700 Exposition Park Dr., Exposition Park* ☎ *323/724–3623* ⊕ *www.californiasciencecenter.org* ✆ *Permanent exhibits free; fees for some attractions, special exhibits, and IMAX screenings vary.*

Cathedral of Our Lady of the Angels

RELIGIOUS SITE | A half block from Frank Gehry's curvaceous Walt Disney Concert Hall sits the austere Cathedral of Our Lady of the Angels—a spiritual draw as well as an architectural attraction. Controversy surrounded Spanish architect José Rafael Moneo's unconventional design for the seat of the Archdiocese of Los Angeles. But judging from the swarms of visitors and the standing-room-only holiday masses, the church has carved out a niche for itself in Downtown L.A.

The plaza in front is glaringly bright on sunny days, though a children's play garden with bronze animals mitigates the starkness somewhat. Head underground to wander the mausoleum's mazelike white-marble corridors. Free guided tours start at the entrance fountain at 1 pm on weekdays. ■TIP→ **There's plenty of underground visitors parking; the vehicle entrance is on Hill Street.** ✉ *555 W. Temple St., Downtown* ☎ *213/680–5200* ⊕ *www. olacathedral.org* ✆ *Free* Ⓜ *Civic Center/ Grand Park.*

The Cecil Hotel

BUILDING | This was once a hotel, but you should absolutely not stay here. But fans of the macabre will find lots to love when they learn about the history of Downtown L.A.'s most notorious lodging. Originally built in 1924, the hotel was once home to multiple serial killers, including the Night Stalker, and the spot of many unsolved murders. The most recent occurred only a few years ago when they found the remains of a tourist inside the hotel's water tower. ✉ *640 S. Main St., Downtown.*

Chinatown

NEIGHBORHOOD | Smaller than San Francisco's Chinatown, this neighborhood near Union Station still represents a slice of East Asian life. Sidewalks are usually jammed with tourists, locals, and residents hustling from shop to shop picking up goods, spices, and trinkets from small shops and miniplazas that line the street. Although some longtime establishments have closed in recent years, the area still pulses with its founding culture. During Chinese New Year, giant dragons snake down the street. And, of course, there are the many restaurants and quick-bite cafés specializing in Chinese feasts. In recent years, a slew of hip eateries like Howlin' Ray's and Majordomo have injected the area with vibrancy.

An influx of local artists has added a spark to the neighborhood by taking up empty spaces and opening galleries along Chung King Road, a faded pedestrian passage behind the West Plaza shopping center between Hill and Yale. Also look for galleries along a little side street called Gin Ling Way on the east side of Broadway. Chinatown has its main action on North Broadway. There are several garages available for parking here that range from $5 to $10 per day. ✉ *Bordered by the 110, 101, and 5 freeways, Downtown* ⊕ *chinatownla.com* Ⓜ *Union Station.*

Chinese American Museum

MUSEUM | Because it's in El Pueblo Plaza, you might assume that this museum features Mexican American art. It's actually the last surviving structure of L.A.'s original Chinatown. Three floors of exhibits reveal the different cultures that have called this area home, as well as how the original residents paved the way for what is now a vibrant and varied Chinatown. Rotating exhibits feature the work of Chinese American artists. ✉ *425 N. Los Angeles St., Downtown* ☎ *213/485–8567* ⊕ *www.camla.org* ✆ *$3* ⊘ *Closed Mon.* Ⓜ *Union Station.*

City Hall of Los Angeles

GOVERNMENT BUILDING | This gorgeous 1928 landmark building is a TV star—it was in the opening scenes of *Dragnet* and served as the Daily Planet building in the original *Adventures of Superman.* During extensive renovations, the original Lindburg Beacon was put back in action atop the hall's 13-story tower. The revolving spotlight, inaugurated by President Calvin Coolidge from the White House via a telegraph key, was used from 1928 to 1941 to guide pilots into the Los Angeles airport. The observation deck, located on the 27th floor, is free to the public and has a stellar view of the greater Los Angeles area. ✉ *200 N. Spring St., Downtown* ☎ *213/485–2121* ⊕ *www.lacity.*

org ⊗ Closed weekends Ⓜ *Civic Center/ Grand Park.*

El Pueblo de Los Angeles

NEIGHBORHOOD | The oldest section of the city, known as El Pueblo de Los Angeles, represents the rich Mexican heritage of L.A. It had a close shave with disintegration in the early 20th century, but key buildings were preserved, and eventually **Olvera Street,** the district's heart, was transformed into a Mexican American marketplace. Today vendors still sell puppets, leather goods, sandals, and woolen shawls from stalls lining the narrow street. You can find everything from salt and pepper shakers shaped like donkeys to gorgeous glassware and pottery.

At the beginning of Olvera Street is the Plaza, a Mexican-style park with plenty of benches and walkways shaded by a huge Moreton Bay fig tree. On weekends, mariachi bands and folkloric dance groups perform. Nearby places worth investigating include the historic Avila Adobe, the Chinese American Museum, the Plaza Firehouse Museum, and the America Tropical Interpretive Center. Exhibits at the Italian American Museum of Los Angeles chronicle the area's formerly heavy Italian presence. ⊠ *Avila Adobe/Olvera Street Visitors Center, 125 Paseo De La Plaza, Downtown* ☎ *213/628–1274* ⊕ *www.elpueblo.lacity. org* ✉ *Free for Olvera St. and guided tours; fees at some museums.*

Exposition Park

CITY PARK | Originally developed in 1872 as an agricultural park, this 160-acre park has a lovely sunken rose garden and three museums—the California African American Museum, the California Science Center, and the Natural History Museum of Los Angeles County—as well as an IMAX theater. There's also Los Angeles Memorial Coliseum where Olympic festivities were held in 1932 and 1984 and where USC games are now played. The newest addition to the park is the Banc of California Stadium,

a 22,000-seat arena that's home to the LAFC soccer club. Good news for commuters: The Metro Expo Line, which connects the Westside to Downtown Los Angeles, has a stop at Exposition Park. ⚠ **Note that the park and neighborhood are sketchy at night.** ⊠ *700 Exposition Park Dr., Exposition Park* ☎ *213/744–2098* ⊕ *expositionpark.ca.gov* Ⓜ *Expo/Vermont Station.*

Geffen Contemporary at MOCA

MUSEUM | The Geffen Contemporary is one of architect Frank Gehry's boldest creations. The largest of the three MOCA branches, with 40,000 square feet of exhibition space, it was once used as a police car warehouse. Works from the museum's permanent collection on display here include the artists Willem de Kooning, Franz Kline, Jackson Pollock, Mark Rothko, and Cindy Sherman. ∎TIP➡ Present your TAP metro card to get two-for-one admission ⊠ *152 N. Central Ave., Downtown* ☎ *213/626–6222* ⊕ *www.moca.org/exhibitions* ✉ *$12; free Thurs. 5–8 and weekends through Mar. 25* ⊗ *Closed Tues.*

GRAMMY Museum

MUSEUM | The GRAMMY Museum brings the music industry to life. Throughout four floors and 30,000 square feet of space, the museum showcases rare footage of GRAMMY performances, plus rotating and interactive exhibits on award-winning musicians and the history of music. A 200-seat theater is great for live events that include screenings, lectures, interviews, and intimate music performances. ⊠ *800 W. Olympic Blvd., Downtown* ☎ *213/765–6800* ⊕ *www. grammymuseum.org* ✉ *$15* ⊗ *Closed Tues.*

★ Grand Central Market

MARKET | Handmade white-corn tamales, warm olive bread, dried figs, Mexican fruit drinks. Hungry yet? This mouthwatering gathering place is the city's largest and most active food market. Treated to a makeover in 2013, Grand Central Market is now the home to various artisanal food vendors. The spot bustles nonstop with locals and visitors surveying the butcher shop's display of everything from lambs' heads to pigs' tails. Produce stalls are piled high with locally grown avocados and heirloom tomatoes. Stop by **Chiles Secos** at stall C-12 for a remarkable selection of rare chilies and spices; **Ramen Hood** at C-2, for sumptuous vegan noodles and broth; or **Sticky Rice** at stall C-5, for fantastic Thai-style chicken. Even if you don't plan on buying anything, it's a great place to browse and people-watch. ⊠ *317 S. Broadway, Downtown* ☎ *213/624–2378* ⊕ *www.grandcentralmarket.com* 🖃 *Free.*

Italian Hall Building

HISTORIC SITE | This landmark, constructed in 1908, is noteworthy because its south wall bears an infamous mural. Famed Mexican muralist David Alfaro Siqueiros shocked his patrons in the 1930s by depicting an oppressed worker of Latin America being crucified on a cross topped by a menacing American eagle. The anti-imperialist mural was promptly whitewashed but was later restored by the Getty Museum. It can be seen on the Italian Hall building today. Today the site functions as a museum and has seven color-coded exhibits on the history of Italian Americans. ⊠ *644 N. Main St., Downtown* ☎ *213/485–8432* ⊕ *iamla. org* 🕙 *Museum closed Mon.* Ⓜ *Union Station.*

Japanese American Cultural and Community Center

CITY PARK | Plenty of traditional and contemporary cultural events make this center well worth the trip. Founded in 1980, JACCC is home to a number of civic and arts organizations. Through the center's basement you reach the James Irvine Garden, a serene sunken space where local plants mix with bamboo, Japanese wisteria, and Japanese maples. The main floor of the museum houses the George J. Doizaki Gallery, which has

2,000 square feet of exhibition space and has housed everything from national treasures of Japan to the Bugaku costumes from the Kasuga Grand Shrine in Nara. An 880-seat theater is known for any number of performing arts shows including Bunraku Puppet Theater and the Grand Kabuki of Japan. ⊠ *244 S. San Pedro St., Downtown* ☎ *213/628–2725* ⊕ *www.jaccc.org* 🕙 *Doizaki Gallery closed Mon. and Tues.; Japanese garden closed Mon.* Ⓜ *Pershing Square.*

Japanese American National Museum

MUSEUM | What was it like to grow up on a sugar plantation in Hawaii? How difficult was life for Japanese Americans interned in concentration camps during World War II? These questions are addressed by changing exhibitions at this museum in Little Tokyo that also include fun tributes to anime and Hello Kitty. Volunteer docents are on hand to share their own stories and experiences. The museum occupies its original site in a renovated 1925 Buddhist temple and an 85,000-square-foot adjacent pavilion. ■**TIP**➔ Take the Metro and get $2 off general admission and a 10% discount at adjoining Chado Tea Room. ⊠ *100 N. Central Ave., off E. 1st St., Downtown* ☎ *213/625–0414* ⊕ *www.janm.org* 🖃 *$12; free Thurs. 5–8* 🕙 *Closed Mon.*

L.A. Live

ARTS VENUE | The mammoth L.A. Live entertainment complex was opened in 2007 when there was little to do or see in this section of Downtown. Since its inception, this once creepy ghost town has become a major hub for sports, concerts, award shows, and more. The first things you'll notice as you emerge from the parking lot are the giant LED screens and sparkling lights, and the buzz of crowds as they head out to dinner before or after a Lakers game, movie, or live show at the Microsoft Theater. There are dozens of restaurants and eateries here, including Los Angeles favorite Katsuya, the spot for sizzling Kobe beef platters

Olvera Street, at the heart of the city's oldest neighborhood, is the place to experience many aspects of L.A.'s Mexican American culture.

and excellent sushi (the crab rolls are not to be missed). ■TIP→ **Park for free on weekdays from 11 am to 2 pm if you eat at one of the dozen or so restaurants here.** ⊠ *800 W. Olympic Blvd., Downtown* ☎ *213/763–5483* ⊕ *www.lalive.com.*

Little Tokyo

NEIGHBORHOOD | One of three official Japantowns in the country—all of which are in California—Little Tokyo is blossoming again thanks to the next generation of Japanese Americans setting up small businesses. Besides dozens of sushi bars, tempura restaurants, and karaoke bars, there's a lovely garden at the Japanese American Cultural and Community Center and a renovated 1925 Buddhist temple with an ornate entrance at the Japanese American National Museum.

On 1st Street you'll find a strip of buildings from the early 1900s. Look down when you get near San Pedro Street to see the art installation called *Omoide no Shotokyo* ("Remembering Old Little Tokyo"). Embedded in the sidewalk are brass inscriptions naming the original businesses, quoted reminiscences from residents, and steel timelines of Japanese American history up to World War II. Nisei Week (a *nisei* is a second-generation Japanese American) is celebrated every August with traditional drums, dancing, a carnival, and a huge parade. ■TIP→ **Docent-led walking tours are available the last Saturday of every month starting at 10:15 am. The cost is $15 and includes entry to the Japanese American National Museum.** ⊠ *Bounded by 1st and 3rd Sts., the 101 and 110 freeways, and LA River, Downtown* ⊕ *www.visitlittletokyo.com* Ⓜ *Civic Center/Grand Park Station.*

Los Angeles Theatre

ARTS VENUE | Built in 1931, the 2,200-seat Los Angeles Theatre opened with the premiere of Charlie Chaplin's classic *City Lights.* Full of glorious French Baroque–inspired details, the six-story lobby is awe-inspiring with its dramatic staircase, enormous fountain, grandiose chandeliers, and ornate gold detailing. You can occasionally witness the old Hollywood glamour by catching a special movie

L.A.'s Chinatown has its share of Chinese restaurants, shops, and cultural institutions, but you'll also find a growing community of artists and galleries.

screening. ✉ *615 S. Broadway, Downtown* ☎ *213/629–2939* ⊕ *www.losangelestheatre.com.*

Million Dollar Theater

ARTS VENUE | The Million Dollar Theater opened in 1918 as part of Sid Grauman's famed chain of movie theaters. This Spanish Baroque–style venue had the special feature of having its own organ. Film stars such as Gloria Swanson, Rudolph Valentino, and a young Judy Garland frequently made appearances. In the '40s, the venue swung with jazz and big band performers including Billie Holiday. The theater is open for special events and is worth a stop if you're walking past to inspect the lavish exterior with entertainment figures carved into the molding. ✉ *307 S. Broadway, Downtown* ☎ *213/617–3600* ⊕ *www.milliondollar.la.*

MOCA Grand Avenue

MUSEUM | The main branch of the Museum of Contemporary Art, designed by Arata Isozaki, contains underground galleries and presents elegant exhibitions. A huge Nancy Rubins sculpture fashioned from used airplane parts graces the museum's front plaza. The museum gift shop offers apothecary items, modernist ceramics, and even toys and games for children to appease any art lover. ◼ **TIP→ Take advantage of the free audio tour.** ✉ *250 S. Grand Ave., Downtown* ☎ *213/626–6222* ⊕ *www.moca.org* 💲 *$15; free Thurs. 5–8* 🕑 *Closed Tues.*

Natural History Museum of Los Angeles County

MUSEUM | **FAMILY** | The hot ticket at this beaux arts–style museum completed in 1913 is the Dinosaur Hall, whose more than 300 fossils include adult, juvenile, and baby skeletons of the fearsome *Tyrannosaurus rex*. The Discovery Center lets kids and curious grown-ups touch real animal pelts, and the Insect Zoo gets everyone up close and personal with the white-eyed assassin bug and other creepy crawlers. A massive hall displays dioramas of animals in their natural habitats. Also look for pre-Columbian artifacts and crafts from the South Pacific, or priceless stones in the

The Artful Los Angeles Metro

Long ago, Los Angeles had an enviable public transportation system known as the Pacific Electric Red Cars, trolleys that made it possible to get around this sprawling city without an automobile. In the mid-1900s, the last of the Red Cars disappeared, and L.A. lost itself in the car culture.

That culture is here to stay, but in recent years, a new rail system has emerged. You can now take the subway through parts of Downtown, Hollywood, Pasadena, and North Hollywood. The Red Line starts at Downtown's Union Station, then curves northwest to Hollywood and on to Universal City and North Hollywood. The Blue and Green light rail lines are designed for commuters. The Gold Line goes from Union Station up to Azusa, stopping in Pasadena. Take the Expo Line from Downtown to Santa Monica, or the Purple Line from Union Station to Koreatown.

When convenient, taking the Metro can save you time and money. If you're worried about being caught in the subway during an earthquake, keep in mind that stations and tunnels were built with reinforced steel and were engineered to withstand a magnitude 8 earthquake.

The Metro Rail stations are worth exploring themselves, and you can sign up for a free docent-led **MTA Art**

Moves tour (☎ 213/922–2738 ⊕ www. metro.net/about/art), which departs from the entrances to the Hollywood & Highland and Union stations. You'll receive a free day pass to ride the rails as you visit the colorful murals, sculptures, and architectural elements that illustrate themes of Los Angeles history.

The Universal City station is next to the site of the Campo de Caheunga, where Mexico relinquished control of California to the United States in 1847. The station features a timeline of the area's past done in the traditional style of colorful Mexican folk art.

The North Hollywood station also celebrates local history, including native Gabrielino culture, many immigrant communities, Amelia Earhart (a local), Western wear designer Nudie, and the history of transportation in L.A. County.

There are film reels on the ceiling of the Hollywood and Vine station as well as original Paramount Pictures film projectors from the 1930s, and floor paving modeled after the yellow brick road from *The Wizard of Oz*. Imposing, glass-clad columns juxtaposed with rock formations can be seen at the Vermont and Beverly station. The old Red Car trolley makes an appearance in the Hollywood and Western station.

Gem and Mineral Hall. Outdoors, the 3½-acre Nature Gardens shelter native plant and insect species and contain an expansive edible garden. ■TIP➔ Don't miss out on the Dino lab, where you can watch paleontologists unearth and clean real fossils. ⊠ 900 W. Exposition Blvd.,

Exposition Park ☎ 213/763–3466 ⊕ www. nhm.org ⊠ $15.

Orpheum Theatre
ARTS VENUE | Opened in 1926, the opulent Orpheum Theatre played host to live attractions including classic comedians, burlesque dancers, jazz greats like Lena Horne, Ella Fitzgerald, and

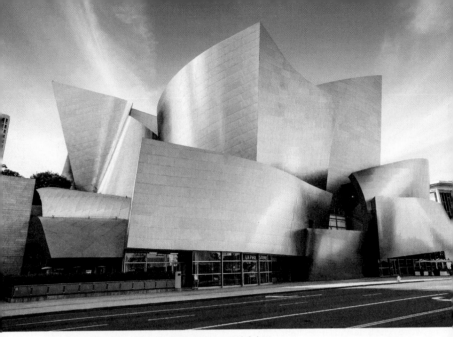

Frank Gehry's Walt Disney Concert Hall was an instant L.A. icon.

Duke Ellington, and later on rock-and-roll performers such as Little Richard. After extensive restorations, the Orpheum once again revealed a stunning white-marble lobby, majestic auditorium with fleur-de-lis panels, and two dazzling chandeliers. A thick red velvet and gold-trimmed curtain opens at showtime, and a white Wurlitzer pipe organ (one of the last remaining organs of its kind from the silent movie era) is at the ready. The original 1926 rooftop neon sign again shines brightly, signaling a new era for this theater. Today the theater plays host to live concerts, comedy shows, and movie screenings. ⌧ *842 S. Broadway, Downtown* ☎ *877/677–4386* ⊕ *www. laorpheum.com.*

Pershing Square

PLAZA | FAMILY | The city's cultures come together in one of its oldest parks, named in honor of World War I general John J. Pershing. Opened in 1866, the park was renovated in the 1990s by architect Ricardo Legorreta and landscape architect Laurie Olin with faded

pastel-color walls, fountains, and towers. However, most Downtown residents and architecture lovers are not fans of the design and have long lobbied for a makeover, which is perennially rumored to be unveiled. From mid-November to mid-January, an outdoor ice skating rink attracts ice skaters and families. ■ **TIP**→ Every Wednesday 10–2 is the Pershing Square Farmers' Market. ⌧ *Bordered by 5th, 6th, Hill, and Olive Sts., Downtown* ☎ *213/847–4970* ⊕ *www.laparks.org/ pershingsquare* ⌧ *Free.*

Richard J. Riordan Central Library

LIBRARY | The nation's third-largest public library, the handsome Richard J. Riordan Central Library was designed in 1926 by Bertram Goodhue. Restored to their pristine condition, a pyramid tower and a torch symbolizing the "light of learning" crown the building. The Cook rotunda on the second floor features murals by Dean Cornwell depicting the history of California, and the Tom Bradley Wing, named for another mayor, has a soaring eight-story atrium.

The library offers frequent special exhibits, plus a small café where you can refuel. Don't ignore the gift shop, which is loaded with unique items for readers and writers. Free docent walking tours are offered Monday through Friday at 12:30, Saturday at 11 and 2, and Sunday at 2. An Art-in-the-Garden tour is on Saturdays at 12:30 pm. A self-guided tour map is also available on the library's website. ⊠ 630 W. 5th St., Downtown ☎ 213/228–7000 ⊕ www.lapl.org ⊠ Free.

Staples Center

ARTS VENUE | Home to the Lakers, the Clippers, the Sparks, and the ice hockey team the Los Angeles Kings, the Staples Center is Downtown's top sports destination. It's also the preferred venue for superstars like Bruce Springsteen, Ariana Grande, and Justin Timberlake. Though not open for visits except during events, the saucer-shaped building is eye-catching. ⊠ 1111 S. Figueroa St., Downtown ☎ 213/742–7100 ⊕ www.staplescenter.com.

Union Station

HISTORIC SITE | Even if you don't plan on traveling by train anywhere, head here to soak up the ambience of a great rail station. Envisioned by John and Donald Parkinson, the architects who also designed the grand City Hall, the 1939 masterpiece combines Spanish Colonial Revival and art deco elements that have retained their classic warmth and quality. The waiting hall's commanding scale and enormous chandeliers have provided the backdrop for countless scenes in films, TV shows, and music videos. Recently added to the majesty are the Imperial Western Beer Company and the Streamliner, two bars that pay homage to the station's original architecture while serving homemade brews and inventive classic cocktails. ■TIP➔ **Walking tours of Union Station are on Saturday at 10 and cost $15.** ⊠ 800 N. Alameda St., Downtown ⊕ www.unionstationla.com.

★ **Walt Disney Concert Hall**

CONCERTS | One of the architectural wonders of Los Angeles, the 2,265-seat hall is a sculptural monument of gleaming, curved steel designed by Frank Gehry. It's part of a complex that includes a public park, gardens, shops, and two outdoor amphitheaters, one of them atop the concert hall. The acoustically superlative venue is the home of the city's premier orchestra, the Los Angeles Philharmonic, whose music director, Gustavo Dudamel, is an international celebrity in his own right. The orchestra's season runs from late September to early June, before it heads to the Hollywood Bowl for the summer. Attached to the hall is Patina, an exquisite fine-dining French restaurant that's the perfect date-night spot for predinner shows. ■TIP➔ **Free 60-minute guided tours are offered on most days, and there are self-guided audio tours.** ⊠ 111 S. Grand Ave., Downtown ☎ 323/850–2000 ⊕ www.laphil.org ⊠ Tours free.

🍴 Restaurants

The Eastside is home to L.A.'s Arts District, Financial District, Chinatown, Little Tokyo, the Theater District, and everything in between. The neighborhood, still dodgy in places, has experienced a culinary renaissance that has rippled through the area, making it a popular dining destination where people come in search of edgy and creative menus that celebrate its eclectic nature. Here you'll find plenty of cozy wine bars, quaint bistros, historical landmarks, ethnic eats, and upscale restaurants that lack pretension.

★ **Bavel**

$$$ | **MIDDLE EASTERN** | Fans of Bestia have been lining up for stellar Mediterranean cuisine at this Arts District hot spot, which is owned by the same restaurateurs. Rose gold stools give way to marble tabletops as the open kitchen bangs out hummus and baba ghanoush spreads, along with flatbreads and lamb

Did You Know?

Fred Harvey opened the last of his historic Harvey House restaurants next to Union Station. Designed by architect Mary Colter, the stunning Navajo-influenced 1930s space appears in films like *The Way We Were* and can be seen during Union Station walking tours.

neck shawarma. **Known for:** Mediterranean cuisine; sceney atmosphere; great vibe. $ *Average main: $40* ✉ *500 Mateo St., Downtown* ☎ *213/232–4966* ⊕ *baveldtla.com.*

Bestia

$$$ | **ITALIAN** | One of the most exciting and popular Italian restaurants in L.A. is housed inside a converted warehouse in the Arts District Downtown. Thirty-somethings flock to this hot spot with an ever-bustling bar and patio. **Known for:** Alla'nduja pizza; being a date spot; upscale modern decor. $ *Average main: $35* ✉ *2121 E. 7th Pl., Downtown* ☎ *213/514–5724* ⊕ *www.bestiala.com* ⊘ *No lunch.*

Bottega Louie

$$ | **ITALIAN** | A Downtown dining staple, this lively Italian restaurant and gourmet market features open spaces, stark white walls, and majestic floor-to-ceiling windows. If the wait is too long at this no-reservations eatery, you can sip on Prosecco and nibble on pastries at the bar. **Known for:** mouthwatering chicken Parm; one-of-a-kind portobello fries. $ *Average main: $25* ✉ *700 S. Grand Ave., Downtown* ☎ *213/802–1470* ⊕ *www.bottegalouie.com.*

★ Broken Spanish

$$$ | **MEXICAN FUSION** | Prepare for a taste explosion at this modern Mexican restaurant. Every dish on the menu is packed with flavor in ways you wouldn't think are possible. **Known for:** modern Mexican; taste explosions; super-friendly staff. $ *Average main: $35* ✉ *1050 S. Flower St., Downtown* ☎ *213/749–1460* ⊕ *brokenspanish.com.*

★ Cole's French Dip

$ | **AMERICAN** | There's a fight in Los Angeles over who created the French dip sandwich. The first contender is Cole's, whose sign on the door says it's the originator of the salty, juicy, melt-in-your-mouth meats. $ *Average main: $10* ✉ *118 E. 6th St., Downtown*

☎ *213/622–4090* ⊕ *www.213hospitality.com/coles.*

The Factory Kitchen

$$$ | **ITALIAN** | The homemade pasta, kneaded from imported Italian flour, is what dreams are made of. The large Arts District spot is carved from a converted warehouse and is held up inside by towering pillars. **Known for:** focaccina calda di recco al formaggio; cannoli. $ *Average main: $32* ✉ *1300 Factory Pl., Downtown* ☎ *213/996–6000* ⊕ *www.thefactorykitchen.com* ⊘ *No lunch weekends.*

Guerrilla Tacos

$ | **MEXICAN FUSION** | What started as a food truck serving gourmet tacos has turned into a brick-and-mortar that also has an excellent (and cheap) bar. East L.A. native chef Wes Avila fires up some of the most inventive tacos in the city—sweet potato with almond chili and feta or the Baja fried cod with chipotle crema. **Known for:** gourmet tacos; cheap drinks; long lines. $ *Average main: $11* ✉ *2000 E. 7th St., Downtown* ☎ *213/375–3300* ⊕ *www.guerrillatacos.com.*

★ Howlin' Ray's

$ | **SOUTHERN** | **FAMILY** | Don't let the hour-long waits deter you—if you want the best Nashville fried chicken in L.A., Howlin' Ray's is worth the effort. Right in the middle of Chinatown, this tiny chicken joint consists of a few bar seats, a few side tables, and a kitchen that sizzles as staff yell out "yes, chef" with each incoming order. **Known for:** spicy fried chicken; classic Southern sides. $ *Average main: $15* ✉ *727 N. Broadway, Suite 128, Downtown* ☎ *213/935–8399* ⊕ *www.howlinrays.com* ⊘ *Closed Mon.*

Langer's Delicatessen-Restaurant

$ | **DELI** | **FAMILY** | This James Beard Award winner not only has the look and feel of a no-frills Jewish deli from New York, it also has the food to match. The draw here is the hand-cut pastrami: lean, peppery, robust—and with a reputation for being the best in town. **Known for:** #19; matzo

ball soup; rugelach. $ *Average main:*
$13 ✉ *704 S. Alvarado St., Downtown*
☎ *213/483–8050* ⊕ *www.langersdeli.com*
⊗ *Closed Sun. No dinner.*

★ Majordomo

$$$ | ECLECTIC | You would never just
stumble upon this out-of-the-way spot
in Chinatown, but world-famous celeb
chef David Chang likes it that way. This
is a dining destination, and it's worth the
trip. **Known for:** minimal design; chuck
short rib with raclette; rice-based drinks.
$ *Average main: $40* ✉ *1725 Naud St.,*
Downtown ☎ *323/545–4880* ⊕ *www.*
majordomo.la.

Original Pantry Cafe

$ | AMERICAN | Opened in 1924 by Dewey
Logan, this classic diner claims to have
never closed in the entirety of its run
and is currently owned by former L.A.
mayor Richard Riordan. Open 24/7, the
diner serves American food for break-
fast, lunch, and dinner, and is known for
cakes, pies, steaks, and chops. **Known for:**
long lines; being always open; amazing
breakfast. $ *Average main: $15* ✉ *877 S.*
Figueroa St., Downtown ☎ *213/972–9279*
⊕ *www.pantrycafe.com.*

Patina

$$$$ | FRENCH FUSION | If you plan on
seeing a show at the Walt Disney Music
Hall, make it a point of adding a dinner at
this fine-dining establishment next door.
Starting off, there's a 58-page bottled
water menu, including the water the
Queen drinks at Buckingham Palace;
another costs $150 and comes from
Norway. **Known for:** cheese cart; French
cuisine; preshow dates. $ *Average main:*
$120 ✉ *Walt Disney Concert Hall, 141 S.*
Grand Ave., Downtown ☎ *213/972–3331*
⊕ *www.patinagroup.com* ⊗ *Closed Mon.*
Ⓜ *Civic Center/Grand Park.*

★ Philippe the Original

$ | AMERICAN | FAMILY | First opened in
1908, Philippe's is one of L.A.'s oldest
restaurants and claims to be the origina-
tor of the French dip sandwich. While the

debate continues around the city, one
thing is certain: the dips made with beef,
pork, ham, lamb, or turkey on a freshly
baked roll stand the test of time. **Known
for:** 50¢ coffee; communal tables; post–
Dodgers game eats. $ *Average main:*
$8 ✉ *1001 N. Alameda St., Downtown*
☎ *213/628–3781* ⊕ *www.philippes.com.*

Q Sushi

$$$$ | JAPANESE | Every night is different
at this elegant *omakase* (chef-selected)
sushi joint. It all depends on what's the
freshest and what's the absolute best.
Known for: omakase; elegance; freshest
fish. $ *Average main: $200* ✉ *521 W. 7th*
St., Downtown ☎ *213/225–6285* ⊕ *www.*
qsushila.com ⊗ *Closed Sun. No lunch*
Sat.

Redbird

$$$ | ECLECTIC | L.A. native Neal Fraser's
modern American restaurant is carved
out of a former rectory with the original
ceiling beams to prove it. Once you move
into the tented and visually stunning
space, you're regaled with a long wine
list and a creative menu that reads from
left to right with small, medium, large,
and extra large dishes. **Known for:** lavish
brunch; generous happy hour; mouthwatering meat. $ *Average main: $40* ✉ *114*
E. 2nd St., Downtown ☎ *213/788–1191*
⊕ *redbird.la.*

71Above

$$$ | ECLECTIC | As its name suggests,
this sky-high dining den sits on the 71st
floor, 950 feet above ground level. With
that elevation come the most stunning
views of any restaurant in L.A., and
the food comes close to matching it.
Known for: sky-high views; fine dining.
$ *Average main: $39* ✉ *633 W. 5th St.,*
71st fl., Downtown ☎ *213/712–2683*
⊕ *www.71above.com* Ⓜ *Pershing Square*
Station.

Shibumi

$$ | JAPANESE | This *kappo* (cooking and
cutting) restaurant in the middle of
Downtown is offering up some of the

Diners at the Wexler's Deli counter inside Grand Central Market

most inventive raw, steamed, grilled, and fried Japanese dishes you'll ever try. Chef David Schlosser serves you personally from the 400-year-old cypress bar. **Known for:** kappo and omakase dining; actual Kobe beef. ⓢ *Average main: $25* ⊠ *815 S. Hill St., Downtown* ☎ *323/484–8915* ⊕ *www.shibumidtla.com* ⊗ *Closed Mon.*

Sushi Gen
$$ | JAPANESE | Consistently rated one of the top sushi spots in L.A., Sushi Gen continues to dole out the freshest and tastiest fish in town. Sit at the elongated bar and get to know the sushi masters while they prepare your lunch. **Known for:** chef recommendations; limited seating; great lunch specials. ⓢ *Average main: $20* ⊠ *422 E. 2nd St., Downtown* ☎ *213/617–0552* ⊕ *www. sushigen-dtla.com* ⊗ *Closed Sun. and Mon. No lunch Sat.*

🛏 Hotels

An ongoing revitalization in Downtown, anchored around the L.A. Live complex, along with a thriving, hipster vibe in Koreatown and Echo Park make these areas a great place to see Los Angeles in transition: think affordable accommodations rubbing elbows with business hotels, streets lined with coffeehouses, and edgy boutiques that can be explored on foot. If you're traveling alone, some parts of Downtown are better to drive rather than walk through after dark.

Ace Hotel Downtown Los Angeles
$$ | HOTEL | The L.A. edition of this bohemian-chic hipster haven is at once a hotel, theater, bar, and poolside lounge, housed in the gorgeous Spanish Gothic–style United Artists building in the heart of Downtown. **Pros:** lively rooftop lounge/pool area, aptly named Upstairs; gorgeous building and views; heart of Downtown. **Cons:** expensive parking rates compared to nightly rates ($36); some kinks in the service; compact rooms.

$ *Rooms from: $239* ✉ *929 S. Broadway, Downtown* ☎ *213/623–3233* ⊕ *www.acehotel.com/losangeles* ⇨ *183 rooms* ⊙ *No meals.*

★ Freehand Los Angeles

$ | HOTEL | Part hotel, part hostel, the Freehand is one of the newest hotels in Downtown Los Angeles and also one of the coolest. **Pros:** range of rooms from lofts to bunk beds; active social scene; great rooftop pool and bar. **Cons:** sketchy area at night around the hotel; free lobby Wi-Fi attracts dubious crowds at times. $ *Rooms from: $100* ✉ *416 W. 8th St., Downtown* ☎ *213/612–0021* ⊕ *freehand-hotels.com/los-angeles* ⇨ *59 shared rooms, 167 private rooms* ⊙ *No meals* Ⓜ *Pershing Square.*

Hotel Figueroa

$$ | HOTEL | After years of renovation, the Hotel Figueroa has finally made its return to the Downtown hospitality scene, and it was well worth the wait. **Pros:** a short walk to Nokia Theatre, L.A. Live, and the convention center; great poolside bar; in-room iPads and complimentary minibar snacks. **Cons:** the area can be sketchy at night; expensive parking ($45/night). $ *Rooms from: $200* ✉ *939 S. Figueroa St., Downtown* ☎ *866/734–6018* ⊕ *www.hotelfigueroa.com* ⇨ *268 rooms* ⊙ *No meals* Ⓜ *Olympic/Figueroa.*

InterContinental Los Angeles Downtown

$$ | HOTEL | First the specs: There are 889 rooms. **Pros:** best views; incredible F&B outlets; top-rate service. **Cons:** too big and impersonal; busy and tricky intersection. $ *Rooms from: $300* ✉ *900 Wilshire Blvd., Downtown* ☎ *213/688–7777* ⊕ *dtla.intercontinental.com* ⇨ *889 rooms* ⊙ *No meals* Ⓜ *7th Street/Metro Center.*

Millennium Biltmore Hotel

$$ | HOTEL | As the local headquarters of John F. Kennedy's 1960 presidential campaign and the location of some of the earliest Academy Awards ceremonies, this Downtown treasure, with its gilded 1923 beaux arts design, exudes ambience and history. **Pros:** 24-hour business center; tiled indoor pool and steam room; multimillion-dollar refurbishment in 2017. **Cons:** pricey valet parking ($45); standard rooms are compact. $ *Rooms from: $200* ✉ *506 S. Grand Ave., Downtown* ☎ *213/624–1011, 866/866–8086* ⊕ *www.millenniumhotels.com* ⇨ *683 rooms* ⊙ *No meals* Ⓜ *Pershing Square.*

The NoMad Hotel

$$ | HOTEL | This stunningly refurbished property used to house the Bank of Italy and touches of the old bank can still be seen throughout—most notably in the lobby bathrooms that are cut out of the original vault. **Pros:** freestanding tubs; smart TVs in rooms; 24-hour gym. **Cons:** sketchy area at night; expensive parking ($48/night). $ *Rooms from: $250* ✉ *649 S. Olive St., Downtown* ☎ *213/358–0000* ⊕ *www.thenomadhotel.com/los-angeles* ⇨ *241 rooms* ⊙ *No meals* Ⓜ *7th Street/Metro Center.*

The Ritz-Carlton, Los Angeles

$$$ | HOTEL | This citified Ritz-Carlton on the 23rd–26th floors of a 54-story tower within Downtown's L.A. Live entertainment complex features skyline views through expansive windows, blond woods, and smartened-up amenities such as flat-screen TVs (including one hidden in the bathroom mirror). **Pros:** designer spa *Jetsons*-esque relaxation room; rooftop pool; daily buffet of five light meals. **Cons:** expensive valet parking ($45); corporate feel; pricey room service. $ *Rooms from: $400* ✉ *900 W. Olympic Blvd., Downtown* ☎ *213/743–8800* ⊕ *www.ritzcarlton.com* ⇨ *123 rooms* ⊙ *No meals.*

The Standard, Downtown L.A

$$ | HOTEL | Built in 1955 as the headquarters of Standard Oil, the building was completely revamped in 2002 under the sharp eye of owner André Balazs, to become a sleek, cutting-edge hotel with spacious guest rooms. **Pros:** 24/7 restaurant; rotating pop-up events; lively rooftop lounge. **Cons:** disruptive

Spa Specialists

Angelenos like to take their time. Here, there's a strong focus on wellness and finding ways to de-stress. Case in point, the ubiquitousness of spas in the city, where residents fit massages into their weekly routine.

When booking a massage, specify your preference for a male or female therapist. Give yourself time to arrive early and relax via steam, sauna, or Jacuzzi depending on the spa's selection. Tip at least 15% to 20%.

Bliss at the W Hollywood. Want that red-carpet glow? Bliss, tucked inside the W Hollywood Hotel, provides superhydrating triple-oxygen-treatment facials that plump and reinvigorate. ⊠ *6250 Hollywood Blvd., Hollywood* ☎ *323/798–1386* ⊕ *www.blissspa.com/locations.*

Chuan Spa at the Langham Huntington. Chinese medicine–influenced therapies at the Huntington Spa help restore balance and harmony to the body via meditative breathing rituals and acupressure. ⊠ *1401 S. Oak Knoll Ave., Pasadena* ☎ *626/585–6414.*

One Spa at Shutters on the Beach. Treatments at Santa Monica's One aim to relax the body and mind. Body treatments here, such as the Moroccan Hammam, turn skin silky soft using all-natural tonics. ⊠ *Shutters on the Beach, 1 Pico Blvd., Santa Monica* ☎ *310/587–1712* ⊕ *www.shuttersonthebeach.com/spa/one-spa.*

Shape House. Well, all the celebs are doing it. For a unique, one-of-a-kind spa treatment, sweat it out inside Shape House. Here you're wrapped in a hot cocoon blanket where you will literally sweat out any impurities in your body. You'll feel amazing after.

⊠ *653 N. Robertson Blvd., West Hollywood* ☎ *855/567–2346.*

Spa at the Beverly Wilshire. Rub elbows with celebs (or play out your *Pretty Woman* fantasies) at the Spa at the Beverly Wilshire with a mani-pedi, followed by an afternoon at the pool. Features include a fabulous rain shower (cascades vary from a cool mist to a brisk Atlantic storm); a mosaic-tile steam room; superstar facial treatments like hydra-facial and the Black Diamond Collection; and oh-so-decadent massages. ⊠ *9500 Wilshire Blvd., Beverly Hills* ☎ *310/275–5200.*

Spa at the Four Seasons, Beverly Hills. Choose your own soundtrack in the deluxe treatment rooms at this spa that concentrates on traditional body treatments in small, seasonally scented private quarters. Try the fabulous inner peace immersion body treatment that begins with a scrub and massage and ends with a Shirodhara treatment. ⊠ *300 S. Doheny Dr., Beverly Hills* ☎ *310/273–2222* ⊕ *www.fourseasons.com/losangeles/spa.*

Spa Montage. The Moroccan decor, ornate steam room, glass-walled sauna, co-ed mineral pool, and indoor Jacuzzi at this hidden Casbah of pampering will keep you relaxed for hours. ⊠ *225 N. Canon Dr., Beverly Hills* ☎ *310/860–7800.*

Waldorf Astoria Spa by La Prairie. This upscale spa in one of the city's most posh areas delivers anti-aging treatments in relaxing treatment rooms. Favorites include the caviar and the gold facials. ⊠ *Waldorf Astoria Beverly Hills, 9850 Wilshire Blvd., Beverly Hills* ☎ *310/860–6666* ⊕ *www.waldorfastoriabeverlyhills.com/spa-health.*

party scene on weekends and holidays; street noise; pricey valet parking ($44). [$] *Rooms from: $200* ✉ *550 S. Flower St., Downtown* ☎ *213/892–8080* 🌐 *www.standardhotels.com/la/properties/downtown-la* 🛏 *207 rooms* 🍴 *No meals* [M] *7th Street/Metro Center.*

Westin Bonaventure Hotel and Suites
$$ | **HOTEL** | **FAMILY** | Step inside the futuristic lobby of L.A.'s largest hotel to be greeted by fountains, an indoor lake and track, and 12 glass elevators leading up to the historic rooms of this 35-story property. Color-coded hotel floors help newcomers navigate the hotel, which takes up an entire city block. **Pros:** spa with shiatsu massage; revolving rooftop lounge; many on-site restaurants. **Cons:** massive hotel might feel too corporate; mazelike lobby and public areas. [$] *Rooms from: $250* ✉ *404 S. Figueroa St., Downtown* ☎ *213/624–1000* 🌐 *westin.marriott.com* 🛏 *1493 rooms* 🍴 *No meals.*

Nightlife

With choice music venues, upscale bars, and divier clubs, Downtown is high on the list of after-dark options.

Baldoria Bar + Kitchen
BARS/PUBS | The perfect neighborhood bar, Baldoria is a Little Tokyo haunt with a big wine list, perfect cocktails, and some of the best Neapolitan pizza in the city. Small in stature, the brick-walled joint projects Lakers games on the wall to local residents and also offers a daily happy hour with cheap food and drinks 4:30–7 pm and a late-night happy hour on Friday and Saturday 11 pm–2 am. And those pizzas? You can learn to make your own as they teach classes three Sundays a month for $30, which includes your pizza, the class, and a glass of wine or beer. ✉ *243 San Pedro St., Downtown* ☎ *213/947–3329* 🌐 *www.baldoriadtla.com.*

Blue Whale
MUSIC CLUBS | This unassuming jazz club in Little Tokyo caters to a serious crowd, bringing progressive and modern jazz to the stage. Although the venue is focused on the music (yes, you may get shushed for talking—that's how small it is), there is a kitchen and bar for snacks and drinks. The club is on the third floor of Weller Court, and the cover runs around $10 to $20. ✉ *Weller Court Plaza, 123 Astronaut E. S. Onizuka St., Suite 301, Downtown* ☎ *213/620–0908* 🌐 *www.bluewhalemusic.com.*

BonaVista Lounge at the Westin Bonaventure
BARS/PUBS | Atop the Westin Bonaventure hotel, L.A.'s best-kept secret cocktail bar revolves 34 floors above the street. With glass walls and views of Downtown, snowcapped mountains, Hollywood, and beyond (on a clear day, you can spot the ocean), there isn't bad seat in the house. Don't eat the food. Drinks are great, if slightly overpriced, but hey, you're paying for a showstopping view. ✉ *404 S. Figueroa St., Downtown* ☎ *213/624–1000* 🌐 *www.marriott.com/hotels/hotel-information/restaurant/laxbw-the-westin-bonaventure-hotel-and-suites-los-angeles* [M] *7th Street/Metro Center.*

Broadway Bar
BARS/PUBS | This watering-hole-meets-dive sits in a flourishing section of Broadway (neighbors include the swank Ace Hotel). Bartenders mix creative cocktails while DJs spin tunes nightly. The two-story space includes a smoking balcony overlooking the street. The crowd is often dressed to impress. ✉ *830 S. Broadway, Downtown* ☎ *213/614–9909* 🌐 *213hospitality.com/broadwaybar.*

Clifton's
THEMED ENTERTAINMENT | Part marketplace, part bazaar of bars, part curio museum, Clifton's is a wild, weird, and glorious establishment. Enter the ground floor and you'll find an indoor forest and a whole lot of grub. Upstairs is a

maze of bars, dance floors, and intimate corners. ✉ *648 S. Broadway, Downtown* ☎ *213/627–1673* ⊕ *www.cliftonsla.com.*

The Edison

BARS/PUBS | The glitz and glam of the Roaring '20s is alive and well in the Edison, where the decor serves as tribute to the power plant that once occupied these premises. Black-and-white silent films are projected onto the walls, and tasty nibbles and artisanal cocktails are served (in a private room, if you prefer). There's live entertainment many nights, from jazz bands to burlesque shows to magic. Closed Sunday–Tuesday. A dress code means no shorts, jerseys, hoodies, flip-flops, tennis shoes, or collarless shirts. ✉ *108 W. 2nd St., Downtown* ☎ *213/613–0000* ⊕ *www. edisondowntown.com.*

★ Golden Gopher

BARS/PUBS | Craft cocktails, beers on tap, an outdoor smoking patio, and retro video games—this bar in the heart of Downtown is not to be missed. With one of the oldest liquor licenses in Los Angeles (issued in 1905), the Golden Gopher is the only bar in Los Angeles with an on-site liquor store for to-go orders—just in case you want to buy another bottle before you head home. ✉ *417 W. 8th St., Downtown* ☎ *213/614–8001* ⊕ *213hospitality.com/project/goldengopher.*

La Cita

DANCE CLUBS | This dive bar may not look like much, but it more than makes up for it with an interesting mix of barflies, urban hipsters, and reasonable drink prices. Friday and Saturday nights, DJs mix Top 40 hits and a tiny dance floor packs in the crowd. For those more interested in drinking and socializing, head to the back patio where a TV plays local sports. Every day has a differently themed happy hour—hip-hop happy hour on Wednesday or rockabilly happy hour on Thursday. Specials vary from $3 Tecates to free pizza. ✉ *336 S. Hill St., Downtown* ☎ *213/687–7111* ⊕ *www.lacitabar.com* Ⓜ *Pershing Square Station.*

Love Song Bar

BARS/PUBS | Lovers of T. S. Eliot and vinyl will find themselves instantly at home inside this cozy establishment named after Eliot's "The Love Song of J. Alfred Prufrock." When not pouring drinks, bartenders often act as DJs, playing records (the best of the '60s through the '80s) in their entirety. As it's housed inside the Regent Theater, the cozy nature of the place can be disrupted when there's a concert scheduled. For those with an appetite, fantastic food can be ordered from the pizza parlor next door—naturally, it's called Prufrock's. ✉ *446 S. Main St., Downtown* ☎ *323/284–5661.*

Redwood Bar & Grill

BARS/PUBS | If you're looking for a place with potent drinks and a good burger, this kitschy bar fits the bill perfectly. Known today as the "pirate bar" because of its nautical decor, the place dates back to the 1940s, when it was rumored to attract mobsters, politicians, and journalists due to its proximity to City Hall, the Hall of Justice, and the original location of the *Los Angeles Times*. There's nightly music from local rock bands, though it comes with a cover charge. ✉ *316 W. 2nd St., Downtown* ☎ *213/680–2600* ⊕ *www.theredwoodbar.com.*

★ Resident

MUSIC CLUBS | Catch a lineup of indie tastemakers inside this converted industrial space, or hang outdoors in the beer garden while trying bites from on-site food truck KTCHN (on cooler evenings you can congregate around the fire pits). A wide variety of draft beers and a specially curated cocktail program are available inside at the bar or at the trailer bar outside. ✉ *428 S. Hewitt St., Downtown* ☎ *213/628–7503* ⊕ *www. residentdtla.com.*

Seven Grand

BARS/PUBS | The hunting lodge vibe makes you feel like you need a whiskey in hand—luckily, this Downtown establishment stocks more than 700 of them.

Attracting whiskey novices and connoisseurs, the bartenders here are more than willing to help you make a selection. Live jazz and blues bands play every night, so even if you're not a big drinker there's still some appeal (although you're definitely missing out). For a more intimate setting, try the on-site **Bar Jackalope,** a bar within a bar, which has a "whiskey tasting library" specializing in Japanese varieties and seats only 18. ✉ *515 W. 7th St., 2nd fl., Downtown* ☎ *213/614–0737* ⊕ *www.sevengrandbars.com* Ⓜ *7th Street/Metro Center.*

★ The Varnish

BARS/PUBS | Beeline through the dining room of Cole's to find an unassuming door that leads to this small, dimly lit bar within a bar. Wooden booths line the walls, candles flicker, and live jazz is performed Sunday through Wednesday. The bartenders take their calling to heart and shake and stir some of the finest cocktails in the city. Those who don't have a drink of choice can list their wants ("gin-based and sweet," "strong whiskey and herbaceous") and be served a custom cocktail. Be warned: patrons requiring quick drinks will want to go elsewhere—perfection takes time. ✉ *118 E. 6th St., Downtown* ☎ *213/265–7089* ⊕ *213hospitality.com/the-varnish.*

🎭 Performing Arts

Ahmanson Theatre

THEATER | The largest of L.A.'s Center Group's three theaters, the 2,100-seat Ahmanson Theatre presents larger-scale classic revivals, dramas, musicals, and comedies like *Into the Woods,* which are either going to or coming from Broadway and the West End. The ambience is a theater lover's delight. ✉ *135 N. Grand Ave., Downtown* ☎ *213/628–2772* ⊕ *www.centertheatregroup.org* Ⓜ *Civic Center/Grand Park Station.*

★ Dorothy Chandler Pavilion

CONCERTS | Though half a century old, this theater maintains the glamour of its early years, richly decorated with crystal chandeliers, classical theatrical drapes, and a 24-karat gold dome. Part of the Los Angeles Music Center, this pavilion is home to the L.A. Opera though a large portion of programming is made up of dance and ballet performances as well. Ticket holders can attend free talks that take place an hour before opera performances. ■ **TIP →** **Reservations for the talks aren't required, but it's wise to arrive early as space is limited.** ✉ *135 N. Grand Ave., Downtown* ☎ *213/972–0711* ⊕ *www.musiccenter.org or www.dorothychandlerpavilion.net.*

East West Players

THEATER | Plays at this Little Tokyo theater focus on the Asian American experience and features an Asian American cast. Its Theatre for Youth Program is a traveling production that promotes racial tolerance and understanding among students. It is also home to the David Henry Hwang Writers Institute. ✉ *120 Judge John Aiso St., Little Tokyo* ☎ *213/625–7000* ⊕ *www.eastwestplayers.org.*

Mark Taper Forum

THEATER | Both dramas and comedies dominate the stage at the Mark Taper Forum, next door to the Ahmanson Theatre in Downtown. A showcase for new and experimental plays, quite a few shows that premiered here have gone on to Broadway and off-Broadway theaters (a number of Pulitzer Prize–winning plays have also been developed here). ✉ *135 N. Grand Ave., Downtown* ☎ *213/628–2772* ⊕ *www.centertheatregroup.org* Ⓜ *Civic Center/Grand Park.*

Microsoft Theater

CONCERTS | The Microsoft Theater is host to a variety of concerts and big-name awards shows—the Emmys, American Music Awards, BET Awards, and the ESPYs. This theater and the surrounding L.A. Live complex are a draw for those

Continued on page 195

Cole's

L.A. STORY

THE CITY'S HISTORY THROUGH ITS BARS

Los Angeles is known as a place where dreams are realized, but it is also a place where pasts are forgotten. Despite what people say about L.A.'s lack of memory, however, there are quite a few noteworthy old-school bars that pay tribute to the city's vibrant past and its famous patrons.

Collectively, these eclectic watering holes have hosted everyone from ex-presidents to rock legends to famed authors and, of course, a continual stream of countless movie stars.

The bars are located in virtually every corner of the city—from Downtown to West Hollywood to Santa Monica.

In terms of character, they run the gamut from dive to dressy and serve everything from top-shelf whisky to bargain-basement beer.

While it's their differences that have kept people coming back through the decades, they all have something in common: Each has a story to tell.

EIGHT OF L.A.'S BEST

Mixing at Cole's

Chez Jay

Cole's

Frolic Room

CHEZ JAY RESTAURANT (1959)
Noteworthy for: Located down the block from the Santa Monica Pier, this steak-and-seafood joint walks the line between celebrity hangout and dive bar.
Signature drink: Martini
Celeb clientele: Members of the Rat Pack, Leonard Nimoy, Sean Penn, Julia Roberts, Renée Zellweger, Owen Wilson, Drew Barrymore
Don't miss: The little booth in the back of the restaurant, known to insiders as Table 10, is a favorite celebrity hideout.
Filmed here: *A Single Man, Goliath*
Join the crowd: *1657 Ocean Ave., Santa Monica, 310/395–1741*

COLE'S (1908)
Noteworthy for: Found inside the Pacific Electric building, touted as Los Angeles's oldest public house, and once the epicenter of the Red Car railway network, this watering hole has its original glass lighting, penny-tile floors, and 40-foot mahogany bar.
Signature drink: Oldfashioned**Celeb clientele:** The men's room boasts that Charles Bukowski and Mickey Cohen once relieved themselves here.

Don't miss: The Varnish at Cole's is an in-house speakeasy with 11 booths that can be accessed through a hidden door marked by a tiny framed picture of a cocktail glass.
Filmed here: *Forrest Gump, L.A. Confidential, Mad Men*
Join the crowd: *118 E. 6th St., Los Angeles, 213/622–4049*

CLIFTON'S REPUBLIC (1931)
Noteworthy for: This historical cafeteria/playground featuring a giant redwood tree in the center and intimidating wildlife taxidermy throughout, serves tasty comfort food and houses three lively bars: the Monarch, the Gothic, and the Pacific Seas.
Signature drink: The Mind Eraser at the Tiki bar; El Presidio at the Monarch; the Hyperion at The Gothic Bar (careful—this one's strong).
Claim to fame: Clifton's whimsical forest-themed dining area inspired Walt Disney to create Disneyland.
Don't miss: The 40's-era Tiki Bar. Located at the top of a secret stairway, it features deliciously strong drinks, dancing ciga-

Chez Jay

Harvelle's

Kibitz Room

Dresden Restaurant

rette girls and the occasional appearance of a sequined mermaid.

FROLIC ROOM (1935)
Noteworthy for: This Hollywood favorite next door to the famed Pantages Theater has served actors and writers from Elizabeth Short to Charles Bukowski.
Signature drink: Cheap Budweiser ($2.75 during happy hour)
Celeb clientele: Kiefer Sutherland
Don't miss: A bowl of popcorn from the old-fashioned machine; the Hirschfeld mural depicting Marilyn Monroe, Charlie Chaplin, Louis Armstrong, Frank Sinatra, and others.
Filmed here: *L.A. Confidential, Southland*
Join the crowd: *6245 Hollywood Blvd., Los Angeles, 323/462–5890*

HARVELLE'S (1931)
Noteworthy for: Located one block off the Third Street Promenade, this dark and sexy jazz bar is said to be the oldest live music venue on the Westside.
Signature drink: The Deadly Sins martini menu offers house made mixes named after the seven sins, from Pride to Lust.

Don't miss: The Toledo Show is a pulse-quickening weekly burlesque-and-jazz performance on Sunday nights.
Join the crowd: *1432 4th St., Santa Monica, 310/395–1676.*

THE KIBITZ ROOM AT CANTER'S DELI (1961)
Noteworthy for: Adjacent to the famous Canter's Deli, which opened in 1948, this Fairfax District nightspot is definitely a dive bar, but that doesn't keep the A-listers away. Joni Mitchell, Jakob Dylan, and Fiona Apple have all played here.
Signature drink: Cheap beer
Celeb clientele: Jim Morrison, Frank Zappa, Juliette Lewis, Julia Roberts, Javier Bardem, Penélope Cruz
Don't miss: The decor is pure retro 1960s, including vinyl booths and a fall-leaf motif on the ceiling.
Filmed here: *I Ought to Be in Pictures, Entourage, Curb Your Enthusiasm, Sunset Strip, Enemy of the State, What's Eating Gilbert Grape*
Join the crowd: *419 N. Fairfax Ave., Los Angeles, 323/651–2030.*

Canter's

In golden days

Pastrami at Canter's

La Dolce Vita

DOLCE VITA (1966)

Noteworthy for: Located in tony Beverly Hills, this staple for northern Italian has a classy clubhouse atmosphere, round leather booths, white tablecloths, and exposed-brick walls.

Signature drink: Martini

Celeb clientele: Members of the Rat Pack; several ex-presidents, including Ronald Reagan. The place prides itself on being a safe haven from pesky paparazzi.

Don't miss: The burgundy-hued round leather booths.

Join the crowd: *9785 Santa Monica Blvd., Los Angeles, 310/278–1845*

MUSSO & FRANK GRILL (1919)

Noteworthy for: This swanky old-timer is called the oldest bar in Hollywood. While that title may spark jealousy among some of its Tinseltown counterparts, there is no doubt that this famed grill conjures Hollywood's halcyon days with its authentic '30s-era decor—and serves a mean martini.

Signature drink: The Mean Martini

Celeb clientele: Charlie Chaplin, Greta Garbo, Ernest Hemingway, F. Scott Fitzgerald, Marilyn Monroe

Don't miss: The red tuxedo-clad waiters are famous in their own right; some have been at the restaurant for more than 40 years.

Filmed here: *Ocean's Eleven, Charlie's Angels 2, Mad Men*

Join the crowd: *6667 Hollywood Blvd., Los Angeles, 323/467–7788*

THE OLDEST RESTAURANT IN HOLLYWOOD Since 1919

looking for a fun night out. The building's emphasis on acoustics and versatile seating arrangements means that all 7,100 seats are good, whether you're at an intimate Neil Young concert or the People's Choice Awards. Outside, the L.A. Live complex hosts restaurants and attractions, including the GRAMMY Museum, to keep patrons entertained before and after shows (though it's open whether or not there's a performance). ⊠ 777 Chick Hearn Ct., Downtown ☎ 213/763–6030 ⊕ www.microsofttheater.com.

The REDCAT (Roy and Edna Disney/Cal Arts Theater)

DANCE | Located inside the Walt Disney Concert Hall, this 288-seat theater serves as a space for innovative performance and visual art in addition to film screenings and literary events. The gallery features changing art installations. Tickets are reasonably priced at $25 and under for most events. ⊠ 631 W. 2nd St., Downtown ☎ 213/237–2800 ⊕ www. redcat.org.

Shrine Auditorium

CONCERTS | Since opening in 1926, the auditorium has hosted nearly every major awards show at one point or another, including the Emmys and the GRAMMYs. Today, the venue and adjacent Expo Hall hosts concerts, film premieres, award shows, pageants, and special events. The Shrine's Moorish Revival–style architecture is a spectacle all its own. ⊠ 665 W. Jefferson Blvd., Downtown ☎ 213/748–5116 ⊕ www.shrineauditorium.com.

🏛 Shopping

Downtown L.A. is dotted with ethnic neighborhoods (Olvera Street, Chinatown, Koreatown, Little Tokyo) and several large, open-air shopping venues (the Fashion District, the Flower Market, Grand Central Market, the Toy District, and the Jewelry District).

It offers an urban bargain hunter's dream shopping experience if you know precisely what you're looking for (like diamonds and gems from the Jewelry District) or if you're willing to be tempted by unexpected finds (piñatas from Olvera Street, slippers from Chinatown, or lacquered chopsticks from Little Tokyo).

Alchemy Works

CLOTHING | This beautifully curated shop specializes in goods by local brands including hats by Janessa Leone, jewelry by Gabriela Artigas, and bags by Clare V., much of which is decidedly contemporary and minimal. There's also an in-store Warby Parker Glass House, where shoppers can try on different styles by the affordable eyewear brand. Besides wearables, Alchemy Works also offers housewares, apothecary items, books and magazines, and more must-haves for modern design lovers. ⊠ 826 E. 3rd St., Downtown ☎ 323/487–1497 ⊕ www. alchemyworks.us.

Hammer and Spear

HOUSEHOLD ITEMS/FURNITURE | This brilliantly decorated shop also acts as a showroom for the owners' interior design business. With dim, moody lighting, luxurious objets d'art (marble bookends, handmade stoneware vessels, and sculptures), and a seamless mix of modern and vintage furniture and textiles, the space is an interior-design junkie's fantasy realized. ⊠ 255 S. Santa Fe Ave., Suite 100, Downtown ☎ 213/928–0997 ⊕ www.hammerandspear.com.

★ The Last Bookstore

BOOKS/STATIONERY | California's largest used and new book and record shop is a favorite for both book lovers and fans of a good photo op, thanks to elements like an archway created from curving towers of books, a peephole carved into the stacks, and an in-store vault devoted to horror texts. Aside from the awesome aesthetics, shoppers will love to get lost in the store's collection of affordable books, art, and music. ⊠ 453

S. Spring St., ground fl., Downtown ☎ 213/488–0599 ⊕ www.lastbookstorela. com Ⓜ Pershing Square Station.

Shopping Streets and Districts

Fashion District

SHOPPING NEIGHBORHOODS | With the influx of emerging designers in this pocket of Downtown, it's become much more than just a wholesale market. Besides containing the plant paradise that is the Los Angeles Flower Market as well as the Fabric District and Santee Alley, the neighborhood now boasts a bevy of boutiques and cool coffee shops, thanks in part to the opening of the Row, a towering complex with curated stores, restaurants, and design space. ✉ Roughly between I–10 and 7th St., and S. Los Angeles St. and S. Central Ave., Downtown ☎ 213/741–2661 ⊕ www. fashiondistrict.org.

Jewelry District

SHOPPING NEIGHBORHOODS | Filled with bargain hunters, these crowded sidewalks resemble a slice of Manhattan with nearly 5,000 individual vendors and businesses. While you can save big on everything from wedding bands to sparkling belt buckles, the neighborhood also offers several more upscale vendors for those in search of super-special pieces. ✉ Between Olive St. and Broadway from 5th to 8th St., Downtown Ⓜ Pershing Square Station.

★ Olvera Street

OUTDOOR/FLEA/GREEN MARKETS | FAMILY | Known as the birthplace of Los Angeles, this redbrick walkway is lined with historic buildings and overhung with grapevines. At dozens of clapboard stalls you can browse south-of-the-border goods—leather sandals, woven blankets, and devotional candles—as well as cheap toys and souvenirs—and sample outstanding tacos. With the musicians and cafés providing the soundtrack, the area is constantly lively. Annual events include a tree lighting ceremony and Día de los Muertos celebrations. ✉ Between Cesar Chavez Ave. and Arcadia St., Downtown ⊕ www.olvera-street.com.

The Row

SHOPPING CENTERS/MALLS | The Row is Downton L.A.'s newest shopping, food, and cultural destination in the venerable L.A. Arts District. Spread across an entire campus, there are around 100 curated boutique stores like Poketo, Bodega, A+R, Charlotte Stone, and Tokyo Bike. Additionally, new restaurants like Rappahannock Oyster Bar and Hayato seem to be popping up weekly. A weekend highlight is Smorgasburg, where every Sunday dozens of food stalls pop up in the next-door parking lot serving tasty favorites across every cuisine imaginable. ✉ 777 Alameda St., Downtown ☎ 213/988–8890 ⊕ rowdtla.com.

Santee Alley

SHOPPING NEIGHBORHOODS | Situated in the Fashion District, Santee Alley is known for back-alley deals on knock-offs of designer sunglasses, jewelry, handbags, shoes, and clothing. Be prepared to haggle, and don't lose sight of your wallet. Weekend crowds can be overwhelming, but there's plenty of street food to keep your energy up. ✉ Santee St. and Maple Ave. from Olympic Blvd. to 12th St., Downtown ⊕ www.thesanteealley.com.

Chapter 8

PASADENA

Updated by
Paul Feinstein

👁 **Sights**
★★★☆☆

🍴 **Restaurants**
★★☆☆☆

🛏 **Hotels**
★★☆☆☆

🏷 **Shopping**
★★☆☆☆

💬 **Nightlife**
★☆☆☆☆

NEIGHBORHOOD SNAPSHOT

GREAT EXPERIENCES

Visit the Huntington Library: In addition to a collection of 18th-century British art, this library has 4 million manuscripts and 700,000 books, including the Gutenberg Bible.

Walk through the Huntington's Botanical Gardens: Set aside a couple of hours to enjoy the expansive lawns and stately trees surrounding the Huntington Library.

See American Craftsmanship at the Gamble House: The teak staircase and cabinetry are just a few of the highlights at this home, built in 1908.

Check Out the Norton Simon Museum: This small museum's fine collection features works by Renoir, Degas, Gauguin, and others.

Hang Out in Old Town Pasadena: Spend the afternoon walking around this 12-block historic town filled with cafés, restaurants, and shops.

QUICK BITES

Lincoln. An adorable café for light breakfast and lunch. They make everything in-house and that includes the pastries and signature cakes. ✉ *1992 Lincoln Ave.*

Pie 'n Burger. This small and charming diner does two things really well—pie and burgers. Most seats are counter-style, with a griddle searing up patties. Burgers are pretty simple but the pies are killer. ✉ *913 E. California Blvd.*

The Raymond 1886. Though carved out of an old cottage, head to the patio (especially for happy hour) as chefs dish out everything from microfarmed oysters and truffle polenta to seared salmon and mac and cheese. ✉ *1250 S. Fair Oaks Ave.*

GETTING HERE

■ **Driving Strategy.** To reach Pasadena from Downtown Los Angeles, drive north on the Pasadena Freeway (I–110). From Hollywood and the San Fernando Valley, use the Ventura Freeway (Highway 134, east), which cuts through Glendale, skirting the foothills, before arriving in Pasadena. There are several city parking lots located in Old Town Pasadena with low rates, all close to Colorado Boulevard, the main drag. On-street parking here is also widely available with few restrictions.

PLANNING YOUR TIME

■ The Huntington Library should command most of your time. Just be sure to keep the summer heat in mind when you visit—the gardens are more pleasant during the cooler morning hours. A stop at the beautiful Gamble House shouldn't take more than an hour, leaving plenty of time for an afternoon visit to the Norton Simon Museum, one of the area's best spots to enjoy world-class art. Unless you're planning on seeing a game or hitting the flea market, you will probably want to skip the Rose Bowl. Head to Old Pasadena in the evening, when the wide boulevards and leafy side streets come to life.

Although seemingly absorbed into the general Los Angeles sprawl, Pasadena is a separate and distinct city. It's best known for the Tournament of Roses, or more commonly, the Rose Bowl, seen around the world every New Year's Day.

But the city has sites worth seeing year-round—from gorgeous Craftsman homes to exceptional museums, particularly the Norton Simon and the Huntington Library, Art Collections, and Botanical Gardens. Note that the Huntington and the Old Mill reside in San Marino, a wealthy, 4-square-mile residential area just over the Pasadena line.

First-time visitors to L.A. only here for a short time might find it hard to get out to Pasadena. However, if you've had your fill of city life and are looking for a nearby escape that feels much farther away than it is, with open space and fresher air, it's the perfect trip.

Start at the **Botanical Gardens,** then spend the afternoon strolling around **Old Town Pasadena,** with shops and restaurants filling its 19th-century brick buildings. Art and architecture lovers shouldn't miss the city's top sight, the **Norton Simon Museum,** most noted for its excellent collection of Degas, as well as works by Rembrandt, Goya, and Picasso. The **Gamble House** is an immense three-story house and one of the country's shining examples of American Arts and Crafts bungalow architecture. The thing that might surprise you the most about visiting Pasadena is that even the drive here—on the freeway, though not during rush hour—is a scenic one. The Pasadena Freeway follows the curves of the arroyo, lined with old sycamores. It was the main road north during the early days of Los Angeles, when horses and buggies made their way through the countryside to the small town of Pasadena. In 1939 the road became the Arroyo Seco Parkway, the first freeway in Los Angeles.

◉ Sights

Castle Green
HOTEL—SIGHT | One block south of Colorado Boulevard stands the onetime social center of Pasadena's elite. This Moorish building is the only remaining section of a turn-of-the-20th-century hotel complex. Today the often-filmed tower (see *The Sting, Edward Scissorhands, The Last Samurai,* and *The Prestige*) is residential. The building is not open to the public on a daily basis, but it does organize two tours a year in June and December. ⊠ *99 S. Raymond Ave., Pasadena* ☎ *626/793–0359* ⊕ *www.castlegreen.com* 🎟 *Tours $30.*

Descanso Gardens
GARDEN | Getting its name from the Spanish word for "rest," this 160-acre oasis is a respite from city life, shaded by massive oak trees. Known for being a smaller, mellower version of the nearby Huntington, Descanso Gardens features denser foliage, quaint dirt paths, and

Pasadena and Environs

GLENDALE

Scholl Canyon
Golf Course

Linda Vista Ave.

Lincoln Ave.

Foothill Fwy.

Arroyo Blvd.

Seco St.

Brookside
Park

210

Men

Ventura Fwy.

TO BURBANK
AND THE STUDIOS
10 mi; 15 - 25 min ←

134

Annandale
Golf Course

Colorado Blvd.

Ave. 64

San Rafael Ave.

Arroyo Blvd.

Yosemite Dr.

La Loma Rd.

Lower
Arroyo
Park

Bellefonte St.

S. Pasadena Ave.

Orange Grove Blvd.

Figueroa St.

Ave. 64

Columbia St.

110 SOUTH
PASADENA
Pasadena Fwy.

York Blvd.

Ave. 54

Mission St.

KEY

1 Exploring Sights

1 Restaurants

TO DOWNTOWN,
LAX ↓

Sights ▼

1 Castle Green **F3**

2 Descanso Gardens **E1**

3 The Gamble House **E3**

4 Huntington Library
Art Collections, and
Botanical Gardens....... **I5**

5 Los Angeles County
Arboretum **J5**

6 Mission San Gabriel
Archangel **J7**

7 Norton Simon
Museum **E3**

8 The Old Mill
(El Molino Viejo)......... **H6**

9 Old Town Pasadena **E3**

10 Rose Bowl **D1**

11 Tournament House
(Wrigley Mansion)...... **E4**

Restaurants ▼

1 The Arbour Pasadena.. **G4**

2 Lincoln **E1**

3 Pie'n Burger............. **G4**

4 The Raymond 1886...... **F5**

5 Union.................... **F3**

The Desert Garden at the mesmerizing Huntington Botanical Gardens

some hilly climbs that can make for good exercise. It's the perfect place to come in search of wonderful scents—between the lilacs, the acres of roses, and the forest of California redwoods, pines, and junipers, you can enjoy all sorts of fragrances. A forest of California live oak trees makes a dramatic backdrop for thousands of camellias and azaleas and the breathtaking 5-acre International Rosarium holding 1,700 varieties of antique and modern roses. A small train ride draws families on weekends. There are also a child's train, a gift shop, and a café. ✉ 1418 Descanso Dr., La Cañada/Flintridge ☎ 818/949–4200 ⊕ www.descansogardens.org 🖃 $9; often free Tues.

The Gamble House

HOUSE | Built by Charles and Henry Greene in 1908, this American Arts and Crafts bungalow illustrates the incredible craftsmanship that went into early L.A. architecture. The term "bungalow" can be misleading, since the Gamble House is a huge three-story home. To wealthy easterners such as the Gambles (as in Procter & Gamble), this type of vacation home seemed informal compared with their mansions back home. Admirers swoon over the teak staircase and cabinetry, the Greene and Greene–designed furniture, and an Emil Lange glass door. The dark exterior has broad eaves, with sleeping porches on the second floor. An hour-long, docent-led tour of the Gamble's interior will draw your eye to the exquisite details. For those who want to see more of the Greene and Greene homes, there are guided walks around the historic Arroyo Terrace neighborhood. Advance tickets are highly recommended. ■ TIP➔ Film buffs might recognize this as Doc Brown's house from Back to the Future. ✉ 4 Westmoreland Pl., Pasadena ☎ 626/793–3334 ⊕ www.gamblehouse.org 🖃 $15 ⊗ Closed Mon.

★ Huntington Library, Art Collections, and Botanical Gardens

GARDEN | If you have time for just one stop in the Pasadena area, be sure to see this sprawling estate built for railroad tycoon Henry E. Huntington in the early 1900s. Henry and his wife, Arabella (who was also his aunt by marriage), voraciously collected rare books and manuscripts, botanical specimens, and 18th-century British art. The institution they established became one of the most extraordinary cultural complexes in the world.

The library contains more than 700,000 books and 4 million manuscripts, including one of the world's biggest history of science collections.

Don't resist being lured outside into the Botanical Gardens, which extend out from the main building. The 10-acre Desert Garden has one of the world's largest groups of mature cacti and other succulents (visit on a cool morning or late afternoon). The Shakespeare Garden, meanwhile, blooms with plants mentioned in Shakespeare's works. The Japanese Garden features an authentic ceremonial teahouse built in Kyoto in the 1960s. A waterfall flows from the teahouse to the ponds below. In the Rose Garden Tea Room, afternoon tea is served (reserve in advance). The Chinese Garden, which is among the largest outside of China, sinews around waveless pools.

The Bing Children's Garden lets tiny tots explore the ancient elements of water, fire, air, and earth. A 1¼-hour guided tour of the Botanical Gardens is led by docents at posted times, and a free brochure with a map and property highlights is available in the entrance pavilion. ⊠ 1151 Oxford Rd., San Marino 🕾 626/405–2100 ⊕ www.huntington.org 🎟 From $25; free admission 1st Thurs. of every month 🕙 Closed Tues.

Los Angeles County Arboretum

GARDEN | Wander through a recreated tropical forest, a South African landscape, or the Australian outback at this arboretum. One highlight is the tropical greenhouse, with carnivorous-looking orchids and a pond full of brilliantly colored goldfish. The house and stables of the eccentric real-estate pioneer Lucky Baldwin are well preserved and worth a visit. Kids will love the many peacocks and waterfowl that roam the property. The most recent addition is a water-harvesting farm, where tall stalks of rainbow corn and vines of passion fruit grow in abundance. ⊠ 301 N. Baldwin Ave., Arcadia 🕾 626/821–3222 ⊕ www.arboretum. org 🎟 $9.

Mission San Gabriel Archangel

MUSEUM | Established in 1771 as the fourth of 21 missions founded in California, this massive adobe complex was dedicated by Father Junípero Serra to St. Gabriel. Within the next 50 years, the San Gabriel Archangel became the wealthiest of all California missions. In 1833 the Mexican government confiscated the mission, allowing it to decline. The U.S. government returned the mission to the church in 1855, but by this time the Franciscans had departed. In 1908 the Claretian Missionaries took charge and poured much care into preserving the rich history. The cemetery here, the first in L.A. County, is said to contain approximately 6,000 Gabrieleno Indians. Tranquil grounds are lushly planted and filled with remnants of what life was like nearly two centuries ago. Public mass is held at the mission Sunday morning at 7 and 9:30, but call ahead as times are subject to change. If you're lucky, you'll hear the six bells that ring out during special services—a truly arresting experience. You can take a self-guided tour of the grounds here by purchasing a map in the gift shop. ⊠ 428 S. Mission Dr., San Gabriel 🕾 626/457–3035 ⊕ www.sangabrielmission.org 🎟 $6.

★ Norton Simon Museum

MUSEUM | As seen in the New Year's Day Tournament of Roses Parade, this low-profile brown building is one of the finest midsize museums anywhere, with a collection that spans more than 2,000 years of Western and Asian art. It all began in the 1950s when Norton Simon (Hunt-Wesson Foods, McCalls Corporation, and Canada Dry) started collecting works by Degas, Renoir, Gauguin, and Cézanne. His collection grew to include works by Old Masters and impressionists, modern works from Europe, and Indian and Southeast Asian art.

Today the Norton Simon Museum is richest in works by Rembrandt, Picasso, and, most of all, Degas.

Head down to the bottom floor to see temporary exhibits and phenomenal Southeast Asian and Indian sculptures and artifacts, where pieces like a Ban Chiang black ware vessel date back to well before 1000 BC. Don't miss a living-artwork outdoors: the garden, conceived by noted Southern California landscape designer Nancy Goslee Power. The tranquil pond was inspired by Monet's gardens at Giverny. ⊠ *411 W. Colorado Blvd., Pasadena* ☎ *626/449–6840* ⊕ *www.nortonsimon.org* ⊠ *$15; free 1st Fri. of month 5–8* ⊙ *Closed Tues.*

The Old Mill (El Molino Viejo)

BUILDING | Built in 1816 as a gristmill for the San Gabriel Mission, the mill is one of the last remaining examples in Southern California of Spanish Mission architecture. The thick adobe walls and textured ceiling rafters give the interior a sense of quiet strength. Be sure to step into the back room, now a gallery with rotating quarterly exhibits. Outside, a chipped section of the mill's exterior reveals the layers of brick, ground seashell paste, and ox blood used to hold the structure together. The surrounding gardens are reason enough to visit, with a flower-decked arbor and old sycamores and oaks. In summer the Capitol Ensemble performs in the garden. ⊠ *1120 Old Mill Rd., San Marino*

☎ *626/449–5458* ⊕ *www.old-mill.org* ⊠ *Free* ⊙ *Closed Mon.*

Old Town Pasadena

NEIGHBORHOOD | This 22-block historic district contains a vibrant mix of restored 19th-century brick buildings interspersed with contemporary architecture. Chain stores have muscled in, but there are still some homegrown shops, plenty of tempting cafés and restaurants, and a bustling beer scene. In recent years, a vibrant Asian food scene has popped up in the vicinity as well. In the evening and on weekends, the streets are packed with people. Old Town's main action takes place on Colorado Boulevard between Pasadena Avenue and Arroyo Parkway. ⊠ *Pasadena* ☎ *626/356–9725* ⊕ *www.oldpasadena.org.*

Rose Bowl

SPORTS VENUE | With an enormous rose on its exterior, this 90,000-plus-seat stadium, is home to the UCLA Bruins, the annual Rose Bowl Game on New Year's Day, and the biggest recording artists in the world. Set at the bottom of a wide arroyo in Brookside Park, the facility is closed except during games, concerts, and special events.

The Rose Bowl Flea Market is held on the grounds the second Sunday of the month, rain or shine, and features antique and vintage finds along with new items from more than 2,500 vendors. Considered one of the best and most eclectic flea markets in the country, it draws hordes of fashion devotees and everyday bargain seekers. Arrive early to beat the crowds, which tend to peak midday. Food and drink are readily available, and parking is free. Admission is $9 per person and gates open at 9 am. ⊠ *1001 Rose Bowl Dr., Pasadena* ☎ *626/577–3100* ⊕ *www.rosebowlstadium.com.*

Did You Know?

Raphael's *Madonna and Child with Book* is part of the wide-ranging collection of the Norton Simon Museum.

Tournament House (Wrigley Mansion)
HOUSE | Chewing gum magnate William Wrigley purchased this white Italian Renaissance–style house in 1914. When his wife died in 1958, Wrigley donated the house to the city of Pasadena under the stipulation that it be used as the headquarters for the Tournament of Roses. The mansion features a green tile roof and manicured rose garden with 1,500 varieties. The interior provides a glimpse of the area's over-the-top style in the early 20th century. Tours of the house are every Thursday from 2 to 3 from February to August; fans of the Rose Parade can see the various crowns and tiaras worn by former Rose Queens, plus trophies and memorabilia. ✉ *391 S. Orange Grove Blvd., Pasadena* ☎ *626/449–4100* 🌐 *www.visitpasadena.com/businesses/tournament-house* 🎟 *Free.*

🍴 Restaurants

With the revitalization of Old Town Pasadena, more people are discovering the beauty of Rose City. They mingle at bistros, upscale eateries, and taco trucks, but are also discovering the newer innovative dining spots that are giving Pasadena a hipper feel.

The Arbour Pasadena
$$$ | MODERN AMERICAN | This new farm-to-table addition to the Pasadena food scene uses all local ingredients to whip up creative cuisine in a chic environment. Upon entry you'll notice a wood-beam ceiling, brick-laden bar, and hanging Edison lights that set the stage. **Known for:** farm-to-table cuisine; local ingredients; chic atmosphere. [$] *Average main: $30* ✉ *527 S. Lake Ave., Suite 120, Pasadena* ☎ *626/396–4925* 🌐 *www.thearbourpasadena.com.*

Lincoln
$ | CAFÉ | This adorable little café should be a go-to for any and all light breakfast and lunch needs. Healthy breakfast bowls get your body moving, while pesto turkey sandwiches fill you up just right. **Known for:** light bites; great patio; strong coffee. [$] *Average main: $15* ✉ *1992 Lincoln Ave., Pasadena* ☎ *626/765–6746* 🌐 *lincolnpasadena.com.*

Pie 'n Burger
$ | DINER | Since 1963, this small and charming diner has done two things really well—pie and burgers. Most seats are counter-style, with a griddle searing up patties. **Known for:** simple burgers; enormous pie slices; retro style. [$] *Average main: $13* ✉ *913 E. California Blvd., Pasadena* ☎ *626/795–1123* 🌐 *pienburger.com.*

The Raymond 1886
$$$ | MODERN AMERICAN | The Raymond 1886 is the coolest kid on the Pasadena block. Carved out of an old cottage, the bar and restaurant has an expansive patio with long wooden tables and hanging lights. **Known for:** solid happy hour; great bar food; expansive patio. [$] *Average main: $30* ✉ *1250 S. Fair Oaks Ave., Pasadena* ☎ *626/441–3136* 🌐 *theraymond.com* 🕒 *Closed Mon.*

★ **Union**
$$$ | ITALIAN | There's a Michelin-quality Italian restaurant hiding in plain sight in Pasadena. The small and homey space is typically filled to the brim as diners await heaven-sent wild mushrooms with G&T polenta or the squid-ink *lumache* (shell pasta) with Maine lobster. **Known for:** superb wine list; great service. [$] *Average main: $31* ✉ *37 E. Union St., Pasadena* ☎ *626/795–5841* 🌐 *www.unionpasadena.com* 🕒 *No lunch.*

🎟 Performing Arts

Fremont Centre Theatre
THEATER | This theater centers on original material and world premieres with

professional actors year-round. The small venue is known for its dedication to diversity and its inclusive atmosphere, with "talkbacks" (Q&As between actors and audience members) after certain shows. Ray Bradbury regularly produced shows here for five years before his death in 2012, including a stage adaptation of *Fahrenheit 451.* ✉ *1000 Fremont Ave., South Pasadena* ☎ *626/441–5977* ⊕ *www.fremontcentretheatre.com.*

The Pasadena Playhouse
THEATER | Exceptional plays and musicals, occasionally featuring known TV and movie actors, are what this theater is mostly known for—that and it's a historical landmark that's been operating as a theater since 1925. The 650-seat playhouse also holds the title of official state theater of California. Tours of the venue are available by appointment. ✉ *39 S. El Molino Ave., Pasadena* ☎ *626/356–7529* ⊕ *www.pasadenaplayhouse.org.*

🛍 Shopping

The stretch of Colorado Boulevard between Pasadena Avenue and Arroyo Parkway, known as Old Town, is a popular pedestrian shopping destination in Pasadena, with retailers such as Crate & Barrel, H&M, and Tiffany's, which sits a block away from Forever 21. A few blocks east on Colorado, the open-air "urban village" known as Paseo Colorado mixes residential, retail, dining, and entertainment spaces along Colorado Boulevard between Los Robles and Marengo avenues. Enter on Colorado or Marengo for free parking.

Elisa B
CLOTHING | This small but well-edited shop stocks casual wear from established basics brands like Michael Stars and Citizens of Humanity alongside high-end designer finds by labels including Opening Ceremony and A.L.C. ✉ *16 E. Holly St., Pasadena* ☎ *626/397–4770* ⊕ *www. elisab.com.*

Gold Bug
GIFTS/SOUVENIRS | Antiques, animal specimens, crystals, and other unique oddities for the eccentric giftees on your list are all found inside this offbeat boutique located just around the corner from bustling Colorado Boulevard, but the main draw here is the jewelry. Funky, whimsical finds like a black beaded bracelet with a diamond-flecked snake-head clasp or a fur-and-chain-mail cuff are stocked alongside more minimal (yet still nature-inspired) pieces, all of which are created by independent designers and made of fine materials like gold or silver and semiprecious stones. ⚠ **No photos allowed inside.** ✉ *34 E. Union St., Pasadena* ☎ *626/744–9963* ⊕ *www.goldbugpasadena.com.*

Pasadena City College Flea Market
OUTDOOR/FLEA/GREEN MARKETS | For bargain hunting, head to the Pasadena City College Flea Market on the first Sunday of each month starting at 8 am. With 400+ vendors, this is a great source for antiques, records, collectibles, furniture, and clothing at prices that won't break the bank. Admission is free and parking is $2 at the adjacent structure. ✉ *1570 E. Colorado Blvd., at Hill Ave., Pasadena* ☎ *626/585–7906* ⊕ *pasadena. edu/community/flea-market.*

★ Rose Bowl Flea Market
OUTDOOR/FLEA/GREEN MARKETS | This massively popular flea market, which happens the second Sunday of each month (rain or shine), deservedly draws crowds that come for deals on goods including mid-century furniture, vintage clothing, pop culture collectibles, books, and music. Food and drink options are on hand to keep shoppers satiated, and general admission is just $9, but VIP/early-bird options are available for a little

extra dough. Bring cash to avoid an inevitable line at the ATM, and feel free to try your hand at haggling. ✉ *1001 Rose Bowl Dr., Pasadena* ☎ *323/560–7469* ⊕ *www.rgcshows.com.*

Vroman's Bookstore

BOOKS/STATIONERY | Southern California's oldest and largest independent bookseller is justly famous for its great service. A newsstand, café, and stationery store add to the appeal. A regular rotation of events including trivia night, kids' story time, author meet-and-greets, crafting sessions, discussions, and more get the community actively involved. ✉ *695 E. Colorado Blvd., Pasadena* ☎ *626/449–5320* ⊕ *www.vromansbookstore.com.*

Chapter 9

LOS FELIZ AND THE EASTSIDE

Updated By
Michelle Rae Uy

👁 Sights	🍴 Restaurants	🛏 Hotels	🛍 Shopping	🍸 Nightlife
★★★☆☆	★★★★★	★★☆☆☆	★★★★☆	★★★★★

A DAY AT GRIFFITH PARK

The 4,100-acre Griffith Park (the largest municipal park and urban wilderness area in the United States) stands out as an oasis in a city covered in cement and asphalt.

On warm weekends, there are parties, barbecues, mariachi bands, and strolling vendors selling fresh fruit. Joggers, cyclists, and walkers course its roadways. There are also top attractions within the park, including the Griffith Observatory and the Los Angeles Zoo.

The park was named after Col. Griffith J. Griffith, a mining tycoon who donated 3,000 acres of land to the city for the park in 1896. It has been used as a film and television location since the early days of motion pictures. One early Hollywood producer advised, "A tree is a tree, a rock is a rock, shoot it in Griffith Park."

GETTING HERE

The park has several entrances: off Los Feliz Boulevard at Western Canyon Avenue, Vermont Avenue, Crystal Springs Drive, and Riverside Drive; from the Ventura/134 Freeway at Victory Boulevard, Zoo Drive, or Forest Lawn Drive; from the Golden State Freeway (I–5) at Los Feliz Boulevard and Zoo Drive. The park is open from 6 am to 10 pm.

Top Experiences

Visit the Griffith Observatory. Griffith Observatory offers breathtaking panoramic views, and the structure itself, whose interior was recently renovated, is a pristinely maintained art deco spectacle. Visit during a scheduled talk or show at the Leonard Nimoy Event Horizon Theater, look through the Zeiss Telescope on a clear night, or check out the Samuel Oschin Planetarium and its incredible dome.

The expansive grounds are open to the public and include a monument dedicated to James Dean; several scenes from *Rebel Without a Cause* were filmed here (if you've never seen the film, it's a definite must-watch before visiting). To see the lights of the city twinkle at night from above, stay late and head up to the Observatory Deck, open until 10 pm every evening except Monday.

Climb Mount Hollywood. There are plenty of scenic routes throughout the park, but one of the best trails is to the top of Mount Hollywood. Park for free at the Griffith Observatory lot and pick up the trail from there. It's an easy half-hour hike to the top. On clear days you'll be able to see all the way to the Pacific Ocean and Catalina Island. About two-thirds of the way up is Dante's View, an

area with benches where you can stop for a break or snack. You'll likely cross paths with horseback riders on the way.

An up-close view of the Hollywood sign from below means hiking a little more than 6 miles round-trip from the parking lot.

Check Out the Los Angeles Zoo and Botanical Gardens. In the northeast corner of the park, the zoo's highlights include a gorilla reserve, a Sumatran tiger, a snow leopard, and an acre dedicated to one of the largest troops of chimpanzees in the United States. In addition, the zoo claims to have more flamingoes than any other zoo worldwide.

Enjoy a Bike Tour. There's a flat, family-friendly 4.7-mile path that runs along Crystal Springs Drive and Zoo Drive. Rentals are available inside the park at **Spokes n' Stuff Bike Shop** (✉ *4730 Crystal Springs Dr., at ranger station parking lot* ☎ *323/653–4099* ⊕ *www.spokes-n-stuff.com*).

See a Concert at the Greek Theatre. The 6,100-seat **Greek Theatre** (☎ *323/665–1927* ⊕ *www.greektheatrela.com*) is an outdoor venue where top artists such as Elton John and Paul Simon have performed.

SOUTH-OF-THE-BORDER FLAVOR

From Cal-Mex burritos to Mexico City–style tacos, Southern California is a top stateside destination for experiencing Mexico's myriad culinary styles.

Many Americans are surprised to learn that the Mexican menu goes far beyond Tex-Mex (or Cal-Mex) favorites like burritos, chimichangas, enchiladas, fajitas, and nachos—many of which were created or popularized stateside. Indeed, Mexico has rich, regional food styles, like the complex mole sauces of Puebla and Oaxaca, and the fresh ceviches of Veracruz, as well as the trademark snack of Mexico City: tacos.

In Southern California, tacos are an obsession, with numerous blogs and websites dedicated to the quest for the perfect taco. They're everywhere—in ramshackle taco stands, roving taco trucks, and strip-mall taquerias,. Whether you're looking for a cheap snack or lunch on the go, SoCal's taco selection can't be beat. But be forewarned: there may not be an English menu. Here we've noted unfamiliar taco terms, along with other potentially new-to-you items from the Mexican menu.

THIRST QUENCHERS

Spanish for "fresh water," *agua fresca* is made from fruit, rice, or seeds blended with sugar and water. Lemon, lime, and watermelon are common flavors. Other varieties include *agua de Jamaica*, flavored with red hibiscus petals; *agua de horchata*, a cinnamon-scented rice milk; and *agua de tamarindo*, a bittersweet variety flavored with tamarind. For a little more kick, try a *michelada*, a beer spiked with lime juice and chili sauce, served in a salt-rimmed glass with ice.

Decoding the menu

Ceviche—Citrus-marinated seafood appetizer from the Gulf shores of Veracruz. Often eaten with tortilla chips.

Chili relleno—Roasted poblano pepper stuffed with ground meat or cheese, then dipped in egg batter, fried, and served in tomato sauce.

Fish taco—A specialty in Southern California, the fish taco is stuffed with grilled or fried whitefish (mahimahi or wahoo), *pico de gallo,* and shredded cabbage.

Gordita—"Little fat one" in Spanish, this dish is like a taco, but the cornmeal shell is thicker, similar to pita bread.

Mole—A complex sauce with Aztec roots made from more than 20 ingredients, including chilies, cinnamon, cumin, anise, sesame seeds, and Mexican chocolate. There are many variations, but the most common is *mole poblano* from the Puebla region.

Quesadilla—A snack made from a fresh tortilla folded and stuffed with simple fillings, then toasted on a griddle. Elevated versions of the quesadilla may be stuffed with sautéed *flor de calabaza* (squash blossoms) or *huitlacoche* (corn mushrooms).

Salsa—A cooked or raw sauce. Popular salsas include *pico de gallo,* a fresh sauce made from chopped tomatoes, onions, chilies, cilantro, and lime; *salsa verde,* made with tomatillos; and *salsa roja,* a cooked sauce made with chilies, tomatoes, onion, garlic, and cilantro.

Sope—A small, fried corn cake topped with ingredients like refried beans, shredded chicken, and salsa.

Taco—Tacos are made from soft corn tortillas filled with chopped onion, cilantro, and salsa with meats like *al pastor* (spiced pork), *barbacoa* (braised beef), carnitas (roasted pork), *cecina* (chili-coated pork), carne asada (roasted, chopped beef), chorizo (spicy sausage), *lengua* (beef tongue), *sesos* (cow brain), and *tasajo* (spiced, grilled beef).

Tamales—Sweet or savory corn cakes that are steamed and filled with cheese, roasted chilies, or shredded meat.

Tlayuda—A Oaxacan dish similar to pizza. Large corn tortillas are baked until hard, then topped with ingredients like refried beans, cheese, and salsa.

Torta—A Mexican sandwich served on a crusty sandwich roll. Fillings include meat, refried beans, and cheese.

9

Los Feliz and the Eastside SOUTH-OF-THE-BORDER FLAVOR

NEIGHBORHOOD SNAPSHOT

TOP REASONS TO GO

■ **Hike at Griffith Park:** This is without a doubt the best place to partake in L.A.'s favorite pastime—exercising. With over 4,210 acres, it's one of the largest urban parks in the country and happens to have one of the most glorious views of the city.

■ **Stargaze at the Griffith Observatory:** Most visitors may flock to this observatory for its mesmerizing panoramas, but the more discerning travelers come for its night sky viewings and star parties.

■ **Get Some Culture at Barnsdall Art Park:** Architecture, art, drama, and wine all come together in one of L.A.'s best-kept secrets, where a day can be spent taking an art class, touring the appealing Frank Lloyd Wright–designed Hollyhock House, and sipping wine.

■ **See a Show at Rockwell Table and Stage:** Put a Hollywood spin to your dinner by watching a riotous comedic or musical stage performance while feasting on delicious, comforting fare.

■ **Eat Your Way Around the Neighborhood:** Los Feliz is home to a host of fantastic restaurants. Indulge in Middle Eastern at Kismet, Italian at Little Dom's, and tacos at the Best Fish Taco in Ensenada.

QUICK BITES

Best Fish Taco in Ensenada. A simple, cheap, unceremonious taco stand with a selection of spicy house-made salsas—a little local treasure. ⊠ *1650 Hillhurst Ave.*

Guisados. The tacos, with handmade tortillas and braised meats, are some of the best in the city—plus each one only costs a few bucks. But you'll have to endure long lines. ⊠ *1261 Sunset Blvd.*

LaMill Coffee. Order up your coffee however you want it (French press, Clover, you name it) and choose from an inventive list of espresso-based drinks. ⊠ *1636 Silver Lake Blvd.*

GETTING HERE

■ When driving from the east, take either I–10 to I–5 heading north or State Route 134 to I–5 heading south; from the west, take I–10 to I–5 heading north or brave the U.S. 101 traffic, getting off in Hollywood then heading east. The closest Metro station is Vermont and Sunset, which puts you within walking distance of Los Feliz's most bustling streets, Vermont and Hillhurst. Metered street parking is available along Vermont and Hillhurst, while some free parking can be found on residential side streets—though pay attention to posted signs.

PLANNING YOUR TIME

■ Los Feliz is a delightfully intimate neighborhood, and it won't take long to tick off its most important highlights. However, a decent, get-your-heart-pumping hike at Griffith Park may take a couple hours or more, and it's definitely worth spending a few more strolling around to experience all of its offerings, including Griffith Observatory. Silver Lake and Echo Park can easily take up a whole lazy day of eating, drinking, and shopping but can also be done in an afternoon.

The neighborhoods in L.A.'s Eastside are talked about with the same oh-my-god-it's-so-cool reverence by Angelenos as Brooklyn is by New Yorkers. These streets are dripping with trendiness—which will delight some and enrage others.

Almost 20 years ago, Los Feliz was the first of these rediscovered, reinvented neighborhoods, then came Silver Lake, then Echo Park. As each one became more expensive, the cool kids relocated, leaving behind their style and influence. Now Highland Park is the center of the oh-so-hip universe. But the epicenter is constantly shifting. No doubt, in the next few years it'll be someplace else.

Los Feliz

In the rolling hills below the stunning Griffith Observatory, Los Feliz is one of L.A.'s most affluent neighborhoods. With Hollywood just a few miles west, its winding streets are lined with mansions belonging to some of the biggest celebrities. In recent years, both Vermont and Hillhurst avenues have come alive with hip restaurants, boutiques, and theaters.

👁 Sights

Barnsdall Art Park
HOUSE | FAMILY | The panoramic view of Hollywood alone is worth a trip to this hilltop cultural center. On the grounds you'll find the 1921 **Hollyhock House,** a masterpiece of modern design by architect Frank Lloyd Wright. It was commissioned by philanthropist Aline Barnsdall

to be the centerpiece of an arts community. While Barnsdall's project didn't turn out the way she planned, the park now hosts the L.A. Municipal Art Gallery and Theatre, which provides exhibition space for visual and performance artists.

Wright dubbed this style "California Romanza" (*romanza* is a musical term meaning "to make one's own form"). Stylized depictions of Barnsdall's favorite flower, the hollyhock, appear throughout the house in its cement columns, roof line, and furnishings. The leaded-glass windows are expertly placed to make the most of both the surrounding gardens and the city views. On summer weekends, there are wildly popular wine tastings and outdoor movie screenings. Self-guided tours are available Thursday through Sunday from 11 to 4. ✉ *4800 Hollywood Blvd., Los Feliz* 🕾 *323/644–6296* ⊕ *www.barnsdall.org* 📧 *Free; house tours $7* 🕑 *House closed Mon.*

★ Griffith Observatory
OBSERVATORY | Most visitors barely skim the surface of this gorgeous spot in the Santa Monica Mountains, but those in the know will tell you there's more to the Griffith Observatory than its sweeping views and stunning Greek Revival architecture. To start, this free-to-the-public mountaintop observatory is home to the Samuel Oschin Planetarium, a

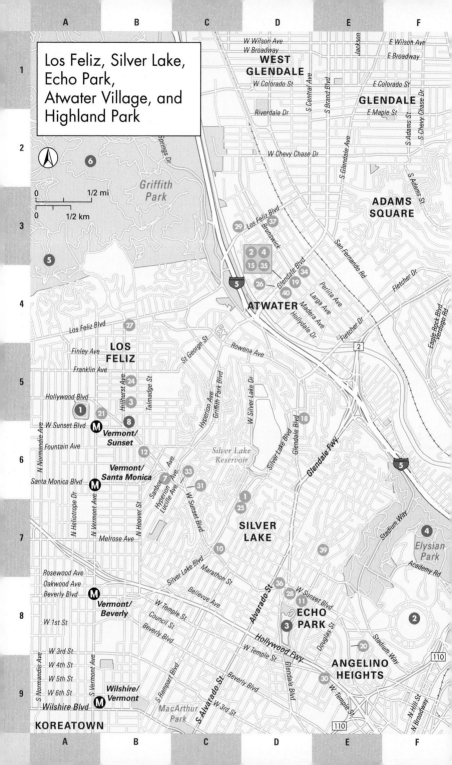

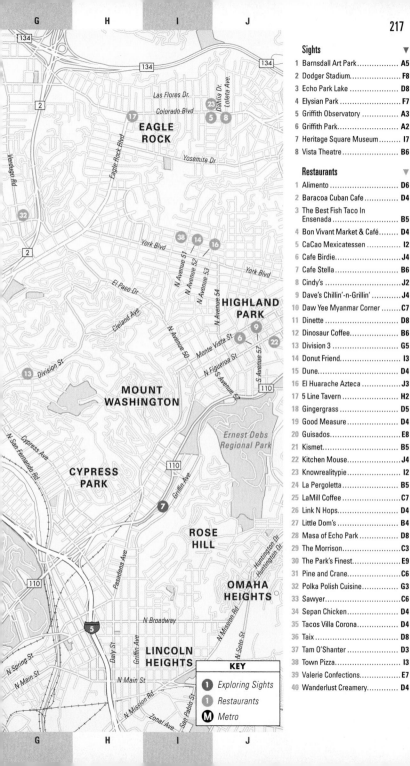

9

Sights ▼

1 Barnsdall Art Park............... **A5**
2 Dodger Stadium.................... **F8**
3 Echo Park Lake **D8**
4 Elysian Park **F7**
5 Griffith Observatory **A3**
6 Griffith Park....................... **A2**
7 Heritage Square Museum........ **I7**
8 Vista Theatre...................... **B6**

Restaurants ▼

1 Alimento **D6**
2 Baracoa Cuban Cafe............. **D4**
3 The Best Fish Taco In
  Ensenada **B5**
4 Bon Vivant Market & Café........ **D4**
5 CaCao Mexicatessen **I2**
6 Cafe Birdie..........................**J4**
7 Cafe Stella **B6**
8 Cindy's **J2**
9 Dave's Chillin'-n-Grillin' **J4**
10 Daw Yee Myanmar Corner **C7**
11 Dinette **D8**
12 Dinosaur Coffee.................... **B6**
13 Division 3 .... **G5**
14 Donut Friend....................... **I3**
15 Dune................................. **D4**
16 El Huarache Azteca **J3**
17 5 Line Tavern **H2**
18 Gingergrass **D5**
19 Good Measure **D4**
20 Guisados............................ **E8**
21 Kismet............................... **B5**
22 Kitchen Mouse.....................**J4**
23 Knowrealitypie **I2**
24 La Pergoletta **B5**
25 LaMill Coffee **C7**
26 Link N Hops........................ **D4**
27 Little Dom's **B4**
28 Masa of Echo Park **D8**
29 The Morrison....................... **C3**
30 The Park's Finest.................. **E9**
31 Pine and Crane.................... **C6**
32 Polka Polish Cuisine.............. **G3**
33 Sawyer.............................. **C6**
34 Sepan Chicken..................... **D4**
35 Tacos Villa Corona................ **D4**
36 Taix **D8**
37 Tam O'Shanter **D3**
38 Town Pizza......................... **I3**
39 Valerie Confections................ **E7**
40 Wanderlust Creamery............. **D4**

Did You Know?

Renovations to the Griffith Observatory have made its interior nearly as spectacular as the views of Hollywood from outside.

state-of-the-art theater with an aluminum dome and a Zeiss star projector that plays a number of ticketed shows. Those spectacular shows are complemented by a couple of space-related exhibits, and several telescopes (naturally), as well as theater programs and events at the Leonard Nimoy Event Horizon Theater. For visitors who are looking to get up close and personal with the cosmos, monthly star-viewing parties with local amateur astronomers are also on hand.

■ TIP→ **For a fantastic view, come at sunset to watch the sky turn fiery shades of red with the city's skyline silhouetted.** ✉ *2800 E. Observatory Ave., Los Feliz* ☎ *213/473–0800* 🌐 *www.griffithobservatory.org* 🕒 *Closed Mon.* ☞ *Observatory grounds and parking are open daily.*

Griffith Park

CITY PARK | FAMILY | The country's largest municipal park, the 4,310-acre Griffith Park is a must for nature lovers, the perfect spot for respite from the hustle and bustle of the surrounding urban areas. Plants and animals native to Southern California can be found within the park's borders, including deer, coyotes, and even a reclusive mountain lion. Bronson Canyon (where the Batcave from the 1960s *Batman* TV series is located) and Crystal Springs are favorite picnic spots.

The park is named after Colonel Griffith J. Griffith, a mining tycoon who donated 3,000 acres to the city in 1896. As you might expect, the park has been used as a film and television location for at least a century. Here you'll find the Griffith Observatory, the Los Angeles Zoo, the Greek Theater, two golf courses, hiking and bridle trails, a swimming pool, a merry-go-round, and an outdoor train museum. ✉ *4730 Crystal Springs Dr., Los Feliz* ☎ *323/913–4688* 🌐 *www.laparks.org/dos/parks/griffithpk* 🎟 *Free; attractions inside park have separate admission fees.*

Vista Theatre

FILM | The Vista, around since 1923, is a single-screen gem that shows brand-new releases and features art deco fixtures and Egyptian-themed details. One of the most affordable theaters in the city, the Vista borders Los Feliz and Silver Lake, and is close to fun bars and restaurants for a pre- or postshow meal or cocktail. ✉ *4473 Sunset Blvd., Los Feliz* ☎ *323/660–6639* 🌐 *www.vintagecinemas.com/vista.*

🍴 Restaurants

This affluent hillside community has a laid-back dining scene. Wine bars, burger joints, and taco stands are among the options for a family night out.

The Best Fish Taco in Ensenada

$ | MEXICAN | FAMILY | In mirroring the taco stands of Ensenada, Mexico—simple, cheap, unceremonious, with a selection of spicy house-made salsas—this little local treasure has achieved what many restaurants serving Baja tacos haven't: an authentic (and delicious) experience. **Known for:** fish-and-shrimp tacos; mango salsa; horchata. [$] *Average main: $6* ✉ *1650 Hillhurst Ave., Los Feliz* ☎ *323/466–5552* 🌐 *www.bestfishtacoinensenada.com.*

Kismet

$ | MEDITERRANEAN | You may feel like you're about to walk into a sauna rather than a restaurant because of its minimalist light-color wood on white paint interior, but Kismet's colorful gorgeous Middle Eastern dishes tell a different story. This James Beard nominee perfectly blends comforting Middle Eastern and Israeli cuisine with Californian flavors and plant-based flair, all served in a modern space. **Known for:** freekeh fritters; jeweled crispy rice with egg yolk; dessert. [$] *Average main: $18* ✉ *4648 Hollywood Blvd., Los Feliz* ☎ *323/409–0404* 🌐 *www.kismetlosangeles.com.*

La Pergoletta

$ | **ITALIAN** | Just look for the swaying Italian flag at a strip mall on Hillhurst and Melbourne, and you'll stumble into La Pergoletta, a cozy little space. Though the decor is decidedly frenzied, it still maintains a chicly rustic quality that looks like it was cobbled together by an Italian *nonna*. **Known for:** fresh pasta you can customize; gnocchi with creamy mushroom sauce; dinner. $ *Average main: $18* ⊠ *1802 Hillhurst Ave., Los Feliz* ☎ *323/664–8259* ⊕ *www.lapergoletta. com.*

Little Dom's

$$ | **ITALIAN** | With a vintage bar and dapper barkeep who mixes up seasonally inspired retro cocktails, an attached Italian deli where you can pick up a pork-cheek sub, and an $18 Monday-night supper, it's not surprising that Little Dom's is a neighborhood gem. Cozy and inviting, with big leather booths you can sink into for the night, the restaurant puts a modern spin on classic Italian dishes such as *burrata* agnolotti and meatballs. **Known for:** ricotta cheese and fresh blueberry pancakes; pizza with sunny-side up egg; breakfast. $ *Average main: $20* ⊠ *2128 Hillhurst Ave., Los Feliz* ☎ *323/661–0055* ⊕ *www.littledoms.com.*

▼ Nightlife

While neighboring Hollywood champions nightclubs, laid-back Los Feliz favors its pubs, quirky neighborhood bars, and casual lounges. The scene is buzzing, especially on weekends, with locals dominating it. But visitors hoping to get away from the rowdiness of Hollywood are always a welcome addition.

Covell

WINE BARS—NIGHTLIFE | Covell is the embodiment of what every unpretentious wine drinker wishes a wine bar should be—laid back. It's thankfully lacking in servers who might turn up their noses should you—for shame!—forget to swirl the glass. But what else would you expect from a spot with shabby furnishings and a vintage motorcycle mounted to the wall? ⊠ *4628 Hollywood Blvd., Los Feliz* ☎ *323/660–4400* ⊕ *www.barcovell. com.*

Dresden Room

PIANO BARS/LOUNGES | This bar's 1940s lounge decor makes it a favorite with folks in Los Angeles. The long-running house band, Marty and Elayne, has entertained patrons for more than three decades. (They found a new generation of fans, thanks to the film *Swingers*.) Other than the entertainment, perhaps the best reason to wander in is to sip on a Blood and Sand cocktail, self proclaimed to be "the world's most tantalizing drink."⊠ *1760 N. Vermont Ave., Los Feliz* ☎ *323/665–4294* ⊕ *www.thedresden. com.*

Good Luck Bar

BARS/PUBS | There's something absolutely appealing about the Chinese-influenced style of this tiki-cum-dive bar's interiors and riotous fruity-yet-potent $12 cocktails. Call it kitschy, consider it too trendy, but if you give it a chance, it will show you a proper good time. ⊠ *1514 Hillhurst Ave., Los Feliz* ☎ *323/666–3524* ⊕ *www. goodluckbarla.com.*

Tabula Rasa Bar

WINE BARS—NIGHTLIFE | This unassuming spot feels less like a wine bar and more of a neighborhood watering hole where the servers take the time to chat with customers rather than somberly educating them on the complexities of wine. Make no mistake: the wine selection is perfection and the snacks are delightful—they simply want to ensure your enjoyment of your wine rather than bow down at the appreciation of their knowledge. ⊠ *5125 Hollywood Blvd., Los Feliz* ☎ *213/290–6309* ⊕ *www.tabularas-abar.com.*

Performing Arts

Though Los Feliz has a bit of a theater scene—mostly a spillover from Hollywood—it's home to a couple of fantastic cinemas and one of L.A.'s best live music venues: the Greek.

Greek Theatre

CONCERTS | With a robust lineup from May through November, acts such as Bruce Springsteen, John Legend, and Aretha Franklin (RIP) have all graced the stage at this scenic outdoor venue. The 5,900-capacity amphitheater is at the base of Griffith Park, and you may want to make a day of it by hiking or stargazing beforehand. There is usually slow, preshow traffic on concert nights, but it'll give you a chance to take in the beautiful park foliage and homes in the Hollywood Hills. Paid lots are available for parking, but wear comfortable shoes and expect to walk, as some lots are fairly far from the theater. Or, park and enjoy cocktails in the trendy and chic Los Feliz neighborhood below before a show, then walk up to the venue. ⌧ *2700 N. Vermont Ave., Los Feliz* ☎ *844/524–7335* ⊕ *www. greektheatrela.com.*

Rockwell Table and Stage

THEATER | Great comfort food, decent cocktails, and a boisterous night of fun await at one of L.A.'s most idiosyncratic nighttime diversions. At the Rockwell Table and Stage performance venue, it's the shows and their hilarious cast that are the main attractions, whether they're doing an unofficial parody of a famous TV show or movie or putting on a political cabaret. ⌧ *1714 N. Vermont Ave., Los Feliz* ☎ *323/669-1550* ⊕ *rockwell-la.com.*

Vintage Los Feliz Theatre

FILM | Los Angeles has an abundance of vintage cinemas that whisk movie lovers back to the Hollywood days of yore, and the Vintage leads the small-screen charge with its three intimate theaters that showcase new releases in 4K. If you're hungry, they have a taco stand and a café serving milk tea. With a prime location on the neighborhood's busiest drag, a perfect Los Feliz evening starts with dinner, ends with drinks, and has the Vintage sandwiched in between. ⌧ *1822 N. Vermont Ave., Los Feliz* ☎ *323/664–2169* ⊕ *vintagecinemas.com/losfeliz.*

Shopping

Stroll past the mansions on Los Feliz Boulevard before hitting the vintage shops and sophisticated boutiques with old-school tendencies—think refurbished brick and classic decor.

La La Ling

CLOTHING | FAMILY | This isn't your average kids' clothing store; La La Ling offers pieces hip enough to be worn by the cool parents it counts as clientele. Shoppers can expect affordable finds like Wu-Tang onesies, rock band tees, and skinny jeans. The store also stocks supplies for the nursery and bath time, plus burp cloths, bibs, swaddlers, and other essentials new mommies and daddies need on the regular. ⌧ *1810 N. Vermont Ave., Los Feliz* ☎ *323/664–4400* ⊕ *www. lalaling.com.*

Skylight Books

BOOKS/STATIONERY | A neighborhood bookstore through and through, Skylight has excellent sections devoted to kids, fiction, travel, food, and it even has a live-in cat. Be sure to browse the Staff Picks section, as the well-informed employees have the inside scoop on new or under-the-radar must-reads. The space also hosts book discussion groups, panels, and author readings with hip literati. Art lovers can peruse texts on design and photography, graphic novels, and indie magazines at Skylight's annex a few doors down. ⌧ *1818 N. Vermont Ave., Los Feliz* ☎ *323/660–1175* ⊕ *www. skylightbooks.com.*

Soap Plant/Wacko

GIFTS/SOUVENIRS | This pop-culture supermarket offers a wide range of items, including rows of books on art and design. But it's the novelty stock that makes the biggest impression, with ant farms, X-ray specs, and anime figurines. An adjacent gallery space, La Luz de Jesus, focuses on underground art. ✉ *4633 Hollywood Blvd., Los Feliz* ☎ *323/663–0122* 🌐 *www.soapplant.com.*

Spitfire Girl

GIFTS/SOUVENIRS | When the person you're shopping for is the nontraditional type, count on this quirky boutique to provide unique goods including taxidermy, printed wood flasks, white magic spell kits, and cheeky socks, much of which is created by Spitfire Girl's own house label. ✉ *1939½ Hillhurst Ave., Los Feliz* ☎ *323/912–1977* 🌐 *www.spitfiregirl.com.*

Vamp

CLOTHING | From well-known designers to up-and-comers and handcrafters who make their shoes in small batches, boutique store Vamp Shoes has a solid collection of footwear for women who appreciate and are not afraid to invest in gorgeous, excellent-quality soles. Inventory here also includes cool bags, hosiery, jewelry, and handcrafted ceramics. ✉ *1951 Hillhurst Ave., Los Feliz* ☎ *323/662–1150* 🌐 *www.vampshoeshop.com.*

Silver Lake

This hilly, mostly residential neighborhood sits southeast of Los Feliz and northwest of Echo Park. Regarded as a bohemian enclave since the 1930s, it was the site of the first large film studio built by Walt Disney. Silver Lake is known for cute boutiques, bougie coffeehouses, and specialty restaurants along its stretch of Sunset Boulevard.

🍴 Restaurants

With plenty of hipster appeal, the eateries of Silver Lake draw an eclectic crowd to its neighborhood hangouts.

★ Alimento

$$ | ITALIAN | There's little surprise that Chef Zach Pollack's soulful Italian masterpiece in Silver Lake features a lot of influences and inspirations; the true Angelenos, after all, grew up in a melting pot. Alimento's dishes are modern takes on traditional Italian cuisine, using locally sourced ingredients and varying in influences—from your classic American to Chinese and Mexican. **Known for:** yellowtail-collar affumicato; chicken liver crostone; dinner only. [$] *Average main: $25* ✉ *1710 Silver Lake Blvd., Silver Lake* ☎ *323/928–2888* 🌐 *www.alimentola.com* ⏲ *Closed Mon. No lunch.*

Cafe Stella

$$$ | FRENCH | This strange den of eclectic decor and peeling paint feels undoubtedly French. Come for the aperitifs (Kir Royal, perhaps?), but stick around for the food for an exquisite blend of French and American bistro cuisine, prepared for lunch and dinner using traditional French technique. **Known for:** brunch; Moroccan eggs; eggs Benedict. [$] *Average main: $34* ✉ *3932 Sunset Blvd., Silver Lake* ☎ *323/666–0265* 🌐 *www.cafestella.com* ⏲ *No brunch Mon.*

Daw Yee Myanmar Corner

$ | BURMESE | Burmese food is hard to find in Los Angeles so it's a good thing that tucked away in a Silver Lake strip mall sits the unassuming Daw Yee Myanmar Corner, a restaurant that's as good as it is rare. The food is an explosion of flavors and textures (there's a lot of roasted peanuts and toasted sesame). **Known for:** tea leaf salad; Burmese cuisine; mohinga. [$] *Average main: $12* ✉ *2837 Sunset Blvd., Silver Lake* ☎ *213/413–0568* 🌐 *www.dawyeesilverlake.com* ⏲ *Closed Tues.*

Dinosaur Coffee

$ | **CAFÉ** | By blending geometrical shapes and horizontal lines together in an airy place with big windows, Dinosaur Coffee has utilized its space well, bringing a touch of the new into a section of Silver Lake that feels a little old. Yet it's more than just the interiors that draw people in—the coffee is excellent, as are the pastries. **Known for:** cappuccino; cold brew; no Wi-Fi. [$] *Average main: $4* ✉ *4334 W. Sunset Blvd., Silver Lake* 🌐 *dinosaurcoffee.com.*

Gingergrass

$ | **VIETNAMESE** | **FAMILY** | With minimalist decor marked by tropical wood banquettes, Silver Lake's bohemian past and uber-trendy present converge at Gingergrass. Traditional Vietnamese favorites emerge from this café's open kitchen, sometimes with a California twist. **Known for:** roasted pork chop with rice; crispy imperial rolls; great desserts. [$] *Average main: $15* ✉ *2396 Glendale Blvd., Silver Lake* ☎ *323/644–1600* 🌐 *www.gingergrass.com.*

LaMill Coffee

$ | **CAFÉ** | These folks take their coffee seriously, sourcing estate-grown beans that are prepared in a variety of ways (French press or Clover, to name but two) and offering an inventive list of espresso-based drinks. To go along with the requisite coffee fix is a menu put together by renowned chef Michael Cimarusti of Providence fame, as well as a serious tea list. **Known for:** blanco y negro; orange-infused cappucino; extensive tea list. [$] *Average main: $14* ✉ *1636 Silver Lake Blvd., Silver Lake* ☎ *323/663–4441* 🌐 *www.lamillcoffee.com.*

Pine and Crane

$ | **TAIWANESE** | **FAMILY** | This is not the typical Chinese restaurant one might expect; it's a fast casual, often locally sourced Taiwanese restaurant housed in a modern setting. The menu changes based on season, the wine and beer list updates constantly, and the tea menu is carefully curated. **Known for:** dan dan noodles; beef rolls; Taiwanese food. [$] *Average main: $12* ✉ *1521 Griffith Park Blvd., Silver Lake* ☎ *323/668–1128* 🌐 *www.pineandcrane.com* 🕒 *Closed Tues.*

Sawyer

$$ | **SEAFOOD** | This Silver Lake seafood spot features high ceilings, exposed brick, a hip crowd, and incredible fish. The lobster roll that comes with Kennebec fries is second to none, and the P.E.I. Black Mussels with Italian sausage will have you ordering extra bread for dipping. **Known for:** seafood boil; oysters; fries. [$] *Average main: $23* ✉ *3709 Sunset Blvd., Silver Lake* ☎ *323/641–3709* 🌐 *www.sawyerlosangeles.com* 🕒 *No brunch weekdays.*

🍸 Nightlife

Silver Lake's best bars can be found in one condensed area, Sunset Junction, the intersection of Sunset and Santa Monica boulevards. If you've spent your day shopping or dining here, return at night when coffee culture takes a breather and makes way for dark eclectic bars patronized by locals and L.A.'s transplant community.

Akbar

BARS/PUBS | This bar's welcoming feel is one of the reasons many people consider it their neighborhood bar, even if they don't live in the neighborhood. The crowd is friendly and inviting, and theme nights attract all sorts of folks, gay or straight. The comedy nights are favorites, as are weekends, when DJs get everyone on the dance floor. ✉ *4356 W. Sunset Blvd., Silver Lake* ☎ *323/665–6810* 🌐 *www.akbarsilverlake.com.*

Cha Cha Lounge

BARS/PUBS | If chaos and the assortment of ill-matched furnishings and decor is something you can forgive—or revel in—then this import from Seattle is a Silver Lake staple you should be partaking in, as there's never a dull moment. Grab your (cheap) poison then meander through the Mexican fiesta-themed bar. Foosball tables, a photo booth, and a vending machine will give you plenty to occupy your time … that is, if you're not already having a swell time. ✉ *2375 Glendale Blvd., Silver Lake* ☎ *323/660–7595* ⊕ *www.chachalounge.com.*

★ 4100

BARS/PUBS | With swaths of fabric draped from the ceiling, this low-lit bar with a bohemian vibe makes it perfect for dates. Groups of locals also come through for the night, making the crowd a plentiful mix of people. The bartenders know how to pour drinks that are both tasty and potent. There's plenty of seating at the tables and stools along the central bar, which gets crowded on the weekends. ✉ *1087 Manzanita St., Silver Lake* ☎ *323/666–4460* ⊕ *213hospitality.com/ project/4100bar.*

The Red Lion Tavern

BREWPUBS/BEER GARDENS | You wouldn't expect old European charm in the hipster enclave of Silver Lake, but Bavarian style is served right alongside irony at the Red Lion Tavern, just as it has for more than 55 years. So, grab a schnitzel and a bratwurst and wander the many rooms chockablock with German memorabilia, and head toward the beer garden for a large selection of German-only beers on draft. ✉ *2366 Glendale Blvd., Silver Lake* ☎ *323/662–5337* ⊕ *www.redliontavern. net.*

★ The Satellite

MUSIC CLUBS | Once known as Spaceland, the Satellite holds nightly shows filled with underground musicians, both touring and local, all trying to make a dent. Many of them play indie rock, punk, or something else outside the mainstream, so it's a must-stop for music fans who abhor the Billboard Top 100. If you're around, make sure to take advantage of the free residencies where bands get to take center stage every Monday for an entire month. ✉ *1717 Silver Lake Blvd.,*

Silver Lake ☎ *323/661–4380* ⊕ *www. thesatellitela.com.*

Silverlake Lounge

MUSIC CLUBS | Rock bands, burlesque, comedy, and even open-mic nights all have a home at the cross-section of Sunset and Silver Lake at a little dive bar called the Silverlake Lounge. This small club with the yellow awning is a neighborhood spot—cash only, by the way—in the best way possible, with cheap drinks and local talent deserving of their time in the limelight. ✉ *2906 W. Sunset Blvd., Silver Lake* ☎ *323/663–9636* ⊕ *www. thesilverlakelounge.com.*

Thirsty Crow

BARS/PUBS | This whiskey bar serves up seasonal cocktails in a fun, rustic environment. Though small, it manages to find space for live musicians and an open-mic night on Saturday. Part of the same hospitality group as Bigfoot Lodge and Highland Park Bowl, this watering hole has a locals-only feel. As local L.A. musician Father John Misty once said, "nothing good ever happens at the goddamn Thirsty Crow," but we think you should go and see for yourself. ✉ *2939 W. Sunset Blvd., Silver Lake* ☎ *323/661– 6007* ⊕ *www.thirstycrowbar.com.*

🛍 Shopping

The action here is concentrated along Sunset Boulevard, where the young and hip come to sip artisanal coffee and peruse the one-of-a-kind wares.

Mohawk General Store

CLOTHING | Filled with a brilliant marriage of indie and established designers, this upscale boutique is a mainstay for the modern minimalist. Pick up the wares of local favorites Black Crane and Jesse Kamm, as well as internationally loved labels like Commes des Garcons, Issey Miyake, and Levi's Vintage Clothing. The Sunset Boulevard store stocks goods for men and women, as well as children, plus accessories and some home goods.

✉ *4011 W. Sunset Blvd., Silver Lake* ☎ *323/522–6459* ⊕ *www.mohawkgeneralstore.com.*

Secret Headquarters

BOOKS/STATIONERY | This could be the coolest comic-book store on the planet, with a selection to satisfy both the geekiest of collectors and those more interested in artistic and literary finds. Rich wood floors and a leather chair near the front window of this intimate space mark the sophisticated setting, which features wall displays neatly organized with new comics and filing cabinets marked DC and Marvel . ✉ *3817 W. Sunset Blvd., Silver Lake* ☎ *323/666–2228* ⊕ *www.thesecretheadquarters.com.*

Silver Lake Wine

WINE/SPIRITS | Boutique wineries from around the world provide this shop with the vintages that fill the floor-to-ceiling racks. Looking unassuming in jeans and T-shirts, the knowledgeable staff can steer you to the right wine or spirits for any occasion. You can wet your whistle at tastings on Monday and Thursday. ✉ *2395 Glendale Blvd., Silver Lake* ☎ *323/662–9024* ⊕ *www.silverlakewine.com.*

Yolk

GIFTS/SOUVENIRS | Stocked with a little bit of everything you'll want to get or give, this shop has a spot-on selection of fresh designer goods. Look for unique kids toys and furnishings, exquisite home accessories, stationeries, and handcrafted items from Californian artisans. ✉ *1626 Silver Lake Blvd., Silver Lake* ☎ *323/660–4315* ⊕ *www.shopyolk.com.*

Echo Park

Silver Lake's edgier older cousin and neighbor, Echo Park is centered on a beautifully restored lakefront park (you can even rent a paddleboat and experience the lake in all its glory). The first residential neighborhood northwest of Downtown Los Angeles, Echo Park has long been under scrutiny for gentrification, along with Highland Park and Silver Lake. This predominantly Latino and Mexican neighborhood has likewise experienced an influx of young artists and industry hopefuls, as well as rent hikes, but it's not devoid of diversity or character. Film buffs take note: it was one of the principal locations of Roman Polanski's film *Chinatown.*

⊙ Sights

Dodger Stadium

SPORTS VENUE | FAMILY | Home of the Dodgers since 1962, it's the third-oldest baseball stadium still in use and has had quite the history in baseball, including Sandy Koufax's perfect game in 1965 and Kirk Gibson's 1988 World Series home run. Not only has it played host to the Dodgers' ups and downs and World Series runs, it's also been the venue for some of the biggest performers in the world, including the Beatles, Madonna, and Beyonce. The stadium can be tough to get into on game day so consider getting dropped off in the park and walking up. Alternately, arrive early as locals tend not to roll up until the third inning. If you have the opportunity to take in a Friday night game, make sure to stick around for the fireworks show that follows—if you're patient, you can even wait in line and watch it from the field. ✉ *1000 Vin Scully Ave., Echo Park* ☎ *866/363–4377* ⊕ *dodgers.mlb.com/la/ballpark* ☉ *Check schedule.*

Echo Park Lake

BODY OF WATER | FAMILY | If this charming little park and its lake of swan boats looks a little familiar to you, it's most likely because you've seen it in one L.A.-shot movie or another (*Chinatown,* for instance). After a major overhaul, the park has blossomed into a beautiful urban landscape, set against the backdrop of the Downtown skyline. Weekends are always bustling, as are mornings when joggers and early risers take laps around the lake. There's a tiny breakfast-slash-lunch spot that serves healthy nosh and good coffee. ✉ *751 Echo Park Ave., Echo Park* 🌐 *www.laparks.org/aquatic/lake/echo-park-lake.*

Elysian Park

HIKING/WALKING | **FAMILY** | Though not Los Angeles's biggest park—that honor belongs to Griffith Park—Elysian comes in second, and also has the honor of being the city's oldest. It's also home to one of L.A.'s busiest and most beloved attractions, Dodger Stadium, home field to the Los Angeles Dodgers. For this reason, baseball fans flock to this 600-acre park for tailgate parties. The rest of the time, however, Elysian Park serves as the Echo Park residents' backyard, thanks to its network of hiking trails, picnic spaces, and public playgrounds. ✉ *929 Academy Rd., Echo Park* 🌐 *www.laparks.org/park/elysian.*

🍴 Restaurants

Echo Park's diversity manifests in its gastronomic scene. While vegan and Mexican restaurants are aplenty, there are other offerings to round it out and satisfy every taste bud, from French to Italian, Japanese to Thai.

Dinette

$ | **CAFÉ** | Coffee shops may be a dime a dozen, but Dinette stands out. First of all, this is a walk-up-window-only establishment, which gives it a nice vintage-diner feel. **Known for:** coffee; avocado toast; waffle with bacon and poached egg. [$] *Average main: $11* ✉ *1608½ Sunset Blvd., Echo Park* ☎ *213/278–0301* 🌐 *dinettela.com* 🕒 *Closed Mon.*

Masa of Echo Park

$$ | **PIZZA** | **FAMILY** | While Masa of Echo Park does do excellent "bistro pizzas," as the restaurant calls them, it's mostly known for their delectable deep-dish pies that may just be the best you'll find this side of Chicago. Be prepared though—it can take a while to get seated and up to 45 minutes to get that deep dish you ordered, so it might be best to call ahead. **Known for:** vegan menu; family-style dining; Italian classics. [$] *Average main: $20* ✉ *1800 W. Sunset Blvd., Echo Park* ☎ *213/989–1558* 🌐 *www.masaofechopark.com.*

The Park's Finest

$ | **BARBECUE** | **FAMILY** | The typical family backyard barbecues scattered throughout Echo Park, which has traditionally overlapped with L.A.'s historic Filipinotown, is transformed into fantastic dining at the Park's Finest. Slow-cooked meats and vinegar-based sauces are topped with *longganisa, ube,* soy sauce, and banana leaves. **Known for:** coconut beef; pulled pork; Filipino-inspired food. [$] *Average main: $15* ✉ *1267 W. Temple St., Echo Park* ☎ *213/481–2800* 🌐 *www.theparksfinest.com.*

Taix

$$ | **FRENCH** | **FAMILY** | Serving French cuisine since 1927—and at its current location since 1962—Taix is the opportunity to peek at a time in L.A. that's mostly disappeared. Dark, wooden tables, intimate booths, low lighting, and portrait-adorned walls all help to set the scene. **Known for:** steak frites; being a local institution; French onion soup. [$] *Average main: $21* ✉ *1911 W. Sunset Blvd., Echo Park* ☎ *213/484–1265* 🌐 *taixfrench.com.*

Valerie Confections

$ | **CAFÉ** | Most cafés treat tea as an afterthought, but at Valerie Confections it's the centerpiece. Different varieties of tea conquer half the menu and many of the morsels advertised only serve to complement the tea. **Known for:** tea; petit fours; baked goods. [$] *Average main: $12* ✉ *1665 Echo Park Ave., Echo Park* ☎ *213/250–9365* 🌐 *valerieconfections.com.*

ⓨ Nightlife

See an up-and-coming local band, bring your own records to the bar, or impress a date in this eclectic neighborhood that manages to maintain its cultural authenticity more so than its neighbor, Silver Lake.

Button Mash

BARS/PUBS | FAMILY | Button Mash hits all the right buttons (sorry), with a wide selection of rotating arcade games, most of which are from the golden age, not to mention a fantastically curated wine and beer list, and a menu put together by the old Starry Kitchen pop-up team that specializes in Asian fusion bar food. Before 9, this bar-cade is all ages, so everyone can be the next pinball wizard between bites of double-fried chicken wings. ⊠ 1391 Sunset Blvd., Echo Park ☎ 213/250–9903 ⊕ www.buttonmashla.com.

★ The Echo and Echoplex

MUSIC CLUBS | These two venues, one sitting on top of the other, are the heart of live music in Echo Park. Both offer a full bar and the ability to order pizza from Two Boots next door as well as recurring themed nights like Part-Time Punks. While they both host cutting-edge music, the Echo usually has up-and-coming local and touring acts whereas more well-known bands play downstairs. ⊠ 1822 Sunset Blvd. , Echoplex entrance at 1154 Glendale Blvd, Echo Park ☎ 213/413–8200 ⊕ www.theecho.com.

El Prado

BARS/PUBS | A small selection of constantly rotating wine and beer ensures you'll get to try something new and interesting each time you visit. A record player serves as the main source of music—while the idea may seem twee, it's the heart of a popular Tuesday night record club, where patrons bring in their own vinyl. ⊠ 1805 W. Sunset Blvd., Echo Park ⊕ www.elpradobar.com.

★ Mohawk Bend

BARS/PUBS | There are so many reasons to stop by Mohawk Bend: 72 craft beers on tap, a wide range of California-only liquor, a vegetarian and vegan-friendly menu that includes tailored-to-your-wants pizza, and a buffalo cauliflower that—rumor has it—started the whole trend. There might be a long line to get into this 100-year-old former theater in the evenings, but it's worth it. ⊠ 2141 Sunset Blvd., Echo Park ☎ 213/483–2337 ⊕ mohawk.la.

The Semi-Tropic

PIANO BARS/LOUNGES | This is a bar that feels more like a café—a place with an atmosphere perfect for studying or relaxing over a cold drink. It has a full menu that boasts everything from churro waffles to customizable charcuterie. Once evening comes around, it becomes alive with DJs spinning vinyl, music showcases, and hip locals indulging in craft beer, well-made cocktails, and fine wines. ⊠ 1412 Glendale Blvd., Echo Park ☎ 213/568–3827 ⊕ www.thesemitropic.com.

The Short Stop

BARS/PUBS | Echo Park's Short Stop is one of the few remaining dive bars in the area, still catering to those who want cheap drinks in a no-frills joint—especially local hipsters and Dodgers fans. There's memorabilia scattered throughout that pay homage to what this once was—a police hangout. ⊠ 1455 W. Sunset Blvd., Echo Park ☎ 213/482–4942.

★ 1642 Beer and Wine

BARS/PUBS | This romantically lit hole-in-the-wall is easy to miss. Perfect for first dates, come here to experiment with craft beers or to warm up with wine. On the first Thursday of every month, get a free tamale with your drink, and hear some live old-time fiddle tunes. ⊠ 1642 W. Temple St., Echo Park ☎ 213/989–6836.

Shopping

With a bit more edge than neighboring Silver Lake, this increasingly cool area has an artsy, do-it-yourself appeal. Secondhand stores squeeze in alongside vegan restaurants, hip dive bars, and friendly boutiques stocked with clothes by local designers.

Esqueleto

JEWELRY/ACCESSORIES | There's a bit of the macabre on display at Esqueleto, but what do you expect from a jewelry boutique with a name meaning "skeleton" in Spanish? But that doesn't mean the light, airy, contemporary shop is stereotypically goth in style; both its design and the inventory it stocks are perfectly polished and selected with a discerningly artistic eye. With a mix of excellent vintage finds and emerging designers (Melissa Joy Manning, Lauren Wolf, and Satomi Kawakita are favorites here), the shop has become a go-to destination for alternative brides' engagement rings and wedding bands. ✉ *1928 W. Sunset Blvd., Echo Park* ☎ *213/947–3508* 🌐 *www.shopesqueleto.com.*

Stories Books and Café

BOOKS/STATIONERY | With an off-the-beaten path collection of new and used literature, a café catering to freelancers and free thinkers, and a back patio that showcases singer-songwriters, Stories Books and Café is an authentic reflection of Echo Park. Readings, signings, and other events are a regular occurrence. ✉ *1716 Sunset Blvd., Echo Park* ☎ *213/413–3733* 🌐 *www.storiesla.com.*

Time Travel Mart

SPECIALTY STORES | **FAMILY** | You probably won't find anything useful in the Time Travel Mart and that's exactly the point. From dinosaur eggs to robot milk, this is a store that touts the ridiculous—all of which should bring back memories of your childhood and maybe a little bit of joy. But that's because the store holds a secret: it's really a fundraiser for the nonprofit 826LA, which tutors neighborhood kids in the back section. So, know when you're buying that totally unnecessary, but absolutely wonderful, samurai umbrella, the proceeds are going to a good cause. ✉ *1714 W. Sunset Blvd., Echo Park* ☎ *213/413–3388* 🌐 *826la.org/store.*

Atwater Village

Alongside nearby Glassell Park and Cypress Park, Atwater Village is one of the seven neighborhoods that make up the Northeast Los Angeles region, christened NELA by some locals. While it mostly mirrors the former two neighborhoods' predominantly residential status, it also swaggers with Los Feliz's upmarket hip vibe. The main thoroughfares of Glendale and Los Feliz boulevards are paved with neighborhood bars, elevated restaurants, and independent coffee shops, not to mention smart boutique shops touting artisanal goods.

Restaurants

Quality trumps quantity in Atwater Village. Expect modest yet eclectic menus stuffed with epicurean delights. Dropping by on a Sunday gives you the option to shop for fresh produce at the farmers' market.

Baracoa Cuban Cafe

$ | **CUBAN** | **FAMILY** | As far as Cuban food goes in Los Angeles, Baracoa's cozy Atwater café, whose interiors loosely resemble an old colonial Spanish square, is perhaps not the most popular, but it's definitely one of the best. This is the kind of non-fancy, home-cooked food that makes you feel good inside, with lovely desserts to boot. **Known for:** bistec ensebollado; platanos fritos; empanadas. [$] *Average main: $15* ✉ *3175 Glendale Blvd., Atwater Village* ☎ *323/665–9590.*

Bon Vivant Market and Café

$$ | **AMERICAN** | Bon Vivant's extensive and eclectic breakfast, lunch, and dinner menu, coupled with its fantastic cocktail menu and charming little marketplace, will almost certainly conquer half a day. Patrons come here and adopt a slow pace, staggering orders of coffee, luscious crepes, small plates, and delicious entrées, while adopting a laissez-faire attitude. **Known for:** cheese and fruit board; brunch; happy hour. $ *Average main: $26* ✉ *3155 Glendale Blvd., Atwater Village* ☎ *323/284–8013* ⊕ *www.bonvivantmarketcafe.com.*

Division 3

$ | **CAFÉ** | **FAMILY** | Who would have thought that a take-out window concept that serves breakfast sandwiches would ever take off? The folks behind Division 3 and, apparently, the entire city of Los Angeles. **Known for:** bacon, egg, and cheddar sandwich; patio seating; hearty deli sandwiches at lunch. $ *Average main: $8* ✉ *3329 Division St., Atwater Village* ☎ *323/987–0500* ⊕ *division3eats.com.*

Dune

$ | **MEDITERRANEAN** | **FAMILY** | Simple, small, and understated, it's easy to miss the best falafel spot in town. Hearty Middle Eastern falafel and chicken shawarma are piled on house-made flatbread. **Known for:** organic green-herb falafel sandwich; fried chicken shawarma sandwich; lunch and dinner. $ *Average main: $12* ✉ *3143 Glendale Blvd., Atwater Village* ☎ *323/486–7073* ⊕ *www.dune.kitchen.*

★ Good Measure

$ | **CONTEMPORARY** | Good Measure's proprietors decided to mix their love of travel with their passion for wine and start their own space offering a by-the-glass selection that spans the globe. The result is this romantic restaurant with an eclectic and excellent wine menu, not to mention an incredible dining menu with a quarterly On Tour section, which explores the food and wines of various regions.

Known for: crispy chicken confit; chickpea fries; desserts. $ *Average main: $18* ✉ *3224 Glendale Blvd., Atwater Village* ☎ *323/426–9461* ⊕ *www.goodmeasure-la.com.*

Link N Hops

$ | **HOT DOG** | Link N Hops is your typical sports bar, almost. There are a couple things that elevate it: excellent hot dog sandwiches and 24 craft beers on tap. **Known for:** Atwater knackwurst; smoked Portuguese Hawaiian; happy hour specials. $ *Average main: $10* ✉ *3111 Glendale Blvd., Atwater Village* ☎ *323/426–9049* ⊕ *linknhops.com.*

The Morrison

$ | **BURGER** | **FAMILY** | The Morrison is a friendly neighborhood Scottish pub, with a bit of an upmarket flair, a kids' menu, and believe it or not, dishes for your canine friends. And, as this is L.A., it serves a damn fine brunch. **Known for:** burgers; dessert menu; cheese fries with bacon jam. $ *Average main: $17* ✉ *3179 Los Feliz Blvd., Atwater Village* ☎ *323/667–1839* ⊕ *www.themorrisonla.com.*

Sepan Chicken

$ | **MIDDLE EASTERN** | Don't knock it until you've tried it. Despite appearances (it looks like a fast-food chicken shack), Sepan Chicken serves one of the best rotisserie chickens in town, or at least this side of Hollywood. **Known for:** Middle Eastern dishes; chicken kebabs; hummus. $ *Average main: $10* ✉ *3324 Glendale Blvd., Atwater Village* ☎ *323/669–0616* ⊕ *sepan-chicken.com.*

Tacos Villa Corona

$ | **MEXICAN** | You likely won't notice this cramped little spot on Glendale Boulevard unless there's a line or you're a fan of the late, great Anthony Bourdain, who was a big fan. About that line—it's almost always there, especially weekend mornings, when Tacos Villa Corona caters to the hangover crowd. **Known for:** chorizo and potato burrito; tacos;. $ *Average* main: $4 ✉ 3185 Glendale Blvd., Atwater Village ☎ 323/661–3458.

Tam O'Shanter

$$$ | **IRISH** | It's a bit of a specific recognition, but Tam O'Shanter is the oldest restaurant run by the same family in the same location in Los Angeles, operating for more than 90 years in its Tudor-style spot—that alone makes this place a worthy addition to any Atwater Village visit. Then there's their delicious food whose $30 prices are completely worth it, not to mention the fact that, once upon a time, it was Walt Disney's favorite restaurant. **Known for:** steak; toad-in-the-hole; Scottish decor. $ *Average main: $32* ✉ *2980 Los Feliz Blvd., Atwater Village* ☎ *323/664–0228* ⊕ *www.lawrysonline. com/tam-oshanter.*

Wanderlust Creamery

$ | **AMERICAN** | **FAMILY** | Eat the entire world in an ice-cream shop. That's the pitch for Wanderlust, which showcases the flavors of the globe in artisanal frozen delights. **Known for:** mango sticky rice vegan ice cream; ube malted crunch; seasonal flavors. $ *Average main: $5* ✉ *3134 Glendale Blvd., Atwater Village* ☎ *323/522–3082* ⊕ *www.wanderlust-creamery.com.*

▼ Nightlife

Unsurprisingly, neighborhood bars pepper Atwater Village. It's an interesting combination of smart, elevated restaurants and unpretentious, very laid-back bars. A night in Atwater may be spent indulging in a lavish feast with friends then topping it off with casual craft beer and cocktails.

Atwater Village Tavern

BARS/PUBS | There's no denying that part of the reason why this charming rectangular joint on Glendale Boulevard has effortlessly established itself as a regular fixture in the neighborhood is its incredible pub food. After all, the fried shrimp tacos, Baja-style, are to die for. But when you toss in the happy hour deals like all-day Mondays, $5 margarita Tuesdays, and $5 shot Fridays, you'll realize this place ain't too shabby as a bar, either. ✉ *3218 Glendale Blvd., Atwater Village* ☎ *323/644–0605* ⊕ *atwatervillagetavern. com.*

★ Bigfoot Lodge

BARS/PUBS | Don't be turned off by the glaring log cabin theme (which is intensified by signature cocktails called Scout's Honor and Roasted Marshmallow). Bigfoot Lodge is beloved by Eastside denizens, and despite appearances, it's every bit a low-key, unpretentious neighborhood bar that specializes in shots and beer and welcomes the occasional tourist that happens to stumble inside. ✉ *3172 Los Feliz Blvd., Atwater Village* ☎ *323/662–9227* ⊕ *www.bigfootlodge.com.*

Golden Road Brewing

BREWPUBS/BEER GARDENS | Sustainability and support of local community has always been a big part of this L.A. brewery's ethos, but more importantly, so is making great food and, of course, excellent beer. With several core brands, as well as a few specialty and seasonal brands, this is a must-stop for any craft beer lover vacationing in the City of Angels. ✉ *5410 W. San Fernando Rd., Atwater Village* ☎ *213/373–4677* ⊕ *goldenroad.la/atwater.*

Moonlight Rollerway Skating Rink

SPORTS VENUE | It seems like every night there's a hubbub at Moonlight Rollerway, whether it's skating to *Purple Rain* for a Prince tribute night, a tricky mannequin challenge, or a Harry Potter–themed skate night. If you're looking for a quick throwback to your childhood or a simple break from life, this is just the ticket. This vintage roller rink also offers affordable lessons, in case you're rusty and need a crash course. ✉ *5110 San Fernando Rd., Atwater Village* ☎ *818/241–3630* ⊕ *moonlightrollerway.com.*

The Roost

BARS/PUBS | Forget all your misconceptions about dive bars, or rather give them a chance, and walk into the Roost, whose comforting elements—a jukebox that comes fully loaded with Tom Petty, Springsteen, and the Allman Brothers Band, cozy leather booths, dimmed lights, and decent hearty food—will make you feel like you've flown back to your hometown for the holidays. The cocktails aren't too shabby either, but do bring cash. ✉ *3100 Los Feliz Blvd., Atwater Village* ☎ *323/664–7272.*

Verdugo Bar

BARS/PUBS | It's hard to decide whether the best thing about this place is its selection of 22 craft beers on tap and menu of "to-go" beer or the large beer garden furnished with picnic tables. It's probably a tie. But be warned, this place can get crowded, but it's worth it, especially on a hot sunny day (so pretty much every day). ✉ *3408 Verdugo Rd., Atwater Village* ☎ *323/257–3408* ⊕ *www.verdugobar.com.*

🛍 Shopping

Atwater Village partakes in the tradition of independent boutique shops boasting a bright, modern look and touting artisanal and locally made goods from small businesses. But it's a small neighborhood, so shopping till you drop may be out of the question, but you can definitely knock off a good couple of hours popping in for a bit of retail therapy.

Potted

FLOWERS | There's something comforting about Potted, like you've just walked into your parents' sunroom or a woodland fairy's home. This is a garden full of colors, nooks and crannies to tuck yourself into, and treasures of the botanic kind waiting to be discovered. It's every plant lover's paradise, but even those who wouldn't consider themselves to be plant fiends will be tempted to spend

a fortune here. ✉ *3158 Los Feliz Blvd., Atwater Village* ☎ *323/665–3801* ⊕ *pottedstore.com.*

Treehaus

CLOTHING | The beauty of Treehaus isn't that it's an independent boutique—Los Angeles has plenty of those—but that it carries a great assortment of retail pieces, from women's and children's clothing to accessories and home goods, all in a cozy rectangular space. ✉ *3153 Glendale Blvd., Atwater Village* ☎ *323/230–6776* ⊕ *www.treehaus.biz.*

Highland Park

In the early 20th century, Highland Park was a bastion for artists who erected numerous Arts and Crafts movement houses. It evolved into a largely immigrant community in the middle of the century and in the last few years has become a hybrid of its history. Local business owners have revived beautiful, historic buildings and turned them into exciting new restaurants, shops, and watering holes that pay ode to the area's past. These stand side by side with long-time establishments that serve up some of the best, and most authentic, tacos in town.

◉ Sights

Heritage Square Museum

MUSEUM | Looking like a prop street set up by a film studio, Heritage Square resembles a row of bright dollhouses in the modest Highland Park neighborhood. Five 19th-century residences, a train station, a church, a carriage barn, and a 1909 boxcar that was originally part of the Southern Pacific Railroad, all built between the Civil War and World War I, were moved to this small park from various locations in Southern California to save them from the wrecking ball. The latest addition, a re-creation of a World War I–era drugstore, has a vintage soda fountain and traditional products. Docents dressed in period costume lead visitors through the lavish homes, giving an informative picture of Los Angeles in the early 1900s. Don't miss the unique 1893 Octagon House, one of just a handful of its kind built in California. ✉ *3800 Homer St., Highland Park* ☎ *323/225–2700* 🌐 *www.heritagesquare.org* 🎟 *$10* 🕒 *Closed Tues.–Thurs. and federal holiday Mon.* ☞ *Tour included with admission price.*

🍴 Restaurants

Highland Park's gastronomic experiences tout an eclectic mix of culinary creations serving Mexican, vegan, Peruvian, and a whole lot of delicious donuts, all punctuated by independent coffee shops. A day along Figueroa, its main strip, will certainly be an epicurean adventure.

CaCao Mexicatessen

$ | **MEXICAN** | CaCao Mexicatessen, opened by local Christie Lujan in 2009, was one of the first places to showcase the creative potential of the street-style taco, offering options such as sea urchin and pork crackling as fillings. With handmade tortillas and a serious commitment to the flavors of Mexico, CaCao has embedded itself as one of the go-to places for Mexican food in Northeast L.A. **Known for:** duck carnitas taco; cochinita pibil taco; vegan tacos. [$] *Average main: $14* ✉ *1576 Colorado Blvd., Highland Park* ☎ *323/478–2791* 🌐 *www.cacaodeli.com* 🕒 *Closed Mon.*

Cafe Birdie

$ | **MEDITERRANEAN** | Though it only opened in 2016, this spacious 1920s spot along this quickly revitalizing stretch of Figueroa has already established itself as a neighborhood bistro frequented by Highland Park residents, as well as folks from nearby neighborhoods. The eclectic menu skillfully blends elements of European, Southern, and Japanese cuisines, tying them together with a fresh California flair and a gorgeous interior inspired by a fictional meeting-of-two-souls narrative. **Known for:** Mediterranean dishes; cocktails; great ambience. [$] *Average main: $19* ✉ *5631 N. Figueroa St., Highland Park* ☎ *323/739–6928* 🌐 *www.cafebirdiela.com.*

Cindy's

$ | **DINER** | **FAMILY** | The husband-and-wife team that took over Cindy's in 2014 never set out to create a trendy space for hipsters looking for their next artisanal fix; they just wanted to make great, accessible food. That's exactly what they've done, and by doing so they've established a neighborhood restaurant with reasonable prices and back-to-basics food that just so happens to look retro cool. **Known for:** brisket hash; house-made condiments; fried chicken and eggs. [$] *Average main: $14* ✉ *1500 Colorado Blvd., Highland Park* ☎ *323/257–7375* 🌐 *cindyseaglerock.com.*

★ Dave's Chillin'-n-Grillin'

$ | **AMERICAN** | **FAMILY** | Dave's Chillin'-n-Grillin' has been making the kind of sandwiches people dream about for more than 10 years. On a couple of griddles, Dave himself often turns out no-nonsense wonders. **Known for:** Rosemary's Turkey; the Pilgrim; the Surf and Turf. [$] *Average main: $12* ✉ *5715 N. Figueroa St., Highland Park* ☎ *323/490–0988* 🕒 *Closed Sun.*

★ Donut Friend

$ | **BAKERY** | When this music-influenced donut shop first opened on York Boulevard in the early days of Highland Park's renaissance, there wasn't much there, and its arrival helped shape the now bustling strip and its vegan inclinations. Donut Friend had evolved into a destination in its own right, touting both a signature and limited menu of purely vegan donuts—which also happen to be inspired by the pop punk and emo music scene—that taste better than Dunkin'. **Known for:** Green Teagan and Sara; Jets to Basil; make-your-own donut. [$] *Average* main: $4 ✉ 5107 York Blvd., Highland Park ☎ 213/995–6191 ⊕ www.donutfriend.com.

El Huarache Azteca

$ | MEXICAN | FAMILY | While you definitely should try the flat shoe-shaped dish El Huarache Azteca is named after—think somewhere between a flatbread and a tostada—you cannot go wrong with any of the other options at this family restaurant that's been a fixture in the area for the last couple decades. Just be aware there's often a wait for the food to come out. **Known for:** huarache; agua fresca; barbacoa de barrego. $ Average main: $10 ✉ 5225 York Blvd., Highland Park ☎ 323/478–9572 ⊕ elhuaracheaztecalive.com ▭ No credit cards.

5 Line Tavern

$ | BURGER | 5 Line Tavern would be just another neighborhood spot in a neighborhood full of neighborhood spots, were it not for its 50 beers on tap, long list of delectable pizzas, burgers, and sandwiches, and a full and diverse bar that has everything from a jalapeño margarita to an 18-year-aged Glenfiddich. If that's not enough incentive, there's a speakeasy hiding in the back. **Known for:** chicken wings; large selection of beers; pizza. $ Average main: $16 ✉ 2136 Colorado Blvd., Highland Park ☎ 323/238–3838 ⊕ www.5linetavern.com.

Kitchen Mouse

$ | DINER | Born in 2014 out of the owner's need for more kitchen space for her growing production catering business, Kitchen Mouse has blossomed into a wildly popular neighborhood restaurant with a cozy rustic-meets-modern look and an inspired, mostly organic vegan-vegetarian menu. The food is bright with vibrant flavors. **Known for:** breakfast and brunch; Morning Glory Bowl; house pancakes. $ Average main: $11 ✉ 5904 N. Figueroa St., Highland Park ☎ 323/259–9555 ⊕ www.kitchenmousela.com.

★ Knowrealitypie

$ | BAKERY | The award-winning Knowrealitypie, hidden in a shop the size of a large walk-in closet, serves homemade pies every Friday through Saturday and only stays open until it sells out, which it often does. So hurry on down to partake in a rotating menu of seasonal savory and sweet pies, turnovers, and other pastries while supplies last. **Known for:** triple cherry cabernet pie; caramel mango passion pie; minipies. $ Average main: $6 ✉ 5106 Townsend Ave., Highland Park ☎ 323/610–2244 ⊕ www.knowrealitypie.com ⊗ Closed Mon.–Thurs.

Polka Polish Cuisine

$$ | POLISH | There's a coziness in Polka Polish Cuisine that can only be matched by a grandmother's living room. The food here, traditional Polish fare, also has that same comfort. **Known for:** royal platter; pierogi; stuffed cabbage. $ Average main: $20 ✉ 4112 Verdugo Rd., Highland Park ☎ 323/255–7887 ⊕ www.polkarestaurant.com ⊗ Closed Mon. and Tues.

Town Pizza

$$ | PIZZA | The red building situated on the corner of York and North Avenue 51 houses a pizzeria that's as quirky and hip as the neighborhood it inhabits. Pizza purists, however, may cringe at some of the toppings, which include beets, corn, and mole. **Known for:** vegan options; mole pizza; the Pig and the Fig. $ Average main: $20 ✉ 5101 York Blvd., Highland Park ☎ 323/344–8696 ⊕ www.townla.com.

🍸 Nightlife

Bars and pubs are everywhere, especially along York Boulevard and North Figueroa Street. Make sure to hit up Highland Park Bowl for a glimpse of what this area used to be more than a century ago.

Block Party

BARS/PUBS | Block Party fills the beer garden need in Highland Park, and it does it very well with a large shuffleboard and a Wii hooked up to a projector, as well as plenty of picnic tables at which to chug (or nurse) beer and wine. The selection, from small-batch and craft vendors, is on point; the more adventurous may want to grab a michelada and *paleta* combo. ✉ *5052 York Blvd., Highland Park* ☎ *323/741–2747* ⊕ *www.blockpartyhlp.com.*

The Hermosillo

BARS/PUBS | The Hermosillo is the kind of laid-back pub every neighborhood should have, with an excellent selection of locally focused draft beer on tap, rotating wine list, and mouthwatering food. To add to its allure, award-winning Highland Park Brewery got its start in the pub's back storage room and is still featured prominently on the menu. ✉ *5125 York Blvd., Highland Park* ☎ *323/739–6459* ⊕ *thehermosillo.com.*

The Hi Hat

MUSIC CLUBS | The only thing left from its previous life as a pool hall are the two tables that greet customers as they enter. Now, it's the epicenter of live music in Highland Park and part of the revitalization of York Boulevard. Its exposed brick walls and pop-up kitchen are the cherry on top of the real treat—the local, underground bands performing here. ✉ *5043 York Blvd., Highland Park* ⊕ *hihat.la.*

Highland Park Bowl

BARS/PUBS | **FAMILY** | Highland Park Bowl was an ambitious restoration project and is now a massive throwback to its Prohibition Era roots as an alcohol-prescribing doctor's office and drugstore with its own bowling alley. That bowling alley remains, complete with the original pin machine. The hooch-pushing doctor and druggist, however, are long gone. But now there's an Italian restaurant that serves excellent pizza made from scratch using a mother dough brought all the way from Italy. ✉ *5621 N. Figueroa St., Highland Park* ☎ *323/257–2695* ⊕ *www.highlandparkbowl.com.*

La Cuevita

PIANO BARS/LOUNGES | Everyone could use a little more mezcal and tequila in their lives, and La Cuevita has a lot of it, often in its collection of tasty cocktails. This Mexican-themed bar—complete with free Taco Tuesdays, a dark red interior, and a picture of a bandito overlooking the patrons—has one of the cheapest happy hours in L.A., marking it the perfect place to start your evening. ✉ *5922 N. Figueroa St., Highland Park* ☎ *323/255–6871.*

★ The Old Chalet

BARS/PUBS | This ski lodge–inspired neighborhood bar may have changed ownership and management, but that doesn't mean that it's gotten a major and pretentious overhaul. In fact, besides its beefed-up whiskey and agave spirit lists (which desperately needed to be updated), new seasonal cocktails, and a new wave of eclectic clientele, it's still pretty much the same neighborhood bar the local residents have come to know and love. Plus, it's got a karaoke night that can't be beat. ✉ *1630 Colorado Blvd., Highland Park* ☎ *323/508–5058* ⊕ *www.theoldchalet.com.*

Sonny's Hideaway

PIANO BARS/LOUNGES | Sonny's Hideaway is the kind of place that does several things at once and does them all well—a stellar cocktail bar with a menu of original and classic drinks, a restaurant that borders on fine dining (albeit with a focus on comfort food), and a local haunt in the heart of York Boulevard. And the decor, which is reminiscent of old Hollywood, ain't so bad either. ✉ *5137 York Blvd., Highland Park* ☎ *323/255–2000* ⊕ *www.sonnyshideaway.com.*

The York

BARS/PUBS | Since 2007, before Highland Park became trendy, the York has been holding its own as the neighborhood bar. It's not just that the aesthetic gives off that neighborhood vibe (think exposed brick and chalkboard menus), but the craft beers on tap are great, and the pub food is delicious—the cheddar burger and the fish-and-chips are favorites. ✉ 5018 York Blvd., Highland Park ☎ 323/255–9675 ⊕ theyorkonyork. wordpress.com.

● Shopping

Figueroa Boulevard isn't buzzing only with bars and restaurants but also with ample opportunities for retail therapy. Small style outposts pave this street, as well as the connecting York Boulevard, with adorable gift shops, record stores, and spots to satisfy your vintage shopping itch.

Galco's Soda Pop Stop

FOOD/CANDY | FAMILY | Galco's, a local fixture in Highland Park for decades, is in some ways a trip down memory lane, carrying over 600 sodas—most of which harken back to the days when soda was a regional affair—and options from all over the world. They also have a collection of retro candies, a soda creation station with more than 100 syrups to choose from, and a selection of alcohol that would put most liquor stores to shame. ✉ 5702 York Blvd., Highland Park ☎ 323/255–7115 ⊕ sodapopstop.com.

Permanent Records

MUSIC STORES | Permanent Records has been a part of the vinyl resurgence since 2013, stocking new and used vinyl for every musical taste and doing it without any snobbery. The record store, which often has in-store performances, also runs its own label that focuses on local bands, limited-edition runs, and reissues. ✉ 5116 York Blvd., Highland Park ☎ 323/739–6141 ⊕ www.permanentrecordsla.com.

TOPO by Kitchen Mouse

FOOD/CANDY | Adjacent to its sister establishment, Kitchen Mouse, is a charming little market stop for all your pastry, grab 'n' go nourishment, and catering needs, complete with a small shop that touts adorable home and gift items. It's a must-stop after you've had your vegan fix at the restaurant. ✉ 5906 N. Figueroa St., Highland Park ☎ 323/474–6184 ⊕ www. kitchenmousela.com/market.

Chapter 10

ORANGE COUNTY AND CATALINA ISLAND

Updated by Kathy A. McDonald

⊙ Sights	🍴 Restaurants	🛏 Hotels	🛍 Shopping	🍸 Nightlife
★★★★★	★★★★☆	★★★★★	★☆☆☆☆	★☆☆☆☆

WELCOME TO ORANGE COUNTY AND CATALINA ISLAND

TOP REASONS TO GO

★ **Disney Magic:** Walking down Main Street, U.S.A., with Sleeping Beauty Castle straight ahead, you really will feel like you're in one of the happiest places on Earth.

★ **Beautiful Beaches:** Surf, swim, paddleboard, or just relax on one of the state's most breathtaking stretches of coastline. Keep in mind the water may be colder and rougher than you expect.

★ **Island Getaway:** Just a short high-speed catamaran ride from the shore, Catalina Island feels 1,000 miles away from the mainland. Wander around charming Avalon, dive or snorkel through the state's first underwater park, or explore the unspoiled beauty of the island's wild interior.

★ **The Fine Life:** Some of the state's wealthiest communities are in coastal Orange County, so spend at least part of your stay here experiencing how the other half lives.

★ **Family Fun:** Ride roller coasters, eat ice cream, bike on oceanfront paths, fish off ocean piers, or try bodysurfing.

1 Disneyland Resort. Once a humble vision of Walt Disney's, Southern California's top family and tourist destination has grown to become a megaresort, with more attractions spilling over into Disney's California Adventure. There's plenty here to entertain kids and adults alike.

2 Knott's Berry Farm. Amusement park lovers should check out this Buena Park attraction, with thrill rides, the *Peanuts* gang, and lots of fried chicken and boysenberry pie.

3 Coastal Orange County. The O.C.'s beach communities may not be quite as glamorous as they appear on TV, but coastal spots like Newport Harbor and Laguna Beach are perfect for chilling out in an oceanfront hotel.

4 Catalina Island. This unspoiled island paradise—with its pocket-size town, Avalon, and large nature preserve—is just off the Orange County coast.

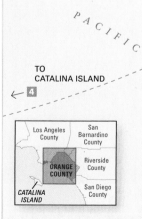

TO
CATALINA ISLAND

With its tropical flowers and palm trees, the stretch of coast between Seal Beach and San Clemente is often called the California Riviera. Exclusive Newport Beach and artsy Laguna are the stars, but lesser-known gems on the glistening coast—such as Corona del Mar—are also worth visiting. Offshore, meanwhile, lies gorgeous Catalina Island, a terrific spot for boating, diving, snorkeling, and hiking.

Few of the citrus groves that gave Orange County its name remain. This region south and east of Los Angeles is now ruled by tourism and high-tech business rather than agriculture. Despite a building boom that began in the 1990s, the area is still a place to find wilderness trails, canyons, greenbelts, and natural environs. Just offshore is a deep-water wilderness that's possible to explore via daily whale-watching excursions.

Planning

Getting Here and Around

AIR TRAVEL

Orange County's main facility is John Wayne Airport Orange County (SNA), which is served by six major domestic airlines and one commuter line. Long Beach Airport (LGB) is served by four airlines, including its major player, JetBlue. It's roughly 20 to 30 minutes by car from Anaheim.

Super Shuttle and Prime Time Airport Shuttle provide transportation from John Wayne and LAX to the Disneyland area of Anaheim. Round-trip fares average about $28 per person from John Wayne and $34 to $80 from LAX.

BUS TRAVEL

The Orange County Transportation Authority will take you virtually anywhere in the county, but it will take time; OCTA buses go from Knott's Berry Farm and Disneyland to Newport Beach. Bus 1 travels along the coast; Buses 701 and 721 provide express service to Los Angeles. Anaheim offers Anaheim Resort Transportation (ART) service that connects hotels to Disneyland Resort, downtown Anaheim, Buena Park, and the Metrolink train center. Rides are $3 each way.

INFORMATION Anaheim Resort Transportation. ☎ 714/563–5287 ⊕ rideart.org.

Orange County Transportation Authority.
☎ 714/636–7433 ⊕ www.octa.net.

CAR TRAVEL

The San Diego Freeway (I–405), the coastal route, and the Santa Ana Freeway (I–5), the inland route, run north–south through Orange County. South of Laguna, I–405 merges into I–5 (called the San Diego Freeway south from this point). A toll road, Highway 73, runs 15 miles from Newport Beach to San Juan Capistrano; it costs $6.22–$8.48 (lower rates are for weekends and off-peak hours) and is usually less jammed than the regular freeways. Do your best to avoid all Orange County freeways during rush hours (6–9 am and 3:30–6:30 pm). Highway 55 leads to Newport Beach. The Pacific Coast Highway (Highway 1) allows easy access to beach communities and is the most scenic route but expect it to be crowded, especially on summer weekends and holidays.

FERRY TRAVEL

There are two ferries that service Catalina Island; Catalina Express runs from Long Beach (about 90 minutes) and from Newport Beach (about 75 minutes). Reservations are strongly advised for summers and weekends. During the winter months, ferry crossings are not as frequent as in the summer high season.

TRAIN TRAVEL

Amtrak makes daily stops in Orange County at all major towns. Metrolink is a weekday commuter train that runs to and from Los Angeles and Orange County.

INFORMATION Amtrak. ☎ 800/872–7245 ⊕ www.amtrak.com. **Metrolink.** ☎ 800/371–5465 ⊕ www.metrolinktrains.com.

⇨ For more information on Getting Here and Around, see Travel Smart Los Angeles.

Restaurants

Much like in L.A., restaurants in Orange County are generally casual, and you'll rarely see suits and ties. However, at top resort hotel dining rooms, many guests choose to dress up.

Of course, there's also a swath of casual places along the beachfronts—seafood takeout, taquerias, burger joints—that won't mind if you wear flip-flops. Reservations are recommended for the nicest restaurants.

Many places don't serve past 11 pm, and locals tend to eat early. Remember that according to California law, smoking is prohibited in all enclosed areas.

Hotels

Along the coast there are remarkable luxury resorts; if you can't afford a stay, pop in for the view at Laguna Beach's Montage or the always welcoming Ritz-Carlton at Dana Point. For a taste of the O.C. glam life, have lunch overlooking the yachts of Newport Bay at the Balboa Bay Resort.

As a rule, lodging prices tend to rise the closer the hotels are to the beach. If you're looking for value, consider a hotel that's inland along the I–405 freeway corridor.

In most cases, you can take advantage of some of the facilities of the high-end resorts, such as restaurants and spas, even if you aren't an overnight guest.

Restaurant and hotel reviews have been shortened. For full information, visit Fodors.com.

WHAT IT COSTS

	$	$$	$$$	$$$$
RESTAURANTS				
	under $20	$20–$30	$30–$40	over $40
HOTELS				
	under $200	$200–$300	$301–$400	over $400

Visitor Information

Visit Anaheim is an excellent resource for both leisure and business travelers and can provide materials on many area attractions. Kiosks at the Anaheim Convention Center act as a digital concierge and allow visitors to plan itineraries and buy tickets to area attractions.

The Orange County Visitors Association's website is also a useful source of information.

INFORMATION Orange County Visitors Association. ⊕ www.visittheoc.com . **Visit Anaheim.** ✉ Anaheim Convention Center, 800 W. Katella Ave., Anaheim ☎ 714/765-2800 ⊕ www.visitanaheim.org.

Disneyland Resort

26 miles southeast of Los Angeles, via I–5.

The snowcapped Matterhorn, the centerpiece of Disneyland, punctuates the skyline of Anaheim. Since 1955, when Walt Disney chose this once-quiet farming community for the site of his first amusement park, Disneyland has attracted more than 650 million visitors and tens of thousands of workers, and Anaheim has been their host.

The resort is a sprawling complex that includes Disney's two amusement parks; three hotels; and Downtown Disney, a shopping, dining, and entertainment promenade. Anaheim's tourist center includes Angel Stadium of Anaheim, home of baseball's 2002 World Series Champion, Los Angeles Angels of Anaheim; the Honda Center (formerly the Arrowhead Pond), which hosts concerts and the Anaheim Ducks hockey team; and the enormous Anaheim Convention Center.

GETTING THERE

Disney is about a 30-mile drive from either LAX or Downtown. From LAX, follow Sepulveda Boulevard south to the I–105 freeway and drive east 16 miles to the I–605 north exit. Exit at the Santa Ana Freeway (I–5) and continue south for 12 miles to the Disneyland Drive exit. Follow signs to the resort. From Downtown, follow I–5 south 28 miles and exit at Disneyland Drive. **Disneyland Resort Express** (☎ 800/828–6699 ⊕ dre.coachusa.com) offers daily nonstop bus service between LAX, John Wayne Airport, and Anaheim. Reservations are not required. The cost is $30 one-way from LAX, and $20 from John Wayne Airport.

SAVING TIME AND MONEY

If you plan to visit for more than a day, you can save money by buying two-three-, four-, and five-day Park Hopper tickets that grant same-day "hopping" privileges between Disneyland and Disney's California Adventure. You get a discount on the multiple-day passes if you buy online through the Disneyland website.

Single-day admission prices vary by date. A one-day Park Hopper pass costs $147–$185 for anyone 10 or older, $141–$177 for kids ages three to nine depending on what day you go. Admission to either park (but not both) is $97–$135 or $91–$127 for kids three to nine; kids two and under are free.

In addition to tickets, parking is $20–$35 (unless your hotel has a shuttle or is within walking distance), and meals in the parks and at Downtown Disney range from $10 to $60 per person.

Disneyland

★ **Disneyland**

AMUSEMENT PARK/WATER PARK | FAMILY |
An imaginative original, Disneyland was an unproven concept when it opened in 1955. But Walt Disney himself could never have predicted the park's success and its beloved place in the hearts of Southern Californians. It is the only one of the parks to have been overseen by Walt himself, has a genuine historic feel, and occupies a unique place in the Disney legend. Expertly run, perfectly maintained, with polite and helpful staff ("cast members" in the Disney lexicon), the park has plenty that you won't find anywhere else—such as the Indiana Jones Adventure ride and Storybook Land, with its miniature replicas of animated Disney scenes from classics such as *Frozen* and *Alice in Wonderland*. Characters appear for autographs and photos throughout the day; times and places are posted at the entrances. Live shows, parades, strolling musicians, fireworks on weekends, and endless snack choices add to the carnival atmosphere. You can also meet some of the animated icons at one of the character meals served at the three Disney hotels (open to the public). Belongings can be stored in lockers just off Main Street; stroller rentals at the entrance gate are a convenient option for families with small tykes. The park's popularity means there are crowds year-round, even on the rare Southern California rainy days. ✉ *1313 S. Disneyland Dr., between Ball Rd. and Katella Ave., Anaheim* ☎ *714/781–4636 guest information* ⊕ *www.disneyland. com* 🖃 *From $97; parking $20.*

PARK NEIGHBORHOODS

Neighborhoods for Disneyland are arranged in geographic order.

MAIN STREET, U.S.A.

Walt's hometown of Marceline, Missouri, was the inspiration behind this romanticized image of small-town America, circa 1900. The sidewalks are lined with a penny arcade and shops that sell everything from tradeable pins to Disney-themed clothing, an endless supply of sugar confections, and a photo shop that offers souvenirs created via Disney's PhotoPass (on-site photographers capture memorable moments digitally—you can access them in person or online via the Disneyland app). Main Street opens half an hour before the rest of the park, so it's a good place to explore if you're getting an early start to beat the crowds (it's also open an hour after the other attractions close, so you may want to save your shopping for the end of the day). **Main Street Cinema** offers a cool respite from the crowds and six classic Disney animated shorts, including *Steamboat Willie*. There's rarely a wait to enter. Grab a cappuccino and fresh-made pastry at the Jolly Holiday bakery to jump-start your visit. Board the **Disneyland Railroad** here to save on walking; it tours all the lands and offers unique views of Splash Mountain, the Grand Canyon, and Primeval World dioramas.

NEW ORLEANS SQUARE

This mini–French Quarter, with narrow streets, hidden courtyards, and live street performances, is home to two iconic attractions and the Cajun-inspired Blue Bayou restaurant. **Pirates of the Caribbean** now features Jack Sparrow and the cursed Captain Barbossa of the blockbuster series, plus enhanced special effects and battle scenes (complete with cannonball explosions). Nearby **Haunted Mansion** continues to spook guests with its stretching room and "doombuggy" rides (there's now an expanded storyline for the beating-heart bride). The *Nightmare Before Christmas* holiday overlay is an annual tradition. This is a good area to get a casual bite to eat; the clam chowder in sourdough bread bowls, sold at the French Market Restaurant and Royal Street Veranda, is a popular choice. Food carts offer everything from just-popped popcorn to churros and even fresh fruit.

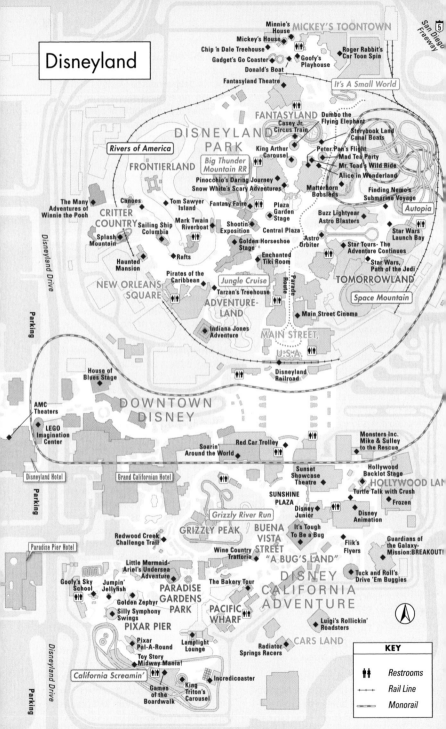

Disneyland

MICKEY'S TOONTOWN

Minnie's House
Mickey's House
Chip 'n Dale Treehouse
Gadget's Go Coaster
Donald's Boat
Fantasyland Theatre
Roger Rabbit's Car Toon Spin
Goofy's Playhouse
It's A Small World

San Diego 5 Freeway

FANTASYLAND
Dumbo the Flying Elephant
Casey Jr. Circus Train
Storybook Land Canal Boats
King Arthur Carousel
Peter Pan's Flight
Mad Tea Party
Mr. Toad's Wild Ride
Alice in Wonderland
Finding Nemo's Submarine Voyage

DISNEYLAND PARK

Rivers of America

FRONTIERLAND
Big Thunder Mountain RR
Pinocchio's Daring Journey
Snow White's Scary Adventures
Matterhorn Bobsleds

Autopia

The Many Adventures of Winnie the Pooh
Canoes
Tom Sawyer Island
Fantasy Faire
Plaza Garden Stage
Buzz Lightyear Astro Blasters
Star Wars Launch Bay

CRITTER COUNTRY
Sailing Ship Columbia
Mark Twain Riverboat
Shootin' Exposition
Central Plaza
Astro Orbitor
Star Tours- The Adventure Continues
Star Wars, Path of the Jedi

Splash Mountain
Rafts
Golden Horseshoe Stage

Haunted Mansion
Enchanted Tiki Room

TOMORROWLAND

Pirates of the Caribbean
Jungle Cruise
Space Mountain

NEW ORLEANS SQUARE
Tarzan's Treehouse

ADVENTURELAND
Main Street Cinema

Indiana Jones Adventure

MAIN STREET, U.S.A.

House of Blues Stage
Disneyland Railroad

AMC Theaters

DOWNTOWN DISNEY

LEGO Imagination Center

Monsters Inc. Mike & Sulley to the Rescue

Soarin' Around the World
Red Car Trolley

Disneyland Hotel

Grand Californian Hotel

Hollywood Backlot Stage
HOLLYWOOD LAND
Turtle Talk with Crush
Frozen

Sunset Showcase Theatre
SUNSHINE PLAZA
Disney Junior
Disney Animation

Paradise Pier Hotel

Grizzly River Run
GRIZZLY PEAK
BUENA VISTA STREET
It's Tough To Be a Bug
Flik's Flyers
Guardians of the Galaxy-Mission:BREAKOUT!

Redwood Creek Challenge Trail
Wine Country Trattoria
"A BUG'S LAND"
Tuck and Roll's Drive 'Em Buggies

Little Mermaid- Ariel's Undersea Adventure
The Bakery Tour
DISNEY CALIFORNIA ADVENTURE

Goofy's Sky School
Jumpin' Jellyfish
PARADISE GARDENS PARK
PACIFIC WHARF

Golden Zephyr
Silly Symphony Swings
Luigi's Rollickin' Roadsters

PIXAR PIER
Pixar Pal-A-Round
Lamplight Lounge
Radiator Springs Racers
CARS LAND

California Screamin'
Toy Story Midway Mania!
Incredicoaster
Games of the Boardwalk
King Triton's Carousel

Disneyland Drive
Parking
Katella Avenue

KEY	
🚻	Restrooms
┼┼	Rail Line
⊏⊐	Monorail

FRONTIERLAND

Between Adventureland and Fantasyland, Frontierland transports you to the wild, wild West with its rustic buildings, shooting gallery, mountain range, and foot-stompin' dance hall. The marquee attraction, **Big Thunder Mountain Railroad,** is a relatively tame roller coaster ride (no steep descents) that takes the form of a runaway mine car as it rumbles past desert canyons and an old mining town. Tour the Rivers of America on the **Mark Twain Riverboat** in the company of a grizzled old river pilot or circumnavigate the globe on the **Sailing Ship Columbia,** though its operating hours are usually limited to weekends. From here, you can raft over to Pirate's Lair on **Tom Sawyer Island,** which now features pirate-themed caves, treasure hunts, and music, along with plenty of caves and hills to climb and explore. If you don't mind tight seating, have a snack at the Golden Horseshoe saloon, where Walt himself used to hang out.

CRITTER COUNTRY

Down-home country is the theme in this shaded corner of the park, where Winnie the Pooh and Davy Crockett make their homes. Here you can find **Splash Mountain,** a classic flume ride with music, and appearances by Brer Rabbit and other *Song of the South* characters. Don't forget to check out your photo (the camera snaps close-ups of each car just before it plunges into the water) on the way out. The patio of the popular Hungry Bear Restaurant has great views of Tom Sawyer's Island and Davy Crockett's Explorer Canoes, which ply the waters on weekends only.

ADVENTURELAND

Modeled after the lands of Africa, Polynesia, and Arabia, this tiny tropical paradise is worth braving the crowds that flock here for the ambience and better-than-average food. Sing along with the animatronic birds and tiki gods in the **Enchanted Tiki Room,** sail the rivers of the world with

Disney's Top Attractions

Indiana Jones: You're at the wheel for this thrilling ride through a cursed temple. Watch out for boulders!

Haunted Mansion: A "doombuggy" takes you through a spooky old plantation mansion.

Matterhorn Bobsleds: At the center of the Magic Kingdom, this roller coaster simulates bobsleds.

Pirates of the Caribbean: Watch buccaneers wreak havoc as you float along in a rowboat.

Space Mountain: This scary-but-thrilling roller coaster is indoors— and mostly in the dark.

joke-cracking skippers on **Jungle Cruise,** and climb the *Disneyodendron semperflorens* (the always-blooming Disney tree) to **Tarzan's Treehouse,** where you can walk through scenes, some interactive, from the 1999 animated film. Cap off the visit with a wild Jeep ride at **Indiana Jones Adventure,** where the special effects and decipherable hieroglyphics distract you while you're waiting in line. There's a single-rider option for a quicker ride. The skewers (some vegetarian options available) at Bengal Barbecue and pineapple whip at Tiki Juice Bar are some of the best fast-food options in the park.

FANTASYLAND

Sleeping Beauty Castle marks the entrance to Fantasyland, a visual wonderland of princesses, spinning teacups, flying elephants, and other classic storybook characters. Rides, and shops such as the princess-themed Bibbidi Bobbidi Boutique, take precedence over restaurants in this area of the park,

Best Tips for Disneyland

■TIP→ As of 2017, all visitors must pass through metal detectors, and bags are searched before entering the Disneyland Resort. Allot 10–15 extra minutes for passing through the security line.

Download the Disneyland app. The app provides access to FASTPASS tickets via the digital MAXPASS, shows attraction wait times in real time, lists entertainment and parade times, and can guide you through the park.

Buy entry tickets in advance. Nearby hotels sell park admission tickets; you can also buy them through Disney's website and the Disneyland app. With package deals, like those offered through AAA, tickets are included.

Lines at ticket booths can take more than an hour on busy days. Save time by buying in advance.

Come midweek. Weekends, especially in summer, are a mob scene. Holidays are crowded, too. A rainy winter weekday is often the least crowded time to visit.

Plan your times to hit the most popular rides. Get to the park as early as possible, even before the gates open, and make a beeline for the top rides before the crowds reach a critical mass. Late evening is when the hordes thin out, and you can catch a special show or parade. Save the quieter attractions for midafternoon.

Use FASTPASS. These passes allow you to reserve your place in line at some of the most crowded attractions (only one at a time). Distribution machines are posted near the entrances of each attraction. Feed in your park admission ticket, and you'll receive a pass with a printed time frame (generally up to 1–1½ hours later) during which you can return to wait in a much shorter line.

Avoid peak mealtime crowds. Start the day with a big breakfast so you won't be too hungry at noon, when restaurants and vendors get slammed. Wait to have lunch until after 1 pm.

If you want to eat at the **Blue Bayou** in New Orleans Square, you can make a reservation up to six months in advance online. Another (cheaper) option is to bring your own snacks. It's always a good idea to bring water.

Check the daily events schedule online or at the park entrance. During parades, fireworks, and other special events, sections of the parks are filled with crowds. This can work in your favor or against you: an event could make it difficult to get around a park—but if you plan ahead, you can take advantage of the distraction to hit popular rides.

Send the teens next door. Disneyland's newer sister park, California Adventure, features more intense rides suitable for older kids (Park Hopper passes include admission to both parks).

but outdoor carts sell everything from churros to turkey legs. Tots love the **King Arthur Carousel, Casey Jr. Circus Train,** and **Storybook Land Canal Boats.** This is also home to **Mr. Toad's Wild Ride, Peter Pan's Flight,** and **Pinocchio's Daring Journey,** all classic movie-theater-dark rides that immerse riders in Disney fairy tales. The Abominable Snowman pops up on the **Matterhorn Bobsleds,** a roller coaster that twists and turns up and around on a made-to-scale model of the real Swiss mountain. Anchoring the east end of Fantasyland is **It's a Small World,** a smorgasbord of dancing animatronic dolls, cuckoo clock–covered walls, and variations of the song everyone knows, or soon *will* know, by heart. Beloved Disney characters like Ariel from *The Little Mermaid* are also part of the mix. Fantasy Faire is a fairy tale–style village that collects all the Disney princesses together. Each has her own reception nook in the Royal Hall. Condensed retellings of *Tangled* and *Beauty and the Beast* take place at the Royal Theatre.

MICKEY'S TOONTOWN

Geared toward small fries, this lopsided cartoonlike downtown, complete with cars and trolleys that invite exploring, is where Mickey, Donald, Goofy, and other classic Disney characters hang their hats. One of the most popular attractions is **Roger Rabbit's Car Toon Spin,** a twisting, turning cab ride through the Toontown of *Who Framed Roger Rabbit?* You can also walk through **Mickey's House** to meet and be photographed with the famous mouse, take a low-key ride on **Gadget's Go Coaster,** or bounce around the fenced-in playground in front of **Goofy's Playhouse.**

TOMORROWLAND

This popular section of the park continues to tinker with its future, adding and enhancing rides regularly. *Star Wars*–themed attractions can't be missed, like the immersive, 3-D **Star Tours – The Adventures Continue,** where you can join the Rebellion in a galaxy far, far away.

Finding Nemo's Submarine Voyage updates the old Submarine Voyage ride with the exploits of Nemo, Dory, Marlin, and other characters from the Disney-Pixar film. Try to visit this popular ride early in the day if you can, and be prepared for a wait. The interactive **Buzz Lightyear Astro Blasters** lets you zap your neighbors with laser beams and compete for the highest score. Hurtle through the cosmos on **Space Mountain** or check out mainstays like the futuristic **Astro Orbiter** rockets, **Star Wars Launch Bay,** which showcases costumes, models, and props from the franchise, and **Star Wars, Path of the Jedi,** which catches viewers up on all the movies with a quick 12-minute film. Disneyland Monorail and Disneyland Railroad both have stations here. There's also a video arcade and dancing water fountain that makes a perfect playground for kids on hot summer days. The Jedi Training Academy spotlights future Luke Skywalkers in the crowd.

Besides the eight lands, the daily live-action shows and parades are always crowd pleasers. Among these is **Fantasmic!,** a musical, fireworks, and laser show in which Mickey and friends wage a spellbinding battle against Disneyland's darker characters. ■ TIP→ **Arrive early to secure a good view; if there are two shows scheduled for the day, the second one tends to be less crowded. A fireworks display lights up weekends and most summer evenings.** Brochures with maps, available at the entrance, list show and parade times.

Disney California Adventure

★ **Disney California Adventure**
AMUSEMENT PARK/WATER PARK | FAMILY |
The sprawling Disney California Adventure, adjacent to Disneyland (their entrances face each other), pays tribute to the Golden State with seven theme areas that re-create vintage architectural styles and embrace several hit Pixar films via engaging attractions. Visitors

Did You Know?

The plain purple teacup in Disneyland's Mad Tea Party ride spins the fastest—though no one knows why.

enter through the art deco–style Buena Vista Street, past shops and a helpful information booth that advises wait times on attractions. The 12-acre Cars Land features Radiator Springs Racers, a speedy trip in six-passenger speedsters through scenes featured in the blockbuster hit. (FASTPASS tickets for the ride run out early most days.) Other popular attractions include the free-falling Guardians of the Galaxy–Mission: BREAKOUT!; World of Color, a nighttime water-effects show; and Toy Story Midway Mania!, an interactive adventure ride hosted by Woody and Buzz Lightyear. At night the park takes on neon hues as glowing signs light up Route 66 in Cars Land and Pixar Pal-A-Round, a giant Ferris wheel on the Pixar Pier. Cocktails, beer, and wine are available; craft beers and premium wines from California are poured. Live nightly entertainment also features a 1930s jazz troupe that arrives in a vintage jalopy. Some rides have a minimum height limit of 40 inches. ⊠ *1313 S. Disneyland Dr., between Ball Rd. and Katella Ave., Anaheim* ☎ *714/781–4636* ⊕ *www.disneyland.com* ⊠ *From $97; parking $20.*

PARK NEIGHBORHOODS
BUENA VISTA STREET
California Adventure's grand entryway re-creates the lost 1920s Los Angeles that Walt Disney encountered when he moved to the Golden State. There's a **Red Car trolley** (modeled after Los Angeles's bygone streetcar line); hop on for the brief ride to Hollywood Land. Buena Vista Street is also home to a Starbucks outlet—within the Fiddler, Fifer and Practical Café—and the upscale Carthay Circle Restaurant and Lounge, which serves modern craft cocktails and beer. The comfy booths of the Carthay Circle restaurant on the second floor feel like a relaxing world away from the theme park outside.

GRIZZLY PEAK
This woodsy land celebrates the great outdoors. Test your skills on the **Redwood Creek Challenge Trail,** a challenging trek across net ladders and suspension bridges. **Grizzly River Run** mimics the river rapids of the Sierra Nevadas; be prepared to get soaked.

Soarin' Around the World is a spectacular simulated hang-gliding ride over internationally known landmarks like Switzerland's Matterhorn and India's Taj Mahal.

HOLLYWOOD LAND
With a main street modeled after Hollywood Boulevard, a fake sky backdrop, and real sound stages, this area celebrates California's film industry. **Disney Animation** gives you an insider's look at how animators create characters. **Turtle Talk with Crush** lets kids have an unscripted chat with a computer-animated Crush, the sea turtle from *Finding Nemo.* The Hyperion Theater hosts **Frozen,** a 45-minute live performance from a Broadway-size cast with terrific visual effects. ■TIP➔ **Plan on getting in line about half an hour in advance; the show is worth the wait.** On the film-inspired ride **Monsters, Inc. Mike & Sulley to the Rescue,** visitors climb into taxis and travel the streets of Monstropolis on a mission to safely return Boo to her bedroom. **Guardians of the Galaxy – Mission: BREAKOUT!,** which opened in summer 2017, replaced the now-closed Twilight Zone Tower of Terror.

CARS LAND
Amble down Route 66, the main thoroughfare of Cars Land, and discover a pitch-perfect re-creation of the vintage highway. Quick eats are found at the Cozy Cone Motel (in a teepee-shape motor court) while Flo's V8 café serves hearty comfort food. Start your day at Radiator Springs Racers, the park's most popular attraction, where waits can be two hours or longer. Strap into a nifty sports car and meet the characters of Pixar's *Cars*; the ride ends in a speedy auto race through the red rocks and

desert of Radiator Springs. ■TIP→ **To bypass the line, there's a single-rider option for Radiator Springs Racers.**

PACIFIC WHARF

In the midst of the California Adventure you'll find 10 different dining options, from light snacks to full-service restaurants. The Wine Country Trattoria is a great place for Italian specialties; relax outside on the restaurant's terrace for a casual bite while sipping a California-made craft beer or wine. Mexican cuisine and potent margaritas are available at the Cocina Cucamonga Mexican Grill and Rita's Baja Blenders, and Lucky Fortune Cookery serves Chinese stir-fry dishes.

PARADISE GARDENS PARK

The far corner of California Adventure is a mix of floating, zigzagging, and flying rides: soar via the **Silly Symphony Swings**; **Goofy's Sky School** rollicks and rolls through a cartoon-inspired landscape; and the sleek retro-styled gondolas of the **Golden Zephyr** mimic 1920s movies and their sci-fi adventures. Journey through Ariel's colorful world on **The Little Mermaid—Ariel's Undersea Adventure.** The best views of the nighttime music, water, and light show, **World of Color,** are from the paths along Paradise Bay. FASTPASS tickets are available. Or for a guaranteed spot, book dinner at the Wine Country Trattoria that includes a ticket to a viewing area to catch all the show's stunning visuals.

PIXAR PIER

This section re-creates the glory days of California's seaside piers, themed with Pixar film characters. If you're looking for thrills, join The Incredibles family on the **Incredicoaster** as the fast moving roller coaster takes its riders from 0 to 55 mph in about four seconds and proceeds through scream tunnels, steeply angled drops, and a 360-degree loop. **Pixar Pal-A-Round,** a giant Ferris wheel, provides a good view of the grounds, though some cars spin and sway for more kicks.

There are also carnival games, an aquatic-themed carousel, and **Toy Story Midway Mania!,** an interactive ride where you can take aim at a series of cartoon targets. Soft-serve ice cream, turkey legs, hot dogs, and churros are readily available for quick snacking. At the **Lamplight Lounge** adults can chill out and overlook the action while sipping on craft cocktails.

OTHER ATTRACTIONS
Downtown Disney District
AMUSEMENT PARK/WATER PARK | FAMILY | The Downtown Disney District is a 20-acre promenade of dining, shopping, and entertainment that connects the resort's hotels and theme parks. **The Void** provides an immersive virtual reality experience with special effects and more; the current game, **Star Wars: Secrets of the Empire**, transforms visitors into participants in an intergalactic battle. Refresh afterward at the bar or dining room at Splitsville, a mid-century modern–style bowling alley serving American comfort food. At **Ralph Brennan's Jazz Kitchen** you can dig into New Orleans–style food and music. Save room for sweets: **Salt and Straw** has gourmet ice cream while **Sprinkles** offers ultrarich cupcakes. Disney merchandise and artwork is showcased at the brightly lit **World of Disney** store. At the megasize **Lego Store** there are hands-on demonstrations and space to play with the latest Lego creations. **Anna and Elsa's Boutique** speedily makes over kids into their favorite character from the hit film *Frozen.* All visitors must pass through a security checkpoint and metal detectors before entering. With a minimum purchase of $20, parking is free for the first three hours. ⊠ *1580 Disneyland Dr., Anaheim* ☎ *714/300–7800* ⊕ *disneyland.disney.go.com/downtown-disney* 🖼 *Free.*

🍴 Restaurants

Anaheim White House
$$$ | ITALIAN | Although a massive fire gutted the Anaheim White House in 2017,

owner Bruno Serato rebuilt and expanded the local landmark known for its specialty pastas. The 1909-built original mansion was the inspiration for the complete renovation. $ *Average main: $38* ✉ *887 S. Anaheim Blvd., Anaheim* ☎ *714/772–1381* ⊕ *www.anaheimwhitehouse.com* ⊗ *No lunch.*

Catal Restaurant and Uva Bar

$$$ | MEDITERRANEAN | Famed chef Joachim Splichal guides his staff to take a relaxed approach at this bi-level Mediterranean spot, where more than 30 wines by the glass, craft beers, and craft cocktails pair well with his Spanish-influenced dishes. Upstairs, Catal's menu has tapas, a variety of flavorful paellas, and charcuterie. **Known for:** people-watching; gourmet burgers; happy hour. $ *Average main: $30* ✉ *Downtown Disney District, 1580 S. Disneyland Dr., Suite 103, Anaheim* ☎ *714/781–3463* ⊕ *www. patinagroup.com.*

Napa Rose

$$$$ | AMERICAN | Done up in a handsome Craftsman style, Napa Rose's rich seasonal cuisine is matched with an extensive wine list, with 1,500 labels and 80 available by the glass. For a look into the open kitchen, sit at the counter and watch the chefs as they whip up such signature dishes as grilled diver scallops and chanterelles, and lamb pot roast topped with a pomegranate mint glaze. **Known for:** excellent wine list; kid-friendly options; gorgeous dining room. $ *Average main: $48* ✉ *Disney's Grand Californian Hotel, 1600 S. Disneyland Dr., Anaheim* ☎ *714/300–7170, 714/781–3463 reservations* ⊕ *disneyland.disney.go.com/ grand-californian-hotel/napa-rose.*

 Hotels

Candy Cane Inn

$ | HOTEL | FAMILY | One of the Disneyland area's first hotels, the Candy Cane is one of Anaheim's most relaxing properties, with spacious and understated rooms

and an inviting palm-fringed pool. **Pros:** proximity to everything Disney; friendly service; free breakfast. **Cons:** dated decor; all rooms face parking lot; no elevator. $ *Rooms from: $179* ✉ *1747 S. Harbor Blvd., Anaheim* ☎ *714/774–5284, 800/345–7057* ⊕ *www.candycaneinn.net* ⤶ *171 rooms* ❙○❙ *Breakfast.*

★ Disney's Grand Californian Hotel and Spa

$$$$ | RESORT | FAMILY | The most opulent of Disneyland's three hotels, the Craftsman-style Grand Californian offers views of Disney California Adventure and Downtown Disney. **Pros:** gorgeous lobby; family friendly; direct access to California Adventure. **Cons:** the $20 self-parking lot is across the street; standard rooms are on the small side; $30 valet parking. $ *Rooms from: $625* ✉ *1600 S. Disneyland Dr., Anaheim* ☎ *714/635–2300* ⊕ *disneyland.disney.go.com/grand-californian-hotel* ⤶ *1019 rooms* ❙○❙ *No meals.*

Doubletree Suites by Hilton Hotel Anaheim Resort-Convention Center

$ | HOTEL | This busy hotel near the Anaheim Convention Center and a 20-minute walk from Disneyland caters to business travelers and vacationers alike. **Pros:** huge suites; walking distance to a variety of restaurants; chocolate chip cookies at check-in. **Cons:** a bit far from Disneyland; pool area is small; $21 daily parking fee. $ *Rooms from: $153* ✉ *2085 S. Harbor Blvd., Anaheim* ☎ *714/750–3000, 800/215–7316* ⊕ *doubletreeanaheim.com* ⤶ *252 rooms* ❙○❙ *No meals.*

Hilton Anaheim

$ | HOTEL | FAMILY | Next to the Anaheim Convention Center, this busy Hilton is the third-largest hotel in Southern California, with a restaurant and food court, hopping lobby lounge with communal tables, a full-service gym, and its own Starbucks. **Pros:** efficient service; fast casual dining options; some rooms have views of the park fireworks. **Cons:** huge size can be daunting; fee to use health club; megasize parking lot. $ *Rooms from: $159* ✉ *777 Convention Way, Anaheim*

☎ *714/750–4321, 800/445–8667* 🌐 *www.hiltonanaheimhotel.com* 🛏 *1572 rooms* 🍴 *No meals.*

Park Vue Inn
$ | HOTEL | FAMILY | Watch the frequent fireworks from the rooftop sundeck at this bougainvillea-covered Spanish-style inn, one of the closest lodgings to the Disneyland Resort main gate. **Pros:** easy walk to Disneyland, Downtown Disney, and Disney California Adventure; free parking until midnight on checkout day; some rooms have bunk beds. **Cons:** all rooms face the parking lot; rooms near the breakfast room can be noisy; inefficient room air conditioners. [$] *Rooms from: $159* ✉ *1570 S. Harbor Blvd., Anaheim* ☎ *714/772–3691, 800/334–7021* 🌐 *www.parkvueinn.com* 🛏 *86 rooms* 🍴 *Breakfast.*

Knott's Berry Farm

25 miles south of Los Angeles, via I–5, in Buena Park.

Knott's Berry Farm
AMUSEMENT PARK/WATER PARK | FAMILY | The land where the boysenberry was invented (by crossing raspberry, blackberry, and loganberry bushes) is now occupied by Knott's Berry Farm. In 1934 Cordelia Knott began serving chicken dinners on her wedding china to supplement her family's income. The dinners and her boysenberry pies proved more profitable than husband Walter's farm, so the two moved first into the restaurant business and then into the entertainment business. The park is now a 160-acre complex with close to 40 rides, dozens of restaurants and shops, arcade games, live shows, a brick-by-brick replica of Philadelphia's Independence Hall, and loads of Americana. Although it has plenty to keep small children occupied, the park is best known for its awesome thrill rides. The boardwalk area is home to several coasters, including the zooming HangTime that pauses dramatically then drops nearly 15 stories, plus water features to cool things off on hot days, and a lighted promenade. And, yes, you can still get that boysenberry pie (and jam, juice—you name it). Buy adult tickets online for a major discount; FastLane wristbands—for quicker access to the most popular rides—cost $70 online. ✉ *8039 Beach Blvd., Buena Park* ✣ *Between La Palma Ave. and Crescent St., 2 blocks south of Hwy. 91* ☎ *714/220–5200* 🌐 *www.knotts.com* 🎟 *$82.*

Park Neighborhoods

THE BOARDWALK

Not-for-the-squeamish thrill rides and skill-based games dominate the scene at the **boardwalk.** Roller coasters—Coast Rider, Surfside Glider, and Pacific Scrambler—surround a pond that keeps things cooler on hot days. **HangTime** towers 150 feet above the boardwalk as coaster cars hang, invert and drop the equivalent of 15 stories. The boardwalk is also home to a string of test-your-skill games that are fun to watch whether you're playing or not, and Johnny Rockets, the park's all-American diner.

CAMP SNOOPY

It can be gridlock on weekends, but kids love this miniature High Sierra wonderland where the *Peanuts* gang hangs out. Tykes can push and pump their own mini-mining cars on **Huff and Puff,** soar around via **Charlie Brown's Kite Flyer,** and hop aboard **Woodstock's Airmail,** a kids' version of the park's Supreme Scream ride. Most of the rides here are geared toward kids only, leaving parents to cheer them on from the sidelines. **Sierra Sidewinder,** a roller coaster near the entrance of Camp Snoopy, is aimed at older children, with spinning saucer-type vehicles that go a maximum speed of 37 mph.

FIESTA VILLAGE

Over in **Fiesta Village** are two more musts for adrenaline junkies: **Montezooma's Revenge,** a roller coaster that goes from 0 to 55 mph in less than five seconds, and **Jaguar!,** which simulates the motions of a cat stalking its prey, twisting, spiraling, and speeding up and slowing down as it takes you on its stomach-dropping course. There's also **Hat Dance,** a version of the spinning teacups but with sombreros, and a 100-year-old **Dentzel carousel,** complete with an antique organ and menagerie of hand-carved animals. In a nod to history, there are restored scale models of the California Missions at Fiesta Village's southern entrance.

GHOST TOWN

Clusters of authentic old buildings relocated from their original mining-town sites mark this section of the park. You can stroll down the street, stop and chat with a blacksmith, pan for gold (for a fee), crack open a geode, check out the chalkboard of a circa-1875 schoolhouse, and ride an original Butterfield stagecoach. Looming over it all is **GhostRider,** Orange County's first wooden roller coaster. Traveling up to 56 mph and reaching 118 feet at its highest point, the park's biggest attraction is riddled with sudden dips and curves, subjecting riders to forces up to three times that of gravity. On the Western-theme **Silver Bullet,** riders are sent to a height of 146 feet and then back down 109 feet. Riders spiral, corkscrew, fly into a cobra roll, and experience overbanked curves. The **Calico Mine** ride descends into a replica of a working gold mine complete with 50 animatronic figures. The **Timber Mountain Log Ride** is a visitor favorite: the flume ride tours through pioneer scenes before splashing down. Also found here is the **Pony Express,** a roller coaster that lets riders saddle up on packs of "horses" tethered to platforms that take off on a series of hairpin turns and travel up to 38 mph. Take a step inside the **Western Trails Museum,** a dusty old gem full of Old West memorabilia and rural Americana, plus menus from the original chicken restaurant and an impressive antique button collection. **Calico Railroad** departs regularly from Ghost Town station for a round-trip tour of the park (bandit holdups notwithstanding).

This section is also home to **Big Foot Rapids,** a splash-fest of white-water river rafting over towering cliffs, cascading waterfalls, and wild rapids. Don't miss the visually stunning show at **Mystery Lodge,** which tells the story of Native Americans in the Pacific Northwest with lights, music, and special effects.

INDIAN TRAILS

Celebrate Native American traditions through interactive exhibits like tepees and daily dance and storytelling performances.

Knott's Soak City Waterpark is directly across from the main park on 13 acres next to Independence Hall. It has a dozen major water rides; **Pacific Spin** is an oversize waterslide that drops riders 75 feet into a catch pool. There's also a children's pool, a 750,000-gallon wave pool, and a funhouse. Soak City's season runs mid-May to mid-September. It's open daily after Memorial Day, weekends only after Labor Day, and then closes for the season.

🍴 Restaurants

Mrs. Knott's Chicken Dinner Restaurant
$$ | **AMERICAN** | **FAMILY** | Cordelia Knott's fried chicken and boysenberry pies drew crowds so big that Knott's Berry Farm was built to keep the hungry customers occupied while they waited. The restaurant's current incarnation (outside the park's entrance) still serves crispy fried chicken, along with fluffy handmade biscuits, mashed potatoes, and Mrs. Knott's signature chilled cherry-rhubarb compote. **Known for:** fried chicken; family friendliness; outdoor dining. [$] *Average main: $22* ✉ *Knott's Berry Farm Marketplace, 8039 Beach Blvd.,*

A mural at Huntington Beach

Buena Park ☎ *714/220–5200* 🌐 *www.knotts.com/california-marketplace/mrs-knott-s-chicken-dinner-restaurant.*

🛏 Hotels

Knott's Berry Farm Hotel
$ | **RESORT** | **FAMILY** | This convenient high-rise hotel is run by the park and sits right on park grounds surrounded by graceful palm trees. **Pros:** easy access to Knott's Berry Farm; plenty of family activities; extra-large swimming pool. **Cons:** lobby and hallways can be noisy; public areas show significant wear and tear; dated room decor. [$] *Rooms from: $129* ✉ *7675 Crescent Ave., Buena Park* ☎ *714/995–1111, 866/752–2444* 🌐 *www.knottshotel.com* 🛏 *320 rooms* 🍴 *No meals.*

The Coast

Running along the Orange County coastline is scenic Pacific Coast Highway (Highway 1, known locally as the PCH). Older beachfront settlements, with their modest bungalow-style homes, are joined by posh gated communities. The pricey land between Newport Beach and Laguna Beach is where ex-Laker Kobe Bryant, novelist Dean Koontz, those infamous Real Housewives of Bravo, and a slew of finance moguls live.

Though the coastline is rapidly being filled in, there are still a few stretches of beautiful, protected open land. And at many places along the way you can catch an idealized glimpse of the Southern California lifestyle: surfers hitting the beach, boards under their arms.

Long Beach

About 25 miles southeast of Los Angeles, via I–110 south.

👁 Sights

★ **Aquarium of the Pacific**
ZOO | **FAMILY** | Sea lions, zebra sharks, and penguins, oh my!—this aquarium focuses on creatures of the Pacific

Ocean and is home to more than 11,000 animals. The main exhibits include large tanks of sharks, stingrays, and ethereal sea dragons, which the aquarium has successfully bred in captivity. The Ocean Theater features the multimedia attraction *Penguins 4D,* a panoramic film that captures the world of this endangered species. Be sure to say hello to Betty, a rescue at the engaging sea otter exhibit. For a non-aquatic experience, head to Lorikeet Forest, a walk-in aviary full of the friendliest parrots from Australia. Buy a cup of nectar and smile as you become a human bird perch. If you're a true animal lover, book an up-close-and-personal Animal Encounters Tour ($109) to learn about and assist in the care and feeding of sharks, penguins, and other aquarium residents; or find out how the aquarium functions with the extensive Behind the Scenes Tour ($19 for adults, not including admission). Certified divers can book a supervised dive in the aquarium's Tropical Reef Habitat ($299). Twice daily whale-watching trips on Harbor Breeze Cruises depart from the dock adjacent to the aquarium; summer sightings of blue whales are an unforgettable thrill. ✉ *100 Aquarium Way, Long Beach* ☎ *562/590–3100* 🌐 *www.aquariumofpacific.org* 🎟 *$30.*

Queen Mary

LIGHTHOUSE | FAMILY | The *Queen Mary,* though berthed, is an impressive example of 20th-century cruise ship opulence and sadly the last of its kind. The beautifully preserved art deco–style ocean liner was launched in 1936 and made 1,001 transatlantic crossings before finally berthing in Long Beach in 1967. Today there are multiple diversions on board from ongoing theatrical performances by illusionist Aiden Sinclair, *Illusions of the Passed: Legends of the Queen Mary,* a wine tasting room, and a daily British-style high tea.

Also on board you can take one of three daily or five weekend tours, such as the informative Glory Days Historical walk or the downright spooky Haunted Encounters tour. (Spirits have reportedly been spotted in the pool and engine room.) You could stay for dinner at one of the ship's restaurants, listen to live jazz in the original first-class lounge, or even spend the night in one of the 347 wood-panel cabins. The ship's neighbor, a geodesic dome originally built to house Howard Hughes's *Spruce Goose* aircraft, now serves as a terminal for Carnival Cruise Lines, making the *Queen Mary* the perfect pit stop before or after a cruise. Anchored next to the *Queen* is the *Scorpion,* a Russian submarine you can tour for a look at Cold War history. ✉ *1126 Queens Hwy., Long Beach* ☎ *877/342–0738* 🌐 *www.queenmary.com* 🎟 *Tours from $16.*

Hotels

Queen Mary Hotel

$ | HOTEL | FAMILY | Experience the golden age of transatlantic travel without the seasickness: a 1936 art deco–style reigns on the *Queen Mary,* from the ship's mahogany paneling to its nickel-plated doors to the majestic Grand Salon. **Pros:** a walkable historic Promenade deck; views from Long Beach out to the Pacific; art deco details. **Cons:** spotty service; vintage soundproofing makes for a challenging night's sleep; mandatory facility fee. [$] *Rooms from: $129* ✉ *1126 Queens Hwy., Long Beach* ☎ *562/435–3511, 877/342–0742* 🌐 *www.queenmary.com* 🛏 *347 staterooms* 🍴 *No meals.*

The Varden

$ | B&B/INN | Constructed in 1929 to house Bixby Knolls Sr.'s mistress, Dolly Varden, this small, historic, European-style hotel, on the metro line in downtown Long Beach, now caters to worldly budget travelers. Compact rooms are mostly white and blend modern touches like flat-screen TVs and geometric silver fixtures with period details like exposed beams, Dakota Jackson periwinkle chairs, and round penny-tile baths. **Pros:** great value for downtown location; discount passes to Gold's Gym across the street; complimentary continental breakfast. **Cons:** no resort services; small rooms; no elevator. [$] *Rooms from: $129* ✉ *335 Pacific Ave., Long Beach* ☎ *562/432–8950* 🌐 *www.thevardenhotel.com* 🛏 *35 rooms* 🍴 *Free Breakfast.*

Newport Beach

6 miles south of Huntington Beach via the Pacific Coast Highway.

Newport Beach has evolved from a simple seaside village to an icon of chic coastal living. Its ritzy reputation comes from mega-yachts bobbing in the harbor, boutiques that rival those in Beverly Hills, and spectacular homes overlooking the ocean.

The city boasts some of the cleanest beaches in Southern California; inland Newport Beach's concentration of high-rise office buildings, shopping centers, and luxury hotels drives the economy. But on the city's Balboa Peninsula, you can still catch a glimpse of a more humble, down-to-earth town scattered with taco spots, tackle shops, and sailor bars.

ESSENTIALS

VISITOR AND TOUR INFORMATION Visit Newport Beach Concierge. ✉ *Atrium Court at Fashion Island, 401 Newport Center Dr.* ☎ *855/563–9767* 🌐 *www.visitnewportbeach.com.*

Sights

Balboa Island
COMMERCIAL CENTER | **FAMILY** | This sliver of terra firma in Newport Harbor boasts quaint streets tightly packed with impossibly charming multimillion-dollar cottages. The island's main drag, Marine Avenue, is lined with equally picturesque cafés and shops. A car-free bike path and boardwalk encircles much of the island for an easy and scenic ramble.

Balboa Peninsula
BEACH—SIGHT | **FAMILY** | Newport's best beaches are on Balboa Peninsula, where many jetties pave the way to ideal swimming areas. The most intense spot for bodysurfing in Orange County, and arguably on the West Coast, known as the **Wedge,** is at the south end of the peninsula. It was created by accident in the 1930s when the Federal Works Progress Administration built a jetty to protect Newport Harbor. **TIP→ Rip currents and punishing waves mean it's strictly for the pros—but it sure is fun to watch an experienced local ride it.** ✉ *2172 E. Ocean Front* 🌐 *www.visitnewportbeach.com/beaches-and-parks/the-wedge.*

Discovery Cube's Ocean Quest
MUSEUM | **FAMILY** | This family-friendly destination has exhibits on the history of the harbor, ocean explorers, and scientific aspects of the Pacific Ocean. Other fun features include a touch tank holding local sea creatures and a lab for kids that encourages innovation. ✉ *600 E. Bay Ave.* ☎ *949/675–8915* 🌐 *www.oceanquestoc.org* 🎟 *$5* 🕒 *Closed weekdays.*

Newport Harbor
BODY OF WATER | **FAMILY** | Sheltering nearly 16,000 small boats, Newport Harbor may seduce even those who don't own a yacht. Spend an afternoon exploring the charming avenues and surrounding alleys; take California's longest-running auto ferry across to Balboa Island. The fare is $2 for car and driver for the scenic crossing. Several grassy areas on the primarily residential Lido Isle have views of the water. To truly experience the harbor, rent an electric boat for a pleasant day cruise or try stand-up paddleboarding in the sheltered waters. ✉ *Pacific Coast Hwy.* 🌐 *www.balboaislandferry.com.*

Newport Pier
MARINA | **FAMILY** | Jutting out into the ocean near 20th Street, Newport Pier

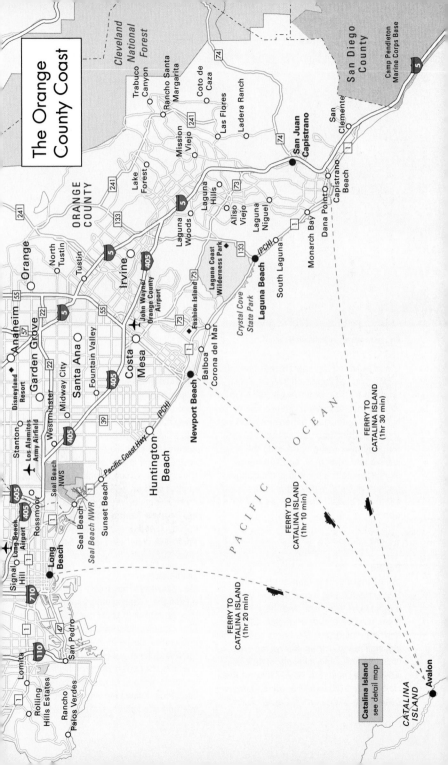

Riding the waves at Newport Beach

is a popular fishing spot. Street parking is difficult, so grab the first space you find and be prepared to walk. Early on Wednesday–Sunday mornings you're likely to encounter dory fishermen hawking their predawn catches, as they've done for generations. On weekends the area is alive with kids of all ages on in-line skates, skateboards, and bikes dodging pedestrians and whizzing past fast-food joints and classic dive bars. ✉ *72 McFadden Pl.*

🍴 Restaurants

Basilic

$$ | **BRASSERIE** | This intimate French-Swiss bistro adds a touch of old-world elegance to the island with its white linen and flower-topped tables. Chef Bernard Althaus grows the herbs used in his classic French dishes. **Known for:** French classics; fine wine; old-school ambience. [$] *Average main: $32* ✉ *217 Marine Ave., Balboa Island* ☎ *949/673–0570* 🌐 *www.basilicrestaurant.com* 🕒 *Closed Sun.*

Bear Flag Fish Co.

$ | **SEAFOOD** | **FAMILY** | Expect long lines in summer at this indoor/outdoor dining spot serving up the freshest local fish (swordfish, sea bass, halibut, and tuna) and a wide range of creative seafood dishes (the Hawaiian-style *poke* salad with ahi tuna is a local favorite). Order at the counter, which doubles as a seafood market, and sit inside the airy dining room or outside on a grand patio. **Known for:** freshest seafood; fish tacos; craft beers. [$] *Average main: $12* ✉ *Newport Peninsula, 3421 Via Lido* ☎ *949/673–3474* 🌐 *www.bearflagfishco.com.*

The Cannery

$$$ | **SEAFOOD** | This 1920s cannery building still teems with fish, but now they go into dishes on the eclectic Pacific Rim menu rather than being packed into crates. Settle in at the sushi bar, in the dining room, or on the patio before choosing between sashimi, freshly shucked oysters, or cilantro-marinated fish tacos. **Known for:** waterfront views; seafood specialties; craft cocktails.

[$] *Average main: $35 ✉ 3010 Lafayette Rd. ☎ 949/566–0060 🌐 www.cannerynewport.com ⏱ Closed Mon. lunch.*

Gulfstream

$$$ | **SEAFOOD** | **FAMILY** | This on-trend restaurant has an open kitchen, comfortable booths, and outdoor seating. The patio is a fantastic place to hang out. **Known for:** oysters on the half shell; local hangout; outdoor patio. [$] *Average main: $33 ✉ 850 Avocado Ave. ☎ 949/718–0188 🌐 www.gulfstreamrestaurant.com.*

3-Thirty-3

$$ | **AMERICAN** | This stylish eatery attracts a convivial crowd—both young and old—for midday, sunset, and late-night dining. A long list of small, shareable plates heightens the camaraderie. **Known for:** happy hour; brunch burritos; generous portions. [$] *Average main: $26 ✉ 333 Bayside Dr. ☎ 949/673–8464 🌐 www.3thirty3nb.com.*

Hotels

Balboa Bay Resort

$$$ | **RESORT** | **FAMILY** | Sharing the same frontage as the private Balboa Bay Club that long ago hosted Humphrey Bogart, Lauren Bacall, and the Reagans, this waterfront resort has one of the best bay views around. **Pros:** exquisite bayfront views; comfortable beds; a raked beach for guests. **Cons:** not much within walking distance; $34 nightly hospitality fee; some rooms have courtyard-only views. [$] *Rooms from: $339 ✉ 1221 W. Coast Hwy. ☎ 949/645–5000 🌐 www.balboabayresort.com 🛏 159 rooms 🍴 No meals.*

Fashion Island Hotel

$$ | **HOTEL** | **FAMILY** | Across a palm tree–lined boulevard from stylish Fashion Island, this 20-story tower caters to business types during the week and luxury seekers on weekends. **Pros:** lively lounge scene; large heated pool; great location. **Cons:** steep valet parking prices; some rooms have views of mall parking; destination fee add-on. [$] *Rooms from: $295 ✉ 690 Newport Center Dr. ☎ 949/759–0808, 877/591–9145 🌐 www.fashionislandhotel.com 🛏 295 rooms 🍴 No meals.*

★ **Lido House, Autograph Collection**

$$ | **RESORT** | **FAMILY** | Close to the Balboa Peninsula, the Lido House is modeled after a New England–style beach cottage, one grand enough to welcome you and all your family and friends. **Pros:** large hot tub and pool deck; lively hotel bar; free bikes to cruise the nearby beach boardwalk. **Cons:** pricey restaurant; $33 resort fee add-on; $40 valet parking. [$] *Rooms from: $300 ✉ 3300 Newport Blvd., Balboa Island ☎ 949/524–8500 🌐 www.lidohouse.com 🛏 130 rooms 🍴 No meals.*

Newport Beach Marriott Hotel and Spa

$$ | **RESORT** | Here you'll be smack in the busy part of town: across from Fashion Island, next to a country club, and with a view toward Newport Harbor. **Pros:** four concierge floors offer enhanced amenities; large spa; across from Fashion Island. **Cons:** sprawling floor plan; small bathrooms; car is essential for exploring beyond Fashion Island. [$] *Rooms from: $229 ✉ 900 Newport Center Dr. ☎ 949/640–4000 🌐 www.marriott.com 🛏 532 rooms.*

Activities

BOAT RENTALS

Balboa Boat Rentals

BOATING | **FAMILY** | You can tour the waterways surrounding Lido and Balboa isles with kayaks ($18 an hour), stand-up paddleboards ($25 for two hours), small motorboats ($75 an hour), and electric boats ($80 to $105 an hour) at Balboa Boat Rentals. *✉ 510 E. Edgewater Ave., Balboa Island ☎ 855/690–0794 🌐 www.boats4rent.com.*

A whimbrel hunts for mussels at Crystal Cove State Park.

BOAT TOURS
Catalina Flyer
TOUR—SPORTS | FAMILY | At Balboa Pavilion, the *Catalina Flyer* operates a 90-minute daily round-trip passage to Catalina Island for $70 in season. Reservations are required; check the schedule, as crossings may be canceled due to annual maintenance. ✉ *400 Main St., Balboa Island* ☎ *949/673–5245* ⊕ *www. catalinainfo.com.*

Hornblower Cruises and Events
TOUR—SPORTS | This operator books three-hour weekend dinner cruises with dancing for $95. The two-hour Sunday brunch cruise starts at $75. Cruises traverse the mostly placid and scenic waters of Newport Harbor. ✉ *2431 W. Coast Hwy.* ☎ *888/467–6256* ⊕ *www. hornblower.com.*

FISHING
Davey's Locker
FISHING | FAMILY | In addition to a complete tackle shop, Davey's Locker offers half-day sport-fishing trips starting at $41.50. Whale-watching excursions begin at $26 for weekdays. ✉ *Balboa Pavilion, 400 Main St., Balboa Island* ☎ *949/673–1434* ⊕ *www.daveyslocker.com.*

🛍 Shopping

★ Fashion Island
STORE/MALL | Shake the sand out of your shoes to head inland to the ritzy Fashion Island outdoor mall, a cluster of arcades and courtyards complete with koi pond, fountains, and a family-friendly trolley—plus some awesome ocean views. It has the luxe department stores Neiman Marcus and Bloomingdale's, plus expensive spots like Jonathan Adler, Kate Spade, and Michael Stars. ✉ *401 Newport Center Dr., between Jamboree and MacArthur Blvds., off PCH* ☎ *949/721–2000, 855/658–8527* ⊕ *www. shopfashionisland.com.*

Laguna Beach

10 miles south of Newport Beach on PCH, 60 miles south of Los Angeles, I–5 south to Highway 133, which turns into Laguna Canyon Road.

Driving in along Laguna Canyon Road from the I–405 freeway gives you the chance to cruise through a gorgeous coastal canyon, large stretches of which remain undeveloped, before arriving at a glistening wedge of ocean. There are 30 coves and beaches to visit, all with some of the cleanest water in Southern California. There's a convenient and free trolley service through town; service is extended on weekends and holidays.

Laguna's welcome mat is legendary. On the corner of Forest and Park avenues is a gate proclaiming, "This gate hangs well and hinders none, refresh and rest, then travel on." A gay community has long been established here; art galleries dot the village streets, and there's usually someone daubing up in Heisler Park. Along the Pacific Coast Highway you'll find dozens of clothing boutiques, jewelry stores, and cafés.

ESSENTIALS
VISITOR AND TOUR INFORMATION Visit
Laguna Beach Visitors Center. ⊠ *381 Forest Ave.* ☎ *949/497–9229, 800/877–1115* ⊕ *www.visitlagunabeach.com.*

◉ Sights

Laguna Art Museum
MUSEUM | This museum displays American art, with an emphasis on California artists from all periods. Special exhibits change quarterly. ⊠ *307 Cliff Dr.* ☎ *949/494–8971* ⊕ *www.lagunaartmuseum.org* ⌚ *$7* ⊙ *Closed Wed.*

Laguna Coast Wilderness Park
HIKING/WALKING | **FAMILY** | The Laguna Coast Wilderness Park is spread over 7,000 acres of fragile coastal territory, including the canyon. The 40 miles of trails are great for hiking and mountain biking, and are open daily, weather permitting. Docent-led hikes are given most weekends. No dogs are allowed in the park. ⊠ *18751 Laguna Canyon Rd.* ☎ *949/923–2235* ⊕ *www.ocparks.com/parks/lagunac* ⌚ *$3 parking.*

★ Main Beach Park
BEACH—SIGHT | **FAMILY** | A stocky 1920s lifeguard tower marks Main Beach Park, where a wooden boardwalk separates the sand from a strip of lawn. Walk along this soft-sand beach, or grab a bench and watch people bodysurfing, playing volleyball, or scrambling around two half-basketball courts. The beach also has children's play equipment. Most of Laguna's hotels are within a short (but hilly) walk. **Amenities:** lifeguards; toilets; showers. **Best for:** sunset; swimming; walking. ⊠ *Broadway at S. Coast Hwy.* ⊕ *www.visitlagunabeach.com.*

1,000 Steps Beach
BEACH—SIGHT | **FAMILY** | Off South Coast Highway at 9th Street, 1,000 Steps Beach is a hard-to-find spot tucked away in a neighborhood with great waves and hard-packed, white sand. There aren't really 1,000 steps down (but when you hike back up, it'll certainly feel like it). Sea caves and tide pools enhance this already beautiful natural spot. The beach is a rare dog-friendly spot. **Amenities:** showers. **Best for:** snorkeling; surfing; swimming. ⊠ *S. Coast Hwy., at 9th St.*

Wood's Cove
BEACH—SIGHT | **FAMILY** | Off South Coast Highway, Wood's Cove is especially quiet during the week. Big rock formations hide lurking crabs. This is a prime scuba-diving spot, and at high tide much of the beach is underwater. Climbing the steps to leave, you can see a Tudor-style mansion that was once home to Bette Davis. Street parking is limited. **Amenities:** none. **Best for:** snorkeling; scuba diving; sunset. ⊠ *Diamond St. and Ocean Way* ⊕ *www.visitlagunabeach.com.*

Looking for shells on Laguna Beach, one of the nicest stretches of sand in Southern California

🍴 Restaurants

Ocean at Main

$$$ | **AMERICAN** | Set in a handsomely renovated former bank from the 1940s, Ocean at Main's dishes are artfully presented and feature the best of California produce. Owned by the O.C.'s favorite chef, Craig Strong (who guided Studio at Montage for almost a decade), there's an expected emphasis on service but without pretension. **Known for:** handsome dining room; local ingredients; California-focused wine list. [$] *Average main: $38* ✉ *222 Ocean Ave.* ☎ *949/715–3870* 🌐 *www.oceanatmain.com.*

Sapphire Laguna

$$ | **INTERNATIONAL** | **FAMILY** | This Laguna Beach establishment set in a historic Craftsman is part gourmet pantry (a must-stop for your every picnic need) and part global dining adventure. Iranian-born chef Azmin Ghahreman takes you on a journey through Europe and Asia with dishes ranging from coconut macaroon pancakes to Malaysian black pepper shrimp. **Known for:** fried chicken sandwich; weekend brunch; pet-friendly patio. [$] *Average main: $27* ✉ *The Old Pottery Place, 1200 S. Coast Hwy.* ☎ *949/715–9888* 🌐 *www.sapphirelaguna.com.*

★ **Studio**

$$$$ | **MODERN AMERICAN** | In a nod to Laguna's art history, Studio has house-made specialties that entice the eye as well as the palate. The restaurant occupies its own Craftsman-style bungalow, atop a 50-foot bluff overlooking the Pacific. **Known for:** attentive service; chef's tasting menu; being great for special occasions. [$] *Average main: $60* ✉ *Montage Laguna Beach, 30801 S. Coast Hwy.* ☎ *949/715–6420* 🌐 *www.studiolagunabeach.com* ⏲ *Closed Mon. No lunch.*

Taco Loco

$ | **MEXICAN** | **FAMILY** | This may look like a fast-food taco stand, and the hemp brownies on the menu may make you think the kitchen's *really* laid-back, but the quality of the food here equals that in many higher-price restaurants. Some

Mexican standards get a Louisiana twist, like Cajun-spiced seafood tacos. **Known for:** vegetarian tacos; sidewalk seating; surfer clientele. $ *Average main: $12* ⊠ *640 S. Coast Hwy.* ☎ *949/497–1635* ⊕ *www.tacoloco.net.*

Zinc Café and Market

$ | VEGETARIAN | FAMILY | Families flock to this small Laguna Beach institution for reasonably priced breakfast and lunch options. Try the signature quiches or poached egg dishes in the morning, or swing by later in the day for healthy salads, house-made soups, quesadillas, or pizzettes. **Known for:** gourmet goodies; avocado toast; busy outdoor patio. $ *Average main: $15* ⊠ *350 Ocean Ave.* ☎ *949/494–6302* ⊕ *www.zinccafe.com* ⊗ *No dinner Nov.–Apr.*

🛏 Hotels

Inn at Laguna Beach

$$$ | HOTEL | FAMILY | This bright yellow local landmark is stacked neatly at the north end of Laguna's Main Beach and it's one of the few hotels in SoCal set almost on the sand. **Pros:** rooftop bar; beach essentials provided; beachfront location. **Cons:** ocean-view rooms are pricey; small hot tub; limited breakfast menu. $ *Rooms from: $379* ⊠ *211 N. Coast Hwy.* ☎ *949/497–9722, 800/544–4479* ⊕ *www.innatlagunabeach.com* ⇌ *70 rooms.*

La Casa del Camino

$$ | HOTEL | The look is Old California at the 1929-built La Casa del Camino, with dark woods, arched doors, and wrought iron in the lobby. **Pros:** breathtaking views from rooftop lounge; personable service; close to beach. **Cons:** some rooms face the highway; frequent events can make hotel noisy; some rooms are very small. $ *Rooms from: $229* ⊠ *1289 S. Coast Hwy.* ☎ *949/497–2446, 855/634–5736* ⊕ *www.lacasadelcamino.com* ⇌ *36 rooms* ❍ *No meals.*

⭐ Montage Laguna Beach

$$$$ | RESORT | FAMILY | Laguna's connection to the Californian plein-air artists is mined for inspiration at this head-turning, lavish hotel. **Pros:** top-notch, enthusiastic service; idyllic coastal location; numerous sporty pursuits available offshore. **Cons:** rates can be more than $1,100 per night for holidays or summer weekends; $50 valet parking; $42 daily resort fee. $ *Rooms from: $695* ⊠ *30801 S. Coast Hwy.* ☎ *949/715–6000, 866/271–6953* ⊕ *www.montagehotels.com/lagunabeach* ⇌ *250 rooms* ❍ *No meals.*

Surf and Sand Resort

$$$$ | RESORT | FAMILY | One mile south of downtown, on an exquisite stretch of beach with thundering waves and gorgeous rocks, this is a getaway for those who want a boutique hotel experience without all the formalities. **Pros:** easy beach access; intimate property; slightly removed from Main Street crowds. **Cons:** pricey valet parking; surf can be quite loud; no air conditioning. $ *Rooms from: $575* ⊠ *1555 S. Coast Hwy.* ☎ *949/497–4477, 877/741–5908* ⊕ *www.surfandsandresort.com* ⇌ *167 rooms* ❍ *No meals.*

🛍 Shopping

Coast Highway, Forest and Ocean avenues, and Glenneyre Street are full of art galleries, fine jewelry stores, souvenir shops, and clothing boutiques.

Adam Neeley Fine Art Jewelry

JEWELRY/ACCESSORIES | Be prepared to be dazzled at Adam Neeley Fine Art Jewelry, where artisan proprietor Adam Neeley creates one-of-a-kind modern pieces. ⊠ *352 N. Coast Hwy.* ☎ *949/715–0953* ⊕ *www.adamneeley.com* ⊗ *Closed Sun. and Mon.*

Art for the Soul

CRAFTS | A riot of color, Art for the Soul has hand-painted furniture, crafts, and unusual gifts. ⊠ *272 Forest Ave.* ☎ *949/675–1791* ⊕ *www.art4thesoul.com.*

Mission San Juan Capistrano

Candy Baron

FOOD/CANDY | FAMILY | Get your sugar fix at the time-warped Candy Baron, filled with old-fashioned goodies like gumdrops, bull's-eyes, and more than 50 flavors of saltwater taffy. ⊠ *231 Forest Ave.* ☎ *949/497–7508* ⊕ *www.thecandybaron. com.*

Fetneh Blake

CLOTHING | Hit Fetneh Blake for pricey, Euro-chic clothes. The emerging designers found here lure Angelenos to make the trek south. ⊠ *427 N. Coast Hwy.* ☎ *949/494–3787* ⊕ *www.fetnehblake. com.*

La Rue du Chocolat

FOOD/CANDY | This shop dispenses chocolate-covered strawberries and handcrafted chocolates in seasonal flavors. ⊠ *Peppertree La., 448 S. Coast Hwy., Suite B* ☎ *949/494–2372* ⊕ *www. larueduchocolat.com.*

San Juan Capistrano

5 miles north of Dana Point, Highway 74, 60 miles north of San Diego, I–5.

San Juan Capistrano is best known for its historic mission, where the swallows traditionally return each year, migrating from their winter haven in Argentina, but these days they are more likely to choose other local sites for nesting. St. Joseph's Day, March 19, launches a week of fowl festivities. Charming antiques stores, which range from pricey to cheap, line Camino Capistrano.

GETTING HERE AND AROUND

If you arrive by train, which is far more romantic and restful than battling freeway traffic, you'll be dropped off across from the mission at the San Juan Capistrano depot. With its appealing brick café and preserved Santa Fe cars, the depot retains much of the magic of early American railroads. If driving, park near Ortega and Camino Capistrano, the city's main streets.

Sights

★ Mission San Juan Capistrano

ARCHAEOLOGICAL SITE | FAMILY | Founded in 1776 by Father Junípero Serra (consecrated as St. Serra), Mission San Juan Capistrano was one of two Roman Catholic outposts between Los Angeles and San Diego. The Great Stone Church, begun in 1797, is the largest structure created by the Spanish in California. After extensive retrofitting, the golden-hued interiors are open to visitors who may feel they are touring among ruins in Italy rather than the O.C. Many of the mission's adobe buildings have been restored to illustrate mission life, with exhibits of an olive millstone, tallow ovens, tanning vats, metalworking furnaces, and the padres' living quarters. The gardens, with their fountains and koi pond, are a lovely spot in which to wander. The bougainvillea-covered Serra Chapel is believed to be the oldest church still standing in California and is the only building remaining in which St. Serra actually led Mass. Mass takes place weekdays at 7 am in the chapel. Enter via a small gift shop in the gatehouse. ✉ 26801 Ortega Hwy. ☎ 949/234–1300 ⊕ www.missionsjc.com ⌨ $10.

San Juan Capistrano Library

LIBRARY | FAMILY | Near Mission San Juan Capistrano is the San Juan Capistrano Library, a postmodern structure built in 1983. Architect Michael Graves combined classical and Mission styles to striking effect. Its courtyard has secluded places for reading. ✉ 31495 El Camino Real ☎ 949/493–1752 ⊕ ocpl.org/libloc/sjc ☉ Closed Fri.

Restaurants

Cedar Creek Inn

$$$ | AMERICAN | FAMILY | Just across the street from Mission San Juan Capistrano, this restaurant has a patio that's perfect for a late lunch or a romantic dinner. The menu is fairly straightforward, dishes are

tasty, and portions are substantial—try the Cobb salad or a burger at lunch, or splurge on the prime rib for dinner. **Known for:** brunch; rich desserts; comfortable seating. Ⓢ *Average main: $30* ✉ *26860 Ortega Hwy.* ☎ *949/240–2229* ⊕ *www.cedarcreekinn.com.*

L'Hirondelle

$$$ | FRENCH | Locals have romanced at cozy tables for decades at this delightful restaurant. Such classic dishes as beef bourguignonne and a New York strip in a black peppercorn and brandy sauce are the hallmark of this French and Belgian restaurant, whose name means "the little swallow." The extensive wine list is matched by an impressive selection of Belgian beers. **Known for:** Sunday brunch; traditional French cuisine; composed salads. Ⓢ *Average main: $35* ✉ *31631 Camino Capistrano* ☎ *949/661–0425* ⊕ *www.lhirondellesjc.com* ☉ *Closed Mon.*

The Ramos House Cafe

$$ | AMERICAN | It may be worth hopping the Amtrak to San Juan Capistrano just for the chance to have breakfast or lunch at one of Orange County's most beloved restaurants, located in a historic board-and-batten home dating back to 1881. This café sits practically on the railroad tracks across from the depot—nab a table on the patio and dig into a hearty breakfast featuring seasonal items, such as the smoked bacon scramble with wilted rocket. **Known for:** southern specialties; weekend brunch; historic setting. Ⓢ *Average main: $20* ✉ *31752 Los Rios St.* ☎ *949/443–1342* ⊕ *www.ramoshouse.com* ☉ *Closed Mon. No dinner.*

🍸 Nightlife

Swallow's Inn

BARS/PUBS | Across the way from Mission San Juan Capistrano you may spot a line of Harleys in front of the down-home and downright funky Swallow's Inn. Despite a somewhat tough look, it attracts all kinds—bikers, surfers, modern-day cowboys, grandparents—for a drink, a casual bite, karaoke nights, and some rowdy live country music. ✉ *31786 Camino Capistrano* ☎ *949/493–3188* ⊕ *www. swallowsinn.com.*

Catalina Island

Just 22 miles out from the L.A. coastline, across from Newport Beach and Long Beach, Catalina has virtually unspoiled mountains, canyons, coves, and beaches; best of all, it gives you a glimpse of what undeveloped Southern California once looked like.

Water sports are a big draw, as divers and snorkelers come for the exceptionally clear water surrounding the island. Kayakers are attracted to the calm cove waters and thrill seekers book the eco-themed zipline that traverses a wooded canyon. The main town, Avalon, is a charming, old-fashioned beach community, where yachts and pleasure boats bob in the crescent bay. Wander beyond the main drag and find brightly painted little bungalows fronting the sidewalks; golf carts are the preferred mode of transport.

In 1919, William Wrigley Jr., the chewing-gum magnate, purchased a controlling interest in the company developing Catalina Island, whose most famous landmark, the Casino, was built in 1929 under his orders. Because he owned the Chicago Cubs baseball team, Wrigley made Catalina the team's spring training site, an arrangement that lasted until 1951.

In 1975, the Catalina Island Conservancy, a nonprofit foundation, acquired about 88% of the island to help preserve the area's natural flora and fauna, including the bald eagle and the Catalina Island fox. These days the conservancy is restoring the rugged interior country with plantings of native grasses and trees. The organization helps oversee the interior's

50 miles of bike trails and 165 miles of hiking trails and helps protect the island's 60 endemic species. Along the coast you might spot oddities like electric perch, saltwater goldfish, and flying fish.

GETTING HERE AND AROUND
FERRY TRAVEL

Two companies offer ferry service to Catalina Island. The boats have both indoor and outdoor seating and snack bars. Excessive baggage is not allowed, and there are extra fees for bicycles and surfboards. The waters around Catalina can get rough, so if you're prone to seasickness, come prepared. Winter, holiday, and weekend schedules vary, so reservations are strongly recommended.

Catalina Express makes an hour-long run from Long Beach or San Pedro to Avalon and a 90-minute run from Dana Point to Avalon with some stops at Two Harbors. Round-trip fares begin at $73.50, with discounts for seniors and kids. On busy days, a $15 upgrade to the Commodore Lounge, when available, is worth it. Service from Newport Beach to Avalon is available through the *Catalina Flyer.* The boat leaves from Balboa Pavilion at 9 am (in season), takes 75 minutes to reach the island, and costs $70 round-trip. The return boat leaves Catalina at 4:30 pm. Reservations are required for the *Catalina Flyer* and recommended for all weekend and summer trips. ■TIP➡ **Keep an eye out for dolphins, which sometimes swim alongside the ferries.**

FERRY CONTACTS Catalina Flyer.
☎ *949/673–5245* ⊕ *www.catalinainfo. com.*

GOLF CARTS
Golf carts constitute the island's main form of transportation for sightseeing in the area; however, some parts of town are off-limits, as is the island's interior. Drivers 21 and over with valid driver's license can rent them along Avalon's Crescent Avenue and Pebbly Beach Road

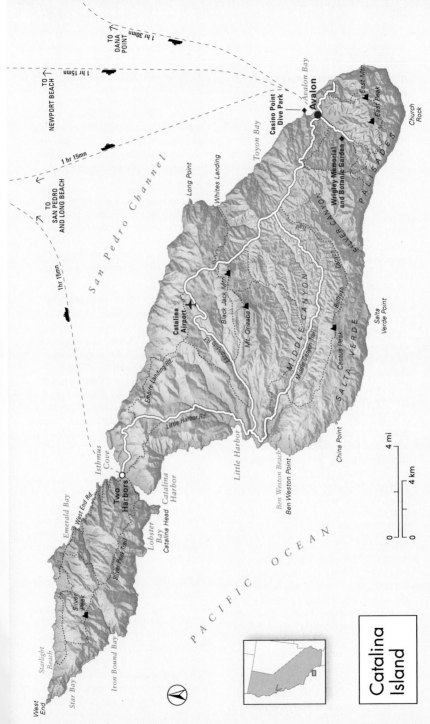

Catalina Island

for about $45 per hour with a $45 deposit, payable via cash only.

GOLF CART RENTALS Island Rentals. ✉ *125 Pebbly Beach Rd., Avalon* ☎ *310/510–1456* ⊕ *www.catalinagolfcartrentals.com.*

HELICOPTER TRAVEL

Island Express helicopters depart from San Pedro (Friday, Saturday, and Sunday only), John Wayne Airport, Burbank Airport, and Long Beach next to the *Queen Mary* (8 am–dusk). The trip from Long Beach takes about 15 minutes and costs $135 one way, $270 round-trip. Reservations a week in advance are recommended; some flights require a minimum passenger load.

TIMING

Although Catalina can be seen in one very hectic day, several inviting hotels make it worth extending your stay for one or more nights. A short itinerary might include breakfast on the pier, a tour of the interior, a snorkeling excursion at Casino Point, or beach day at the Descanso Beach Club and a romantic waterfront dinner in Avalon.

After late October, rooms are much easier to find on short notice, rates drop dramatically, and many hotels offer packages that include transportation from the mainland and/or sightseeing tours. January to March you have a good chance of spotting migrating gray whales on the ferry crossing.

TOURS

Santa Catalina Island Company runs nine land tours and six ocean tours, including the *Flying Fish* boat trip (summer evenings only); a comprehensive inland motor tour; a tour of Skyline Drive; several Casino tours; a scenic tour of Avalon; a glass-bottom-boat tour; an undersea tour on a semisubmersible vessel; an eco-themed zipline tour that traverses a scenic canyon; a speedy Ocean Runner expedition that searches for all manner of sea creatures and a fast Cyclone boat tour that takes you to the less populated center of the island, Two Harbors. Reservations are highly recommended for the inland tours. Tours cost $14 to $129. There are ticket booths on the Green Pleasure Pier, at the Casino, in the plaza, and at the boat landing. Catalina Adventure Tours, which has booths at the boat landing and on the pier, also arranges excursions at comparable prices.

The Catalina Island Conservancy organizes custom ecotours and hikes of the interior. Naturalist guides drive open Jeeps through some gorgeously untrammeled parts of the island. Tours start at $70 per person for a two-hour trip (two-person minimum). The tours run year-round.

ESSENTIALS

VISITOR AND TOUR INFORMATION
Catalina Adventure Tours. ☎ *877/510–2888* ⊕ *www.catalinaadventuretours.com.* **Catalina Island Chamber of Commerce and Visitors Bureau.** ✉ *1 Green Pleasure Pier, Avalon* ☎ *310/510–1520* ⊕ *www. catalinachamber.com.* **Catalina Island Conservancy.** ✉ *125 Claressa Ave., Avalon* ☎ *310/510–2595* ⊕ *www.catalinaconservancy.org.* **Santa Catalina Island Company.** ☎ *877/778–8322* ⊕ *www.visitcatalinaisland.com.*

Avalon

A 1- to 2-hour ferry ride from Long Beach, Newport Beach, or San Pedro; a 15-minute helicopter ride from Long Beach or San Pedro, slightly longer from Santa Ana.

Avalon, Catalina's only real town, extends from the shore of its natural harbor to the surrounding hillsides. Its resident population is about 3,800, but it swells with tourists on summer weekends. Most of the city's activity, however, is centered on the pedestrian mall on Crescent Avenue, and most sights are easily reached on foot. Private cars are restricted and rental cars aren't allowed, but taxis, trams, and shuttles can take you anywhere you need to go. Bicycles, electric bikes, and golf carts can be rented from shops along Crescent Avenue.

◉ Sights

★ Casino

BUILDING | This circular white structure is one of the finest examples of art deco architecture anywhere. Its Spanish-inspired floors and murals gleam with brilliant blue and green Catalina tiles. In this case, *casino,* the Italian word for "gathering place," has nothing to do with gambling. First-run movies are screened nightly at the Avalon Theatre, noteworthy for its classic 1929 theater pipe organ and art deco wall murals. The circular ballroom once famously hosted 1940s big bands and is still used for gala events.

The Santa Catalina Island Company leads three tours of the Casino—the 30-minute basic tour ($14), the 90-minute behind-the-scenes tour ($28), which leads visitors through the green room and into the Wrigleys' private lounge, and a weekend nights evening tour ($45), where guests enjoy wine on the scenic terrace after touring the historic building. ⊠ *1 Casino Way* ☎ *310/510–0179 theater* ⊕ *www. visitcatalinaisland.com.*

Casino Point Dive Park

BEACH—SIGHT | FAMILY | In front of the Casino are the crystal-clear waters of the Casino Point Dive Park, a protected marine preserve where moray eels, bat rays, spiny lobsters, harbor seals, and other sea creatures cruise around kelp forests and along the sandy bottom. No need to don a wetsuit: the brilliantly orange garibaldi, California's state marine fish, can sometimes be viewed from the seawall. It's a terrific site for scuba diving, with some shallow areas suitable for snorkeling. Equipment can be rented on and near the pier. The shallow waters of Lover's Cove, east of the boat landing, are also good for snorkeling. ⊠ *Avalon.*

Where the Buffalo Roam ◉

Zane Grey, the writer who put the Western novel on the map, spent a lot of time on Catalina, and his influence is still evident in a peculiar way. As the story goes, when the movie version of Grey's book *The Vanishing American* was filmed here in 1924, American bison were ferried across from the mainland to give the land that Western plains look. After the crew packed up and left, the buffalo stayed, and a small herd of about 150 still remains, grazing the interior and reinforcing the island's image as the last refuge from SoCal's urban sprawl.

Catalina Island Museum

LOCAL INTEREST | FAMILY | The exterior of the Catalina Island Museum is a nod to Catalina Island's developer William Wrigley Jr.—it's modeled after Wrigley Field in Chicago. Inside, the museum traces the island's history from it's precontact days and native Chumash to its role in Hollywood history and beyond. Two galleries host traveling exhibitions. The view from the outside terrace takes in lovely Avalon and its picturesque harbor. A small gift shop offers reproductions of the island's signature colorful Catalina pottery tiles. ⊠ *217 Metropole Ave.* ☎ *310/510–2414* ⊕ *www.catalinamuseum.org* ⊠ *$17.*

Green Pleasure Pier

LOCAL INTEREST | FAMILY | Head to the Green Pleasure Pier for a good vantage point of Avalon. On the pier you can find the visitor information, snack stands, and scads of squawking sea gulls. It's also the landing where visiting cruise-ship passengers catch tenders back out to their ship. ⊠ *End of Catalina Ave.*

Wrigley Memorial and Botanic Garden
GARDEN | Two miles south of the bay is Wrigley Memorial and Botanic Garden, home to plants native to Southern California. Several grow only on Catalina Island—Catalina ironwood, wild tomato, and rare Catalina mahogany. The Wrigley family commissioned the garden as well as the monument, which has a grand staircase and a Spanish-style mausoleum inlaid with colorful Catalina tile. Wrigley Jr. was once buried here but his remains were moved to Pasadena during World War II. ✉ *Avalon Canyon Rd.* ☎ *310/510–2897* 🌐 *www.catalinaconservancy.org* 🎟 *$8.*

🍴 Restaurants

Bluewater Grill
$$ | **SEAFOOD** | **FAMILY** | Overlooking the ferry landing and the entire harbor, the open-to-the-salt-air Bluewater Grill offers freshly caught fish, savory chowders, and all manner of shellfish. If they're on the menu, don't miss the swordfish steak or the sand dabs. **Known for:** fresh local fish; happy hour (October–May); harbor views. [$] *Average main: $27* ✉ *306 Crescent Ave.* ☎ *310/510–3474* 🌐 *www.bluewater-grill.com.*

Descanso Beach Club
$ | **AMERICAN** | **FAMILY** | Set on an expansive deck overlooking the water, Descanso Beach Club serves a wide range of favorites: buffalo wings, hamburgers, salads, nachos, and tacos are all part of the selection. Watch the harbor seals frolic just offshore while sipping the island's super-sweet signature cocktail, the Buffalo Milk, a mix of fruit liqueurs, vodka, and whipped cream. **Known for:** tropical beach vibe; scenic views; chic cabana rentals. [$] *Average main: $15* ✉ *Descanso Beach, 1 Descanso Ave.* ☎ *310/510–7410.*

The Lobster Trap
$$ | **SEAFOOD** | Seafood rules at the Lobster Trap—the restaurant's owner has his own boat and fishes for the catch of the day and, in season, spiny lobster. Ceviche is a great starter, always fresh and brightly flavored. **Known for:** locally caught seafood; convivial atmosphere; locals' hangout. [$] *Average main: $26* ✉ *128 Catalina St.* ☎ *310/510–8585* 🌐 *catalinalobstertrap.com.*

🛏 Hotels

Aurora Hotel
$$ | **HOTEL** | In a town dominated by historic properties, the Aurora is refreshingly contemporary, with a hip attitude and sleek furnishings. **Pros:** trendy design; quiet location off main drag; close to restaurants. **Cons:** standard rooms are small, even by Catalina standards; no elevator; small bathrooms. [$] *Rooms from: $270* ✉ *137 Marilla Ave.* ☎ *310/510–0454* 🌐 *www.auroracatalina.com* 🔑 *18 rooms* 🍽 *Breakfast.*

Hotel Vista del Mar
$$ | **HOTEL** | **FAMILY** | On the bay-facing Crescent Avenue, this third-floor property is steps from the beach, where complimentary towels, chairs, and umbrellas await guests. **Pros:** comfortable beds; central location; in-room fireplace. **Cons:** no restaurant or spa facilities; few rooms with ocean views; no elevator. [$] *Rooms from: $235* ✉ *417 Crescent Ave.* ☎ *310/510–1452, 800/601–3836* 🌐 *www.hotel-vistadelmar.com* 🔑 *14 rooms* 🍽 *Breakfast.*

Mt. Ada
$$$$ | **B&B/INN** | If you stay in the mansion where Wrigley Jr. once lived, you can enjoy all the comforts of a millionaire's home—at a millionaire's prices. **Pros:** timeless charm; shuttle from heliport and dock; incredible views. **Cons:** smallish rooms and bathrooms; expensive; queen-size beds only. [$] *Rooms from: $480* ✉ *398 Wrigley Rd.* ☎ *310/510–2030, 877/778–8322* 🕒 *Closed mid-Jan.–early Feb.* 🔑 *6 rooms* 🍽 *Some meals.*

Pavilion Hotel

$$ | HOTEL | FAMILY | This mid-century modern–style hotel is Avalon's most citified spot, though just a few steps from the sand. **Pros:** centrally located, steps from the beach and harbor; friendly staff; plush bedding. **Cons:** no pool; rooms near stairs can be noisy; some rooms fully shaded. [$] *Rooms from: $265* ✉ *513 Crescent Ave.* ☎ *310/510–1788, 877/778–8322* 🌐 *www.visitcatalinaisland.com* 🛏 *71 rooms* 🍴 *Breakfast.*

Portofino Hotel

$$ | HOTEL | FAMILY | Steps from the Green Pleasure Pier, this European-style hotel creates an intimate feel with brick courtyards and walkways and suites named after Italian cities. **Pros:** romantic; close to beach; incredible sundeck. **Cons:** ground-floor rooms can be noisy; some rooms are on small side; no elevator. [$] *Rooms from: $209* ✉ *111 Crescent Ave.* ☎ *310/510–0555, 888/510–0555* 🌐 *www.hotelvillaportofino.com* 🛏 *35 rooms* 🍴 *Breakfast.*

Activities

BICYCLING

Brown's Bikes

BICYCLING | FAMILY | Look for rentals on Crescent Avenue and Pebbly Beach Road, where Brown's Bikes is located. Beach cruisers start at $25 per day, mountain bikes are $30 per day, and electric bikes are $50 for a day rental and a good choice for Catalina's hills. ✉ *107 Pebbly Beach Rd.* ☎ *310/510–0986* 🌐 *www.catalinabiking.com.*

DIVING AND SNORKELING

The Casino Point Underwater Park, with its handful of wrecks and ample sea life, is best suited for diving. Lover's Cove is better for snorkeling (but you'll share the area with glass-bottom boats). Both are protected marine preserves.

Catalina Divers Supply

SCUBA DIVING | Head to Catalina Divers Supply to rent equipment, sign up for guided scuba and snorkel tours, and attend certification classes. It also has an outpost at the Dive Park at Casino Point that offers gear rental and tank air fills. ✉ *7 Green Pleasure Pier* ☎ *310/510–0330* 🌐 *www.catalinadiverssupply.com.*

Index

A

A.O.C. ✕, 112
Abbot Kinney Boulevard, 76
Abigaile Restaurant and Brewery/
Alta House ✕, 90
Ace Hotel Downtown Los Angeles
🔲, 185–186
Adamson House and Malibu Lagoon
Museum, 83
Ahmanson Theatre, 190
Air travel, 38–39, 50, 240
Alimento ✕, 222
Ambrose, The 🔲, 69
American Rag Cie (shop), 119
Amoeba Records (shop), 143
Anaheim White House ✕, 250–251
ANdAZ West Hollywood 🔲, 115
Angelini Osteria ✕, 112
Angels Flight Railway, 172
Animal ✕, 112
Annenberg Community Beach House,
63, 66
Aquarium of the Pacific, 254–255
Arbour Pasadena, The ✕, 206
ArcLight, 142
Art galleries
Beverly Hills and the Westside, 97,
111–112
Santa Monica, 66
Atwater Village, 228–231
Aurora Hotel 🔲, 270
Avalon (Catalina Island), 268–272
Avila Adobe, 172

B

Balboa Bay Resort 🔲, 259
Balboa Island, 256
Balboa Peninsula, 256
Baracoa Cuban Cafe ✕, 228
Barnsdall Art Park, 215
Bars, 191–194. ⇨ See also Nightlife and
performing arts under specific areas
Baseball, 33, 225
Basilic ✕, 258
Basketball, 33
Bavel ✕, 181, 183
Bay Cities Italian Deli ✕, 67
Bayside Hotel 🔲, 69
Bazaar by José Andrés, The ✕, 102
Bea Bea's ✕, 148
Beach House at Hermosa 🔲, 90
Beaches
Orange County and Catalina Island, 256,
261, 269
Santa Monica, 75, 76, 83, 85–87,
89–90, 91
Bear Flag Fish Co. ✕, 258
Bergamot Station (gallery), 66

Best Fish Taco in Ensenada, The
✕, 219
Bestia ✕, 183
Beverly Hills, West Hollywood, and
the Westside, 16, 96–122
lodging, 103, 106–107, 115–116
nightlife and performing arts, 116–118
restaurants, 96, 101–103, 112–115
shopping, 107–109, 111–112, 119–122
sightseeing, 97, 100–101, 109–112
transportation, 96
Beverly Wilshire, a Four Seasons
Hotel 🔲, 103
Bicycling, 71–72, 80–82, 211, 272
Bigfoot Lodge (bar), 230
Binoculars Building, 76
Bluewater Grill ✕, 270
BOA Steakhouse ✕, 112
Boat and ferry travel, 241, 266
Boat rentals, 259–260
Boiling Crab, The ✕, 162
Bon Vivant Market and Café ✕, 229
Botanical Gardens, 199, 202–203,
211, 270
Bottega Louie ✕, 183
Bowling, 145
Bradbury Building, 172–173
Brentwood, 91–94
Brentwood Country Mart, 94
Brig, The (bar), 78
Broad Museum, The, 173
Broadway (Downtown Los Angeles), 169
Broken Spanish ✕, 183
Burbank, 148–151
Bus travel, 39, 50, 240–241
Bus tours, 51

C

CaCoa Mexicatessen ✕, 232
Cactus Taqueria #1 ✕, 133
Cafe Birdie ✕, 232
Café Gratitude ✕, 133
Café Sierra ✕, 146
Cafe Stella ✕, 222
California African American
Museum, 173
California Science Center, 173
Candy Cane Inn 🔲, 251
Cannery, The ✕, 258–259
Canter's ✕, 112–113
Car rentals, 41
Car travel, 39–41, 50
Casino, 269
Casino Point Dive Park, 269
Cassell's Hamburgers ✕, 162
Castle Green, 199
Catal Restaurant & Uva Bar ✕, 251
Catalina Island, 266–272. ⇨ See also
Orange County and Catalina Island
Catalina Island Museum, 269
Catch LA ✕, 113
Cathedral of Our Lady of the Angels,
169, 173–174
Cecil Hotel, The, 174
Cedar Creek Inn ✕, 265

Centanni Trattoria ✕, 148
Chamberlain 🔲, 115
Channel Road Inn 🔲, 69
Chateau Marmont 🔲, 115
Chez Jay Restaurant (bar), 72, 192
Children's activities, 32. ⇨ See also
under specific areas
Chinatown, 169, 174
Chinese American Museum, 174
Cindy's ✕, 232
City Hall of Los Angeles, 174–175
Cleo ✕, 113
Clifton's Republic (bar), 192–193
Climate, 43
Coast, The, 254–266
Cole's (bar), 192
Cole's French Dip ✕, 183
Comedy clubs, 117, 141, 149
Concert halls, 164
Connie and Ted's ✕, 113
Contacts, 50
Cow's End Café, The ✕, 77
Craft and Folk Art Museum, 157
Craig's ✕, 113
Crescent Beverly Hills, The 🔲,
103, 106
Crossroads ✕, 113
Crustacean ✕, 102
Cuisine, 24–25, 212–213
Culver City, 165
Culver Hotel, 165
Culver Studios, 165
Currency. ⇨ see Money matters
Custom Hotel 🔲, 71
Customs and duties, 43
CUT ✕, 102

D

Dan Blocker Beach, 83, 85
Dan Tana's ✕, 113
Dave's Chillin'-n-Grillin' ✕, 232
Daw Yee Myanmar Corner ✕, 222
Descanso Beach Club ✕, 270
Descanso Gardens, 199, 202
Dinette ✕, 226
Dining. ⇨ See Restaurants; under
specific areas
Dinosaur Coffee ✕, 223
Dirty Laundry (bar), 139
Discovery Cube's Ocean Quest, 256
Disney Studios, 128
Disneyland, 243–247
Disneyland Resort, 242–252
Disney's California Adventure, 247,
249–252
Disney's Grand Californian Hotel and
Spa 🔲, 251
Diving, 272
Division 3 ✕, 229
Dockweiler Beach, 88
Dodger Stadium, 225
Dolby Theatre, 125, 128–129
Dolce Vita (bar), 194

Dongpo ✕ , 146
Donut Friend ✕ , 232–233
Dorothy Chandler Pavilion, 190
Doubletree Guest Suites by Hilton
    Hotel Anaheim Resort-Convention
    Center ⊡ , 251
Downtown, 17, 168–196
lodging, 185–186, 188
nightlife and performing arts, 188–195
restaurants, 168, 169, 175–176, 181,
    183–185
shopping, 169, 175–176, 195–196
sightseeing, 169, 172–181
transportation, 168, 179
Dream Hollywood ⊡ , 136
Duke's Barefoot Bar, 87
Dune ✕ , 229
Duties, 43

E

East West Players, 190
Eastside, 17. ⇨ See also Los Feliz and
    the Eastside
Echo and Echoplex, The (bar), 227
Echo Park, 225–228
Echo Park Lake, 225–226
Egyptian Theatre, 129
El Capitan Theatre, 128, 129, 142
El Coyote Mexican Food ✕ , 113–114
El Huarache Azteca ✕ , 233
El Molino Viejo (The Old Mill), 204
El Pueblo de Los Angeles, 169, 175
El Rey Theater, 117
El Segundo, 88–89
Elysian Park, 226
Emergencies, 40, 50
Exposition Park, 175

F

Factory Kitchen, The ✕ , 183
Fairmont Miramar Hotel & Bunga-
    lows Santa Monica ⊡ , 69
Farmer's Daughter Hotel ⊡ , 115
Farmers Market, 109
Fashion District, 196
Fashion Island, 260
Fashion Island Hotel ⊡ , 259
Father's Office ✕ , 68
Ferry travel, 241, 266
Film, 72–73, 142
Firefly ✕ , 144
Fishing, 260
5 Line Tavern ✕ , 233
Flea markets, 207–208
Football, 33
Forma Restaurant and Cheese Bar
    ✕ , 68
4100 (bar), 224
Four Seasons Hotel, Los Angeles at
    Beverly Hills ⊡ , 106
Fox Plaza, 97
Fred Segal (shop), 120
Freehand Los Angeles ⊡ , 186
Freeway driving, 40–41

Fremont Centre Theatre, 206–207
Frolic Room (bar), 193

G

Gagosian Gallery, 97
Galley, The (bar), 72
Gamble House, 199, 202
Garland, The ⊡ , 152–153
Geffen Contemporary at MOCA,
    169, 175
Georgian Hotel, The ⊡ , 69
Getty Center, 91–92
Getty Villa Malibu, 75
Gingergrass ✕ , 223
Gjelina ✕ , 77
Golden Gopher (bar), 189
Golf carts, 266–267
Good Measure ✕ , 229
Good Neighbor Restaurant ✕ , 144
Good Times at Davey Wayne's
    (bar) 140
Grammy Museum, 175
Grand Central Market, 169, 175–176
Greek Theatre, 211, 221
Green Pleasure Pier, 269
Greenblatt's Deli ✕ , 114
Grey, Zane, 269
Greystone Mansion, 97, 100
Griffith Observatory, 211, 215, 219
Griffith Park, 219
Grove, The, 109
Grub ✕ , 133
Guelaguetza ✕ , 162
Guerrilla Tacos ✕ , 183
Guided tours, 51, 179, 268
Guinness World of Records Museum,
    129
Gulfstream ✕ , 259
Gwen ✕ , 133

H

Harvelle's (bar), 72, 193
Hayat's Kitchen ✕ , 152
Health, 48
Helicopter travel, 268
Here's Looking At You ✕ , 162
Heritage Square Museum, 231–232
Hermosa Beach, 89–90
Hide Sushi ✕ , 163
Highland Park, 231–235
Hiking, 138
Hilton Anaheim ⊡ , 251–252
Historic Core (Downtown Los Angeles),
    169
Hockey, 33
Hollyhock House, 215
Hollywood and the studios, 16,
    124–154
lodging, 136–138, 145, 148, 149, 152–153
nightlife and performing arts, 138–142,
    145, 149, 153
restaurants, 124, 132–136, 137, 144–145,
    146, 148–149, 152
shopping, 143–144, 151, 153–154

sightseeing, 125–132, 146, 148, 151
sports and outdoor activities, 138
transportation, 124
Hollywood Bowl, 128, 142
Hollywood Bowl Museum, 129
Hollywood Forever Cemetery,
    129–130
Hollywood Heritage Museum, 130
Hollywood Museum, 130
Hollywood Roosevelt Hotel ⊡ , 136
Hollywood Sign, 131
Hollywood Walk of Fame, 128, 131
Hollywood Wax Museum, 131
Hornblower Cruises and Events, 76
Hot Stone Slow Food from Korea
    ✕ , 144
Hotel Amarana Burbank ⊡ , 149
Hotel Casa del Mar ⊡ , 69–70
Hotel Erwin ⊡ , 78
Hotel Figueroa ⊡ , 186
Hotel Normandie ⊡ , 162–163
Hotel Shangri-La ⊡ , 70
Hotel Vista del Mar ⊡ , 270
Hotels. ⇨ See also Lodging under
    specific areas
price categories, 47, 242
Howlin' Ray's ✕ , 183
Huckleberry Bakery and Cafe ✕ , 68
Huntington Library, Art Collections,
    and Botanical Gardens, 202–203
Huntley Santa Monica Beach ⊡ , 70
Hurry Curry of Tokyo ✕ , 163

I

Immunizations, 43
In-N-Out Burger ✕ , 137
Inn at Laguna Beach ⊡ , 263
Inspiration Point, 75
InterContinental Los Angeles Down-
    town ⊡ , 186
Italian Hall Building, 176
Itineraries, 57–59, 82

J

Japanese American Cultural and
    Community Center, 176
Japanese American National
    Museum, 176
Jean-Georges Beverly Hills ✕ ,
    102–103
Jewelry District, 196
Jitlada ✕ , 133
Joan's on Third ✕ , 114

K

Kibitz Room at Canter's Deli (bar), 193
Kinney, The ⊡ , 78
Kismet ✕ , 219
Kitchen Mouse ✕ , 233
Knott's Berry Farm (theme park),
    252–254
Knott's Berry Farm Hotel ⊡ , 254
Knowrealitypie ✕ , 233

Kobawoo House ✕, 162
Koreatown, 16–17, 161–166. ⇨ See also Mid-Wilshire and Koreatown

L

L.A. Live, 176–177
La Brea Tar Pits Museum, 157, 160
La Casa del Camino 🏨, 263
La Pergoletta ✕, 220
Laguna Art Museum, 261
Laguna Beach, 261–264
Laguna Coast Wilderness Park, 261
LaMill Coffee ✕, 223
Langer's Delicatessen-Restaurant ✕, 183–184
Las Tunas Beach, 85
Last Bookstore, The, 195–196
Laurel Canyon, 151
Le Meridien Delfina Santa Monica 🏨, 70
Legends Beach Bike Tours, 71–72
Lemonade ✕, 137
Leo Carrillo State Park, 85
L'Hirondelle ✕, 265
Lido House, Autograph Collection 🏨, 259
Lighthouse Cafe ✕, 90
Lincoln ✕, 206
Line, The 🏨, 163–164
Link N Hops ✕, 229
Little Dom's ✕, 220
Little Tokyo, 169, 177
Lobster Trap, The ✕, 270
Lodging, 45–47
amenities 242
children, 47
neighborhoods, 46
parking, 47
price categories, 47, 242
reservations, 45
services, 45, 47
Loews Hollywood 🏨, 136
Loews Santa Monica Beach Hotel 🏨, 70
London West Hollywood at Beverly Hills, The 🏨, 115–116
Long Beach, 254–256
Los Amigos ✕, 149
Los Angeles County Arboretum, 203
Los Angeles County Museum of Art (LACMA), 160
Los Angeles International Airport (LAX) area lodging, 71
Los Angeles Museum of the Holocaust, 109, 111
Los Angeles Theatre, 177–178
Los Angeles Zoo and Botanical Gardens, 211
Los Feliz and the Eastside, 17, 210–234
nightlife and the performing arts, 220–221, 222–224, 227, 230–231, 233–235
shopping, 221–222, 224–225, 228, 231, 235
sightseeing, 210–211, 215, 219, 222, 225–226, 231–232

restaurants, 214, 219–220, 222–223, 226, 228–230, 232–233
transportation, 210, 214
Luv2Eat Thai Bistro ✕, 133

M

Magic Castle Hotel 🏨, 136
Main Beach Park, 261
Main Street (Santa Monica), 66
Majordomo ✕, 184
Malibu, 83–88
Malibu Beach Inn 🏨, 87
Malibu Lagoon State Beach, 85
Malibu Pier, 85
Mama Shelter 🏨, 137
Manhattan Beach, 89
Mantee Café ✕, 144
Margot ✕, 166
Marina del Rey, 76
Mark Taper Forum, 190
Marouch ✕, 133
Masa of Echo Park ✕, 226
Mastro's Ocean Club ✕, 87
Maude ✕, 103
Maxfield (shop), 120
Meals by Genet ✕, 160
Mélisse ✕, 68
Melrose Avenue, 111
Merkato Ethiopian Restaurant and Market ✕, 160–161
Metro Rail, 41, 50, 179
Miceli's ✕, 145
Michael's Santa Monica ✕, 68
Microsoft Theatre, 190, 195
Mid-Wilshire and Koreatown, 16–17, 156–166
lodging, 162–164
nightlife and performing arts, 164
restaurants, 156, 160–161, 162, 163, 166
shopping, 162, 164
sightseeing, 157, 160
transportation, 156
Milk Bar LA ✕, 114
Millenium Biltmore Hotel 🏨, 186
Million Dollar Theater, 178
Miracle Mile, 157–161
Mission San Gabriel Archangel, 203
Mission San Juan Capistrano, 265
MOCA Grand Avenue, 178
Mofongo's ✕, 152
Mohawk Bend (bar), 227
Moment Hotel 🏨, 137
Mondrian Los Angeles 🏨, 116
Money matters, 48–49
Montage Beverly Hills 🏨, 106
Montage Laguna Beach 🏨, 263
Monty's Good Burger ✕, 162
Moonshadows (bar), 87–88
Morrison, The ✕, 229
Mt. Ada 🏨, 270
Mount Hollywood, 211
Mr. C. Beverly Hills 🏨, 106
Mrs. Knott's Chicken Dinner Restaurant ✕, 253–254

MTA Art Moves, 179
Mulholland Drive, 151
Muscle Beach, 76
Museum of Jurassic Technology, 165
Museum of Tolerance, 100
Museums
Adamson House and Malibu Lagoon Museum, 83
Broad Museum, 173
California African American Museum, 173
California Science Center, 173
Catalina Island Museum, 269
Chinese American Museum, 174
Craft and Folk Art Museum, 157
Discovery Cube's Ocean quest, 256
Geffen Contemporary at MOCA, 169, 175
Getty Center, 91–92
Getty Villa Malibu, 75
Grammy Museum, 175
Greystone Mansion, 97, 100
Guinness World of Records Museum, 129
Heritage Square Museum, 231–232
Hollywood Bowl Museum, 129
Hollywood Heritage Museum, 130
Hollywood Museum, 130
Hollywood Wax Museum, 131
Huntington Library, Art Collections, and Botanical Gardens, 202–203
Japanese American Cultural and Community Center, 176
Japanese American National Museum, 176
La Brea Tar Pits Museum, 157, 160
Laguna Art Museum, 261
Los Angeles County Museum of Art (LACMA), 160
Los Angeles Museum of the Holocaust, 109, 111
MOCA Grand Avenue, 178
Museum of Jurassic Technology, 165
Museum of Tolerance, 100
Natural History Museum of Los Angeles County, 178–179
Norton Simon Museum, 199, 203–204
Paley Center for Media, 100–101
Petersen Automotive Museum, 157, 160
Ripley's Believe It or Not, 132
Skirball Cultural Center, 92
Will Rogers State Historic Park and Museum, 75
Musso & Frank Grill, 140, 194

N

Napa Rose ✕, 251
Nate 'n' Al's ✕, 103
Natural History Museum of Los Angeles County, 178–179
Newport Beach, 256–260
Newport Beach Marriott Hotel and Spa 🏨, 259
Newport Harbor, 256
Newport Pier, 256, 258
Nice Guy, The ✕, 114
Nicholas Canyon Country Beach, 85–86
Nightlife, 47–48. ⇨ See also under specific areas
Nijiya Market ✕, 163
N/naka ✕, 166
Nobu Malibu ✕, 87

NoHo Arts District, *151*
NoMad Hotel, The ⊡ , *186*
North Hollywood, *151–154*
Norton Simon Museum, *199, 203–204*
Nozawa Bar ✕ , *103*
Nuart, *72*

O

Ocean at Main ✕ , *262*
Old Chalet, The (bar), *234*
Old Mill, The (El Molino Viejo), *204*
Old Town Pasadena, *199, 204*
Olvera Street, *175, 196*
1,000 Steps Beach, *261*
Orange County and Catalina Island,
    240–272
beaches, *256, 261, 269*
lodging, *241, 251–252, 254, 255–256, 259,
    263, 270, 272*
nightlife and performing arts, *265–266*
restaurants, *241, 250–251, 253–254,
    258–259, 262–263, 265, 270*
shopping, *260, 263–264*
sports and outdoor activities, *259–260, 272*
transportation, *240–241, 266, 268*
visitor information, *242, 268*
Original Pantry Cafe ✕ , *184*
Orpheum Theatre, *179–180*
Osteria Mozza ✕ , *135*
Otheroom, The (bar), *78–79*

P

Pablito's Kitchen ✕ , *149*
Pacific Design Center, *109, 111*
Pacific Palisades, *74–75*
Paley Center for Media, *100–101*
Palihotel ⊡ , *137–138*
Palihouse Santa Monica ⊡ , *70*
Palihouse West Hollywood ⊡ , *116*
Pantages Theatre, *131–132, 142*
Papilles Bistro ✕ , *135*
Paramount Pictures, *132*
Park Vue Inn ⊡ , *252*
Parking, *47, 73*
Park's Finest, The ✕ , *226*
Pasadena, *17, 198–208*
nightlife and performing arts, *206–207*
restaurants, *198, 206*
shopping, *207–208*
sightseeing, *199, 202–206*
transportation, *198*
Pasadena Playhouse, *207*
Passports, *43*
Patina ✕ , *184*
Pavilion Hotel ⊡ , *272*
Peninsula Beverly Hills ⊡ , *106*
Performing arts, *48.* ⇨ *See also*
    Nightlife and performing arts under
    specific areas
Pershing Square, *180*
Petersen Automotive Museum,
    157, 160
Petit Trois ✕ , *135*
Petite Taqueria ✕ , *114*
Petty Cash Taqueria ✕ , *114*

Philippe the Original ✕ , *184*
Pie 'n Burger ✕ , *206*
Pierce Brothers Westword Village
    Memorial Park and Mortuary, *101*
Pine and Crane ✕ , *223*
Pink's Hot Dogs ✕ , *135*
Pizzeria Mozza ✕ , *135*
Polka Polish Cuisine ✕ , *233*
Portofino Hotel ⊡ , *272*
Portofino Hotel & Yacht Club ⊡ ,
    90–91
Porto's Bakery ✕ , *149*
Price categories
dining, *45, 242*
lodging, *47, 242*
Providence ✕ , *135*
Public transport, *41, 50, 179*
Purple Orchard (bar), *89*

Q

Q Sushi ✕ , *184*
Queen Mary (ocean liner), *255*
Queen Mary Hotel ⊡ , *255*

R

Ramos House Cafe, The ✕ , *265*
Rancho Palos Verdes, *91*
Raymond 1886, The ✕ , *206*
Ray's and Stark Bar ✕ , *161*
Redbird ✕ , *184*
REDCAT, The (Roy and Edna Disney/Cal
    Arts Theater), *195*
Redondo Beach, *90–91*
Reel Inn ✕ , *87*
Republique ✕ , *114*
Resident (club), *189*
Restaurants, *30–31.* ⇨ *See also under*
    specific areas
children in, *44*
cuisine, *24–25, 212–213*
dress, *44–45*
hours, *44*
local chains, *137*
price categories, *45, 242*
smoking in, *44*
reservations, *44*
taxes, *45*
tipping, *45*
Ricardo Montalbán Theatre, *142*
Richard J. Riordan Central Library,
    180–181
Ride-sharing, *42*
Ripley's Believe It or Not, *132*
Ritz Carlton, Los Angeles ⊡ , *186*
Robert H. Meyer Memorial State
    Beach, *86*
Rockwell Table and Stage, *221*
Rodeo Drive, *97, 101*
Rodini Park ✕ , *152*
Roscoe's House of Chicken and
    Waffles ✕ , *135*
Rose Bowl, *204*
Rose Bowl Flea Market, *207–208*
Rose Cafe ✕ , *77–78*

Row, The, *196*
Rustic Canyon Wine Bar and Sea-
    sonal Kitchen ✕ , *68*

S

Safety, *49*
Salt Air ✕ , *78*
San Juan Capistrano, *264–266*
San Juan Capistrano Library, *265*
Santa Monica and the beaches,
    16, 62–94
lodging, *69–70, 78, 87, 89, 90–91*
nightlife and performing arts, *72–73,*
    78–79, 87–88, 89, 90
restaurants, *62, 67–69, 77–78, 87, 92*
shopping, *73–74, 79, 83, 88, 94*
sightseeing, *63, 66–67, 75–77, 83–87, 88,*
    89–90, 91–92
sports and outdoor activities, *71–72, 80–83*
transportation, *62*
Santa Monica Boulevard, *111*
Santa Monica Pier, *66–67*
Santa Monica Pier Aquarium, *67*
Santa Monica Place, *67*
Santa Monica Playhouse, *73*
Santa Monica Seafood ✕ , *68*
Santee Alley, *196*
Sapphire Laguna ✕ , *262*
Satellite (bar), *224*
Sawtell Boulevard, *163*
Sawyer ✕ , *223*
Scooter tours, *51*
Sea Shore Motel ⊡ , *70–71*
Sepan Chicken ✕ , *229*
71Above ✕ , *184*
Shade ⊡ , *89*
Sheraton Gateway Los Angeles
    Hotel ⊡ , *71*
Sheraton Universal ⊡ , *148*
Shibumi ✕ , *184–185*
Shopping. ⇨ *See under specific*
    areas
Shore Hotel ⊡ , *71*
Shrine Auditorium, *195*
Shutters on the Beach ⊡ , *71*
Sightseeing tours, *51, 179, 268*
Silver Lake, *222–225*
1642 Beer and Wine (bar), *227*
Skateboarding, *83*
Skirball Cultural Center, *92*
Sky's Gourmet Tacos ✕ , *161*
SLS Hotel at Beverly Hills ⊡ , *106*
Smoking, *44*
Snorkeling, *272*
Sony Pictures Studios, *165*
Spadena House, *101*
Spago Beverly Hills ✕ , *103*
Spas, *164, 166, 187*
Special–interest tours, *51*
Sports and the outdoors, *33.* ⇨ *See*
    also under specific areas; specific sports
Sportsmen's Lodge ⊡ , *145*
Spumante Restaurant ✕ , *152*
Sqirl ✕ , *135–136*
Standard, The ⊡ , *116*

Standard Downtown L.A., The ⌷, 186, 188
Staples Center, 181
Strand bike path, 80–82
Stout ✕, 136
Studio ✕, 262
Studio City, 144–145
Subway travel, 179
Sunset Boulevard, 111
Sunset Marquis Hotel and Villas ⌷, 116
Sunset Plaza, 111
Sunset Strip, 52–56, 109
Sunset Tower Hotel ⌷, 116
Surf and Sand Resort ⌷, 263
Sushi Gen ✕, 185
Swingin Door Texas BBQ, The ✕, 152

T

Taco Loco ✕, 262–263
Tacos Villa Corona ✕, 229–230
Taix ✕, 226
Tam O'Shanter ✕, 230
Tar and Roses ✕, 69
Taxes, 45, 49
Taxis, 42, 50
TCL Chinese Theatre, 125, 128, 132
TeaPop ✕, 152
Terranea ⌷, 91
Tesse ✕, 114–115
Theater, 190, 195, 206–207, 221
Third Street Promenade, 67
Three Broomsticks/Hog's Head ✕, 146
3-Thirty-3 ✕, 259
Timing the visit, 43
Tipping, 45, 49
Tommy's ✕, 137
Topanga State Beach, 86
Topanga State Park, 86
Toscana ✕, 92
Tournament House, 206
Tours and packages, 51, 179, 268
Town Pizza ✕, 233
Train travel, 42, 50, 179, 241
Transportation, 38–42, 50, 179
Trapeze School of New York, 72
Trois Mec ✕, 136
Tsujita L.A. Artisan Noodles ✕, 163

U

Union ✕, 206
Union Station, 181
Universal City, 145–148
Universal Studios Hollywood, 128, 146
UnUrban Coffee House, 72
Upright Citizens Brigade (comedy club), 141
Urth Caffé Melrose ✕, 115

V

Valerie Confections ✕, 226
Varden, The ⌷, 255–265
Varnish, The (bar), 190
Venice, 76–79, 83
Venice Beach Boardwalk, 76–77
Venice Beach House ⌷, 78
Venice Skatepark, 83
Venice Whaler ✕, 78
Vespertine ✕, 166
Viceroy L'Ermitage Beverly Hills ⌷, 106
Viceroy Santa Monica ⌷, 71
Vintage Los Feliz Theatre, 221
Virginia Robinson Gardens, 101
Visas, 43
Visitor information, 49, 50. ⇨ See also under specific areas
Vista Theatre, 219

W

Waldorf Astoria Beverly Hills ⌷, 106–107
Walking tours, 51
Wallis Annenberg Center for the Performing Arts, 101
Walt Disney Concert Hall, 169, 181
Wanderlust Creamery ✕, 230
Warner Bros. Studios, 128, 148
Wasabi at CityWalk ✕, 146, 148
Weather, 43
West Hollywood, 16, 109–122. ⇨ See also Beverly Hills, West Hollywood, and the Westside
West Hollywood Design District, 111–112
West Hollywood Library, 112

Westin Bonaventure Hotel & Suites ⌷, 188
Westside. ⇨ see Beverly Hills, West Hollywood, and the Westside
Westward Beach–Point Dune, 86
Will Geer Theatricum Botanicum, 88
Will Rogers State Beach, 75
Will Rogers State Historic Park and Museum, 75
Wood's Cove, 261
Wrigley Memorial and Botanical Garden, 270
Wurstküche ✕, 137

Z

Zankou Chicken ✕, 137
Zinc Café & Market ✕, 263
Zoos, 211
Zuma Beach Park, 86–87

Photo Credits

Front Cover: Jill Krueger [Description: LA Skyline view from Griffith Observatory.]. Back cover, from left to right: Chebyshev007/Dreamstime. com, Jill Krueger, Shawnhemp/Dreamstime.com. Spine: JingleBeeZ Photo Gallery/Shutterstock. Interior, from left to right: Jill Krueger (1). Jill Krueger (2-3). ames sf/Flickr, [CC BY 2.0] (5). Chapter 1: Experience Los Angeles: Jill Krueger (6-7). Courtesy of Walt Disney Concert Hall (8). Visit Santa Monica (9). Paul Hiffmeyer/Disney Enterprises (9). Courtesy of Los Angeles County Museum of Art (10). Matt Marriott/Courtesy of Los Angeles Tourism (10). Jamie Pham Photography/Alamy Stock Photo (10). Hamilton Pytluk/Universal Studios Hollywood (10). Mike Kelley/Courtesy The Broad (11). Lux Blue/shutterstock (11). Courtesy of Los Angeles Tourism (12). Courtesy of Los Angeles Tourism (12). Courtesy of Los Angeles Tourism (12). Matt Marriott/Courtesy of Los Angeles Tourism (13). Courtesy of Los Angeles Tourism (14). Briana Edwards/Paramount studios (14). Eric Glenn/shutterstock (14). Joseph Sohm/shutterstock (14). Courtesy of Griffith Observatory (15). OLOS/shutterstock (15). Donald Riddle Images, All Rights Reserved (20). divanov/shutterstock.com (20). Courtesy of Santa Monica Pier (20). Jill Krueger (20). Sean Pavone/shutterstock (20). Rosana Scapinello/Dreamstime (22). Kim.jihoon/shutterstock (22). Courtesy of Los Angeles Tourism (22). Jon Bilous/Dreamstime.com (22). Jill Krueger (23). www.nicholasnicholas.com (24). Bella Marie Adams/Melrose Umbrella Co (25). Jill Krueger (26). Mitchblatt/Dreamstime.com (27). Pinz Bowling Center (28). www.nicholasnicholas.com (28). courtesy of the hollywood roosevelt (28). courtesy of the grove (28). Catch Hospitality Group (29). Henry Hargreaves (29). ROB STARK (29). courtesy of chateau marmont (29). Tina Whatcott (30). Courtesy of Cole's French Dip (31). Chapter 2: Travel Smart Los Angeles: Heeb Christian/agefotostock (52). stevelyon/Flickr, [CC BY 2.0] (53). Neil Emmerson/age fotostock (53). Kjetil Ree/Wikimedia Commons (54). IK's World Trip/Flickr, [CC BY 2.0] (54). Hyatt (55). Stepan Mazurov/Flickr, [CC BY 2.0] (55). mertxe iturrioz/Flickr, [CC BY 2.0] (55). Mike Simpson/iStockphoto (56). **viv**/Flickr [CC BY 2.0] (56). Chapter 3: Santa Monica and the Beaches: Appalachianviews/Dreamstime.com (61). Asterixvs/Dreamstime.com (66). Richard Ross with the courtesy of the J. Paul Getty Trust (74). jonrawlinson/Flickr [CC BY 2.0] (77). Naki Kouyioumtzis/agefotostock (80). ames sf/Flickr, [CC BY 2.0] (81). Pygmy Warrior/Flickr, [CC BY 2.0] (81). alonzoD/Flickr (81). Anton J. Geisser/agefotostock (81). Courtesy of J. Paul Getty Trust (93). Chapter 4: Beverly Hills, West Hollywood, and the Westside: F11photo/Dreamstime.com (95). Nito100/Dreamstime.com (100). Courtesy of Annenberg Space for Photography (102). Scott Leigh/iStockphoto (104-105). Stella Levi/iStockphoto (110). Chapter 5: Hollywood and the Studios: Sepavo/Dreamstime.com (123). Chicco7/Dreamstime.com (128). Gary Bembridge/Flickr, [CC BY 2.0] (130). Davel5957 (134). DAVID SPRAGUE (147). Chapter 6: Mid-Wilshire and Koreatown: Let Go Media/Shutterstock (155). Michael Gordon/Shutterstock (161). Chapter 7: Downtown Los Angeles: Eddie Hernandez Photography (167). Biansho/Dreamstime.com (172). Usataro/Dreamstime.com (177). Gerry Boughan/Dreamstime (178). f11photo/Shutterstock (180). Lilyling1982/Dreamstime.com (182). Jakob N. Layman (185). michael balderas/iStockphoto (191). Trujillo Paumie (191). tannazie/Flickr, [CC BY 2.0] (192). Tamsin Slater/Flickr, [CC BY 2.0] (192). Atomazul/Dreamstime.com (192). Trujillo Paumie (192). Chez Jay (193). Meg Butler (193). bORjAmATiC/Flickr, [CC BY 2.0] (193). Truillo Paumie (193). rawkblog.blogspot.com/flickr, [CC BY 2.0] (194). arnoldinuyaki/flickr, [CC BY 2.0] (194). Never Cool in School/ eslie Kalohi/Flickr, [CC BY 2.0] (194). Howard Wise (194). Musso and Frank Grill (194). Public Domain (194). Chapter 8: Pasadena: Kit_Leong/istockphoto (197). 2000-2016 Pasadena Convention & Visitor Bureau (202). wikipedia.org (205). Chapter 9: Los Feliz and the Eastside: yhelfman/shutterstock (209). David Livingston/iStockphoto (210). Clinton Steeds/Flickr [CC BY 2.0] (211). wolfsavard/Flickr, [CC BY 2.0] (211). wisley/Flickr, [CC BY 2.0] (212). Gonzalo Rivero/wikipedia.org (213). tannaz/Flickr, [CC BY 2.0] (213). Jill Krueger (218). Chapter 10: Orange County and Catalina Island: Robert Holmes (237). www.ericcastro.biz/Flickr [CC BY 2.0] (248). Robert Holmes (254). Scott Vickers/iStockphoto (258). www.rwongphoto.com/Alamy (260). Brett Shoaf/Artistic Visuals Photography (262). Lowe Llaguno/Shutterstock (264). Backyard Production/istockphoto (271). All author photos are courtesy of the writers.

*Every effort has been made to trace the copyright holders, and we apologize in advance for any accidental errors. We would be happy to apply the corrections in subsequent printings of this publication.

Notes

Notes